Deploying and Managing a Cloud

Infrastructure

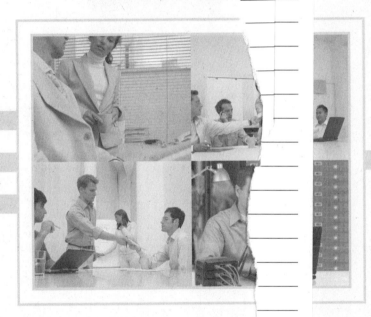

W

Deploying and Managing a Cloud Infrastructure

Real World Skills for the CompTIA Cloud+™ Certification and Beyond

Zafar Gilani

Abdul Salam

Salman Ul Haq

SYBEX®

A Wiley Brand

Acquisitions Editor: Kenyon Brown
Development Editor: Tom Cirtin
Technical Editor: Kunal Mittal
Production Editor: Christine O'Connor
Copy Editor: Judy Flynn
Editorial Manager: Pete Gaughan
Production Manager: Kathleen Wisor
Associate Publisher: Jim Minatel
Media Supervising Producer: Rich Graves
Book Designers: Judy Fung and Bill Gibson
Compositor: Craig Woods, Happenstance Type-O-Rama
Proofreader: Kim Wimpsett
Indexer: Nancy Guenther
Project Coordinator, Cover: Patrick Redmond
Cover Image: Wiley

I dedicate this book to my family and my alma maters: NUST, UPC, and KTH.
—Zafar Gilani

This book is dedicated to my father and mother, for their kindness and devotion and for their endless support when I was busy writing this book. Without their prayers and support, it would not have been possible for me to complete this book.
—Abdul Salam

I dedicate this book to my father. May he live a long and happy life.
—Salman Ul Haq

Acknowledgments

I thank Thomas Cirtin, Kenyon Brown, Christine O'Connor and the rest of Wiley's editorial team for their important comments and suggestions.

—Zafar Gilani

I would like to express my gratitude to Ms. Asifa Akram, for her support, patience, and encouragement throughout the project. It is not often that one finds an advisor and friend who always finds the time to listen to the little problems and roadblocks that unavoidably crop up in the course of performing research. Her technical advice was essential to the completion of this book and has taught me innumerable lessons and insights on the writing of this technical ebook.

—Abdul Salam

I would like to thank my family for giving me the time and space required to complete chapters of this book. The awesome team at Wiley has perfectly managed the execution of this book, especially Thomas Cirtin for reviewing the manuscripts and Jeff Kellum, who initially started with the project but is no longer with Wiley. Finally, I would like to thank Zafar for keeping everyone engaged.

—Salman Ul Haq

About the Authors

Zafar Gilani   is a full-time researcher and a PhD candidate at the University of Cambridge Computer Laboratory. Prior to starting his doctoral degree program in 2014, he successfully completed his master of science degree in the field of distributed computing. During that time, he was an Erasmus Mundus scholar at Universitat Politècnica de Catalunya (UPC) and Kungliga Tekniska högskolan (KTH) from 2011 to 2013. For his master's thesis research, he worked on spatio-temporal characterization of mobile web content at Telefonica Research, Barcelona. One of the technological use cases of his research became the basis for developing mobile web content pre-staging for cellular networks.

Prior to starting master's studies, he worked at SLAC National Accelerator Laboratory as a visiting scientist from 2009 to 2011. At SLAC he was involved in the research and development of Internet performance monitoring techniques and applications for geo-location of IP hosts. He graduated from NUST School of Electrical Engineering and Computer Science with a bachelor of science in computer science in 2009. He worked on providing InfiniBand support to MPJ Express (a Java-based MPI-like library) as his bachelor of science thesis research work. He can be reached on LinkedIn and at zafar.gilani@cl.cam.ac.uk.

Abdul Salam   is a senior consultant with Energy Services. He has more than seven years of broad experience in cloud computing, including virtualization and network infrastructure. Abdul's previous experience includes engineering positions at multinational firms. Abdul has authored numerous blogs, technical books and papers, and tutorials as well as web content on IT. He earned a bachelor degree in information technology followed by a master of business administration in information technology and technical certifications from Cisco and Juniper Networks. You can contact him at LinkedIn.

Salman Ul Haq   is a techpreneur and chief hacker at TunaCode. His interest in cloud computing grew when Amazon launched Amazon Web Services (AWS), which ushered in the modern cloud. His core expertise is in building computer vision systems and APIs for the cloud. He is co-inventor of CUVI and gKrypt SDKs. His other interests include big data, especially when combined with advanced AI in the cloud, and data security in the cloud. He can be reached at salman@programmerfish.com.

Contents at a Glance

Contents

Table of Exercises

CompTIA.

It Pays to Get Certified

In a digital world, digital literacy is an essential survival skill.

Certification demonstrates that you have the knowledge and skill to solve technical or business problems in virtually any business environment. Certifications are highly valued credentials that qualify you for jobs, increased compensation, and promotion.

LEARN		CERTIFY	WORK

IT is Everywhere	IT Knowledge and Skills Get Jobs	Job Retention	New Opportunities	High Pay-High Growth Jobs
IT is mission critical to almost all organizations and its importance is increasing.	Certifications verify your knowledge and skills that qualifies you for:	Competence is noticed and valued in organizations.	Certifications qualify you for new opportunities in your current job or when you want to change careers.	Hiring managers demand the strongest skill set.
• 79% of U.S. businesses report IT is either important or very important to the success of their company	• Jobs in the high growth IT career field • Increased compensation • Challenging assignments and promotions • 60% report that being certified is an employer or job requirement	• Increased knowledge of new or complex technologies • Enhanced productivity • More insightful problem solving • Better project management and communication skills • 47% report being certified helped improve their problem solving skills	• 31% report certification improved their career advancement opportunities	• There is a widening IT skills gap with over 300,000 jobs open • 88% report being certified enhanced their resume

- **CompTIA Cloud+ certification** designates an experienced IT professional equipped to provide secure technical solutions to meet business requirements in the cloud.
- Certifies that the successful candidate has the knowledge and skills required to understand standard cloud terminologies and methodologies to implement, maintain, and support cloud technologies and infrastructure.
- Job roles include System Administrator, Network Administrator and Storage Administrator among many others.
- **The market for cloud related jobs is growing** with annual cloud market growth of almost 30% projected by research group IDC over the next several years.

Steps to Getting Certified and Staying Certified

Review Exam Objectives	Review the certification objectives to make sure you know what is covered in the exam. http://certification.comptia.org/examobjectives.aspx
Practice for the Exam	After you have studied for the certification, take a free assessment and sample test to get an idea of what type of questions might be on the exam. http://certification.comptia.org/samplequestions.aspx
Purchase an Exam Voucher	Purchase your exam voucher on the CompTIA Marketplace, which is located at: http://www.comptiastore.com/
Take the Test	Select a certification exam provider and schedule a time to take your exam. You can find exam providers at the following link: http://certification.comptia.org/Training/testingcenters.aspx
Stay Certified! Continuing Education	The CompTIA Cloud+ certification is valid for three years from the date of certification. There are a number of ways the certification can be renewed. For more information go to: http://certification.comptia.org/getCertified/stayCertified.aspx

How to Obtain More Information

Visit CompTIA online   www.comptia.org to learn more about getting CompTIA certified.

Contact CompTIA   Call 866-835-8020 ext. 5 or email questions@comptia.org.

Connect with us   We're on LinkedIn, Facebook, Twitter, Flickr, and YouTube.

Introduction

Cloud computing is reality now, defining how IT is handled not only in large, medium, and small enterprises but also in—consumer—facing businesses. The *cloud* itself is a familiar cliché, but when you attach *computing*, it brings with it a slew of services, vendors, and such, and the horizon includes virtual server providers, hosting providers, virtual storage and networking providers, hypervisor vendors, and private/public cloud providers.

The enterprise IT landscape has always been well-defined and segmented. Cloud computing initially started with replacing the traditional IT model; any business that had anything to do with computers and software (and that was almost 100 percent of businesses around the world) would need to acquire physical servers (often racks of them, depending on the size of the business) and storage and networking components. The business then had to construct a specially designed data center to deploy the components then configure, support, and manage the data center. Specialized IT skills were needed for executing a data center and managing it. Only large-scale enterprises and well-funded businesses could afford to undertake this. Even for large enterprises that had their own massive data centers for distributing enterprise applications to the workers and storing business data, operating the data center itself was a distraction that added to costs.

Cloud computing is a natural transition from this legacy model of enterprise IT to a world where computing can be sold and purchased just like any other commodity, where consumers would pay only for what they use, without steep up-front bills. You can now "order" 100 virtual servers and build enough computing capacity to run an application consumed by 100 million users over the Internet without owning a single server or writing a huge check to cover up-front costs. The cloud has not only ushered in a new age for enterprise IT, it has become the enabler technology for the Internet startups of today. It would be safe to say that a lot of very well-known Internet businesses wouldn't be possible if there were no cloud.

Who Should Read This Book

The global cloud market is expected to reach $270 billion by 2020. With most government and corporate IT moving into the cloud, this is the perfect time to equip yourself with the right skills to thrive in cloud computing.

Even though cloud computing has significantly lowered the barrier for businesses to use IT resources on demand, this does not mean that you can create your company's virtual data center in the cloud with just a few clicks. Building the right cloud infrastructure and efficiently managing and supporting it requires specialized skills. In addition to cloud practitioners, this book is for IT students who want to take a dive into understanding the concepts behind some of the key technologies that power modern cloud solutions and are essential for deploying, configuring, and managing private, public, and hybrid cloud environments.

Additionally, the topics covered in this book have been selected to address the CompTIA Cloud+ certification CV0-001, as indicated in the title of the book.

If you're preparing for the CompTIA Cloud+ certification CV0-001, this book is ideal for you. You can find more information about the CompTIA Cloud+ certification here:

http://certification.comptia.org/getCertified/certifications/cloudplus.aspx

How This Book is Organized

The topics in this book were chosen to cover a wide range of cloud technologies, deployment scenarios, and configuration issues as well as fundamental concepts that define modern cloud computing. Every chapter begins with an introduction and a list of the topics covered within it. To enhance your learning experience, we've included hands-on exercises and real-world scenarios. The book also includes a practice exam that covers the topics presented in each chapter, which will help you prepare well for the certification exam.

Chapter 1, "Understanding Cloud Characteristics," starts off with a detailed overview of the key terms related to cloud computing, including discussions of elasticity, metering/billing with the pay-as-you-grow model, network access, multitenancy, and a hybrid cloud scenario with cloud bursting, rapid deployment, and automation. The chapter also covers key concepts in object-based storage systems, including object IDs, metadata, access policies, and enabling access through REST APIs.

Chapter 2, "To Grasp the Cloud—Fundamental Concepts," takes a dive into the key piece of technology that makes it possible to enable cloud computing—virtualization. This chapter covers Type 1 and Type 2 hypervisors and their differences plus popular open-source and proprietary hypervisors that are available today with an overview of their key features. It also covers consumer versus enterprise use cases and workstation versus infrastructure virtualization. We discuss the key benefits of virtualization, like shared resources, elasticity, and complete resource pooling, including compute, storage, and network. The chapter ends with a discussion of the fundamentals of cloud computing in the context of virtualization technology.

Chapter 3, "Within the Cloud: Technical Concepts of Cloud Computing," takes a dive into the technical aspects of scalable computing, which include a comparison of traditional and cloud infrastructures, selecting the right infrastructure for building your own cloud, scaling and optimizing a data center, and economies of scale. At the end of the chapter, there's a section on cloud infrastructure, which covers open-source and proprietary solutions and includes a discussion on choosing between creating in-house tools or selecting third-party solutions and what drives the build versus buy decisions when it comes to cloud infrastructure.

Chapter 4, "Cloud Management," includes a plethora of scenarios, use cases, and issues associated with managing deployment and ongoing support for your cloud implementation. Broadly, this includes managing your own cloud, managing workloads in the cloud, and managing business data assets that live in the cloud, including data migration and secure storage and access of the data. The cloud is device agnostic, so controlling and managing access to the cloud by a plethora of devices—a concept known as BYOD—is also discussed.

Chapter 5, "Diagnosis and Performance Monitoring,"   discusses the aspects of a cloud implementation that you'll want to gauge and monitor. This includes performance metrics across compute (e.g., IOPS and load balancing), network (e.g., latency and bandwidth), and storage (e.g., file system performance and caching) resources. We also discuss best practices to achieve optimal performance with the hypervisor and common failure scenarios.

Chapter 6, "Cloud Delivery and Hosting Models,"   dives into the three main types of clouds in terms of delivery and access: public, private, and hybrid. On-premise and off-premise hosting options are discussed for all three types. At the end of the chapter is a discussion of the security and functionality aspects of these models.

Chapter 7, "Practical Cloud Knowledge: Install, Configure, and Manage,"   provides hands-on practical knowledge of the intricacies of setting up and managing your own cloud infrastructure. The chapter includes key discussions on creating a complete virtualized data center and configuring virtual compute, storage, and networking components. We'll discuss migrating existing data and compute workloads to a newly built cloud and provide an overview of the key virtual components of the cloud.

Chapter 8, "Hardware Management,"   walks through the physical hardware components that make up a cloud. Pros and cons of hardware design choices are discussed, including compute (e.g., number of cores and parallelism), storage (e.g., magnetic/spinning disk versus SSD), and networking (e.g., NIC quantities, types, and speed). Toward the end of the chapter, there's an in-depth discussion of cloud storage options.

Chapter 9, "Storage Provisioning and Networking,"   dives deep into creating virtualized storage, managing storage security and access, and provisioning models. We'll show you how to configure networking for the cloud, including how to create and configure multiple virtual networks within the same cloud, how to configure remote access to the cloud over the network, and how to optimize network performance. The chapter also includes some common troubleshooting scenarios as well as a discussion of selecting the right networking protocols and networking monitoring and alert mechanisms.

Chapter 10, "Testing and Deployment: Quality Is King,"   focuses on how QoS defines the success of the cloud. This chapter walks through extensive testing criteria for compute, storage, networking, and security/penetration. Test automation is also discussed. Deployment-related aspects like HA, multipathing, and load balancing are discussed toward the end of the chapter.

Chapter 11, "Cloud Computing Standards and Security,"   discusses the importance of standards for cloud implementation and management. The bigger portion of the chapter addresses the important topic of security in the cloud, including a discussion of the technical tools used to implement foolproof security for a cloud infrastructure. Encryption technologies are discussed along with implementation strategies for encryption in all states—communication, usage, and storage.

Chapter 12, "The Cloud Makes It Rain Money: The Business in Cloud Computing," discusses the various business models for distributing cloud services, including IaaS, SaaS, DaaS, and PaaS. Enterprise applications and collaboration and telepresence tools are discussed from a business perspective. Disaster recovery, an important responsibility of every cloud service provider, is discussed at length, including redundancy, geographical diversity, and mission-critical application requirements. More recent trends within cloud computing, like the freelance movement and BYOD, are discussed toward the end of the chapter.

Chapter 13, "Planning for Cloud Integration: Pitfalls and Advantages," takes a broader look at the technical aspects to consider while making the transition to the cloud. This includes making the right choice for the type of cloud to adopt and modifying the organizational structure to adapt to the new IT trends. Common pitfalls encountered along the road to cloud adoption are also discussed.

If you think you've found a technical error in this book, please visit http://sybex .custhelp.com. Customer feedback is critical to our efforts at Sybex.

Interactive Online Learning Environment and Test Bank

This book provides access to relevant study tools and a test bank in an interactive online learning environment, making it an ideal exam prep guide for this challenging, but rewarding certification. Items available among the study tools and test bank include the following:

Practice Exam   This book comes with a 76-question practice exam to help you test your knowledge and review important information.

Electronic Flash Clards   This book also includes 113 questions in a flash card format (a question followed by a single correct answer). You can use these questions to review your knowledge and understanding of concepts.

Glossary   The key terms from this book, and their definitions, are available as a fully searchable PDF you can save to your device and print out.

NOTE   You can access the online learning environment and test bank at http://sybextestbanks.wiley.com.

Chapter

1

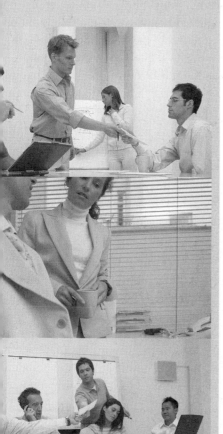

Understanding Cloud Characteristics

TOPICS COVERED IN THIS CHAPTER INCLUDE:

✓ **Basic terms and characteristics**

- Elasticity
- On-demand/self-service
- Pay-as-you-grow
- Chargeback
- Ubiquitous access
- Metering and resource pooling
- Multitenancy
- Cloud bursting
- Rapid deployment
- Automation

✓ **Object storage concepts**

- ObjectID
- Metadata
- Extended metadata
- Data/blob
- Policies
- Replication
- Access control

Thomas J. Watson, the founder of IBM, remarked in the early 1940s, "I think there is a world market for about five computers."

Even though that comment was referring to a new line of "scientific" computers that IBM built and wanted to sell throughout the United States, in the context of the cloud, the idea behind it still applies. If you think about it, most of the world's critical business infrastructure relies on a handful of massive—really massive—data centers spread across the world. Cloud computing has come a long way, from early mainframes to today's massive server farms powering all kinds of applications.

This chapter starts off with overview of some of the key concepts in cloud computing. Broadly, the standard features of a cloud are categorized into compute, storage, and networking. Toward the end of the chapter, there's a dedicated section on elastic, object-based storage and how it has enabled enterprises to store and process big data on the cloud.

Basic Terms and Characteristics

Before we begin, it's important to understand the basic terms that will be used throughout the book and are fundamental to cloud computing. The following sections will touch upon these terms to give a feel for what's to follow in later chapters.

Elasticity

Natural clouds are indeed elastic, expanding and contracting based on the force of the winds carrying them. The cloud is similarly elastic, expanding and shrinking based on resource usage and cloud tenant resource demands. The physical resources (computing, storage, networking, etc.) deployed within the data center or across data centers and bundled as a single cloud usually do not change that fast. This elastic nature, therefore, is something that is built into the cloud at the software stack level, not the hardware.

The classic promise of the cloud is to make compute resources available on demand, which means that theoretically, a cloud should be able to scale as a business grows and shrink as the demand diminishes. Consider here, for example, Amazon.com during Black Friday. There's a spike in inbound traffic, which translates into more memory consumption, increased network density, and increased compute resource utilization. If Amazon.com had, let's say, 5 servers and each server could handle up to 100 users at a time, the whole deployment would have peak service capacity of 500 users. During the holiday season, there's an influx of 1,000 users, which is double the capacity of what the current deployment can handle. If Amazon were smart, it would have set up 5 additional (or maybe 10) servers within its data center in anticipation of the holiday season spike. This would mean physically provisioning 5 or 10 machines, setting them up, and connecting with the current deployment of 5 servers. Once the season is over and the traffic is back to normal, Amazon doesn't really need those additional 5 to 10 servers it brought in before the season. So either they stay within the data center sitting idle and incurring additional cost or they can be rented to someone else.

What we just described is what a typical deployment looked like pre-cloud. There was unnecessary physical interaction and manual provisioning of physical resources. This is inefficient and something that cannot be linearly scaled up. Imagine doing this with millions of users and hundreds or even thousands of servers. Needless to say, it would be a mess.

This manual provisioning is not only inefficient, it's also financially infeasible for startups because it requires investing significant capital in setting up or co-locating to a data center and dedicated personnel who can manually handle the provisioning.

This is what the cloud has replaced. It has enabled small, medium, and large teams and enterprises to provision and then decommission compute, network, and memory resources, all of which are physical, in an automated way, which means that you can now scale up your resources just in time to serve the traffic spike and then wind down the additional provisioned resources, effectively just paying for the time that your application served the spike with increased resources.

This automated resource allocation and deallocation is what makes a cloud elastic.

On-Demand Self-service/JIT

On-demand self-service can be thought of as the end point of an elastic cloud, or the application programming interface (API) in strict programming terminology. In other words, elasticity is the intrinsic characteristic that manifests itself to the end user or a cloud tenant as on-demand self-service, or *just in time (JIT)*.

Every cloud vendor offers a self-service portal where cloud tenants can easily provision new servers, configure existing servers, and deallocate extra resources. This process can be done manually by the user, or it can also be automated, depending upon the business case.

Let's look again at our Amazon.com example to understand how JIT fits in that scenario and why it's one of the primary characteristics of a cloud. When the devops (development and operations) personnel or team figures out that demand would surge during the holiday season, they can simply provision 10 more servers during that time, either through a precooked shell script or by using the cloud provider's web portal. Once the extra allocated resources have been consumed and are no longer needed, they can be deallocated through another custom shell script or through the portal. Every organization and team will have its own way of doing this.

With automated scripting, almost all major cloud vendors now support resource provisioning based on JavaScript Object Notation (JSON). Here is an example pseudo-JSON object that can be fed to an HTTPS request to spin up a new server:

```
{
        request-type        : "provision-new",
        template-name       : "my-centos-template",
        total-instances     : "10",
}
```

This script can and will of course be more comprehensive. We wrote it just to give you an idea of how simple and basic it has become to spin up and shut down servers.

Templating

Templating is a nice way to spin up preconfigured servers that hit the ground running. Let's consider a real example: Suppose you are part of a project that provides smart video analytics to advertisers. It is distributed as a web app running on the cloud. The app spans across several languages, frameworks, backend processing engines, and protocols. Currently, it runs atop Ubuntu Linux servers. Web apps that process and serve videos can typically clog servers pretty quickly. The web app that the devops team has written has a "soft installation," which bundles required frameworks and libraries into a neat deployment script.

Now, when you anticipate (or predict) a traffic spike or even an abnormal increase in app consumption, you have to spin new instances and join them with the whole deployment network running several servers for DB, process, CDN, front end, and so on. You have cooked a nice "image" of your deployment server, which means that whenever you have to spin a new instance to meet increased user demand, you simply provision a new instance and provide it with this ready-to-run template. Within 20 to 30 seconds, you have a new member in this small server family ready to serve users. This process is automated through your custom provisioning script, which handles all the details like specifying the template, setting the right security for the instance, and allocating the right server size based on the memory, compute resources, storage, and network capacity of the available server sizes.

Once the request is sent, it is not queued; instead it's served in real time, which means that the physical (actually in a virtualized environment, but more on that in Chapter 2, "Terms Loosely Affiliated with Cloud Computing") compute resources are provisioned from the pool of seemingly infinite servers. For a typical deployment, all this would take is not more than 2 minutes to spin up 100 or more servers. This is unprecedented in computing and something that played a key role in accelerated adoption of the cloud.

EXERCISE 1.1: JIT PROVISIONING ON AWS

As a real-world example, let's walk through the process of provisioning a Linux server on *Amazon Web Services (AWS),* shown in the following screen shot. This assumes that you already have signed up for an AWS account and logged into the dashboard:

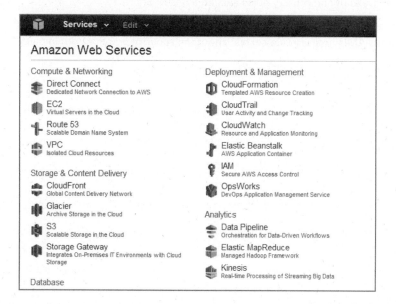

1. Once you have logged into the AWS dashboard, select EC2 and then Launch Instance.

It's a seven-step process to configure and launch a single or multiple instances, although if you have your template prepared already, it's as simple as a one-step click and launch operation.

Back to launching our new instance from scratch.

EXERCISE 1.1: JIT PROVISIONING ON AWS *(continued)*

2. First you will have to specify the Amazon Machine Image (AMI), which is Amazon's version of a template used to spin up a preconfigured customized server in the cloud. In AWS, you can select a vanilla OS or your own template (AMI), or you can select from hundreds of community AMIs available on AWS.

   It is, however, recommended not to spin mission-critical applications on top of shared community AMIs until you are certain about the security practices put in place.

3. Next, select the size of the instance.

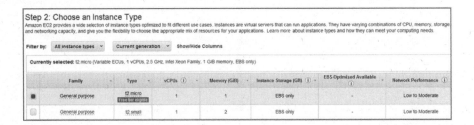

   AWS has a set of fixed compute resource servers.

4. You can get started with selecting the hardware and networking configurations you need and then add more resources on top of that while configuring the instance.

Pay as You Grow

One of the primary "promises" of the cloud, and also what contributed significantly to the early adoption of it, was the pay-as-you-go model, which has been slightly tweaked, in fact, and just renamed to pay as you grow. A decade ago, startups needed to have substantial financial muscle to invest in initial data center setup. This is not an easy feat. A specialized skill set is needed to properly set up, configure, and manage a server infrastructure. There were two problems—steep financial cost and unnecessary and unneeded complexity. Smaller startups and engineering teams could just co-locate with an operational data center and set up a few servers to start with to control cost, at least until the product was validated and experiencing initial adoption. This is precisely when things go bad, infrastructure wise.

When YouTube started adding new users and the team started experiencing exponential growth, most of their time was spent in keeping the product (website) responsive and alive. This meant adding dozens of servers every day into the data center and dealing with the increased complexity and maintenance. They were in Silicon Valley with easy access to hardware they could purchase over the counter and plug into their co-located data center. Imagine scaling your application in a physical location where provisioning new servers would mean a lead time of a few or several days. This is a familiar story with most of the web startups pre-cloud, or pre-AWS to be more precise.

Another angle to the financial component of this equation is to look at both expansions and contractions in the usage of the product/service. In times of spikes, you will need to make investments into infrastructure to plug in more servers, but what happens when the spike normalizes or, worse, goes into a valley (steep decline in application/service usage)? If you had not played your infrastructure cards right, you would end up with dozens or maybe hundreds of servers you do not need anymore, but you have to keep them operational within the data center just in case another usage spike knocks on the door.

Naturally, not every startup will have the financial and technical expertise needed to set up initial infrastructure and start serving end users. This is the case with every consumer-facing startup, where predictions of usage patterns may not be anywhere near accurate and hence the engineering team will have no solid data to base their resource provisioning or infrastructure setup on. This may not hold true for most enterprises where usage density is prior knowledge, as is scaling out. But then, large enterprise where the primary use case is internal enterprise applications being consumed by the workforce were not the initial targets for the cloud. It's only now that large enterprises and financial institutions have started to move to the cloud or building their own private cloud on which to host enterprise applications.

Pay-as-You-Grow Theory vs. Practice

In theory, pay as you grow would mean that the cost/user would be treated as a constant and scaling out would mean a linear increase in cloud infrastructure and resource usage bills. Let's consider the launch of awesome-product.com. Initially, in the pregrowth phase, there are on average 100 users who interact with the product monthly. The cloud engineer or team at awesome-product.com calculates the cost incurred per user to be $1/month. This includes the network bandwidth, storage, compute cycles (CPU/GPU usage), content distribution network (CDN), and DB cost components. Awesome-product.com has an SLA with AWS, where the whole product is hosted. In its third month, it starts to experience growth and users start accessing its product in droves. Adoption increases and now it has 10,000 users. If you scale the cost linearly, you will simply have $1 × 10 thousand to estimate the monthly cloud infrastructure cost based on a pay-as-you-grow model. This does not usually hold true because the cost/user can be treated as a constant only in a deployment serving a limited user base, or 100 initial users in this example.

Practically, what happens—and this is something that engineers can easily relate to—is that the cost/user also gradually increases as more users are added. At a finer technical level, this increase in cost/user is due to increased number of users being put on the same server even when you are scaling out servers. Within networking, it's a given that when more users start accessing the limited network backbone on a single server, performance and capacity changes negatively. This would mean that even if the servers are optimally configured, packing more users into the servers as you experience growth would negatively impact performance, and hence you will need additional servers to keep delivering the same experience. These additional infrastructure resources would translate into increased cost/users.

Alternately, if the SLA specifies a non-licensing-based model (where a fixed set of compute, network, and storage resources are locked in and instead of fewer users in the initial stages, the cost/user component grows when there is user growth) and instead works on a growth-based model, additional compute, network, and storage resources are added into your "virtual cluster" whenever they're needed during the growth stage or released back into the main pool when they're not needed. This model would compute the cost/user based not on the total cost of the cloud infrastructure in the early stages but rather on the optimal number of users/server and whether the network would optimally handle usage spikes (something the cloud provider will have to specify). This type of cost analysis would yield a more optimal overall cost and stick true to the pay-as-you-grow paradigm.

Chargeback

Chargeback is a common term in the financial world. In IT, and specifically in cloud computing, *chargeback* refers to implementing a resource usage model where customers or users of the cloud resources can be billed based on predetermined granular units of compute, storage, networking, or other resource consumption. Every public cloud provider has a chargeback model implemented. Without chargeback, these public cloud providers will not be able to keep operating commercially.

AWS, for example, displays a price list for every cloud resource it offers—X dollars for every hour you keep a virtual machine, Y dollars for every GB you put on the network, and so on. This would mean that its chargeback model would keep a tab on the precise resource usage by every one of its customers and bill them accordingly. Chargeback is what makes the pay-as-you-go model of cloud computing possible.

Some cloud providers, like Amazon (AWS), Microsoft (Azure), and Google (Google Cloud), provide a set of resources for free initially, but this doesn't mean they have metering enabled for those resources. Amazon, for example, gives a micro instance for free for the first year coupled with storage, bandwidth, and a few more resource offerings, but you can always log into your cloud management console and check precise usage.

Chargeback helps cloud tenants in some of the following ways:

- Determining precise usage to plan for growth and provision new resource.
- Knowing your product's overall resource footprint, which may help you become greener
- Optimizing resource usage based on real usage data sourced from the cloud provider
- Budgeting cloud infrastructure

Implementing Chargeback

The backend implementation of the chargeback model would need to have at least the following characteristics:

Scalable   The resource consumption monitoring component, which keeps tabs on the whole data center or across data centers of the cloud provider, would need to be scalable at the cloud scale with tens of billions of resource usage transactions happening every day. The metering component itself would be a huge big data problem to solve.

Atomic Precision   Cloud vendors charge for every hour of compute resources tenants utilize. Big public cloud vendors may have hundreds of thousands of servers and millions of tenants on their platform. Implementing precision into the resource monitoring component is crucial because when added up, even very small inaccuracies may translate into millions of dollars' worth of lost billing.

Fluid   Pricing models for cloud resources change. New offers and promotions have to be taken into account. This would mean that the price compute layer on top of the metering component would need to be flexible to incorporate changes into the pricing model.

Capable of Analytics   Billions of resource transactions happen across public clouds every day. All these transactions would need to be unified into easily consumable analytics for the cloud provider to determine usage patterns, conduct auditing, discover possible leaks, and lead toward more optimized cloud infrastructure. This is a big data problem where perhaps tens of terabytes of data would need to be ingested and analyzed every day.

Ubiquitous Access

Every public cloud tenant or user should be able to connect to the platform and operate their account over the Internet regardless of location or network technology, as long as the technology is commonly used and supported by the cloud provider. The same would hold true for custom private cloud implementations, with the only change being that the cloud is usually locked behind a firewall with only authorized users allowed access. This is what ubiquitous access guarantees. However, this does not mean that the public cloud providers would not account for security consideration or honor the access limits set by a user.

In years past, users would have to go to a specialized physical location where a mainframe was hosted or where thin clients were available to be able to get on the legacy cloud platform and use or perform maintenance operations. Today, you can, for example, connect to your Amazon cloud account anywhere and perform every operation that's available.

There are a couple of aspects that have to be kept in mind regarding ubiquitous access:

Security   Cloud tenants typically connect with the cloud provider for resource management over the network. The most popular way is to use Secure Shell (SSH) to access your cloud account and perform operations. Most cloud providers enable users to allow or block network IP addresses and ports. This would not mean that the cloud provider is not offering ubiquitous access or pseudo-ubiquitous access.

Security has become one of the top concerns within the cloud, and therefore security is something that has to be prioritized over easy access. This wouldn't make a cloud less ubiquitous because the vendor enables tenants to customize their access levels based on their security concerns.

Ubiquitous Network   Cloud tenants should be able to connect to the platform regardless of how the internal network backbone is implemented within the vendor's data centers. Every major public cloud vendor has geographically distributed data centers across continents, and tenants can provision resources in any of the available zones based on the physical proximity of their majority user base. Access to the cloud platform for the tenants should be abstracted from the underlying details of how the network requests would be routed to the right data center.

Metering Resource Pooling

There are two types of cloud infrastructure offerings: bare metal and virtual (with further divisions within virtual). With a bare metal infrastructure, the physical server would be allocated with the same specification you placed an order for. This is popular among scientific- and compute-based financial users because they need the performance that bare metal would guarantee; the cloud vendor would make a commitment to not onboard multiple tenants to the same physical servers. However, these users form a tiny subset of the overall user base of cloud vendors, and therefore cloud offerings are not geared toward allocating silicon instead of virtual machines. Also, on the scale of the cloud, rolling out a bare metal offering would be complex and not only incur additional cost but also diminish profits for the cloud vendors. This is one of the reasons Amazon does not offer bare metal cloud instances.

Resource pooling refers to virtualizing the physical resources available in the cloud vendor's centers. From *virtual machines (VMs)* to software defined networking (SDNs), the physical layer has been totally abstracted, not only from the tenants but also from the infrastructure and data center engineering teams within the cloud vendors.

Virtualization brings in a whole new set of challenges when it comes to metering the resources consumed by individual tenants. Keep in mind that metering is critical to cloud vendors' operations and commercial viability and any inaccuracy could result in massive losses in the form of unbilled resources.

🌐 **Real World Scenario**

Metering Pooled Resources

Consider this scenario to understand the complexity in metering pooled resources. When a physical machine is virtualized, it enables spinning up and shutting down multiple operating system (OS) instances almost in real time. Although virtualization providers like VMware do provide mechanisms to allocate resources on a server (compute, storage, and network) at a granular level, there would be overflow based on the number of VMs running on a physical server at any given moment. If a dual Intel Xeon server with IB ports and SSD storage has just a single VM running, the application running on the VM would definitely give its best performance. However, when the server gets saturated with the maximum number of VMs that may be spun up, the resources would be strictly rationed.

The cloud vendor would need to have metering built in so it can account for pooled resource utilization at the atomic level. This resource metering would have to implemented on top of the VM resource monitoring and not at the level of bare metal.

Multitenancy

Data centers of cloud vendors are deeply virtualized, which translates into the ability of the vendor to pack multiple users or tenants into the same physical servers. This is what's referred to as multitenancy within the cloud.

Single-Instance Model

Multitenancy is often used with the term *single-instance model*. They both refer to the same feature of the popular definition of the cloud where physical resources are virtualized; the physical layer is completely abstracted and offered as billable units of compute, storage, and network resources. In this model, the applications of multiple tenants belonging to different companies reside on the same physical server but are segregated at the VM level so that data, software, and custom applications and configurations running on one tenant's cloud account are not accessible to the other tenant. This segregation is implemented within the virtualization layer, which ensures that data and access cannot leak between multiple VMs running on the same server.

Customized Configurations

Every application has unique requirements for tweaking the software it's running on. This includes, for example, configuring a web server running on top of the cloud VM allocated for the application. Multitenancy would not stop a tenant from customizing software running on top of its cloud instance. This is one level above the VM segregation we just talked about. Multitenant clouds usually offer units of resources that "look like" actual physical units but are actually a portion of the actual physical resource. For example, AWS offers instances that specify the number of cores you will get but not the type of CPU. The *Amazon Elastic Compute Cloud (EC2)* micro instance has an older-generation Xeon-based server, but Amazon does not offer the actual Xeon CPU as a unit of resource. Rather, it offers x number of cores as the billable compute unit because the virtualization layer running on top of the actual physical resource partitions the CPU into a given number of virtual machines, each of which will have access to the same CPU but not be able to share the same compute load. The same happens with network and storage. Your application's backend database may reside on the same physical storage as your competitor's, but the data cannot seep through and cross the boundaries set by the VM.

Having said this, not all clouds are multitenant. Let's take a quick look at the much smaller niche segment, single-tenant clouds, and some of the aspects that need to be properly analyzed when adopting either a single-tenant or multitenant cloud configuration.

Single-Tenant Cloud

With a single-tenant cloud, every tenant has physical and not virtual boundaries around the allocated resource pool. This is common in bare metal cloud offerings where the vendor guarantees physical resource allocation for a tenant and commits to not packing multiple users on the same pool of physical resources. Offering single tenancy within a bare metal cloud offering is relatively easier than offering single tenancy or physical segregation within a virtualized cloud offering.

In a virtualized cloud, single tenancy may be implemented by ensuring that a tenant's VMs cannot be packed with another tenant's VMs. To get a fair understanding, consider this example: Your application awesome-app.com has spun 20 VMs, or EC2 instances on the Amazon cloud. If the physical server on top of which your EC2 instance is running can pack in 6 VMs in a single server, that would mean your instances would be distributed among at least 4 physical servers. Now, one of those servers would still have the capacity to pack in 4 more VMs after your last 2 VMs are packed into it. Because Amazon does not offer or guarantee single tenancy, this would mean that the virtualization layer can pick any other 4 VMs from another tenant or multiple tenants and pack them into the same physical server where your VMs are running.

Cost Optimization

In the preceding example, consider that Amazon did offer single tenancy; that would mean that the last physical server would have only 2 VMs running on it while it has the capacity of 6. The virtualization layer may intelligently expand the allocated resources of those last 2 instances to span and utilize the complete compute, storage, and network resources available on that physical server. But if this does not happen, Amazon would have idle resource packets sitting around in its data centers and this would lead to lost revenue. Therefore, single tenancy would incur more operational costs and reduced revenue because the available resources are not completely utilized.

Security

One of the primary reasons to go for single tenancy is security. Some regulations within healthcare (HIPAA/HITECH) and finance (PCI-DSS) demand that personally identifiable data or critical financial information be physically segregated to prove that it's properly secured. This has been one of the stumbling blocks in the adoption of the cloud, especially public cloud solutions within the healthcare and financial sectors. The remedy to this challenge is to encrypt all critical data before it leaves a controlled premises (company) and heads to the cloud. In response to this challenge, the public cloud providers offer single-tenant dedicated encryption key managers that run on instances with physical boundary segregation from other tenants, ensuring that data security keys are housed in a physically separate server.

Cloud Bursting

Typically, there are three different cloud deployment strategies: private cloud deployment, public cloud deployment, and hybrid. Cloud bursting is used with the hybrid cloud deployment strategy, where the deployment utilizes a mix of an in-house private cloud and a public cloud, as the term *hybrid* suggests.

Cloud bursting is something that mainly enterprise cloud tenants would have to implement because most of the consumer-facing web applications run completely on public clouds.

In enterprise cloud deployment, a typical use case would be catering to applications that are workforce facing, like enterprise resource planning (ERP) and internal financial and management applications. These applications would have a set of defined users and predictable future resource requirements. Then there are applications for the enterprise that are either consumer facing or the kind that can experience sudden spikes in use. Because the private cloud deployment would entail a company's own data center with a set number of physical servers, catering to these spikes in usage would mean adding more physical resources into the data center. The other option would be to implement cloud bursting, which would mean that whenever there's a spike in usage beyond the capacity of the physical resources available within the company's private cloud, the additional users would all be routed to the public cloud.

When you're implementing the cloud bursting strategy, you would need to consider transparent switching, load balancing, and security.

Transparent Switching

Enterprise applications running on top of the private cloud usually do not implement the automated switching required when the private cloud runs out of resources. This switching happens between the virtualization and application layer. For example, Amazon Virtual Private Cloud (Amazon VPC) allows for a private cloud to connect with compute/storage/ networking resources allocated inside Amazon's cloud through a VPN connection.

Another interesting company that sensed the need to deploy hybrid clouds and to be able to transparently switch between them based on their performance or business considerations is CloudSwitch. It operates along with VMware virtualization layers and enables cloud administrators or data center engineering teams to automate the switch between the enterprise's private cloud and an already configured public cloud.

Load Balancing

Implementing cloud bursting would allow for smart load balancing for performance-sensitive applications. Whenever the requests increase the available capacity, the additional load is shifted on to the public cloud, and as the number of requests for an application decrease, the transparent switching mechanism would automatically move the load back into the private data center along with all the persistent data.

In addition to demand, there are other operational scenarios in which cloud bursting would fit well, such as, for example, upgrading components within the data center or upgrading the complete data center. In such a scenario, the complete load of the enterprise would be routed to the public cloud while the private cloud's data center gets updated. Generally, this would involve experiencing downtime if the right cloud augmentation or bursting strategy is not implemented.

Security

A hybrid cloud deployment may not enable cloud bursting or switching to a public cloud every application running on top of it. In cases where applications operate on business- or customer-sensitive data elements, the apps would have to be kept inside the controlled premises of the private cloud data center to ensure security of the sensitive data. This important aspect needs to be considered when a cloud switching strategy is implemented in a hybrid cloud deployment.

Rapid Deployment

In an ideal world, or maybe in the near future, the IT world would have zero-time deployment, which means that you can construct a basic use case application and provision cloud resources for it within no time. Rapid deployment, not zero-time deployment, refers to this ability of a cloud vendor to instantly construct a whole stack of technologies, frameworks, backend data bases, and third-party tools and software along with the required compute, storage, and networking resources and deploy this in a fully automated way.

Traditionally, deploying enterprise applications and software involved several phases and validation tests and required the involvement of a team of engineers to overlook the deployment of the application. A competitive business landscape and the need to keep on innovating has stripped even the biggest of enterprises of the luxury to have deployments of applications take several days. This is true for the majority of the use cases that these applications target, but not all. Applications that are critical to an enterprise may have a rapid deployment strategy built in but would have rigorous validation and usability tests before the deployment is complete.

Rapid deployment comes in many forms and shapes. One of the most common examples is Amazon's AMI marketplace. When launching a new EC2 compute instance on AWS, you can either select a vanilla operating system to run on top of the instance or select one of the many preconfigured instances for your specific use case. One use case author Salman Ul Haq generally encounters is having an instance with computer vision libraries, MEAN stack (MongoDB, ExpressJS, AngularJS, and Node.js), nginx, and a bunch of other tools, databases, and frameworks preinstalled.

This is not a common use case for most tenants, and there was no public Amazon machine instance (AMI) available in the marketplace, so Salman built one of his own. Once he has a machine running with the right kind of boilerplate set up, all he has to do is create a template out of it or create an AMI. Every time he needs additional compute resources for his application, he simply fires up an instance with the already saved AMI. This is not fully automated because he will still have to configure other tools and frameworks on top of it to make his application work on it.

Application-Specific Rapid Deployment Strategy

Every application has its own unique set of requirements and configurations. Therefore, no single universal rapid deployment strategy would fit all use cases. The base resources a tenant can allocate within a public cloud provide the boilerplate on which to deploy and configure your application, but to have a truly one-click deployment, your engineering team would need to implement its own deployment scripts.

In addition to offering cloud resources, vendors offer fully managed and hosted solutions. These solutions are often industry specific (or scale vertically) and bundle everything from the lowest-level hardware resources required to application-level details, all completely managed by the cloud provider. An example would be Google's BigQuery offering, which enables anyone to load a big dataset and analyze it and just pay for the resources they consume. These hosted services use pricing calculators to estimate the cost of using the hosted solution for a specific use case. However, fully managed and hosted solutions do not give the same level of flexibility when it comes to configuring the application or software suite you're consuming.

A rapid deployment strategy would have at least the characteristics discussed in the following sections.

Resource Provisioning

Smart resource provisioning would mean determining the required compute, storage, networking, and other resources to spin up an application. This calculation would be based either on a set configuration that specifies how much resources are needed or on a set pattern.

Installation and Configuration

Automated installation scripts or tools would have to be executed once cloud resources are provisioned. Automated installation would mean installing and configuring all the required third-party software, libraries, and tools the application needs. A common practice is to write the installation script once and then package it inside the application so that once you allocate a cloud instance or a set of instances, you simply deploy the app and it installs itself.

Integration

Applications, especially enterprise applications, seldom exist in isolation. Your CRM is connected with your ERP, which is connected with your accounting software. In this interconnected world of enterprise and consumer applications, you will have to make sure that when you deploy a new application, it automatically takes care of all the integration complexities that arise from it. Usually the applications are implemented in a modular way such that the interconnected applications talk to each other through a generic protocol such as, for example, a REST API. This way, deploying a new application or updating an existing application will not break down the whole application ecosystem and would just impact a part of the complete deployment.

Object Storage Concepts

To understand the scale of persistent data stored on the cloud and added every day, consider this statement from Eric Schmidt, CEO of Google: "Every two days now we create as much information as we did from the dawn of civilization up until 2003."

This amounts to roughly over 5 exabytes (yes, *exa*) of data that humanity has generated. Most of this data is in either private or public clouds somewhere.

The scale is unique in the sense that never in humanity did we have the need to store such a humongous amount of data in a centralized place or data center. This scale of data presents unique challenges for both storing and read/write operations on the data.

File-Based Data Storage

Traditional file storage systems were created with human readability in mind. The hierarchical layout of the various legacy file systems was designed for a limited scale of storage. There were several advantages of going this route:

Layered Organization of Data Files   It's easier to have data (text, video, audio, structured, and unstructured) files organized into layers with a hierarchical structure.

Structure Definition   It's easier to express structure of both structured and unstructured data when it's organized into multiple levels. Consider the example of storing your family photos. You may have a high-level folder named Family Photos with subfolders either for every member of the family or based on location or event. This hierarchy can theoretically continue till infinity. Imagine if you were not allowed to create subfolders and just had one single folder to keep all your data. Accessing that data manually would be a nightmare.

Despite these and many more advantages that have made the hierarchical file systems so popular throughout the past decades, they fall acutely short when it comes to the scale of data storage and read/write operations at which the cloud operates. Read/write latency, lack of APIs, and scalability are among the challenges we would have if we stuck with legacy hierarchical file systems.

Read/Write Latency

Legacy file systems like NTFS have an elaborate mechanism to access data stored on the physical medium (magnetic or SSDs). Because the data is available in a hierarchical structure, reading it would require first decoding the hierarchy and computing the actual physical address of the memory blocks on the physical storage medium.

Any system that has to access data from a storage device would have to compute the address of the required memory blocks and go through a similar process, but with legacy file systems, there are additional hops required because of the hierarchic layout. This additional processing may be tolerable in individual machine or even small-scale cluster deployment, but it becomes a significant showstopper when we scale it to the cloud level where petabytes of data elements are processed every single day, often across data centers that are physically separated.

Lack of APIs

The cloud is one big application programming interface (API). Almost every resource available on the cloud can be reserved, provisioned, consumed, and discarded through vendor APIs. The reason for creating API abstractions over all the cloud infrastructure and service resources any vendor offers is that the cloud was made for the Web. In contrast, legacy file systems were not primarily made for the Web. Early systems like FAT16 and 32 were primary made for single users, with little or no network connectivity considerations kept in focus while they were developed. This is the reason we had NTFS and then more protocols with focus on a clustered data storage system, where data would need to be accessed over the network and end users would no longer be able to control the actual physical storage medium where the data would be stored.

The cloud is a virtualized abstraction over a group of servers interconnected with a high-speed network. In a virtualized environment, you never know how much physical resources have been allocated to you. The VM that the cloud provider has spun up on your request and made available to you is a complete abstraction over the actual compute, storage, and networking resources available within the vendor's data centers.

The cloud would not have survived if we did not have object-based storage. But then object based storage is also one of the stumbling blocks that prevents cloud migration for enterprises with legacy applications running in-house, which are deeply integrated and rely on legacy data storage systems. Often, these organizations have to write gateway components to translate between internal data access protocols and external object-based storage on the cloud.

Scalability

It would be obvious from the previous two challenges, but to elaborate further, legacy data storage and access systems and protocols were not made for big data. The term *big data* is not used here in the popular sense of the word but to express the scale component of the big data (there are three features that classify big data: speed, scale, and frequency).

Facebook alone gets millions of photos added onto the platform every day. The scale (hundreds of terabytes or more), frequency (every day), and speed (throughout the day) would definitely qualify this scale at which data gets pushed into the Facebook platform as big data. Now imagine if Facebook were storing this massive trove of data on a legacy hierarchical file system. It would be a nightmare to create the hierarchy and a bigger nightmare to push changes and updates in the hierarchy because the change would have to be propagated to every single level within it.

Object Storage

The cloud needed a data storage mechanism that is flat, not hierarchical. It needed what we call object-based storage. Each data element, structured or unstructured, lives on the same level. In a way, object-based storage is also hierarchical, but with one level.

If you have a background in the object-oriented programming (OOP) paradigm, made popular first by the Java language (but all modern programming languages support OOP concepts), you know that everything would be thought of as an object. Imagine building a customer relationship management (CRM) system. Once the technical-business analyst captures the functionality requirements, the technical analyst, as part of their job to map the functional requirements to technical requirements, would identify and extract entities and map them as "objects." Even though these objects are not the same as objects in the object-based data storage systems, the concept is the same. However, OOP supports hierarchy of objects with multiple levels of inheritance, whereas object-based storage is flat. Object-based storage is often used interchangeably with document-based storage because every object could be thought of as a document.

Structured vs. Unstructured Data

Storage systems and protocols that were primarily made for networked data storage systems were either too complex to integrate into an application or not scalable to hundreds of billions of data elements. These systems mainly catered to unstructured data elements like textual data (documents, text blobs) and visual/audio data (photos, videos, audio files) within an enterprise. They were not designed for consumer applications. Even today, a lot of valuable data sits in silos within enterprises and is often not accessible to other teams and departments within the same organization. This is an indicator of the complexity, both technical and the complexity of the red tape, required for easy access to the data.

Relational database management systems (RDBMSs) primarily dominated storage, read/write access, and transactions over structured data. The RDBMS would manage the data stored across a networked storage system and consumers of this data would have access to it through SQL or SQL-like queries. This was the norm pre-cloud. This is a particularly good scheme for data storage, but it only works with structured data with relationships and hierarchies explicitly defined. However, most of the data that is generated every day is not structured. A huge chunk of the data being generated every day consists of plethora of visual and audio files, billions of web pages on the Internet, and the plethora of sensors within wearable devices, and so on, generating data at high frequency. We need a better way to organize this data and enable fast access (read/write) to it.

REST APIs

REST APIs are the language of the cloud. As discussed previously, every single resource a public or private cloud offers can be consumed through REST API calls.

Object ID

Since object-based storage means that every data element or object would be at the same level (flat storage), every object gets a unique identifier, which is used to access the object from the pool. The physical storage medium is completely abstracted from the consumer of the data because you do not have to specify a network address or path to fetch a data element. The system would know where the object is stored in the pool based on the ID you provided. This is a huge step up from legacy data storage systems where you would have to first ping the network storage system, then query it to fetch the address of the data elements you wanted to access, and then take care of the minute details of the data transaction in order to have the data read into the application. This has been replaced by a simplistic object ID–based data object access.

Even though object storage has not been standardized like other technologies and frameworks, every public cloud vendor incorporates the primary set of features for object-based storage we've been discussing. There are several startups and enterprise data companies that have rolled out object data storage system products that target customers looking into building private clouds. Often, as already mentioned, these enterprise companies would need to have a gateway between their legacy data storage systems and the new cloud-based object data storage system until they completely migrate to the cloud. Companies like Infinity Storage and SwiftStack have object storage gateway products that can be used with object storage products from HP, IBM, and a host of other companies. Covering the features of object storage products from these companies is beyond the scope of this book, but once you're comfortable with the concepts of object-based storage, it would be easy to adopt and deploy any product.

In the following sections, we'll cover the essential characteristics of object-based data storage, and for this, we will use Amazon Simple Storage Service (S3) to explain the concept in a practical manner. Other public cloud providers, like Microsoft Azure, Google Cloud, Rackspace, and DigitalOcean, have their own object-based storage options. Then there are third-party solutions for document-based storage like MongoDB, AeroSpike, and so on. These document-based "databases" implement the core characteristics of object-based storage and can be either deployed on your custom cloud instance or consumed as a hosted solution offered by several startups. The startup behind MongoDB, for example, offers hosted MongoDB service as well.

Let's get started with our example of Amazon S3 storage. S3 is a persistent data storage offering from Amazon. It is perhaps one of the most popular and earliest implementations of object storage service on a public cloud.

Object Life Cycle on Amazon S3

Amazon's RESTful API, which has client libraries for multiple languages like JavaScript, Java, C#, and PHP, can be used to manage the complete life cycle of an object. Objects are put into "buckets,"' which are kind of super objects and need to have unique names. No two users on the Amazon public cloud can have buckets with the same name. The buckets are arranged in a flat address space with unique names. This would mean that two objects can have the same name in two different buckets.

Object creation and read and deletion operations can be performed through the S3 REST API. You can put in an infinite amount of objects or data elements, at least theoretically, with constant access time, which indicates true scalability of the platform. An object is not limited by size either; you can have an object as small as 1 byte and as big as 5 terabytes each. This limit is imposed by Amazon and may vary with different public and private cloud providers. Because it's a service from Amazon, you do not have access to the fine-grain configurations like putting limits on the maximum size of an object, but you can still decide on object storage policies and put security-based limitations, as we'll discuss in the next sections.

Metadata

Instead of a centralized lookup table for storing *metadata* for every file or data element in the storage system, the metadata of every object is embedded right with the object in the flat address space. This guarantees that as scale of the data element or blobs increases, access times are not affected. Data organization is truly decentralized.

The way metadata is defined is also flat. Key-value pairs are used to define characteristics of an object. The object storage backend does not discriminate between different types of data since they are all treated as objects.

Enabling association of metadata for objects stored on Amazon S3 or any other object storage system enabled application developers and engineers to define properties of objects. There's no limit to how many key-value pairs you can define for a single object, but more key-value pairs would mean the size of the metadata of an object would increase and possible increased latency when objects are accessed over the network or the Internet.

Some metadata is created by the provider at the time of object creation and maintained throughout the life cycle of the object. This normally includes the creation/update date and size of the object. Additional metadata may include a flag indicating whether you want the data within the object to be encrypted before it's stored on the physical medium. Another form of associated system metadata is the MD5 checksum of the object's raw data, which is used to establish authenticity of the object when it's accessed and downloaded to a client machine. Encryption has become a necessity, and every public cloud provider now has it built in, with the option to turn it on or off. Cloud tenants can also pick and choose which buckets, for example, to encrypt and which buckets to leave as is. An important thing to note here is that this type of system-generated metadata is derived from the security policy the tenant has specified. System metadata key-value pairs cannot be modified by the cloud tenant. Table 1.1 lists some of the system defined metadata.

TABLE 1.1   Example of system-defined metadata

Key	Value
Date	Object creation date stamp
Content-Length	Size of the object in bytes
Last-Modified	Update/modification date stamp
Content MD-5	MD5 checksum

On top of this metadata, the tenant can create additional key-value pairs. For example, if you are operating a video site, a straightforward way to maintain information about the media files you have stored as objects on S3 would be to create key-value pairs for each piece of information you would like to associate with a media file, which may include title, genre, length in seconds, and a short description of the media file, as shown in Table 1.2. This way, you would just keep the object ID of this media file in another database and whenever you access the media file, you would simply fetch the metadata of it to fill in the details.

TABLE 1.2   Example of user-defined metadata

Key	Value
Title	Title of the video file
Length	Length in seconds of the video file
Genre	Genre information
Short-Description	Short description of the video

Legacy file storage systems do not expose the metadata of a file other than what the operating system reveals. The concept of defining custom metadata for a file is also alien to legacy file systems.

Data/Blob

In the world of structured data, a blob is considered a lump of raw data that cannot be operated on. Even though there is structure in every type of data that exists today, the definition of *structure* in terms of data is limited to data elements that can be operated on by a database system. A list of patient names, their addresses, and SSNs would be an example of structured data, whereas X-ray files, 3D scan files, and such visual data would be classified as unstructured data.

Any database system would be able to run SQL queries on the structured data and treat unstructured data as a lump that can be identified by some form of associated structured data, like an ID or patient name in this case. You cannot "sort" X-ray images based on their brightness or some other image-related characteristic, but you can always sort a patient list based on ascending order of SSNs.

An RDBMS is one of the most inefficient ways to store unstructured data. Consider a typical example of a customer table with the following columns:

serial_no	checkin_date	SSN	treatment_id

Suppose you are building an online electronic medical record (EMR) application and you have to keep a record of every test and its result, including all imagery/audio data of the patient within the system, and be able to fetch them on demand. This would mean that you insert all this "unstructured" data as blobs into the database and hurt the overall query performance because a single row of maybe a few kilobytes has now bloated to anywhere from a few megabytes to hundreds of megabytes or even GBs. This would be the most inefficient but highly convenient way to do this because all your information of any given patient is centralized into the database. Databases were just not made to embrace unstructured data; this was always an afterthought or a default option to construct your application quickly and forego performance.

Within the cloud, your data is considered a blob and put into the same pool as any other structured or unstructured data element. The recommended practice, though, is to store structured data into document-based storage and route unstructured data into Amazon S3, Microsoft Azure Storage, or Google Cloud Storage.

Extended Metadata

As we discussed previously, the association of metadata with an object, both *system-generated metadata* and *custom key-value metadata* created by the user, helps in associating added information, especially with unstructured data objects. Extended metadata primarily consists of a unique identifier for every single object in the pool of the cloud vendor, which helps in fetching the object regardless of where it's physically located.

In the case of Amazon S3, this would be the object ID with which you can query the object for read/modify/delete. This extended metadata also becomes part of the system-generated metadata since the unique identifier of the object is generated by the system to ensure its uniqueness and coherence with the ID generation scheme.

Physical Layer Abstraction

Extended metadata allows for thorough abstraction of physical storage devices and the whole underlying storage fabric from the end user or cloud tenant. This also enables the cloud provider to offer replication and ensure high availability (HA) and data loss prevention even when multiple servers across data centers experience downtime or, worse, crash.

When you create an object and push it to the public cloud for storage, you do not have to specify the location where you would want the object to be stored. Instead, when you make the PUT REST API call for pushing the object, you get a unique identifier as a response. This ID is persistent throughout the life of the object. Similarly, when you want to fetch that object and consume the data, all you have to do is make a GET call to the object storage's REST API and specify the unique ID.

The data object may have hopped several physical storage locations and may have been replicated several times, but these operational details are abstracted from the consumer of this data object and you get the data back in response to your GET call to the storage API. This not only removes all complexity from data storage and access but also gives the cloud vendor the flexibility to transition backend storage systems without adding any complexity or even changing the API call signatures.

Data Residency

Public cloud providers are generally not bound to ensure that objects pushed by tenants or end users are stored in a specific region or data center or physical storage. However, a higher-level physical distribution is visible to the tenants and can be configured to keep data objects closest to the end users. For example, Amazon offers the choice of zones that indicate their data centers spread across the world. If you specify your S3 buckets to be placed in the West-1 zone, you would know that end users on the U.S. West Coast would be closest in distance to your data.

Policies

Most of the finer lower-level details and configurations are abstracted from the end user as we discussed previously. But not every cloud tenant will have the same set of use cases and configurations for object data storage. The cloud provider has to expose some of the configurations that directly impact the applications a tenant is running, and these applications are consuming the data elements stored in the cloud provider's object storage system.

Policies are one way to configure the access of data and also impact its life cycle. Users can set policies that apply to the whole account (or every S3 bucket the user creates, in the case of Amazon) or specify individual policies for separate pools of objects.

Group policies can be broadly related to file permissions that users can set for individual files or folders. Not every data object your application sends off to the cloud for storage is meant to be publicly available. This authentication and authorization for accessing your data objects can be implemented with policies that limit access to your data objects to a set number of users.

Object Access Policy   Cloud tenants can limit the access of their data objects by configuring Object Access Authorization Policy on a pool of their objects or on the whole account. This access could, for example, be limited to a specific application that provides a token string every time it makes a request to fetch an object from the secure bucket.

Another common use case for implementing an object access authorization policy is to enforce access limitation. Websites distributing content over the Internet may not want to pay for the bandwidth resulting from requests originating from a specific region. They can erect this access wall by implementing an access policy, filtering every request through their application, and denying object read/write/delete requests based on the location where the request originated.

Life Cycle Management   Almost every cloud provider now enables tenants to choose between magnetic-based physical storage or SSD-based storage devices. Applications that demand faster data element read/writes would choose to go with faster but more expensive SSDs or a hybrid storage model that combines SSDs for performance-critical data and magnetic disk-based storage for other data. There are further offerings within the magnetic rotating disk category too.

Your application, for example, holds terabytes of video data of your combined user base. You realize that videos that are three months old are not accessed much. This would mean that as videos become older than three months, they can be migrated from S3 to the much cheaper Glacier. This life cycle of a data objects, which is based on the life of the object, can be implemented as part of a life cycle policy. Amazon, for example, offers the following policy options for objects stored in S3:

Life Cycle   Specified life cycle of the object. You can even choose to delete an object after a specified period of time. Previously, this had to be implemented within the application, which would run an age check on every object stored and pick out objects for deletion.

Versioning   Just as with a source control that tracks every change you commit to a file, with the ability to reverse to a previous version, you can set policy to track modifications your application makes to a data object. This can also be used to track the authenticity of a data object and determine if any object has been tempered with.

CORS   A common use case is applications consuming their own data or websites consuming their own data. This is enforced through CORS, which stands for cross-origin resource sharing and enables object owners (cloud tenants) to specify whether the GET request for the object can be originated from only a specific domain or set of domains or made available publicly.

ACL   Access control lists are a way to limit access to an object to a set of users. This is different than setting CORS configuration.

Replicas

Data backup is a routine procedure within enterprises that prevents complete data loss. Replication is a primary feature in any network-based storage system. Object-based storage systems in the cloud are no exception. Data critical to the business would need to be replicated with the latest version of the object maintained at every replicated location. The cloud provider abstracts the replication details from the end user to enable users to choose between low-cost storage options that have less or no replication or more-expensive object storage offerings that have more replication.

 Real World Scenario

Real-Time Replication vs. Passive Backup

Cloud tenants can choose to implement either real-time replication or passive backup, based on the data requirements of their business. Passive backups are often the most cost-effective options available for businesses to perform regular backups of all data on the cloud. In a hybrid cloud deployment, the data would often be backed up on the public cloud while being generated and consumed in the private cloud. This data archiving strategy works well when data and access to it is not critical.

Data replication in real time would mean that latest version of the data object is always available, even if one of multiple replication points face downtime. This replication is managed by the cloud provider and abstracted from the tenant. Cloud tenants can enforce data replication requirements in service-level agreements (SLAs).

Summary

A cloud is a huge pool of consolidated hardware resources that are abstracted from the OS and the applications that are deployed on top of it. The key features of a cloud include its ability to scale up and down based on usage and demand. Fine-grain elasticity is earmarked by significantly lower startup costs compared to deploying your own infrastructure. The hardware resources are completely isolated from tenants, which enables ubiquitous access to the cloud.

With the pay-as-you-grow model, users can start up with very little cost and pay only for the resources they utilize. A single physical server and the whole data center can accommodate multiple tenants with fine-grain boundary/segmentation.

Tenants can spin up new instances and deploy their applications in no time with preconfigured deployment scripts. This deployment automation enables upgrading applications and maintenance without service disruption.

Along with compute and networking, storage is abstracted from the cloud tenants. The concept of object storage has emerged from the need to store, query, and serve enormous amounts of data stored by millions of tenants on the public clouds. This flat storage model treats every piece of data as an object that carries a unique ID with which it can be pulled from the underlying storage through object storage APIs available with every major public cloud provider and a host of object storage API products for private cloud providers.

Chapter Essentials

Elastic, Ubiquitous, and Multitenant Characteristics of the Cloud   The cloud could be thought of as a large pool of compute, storage, and networking resources that can be sliced and diced with tenants only paying for what they consume. Resources can be easily scaled up/down, and applications do not need to be aware of the physical hardware they're running on. Several users can be accommodated in the same data center with segmentation implemented so that data and applications of a user are not visible/consumed by other users.

Low Startup Cost   You pay only for the resources you consume. With limited users initially, the costs are low, and they grow as users increase.

Rapid Deployment   Tenants need to engineer the deployment scripts, which can then be used to rapidly deploy applications on new VMs and manage updates without disrupting service.

Flat Object Storage   In contrast to the hierarchical address space of traditional file systems, the object storage concept of the cloud consolidates all available storage and puts data on a flat address space. Every element of data is treated as a unique object with its own identifier, and additional operational/business information is attached to the object as metadata.

Chapter

2

To Grasp the Cloud—Fundamental Concepts

TOPICS COVERED IN THIS CHAPTER INCLUDE:

✓ **Cloud computing clarified—what it is and what it's not**

- History and background
- True nature of the cloud

✓ **Virtualization and scalability**

- Type 1 and Type 2 cloud hypervisors
- Proprietary vs. open-source hypervisors
- Consumer vs. enterprise use cases
- VDI vs. IaaS
- Benefits of hypervisors

✓ **Foundations of cloud computing**

- Infrastructure
- Platform
- Applications
- Enabling services

This chapter covers some of the fundamentals of Cloud computing. Virtualization is at the core of Cloud technology and will be discussed at length though this chapter.

The True Nature of the Cloud

There are some distinct characteristics that define the modern cloud. The following sections provide an overview of some of these characteristics, which are covered in detail in later sections.

History and Background

The cloud is not a new concept; in fact, it has been around since people starting using computers. Therefore, we often refer to the modern version of cloud computing as "the second birth of the cloud." In their first life, they were known as mainframes, computers that occupied enormous spaces. They were stuffed in large rooms akin to modern server rooms and had multi-access capabilities because they were expensive and individual users could not afford them. Therefore, big businesses and educational entities usually had a single mainframe to which multiple users could connect. Features that we take for granted today were not present in those bulky computers, but they did enable multiple users to connect to them and run compute jobs (literal compute jobs like math computations, not the type of compute jobs we run in today's servers). This was the first wave of cloud computing, but it stemmed from limitations in technology in the late '50s and early '60s, not any "need" for huge computers. This limitation vanished with the advent of PCs, which spelled the end of the first wave of the cloud. The following photo shows an early IBM mainframe.

Even though the first generation of mainframe computers don't compare to today's cloud, they do share the access and usage mechanism to some extent—hosted in dedicated rooms (modern-day data centers) and served through terminals that can be connected to them with multiple users (now scalable to hundreds of millions) who can deploy compute jobs on them.

Contrary to popular belief, the modern generation of IBM mainframes are still very much in use in a significant number of large organizations, running critical applications, storing sensitive data, and executing many millions of transactions every single day. The scale and penetration of IBM's mainframes was revealed in an antitrust investigation into IBM's mainframe business line initiated by the EU Commission. You can find out more at

```
http://europa.eu/rapid/press-release_IP-10-1006_en.htm?locale=en
```

Elastic

This is a fundamental property that differentiates a cloud from any other "internetworked collection of servers." Elasticity enables cloud tenants to spin new virtual servers on demand and on the fly. This way, compute resources can be seamlessly scaled up and down based on demand. The fact that Amazon named its cloud product *Elastic* Compute Cloud (EC2) is a perfect example of how important this property is.

Massive

Amazon has several data centers spread across multiple physical locations across the globe. A single data center houses thousands and sometimes tens of thousands of physical servers connected together through a high-speed network, and the data center is connected to a high-speed Internet backbone. The scale at which public cloud providers operate is staggering; never before in the history of computing have we had these huge data centers accommodating tens of thousands of physical servers. Microsoft Azure and Google Cloud have similar massive data centers, as do companies that do not sell computing resources but have huge compute resource requirements for their own products. A perfect example would be Facebook, which also has huge data centers spread across the world.

On Demand

The ability to set up and operate virtual servers ubiquitously and without the need to provision any physical server resources is an intrinsic property of the cloud. A cloud tenant can allocate networking, storage, bandwidth, and compute resources on demand based on its own requirements or provisioning policies. All major public cloud vendors have enabled High Availability (HA) and ubiquitous access, which enables tenants to spin up new virtual servers whenever needed and spin them down when demand goes down. Compute resources on the cloud can be set up with on-demand (highest priced), spot (bidding based on available compute resource pool and other bidders), and reserved (commitment to keep using the virtual server for a set period of time) pricing models.

Virtualized

Virtualization allows for efficient use of available compute, storage, and networking hardware and packs in more users without decreasing the experience for a single inhabitant. We will talk more about virtualization in Chapter 7, "Practical Cloud Knowledge: Install, Configure, and Manage Virtual Machines and Devices," where we go through deployment and management of VMs.

Secure

The ability to have fine-grained control and advanced monitoring enabled makes the cloud generally secure. There haven't been many instances of security breaches on any of the major cloud environments. Let's consider a real-world scenario.

A cloud electronic medical record (EMR) application stores and processes electronic protected health information (ePHI) in the cloud. Any breach of a patient's ePHI must be reported and the storage entity is often fined. Therefore, the need to keep ePHI secure in the cloud is a high priority and can become an obstacle for an EMR application vendor attempting to increase adoption of the application.

To enable increased security for sensitive data assets, public cloud vendors now provide the ability to have single-tenant virtual servers and dedicated servers for hardware encryption and key management. A single-tenant virtual server is located on a physical server that will not spin up virtual servers for any other tenant. These virtual server instances cost more because available compute resources on the dedicated server cannot be monetized. For the application vendors, this adds another layer of security since no external process will have access to the same physical storage and memory resources, which are the most effective entry points for hackers to gain access to encryption keys and data assets.

Security is now among the top five concerns of companies weighing the adoption of a cloud solution at some level and companies that have already deeply embraced the cloud within their IT fabric. There is a heightened awareness for ensuring security of all data that goes into the cloud for archiving as well as for use within business applications that also run off the cloud. This is one of the primary reasons we see a plethora of cloud data security vendors popping up across the cloud domain.

Always Available

No server vendor can guarantee 100 percent uptime. As you can see in Table 2.1, even 99.99 percent uptime would translate into about an hour of downtime over a year.

TABLE 2.1   Availability and downtimes

Availability %	Downtime/year	Downtime/month	Downtime/week
90% (one nine)	36.5 days	72 hours	16.8 hours
95%	18.25 days	36 hours	8.4 hours
97%	10.96 days	21.6 hours	5.04 hours
98%	7.3 days	14.4 hours	3.36 hours
99%	3.65 days	7.2 hours	1.68 hours
99.5%	1.83 days	3.6 hours	50.4 minutes
99.95%	4.38 hours	21.56 minutes	5.04 minutes
99.99%	52.56 minutes	4.32 minutes	1.01 minutes
99.999%	5.26 minutes	25.9 seconds	6.05 seconds

This is not trivial for a web-scale business or social application serving hundreds of millions of users across the globe 24 hours a day, especially transaction and payment gateway systems Therefore, modern clouds are required to have failover support and mechanisms to ensure maximum availability.

In 2011, Amazon's US-EAST data centers tripped for more than 24 hours. Hundreds of applications serving hundreds of millions of users got affected. Even though Amazon operates several massive data centers across North America, Europe, and Asia, a number of very popular applications were completely taken down because of the outage. This confirms that complete reliability on the cloud vendors for smooth failover support is not advisable. If these applications (popular social app Reddit was among them) had implemented their own failover mechanism upon the software stack on top of Amazon's EC2 service, they would have been able to get back live within an hour of the outage. Add up the lost revenue and reputation and you realize why it is important to ensure failover yourself, even if your cloud vendor guarantees it.

Virtualization and Scalability

Virtualization is the enabling technology for the cloud. This is what enables data centers to populate tens of thousands of physical servers and then completely automate virtual server creation, use, and deletion.

The True Definer of Cloud Computing

How do you make a cloud? What is the difference between a bunch of servers that are connected together and a bunch of servers that are connected together through a high-speed network and running separate OSs but have the ability to talk to each other through standard messaging protocols like MPI or OpenMP? The difference is virtualization. To give you a glimpse into the difficulty of qualifying this setting as a cloud, consider the sidebar "Virtualization vs. Bare Metal."

 Real World Scenario

Virtualization vs. Bare Metal

Author Salman Ul Haq has recently been developing an image processing API that would run on the cloud and would be able to process millions of images on the fly, performing computer vision magic like giving you relevant tags for every photo you send to it based on the content it analyses within the images. He went with Amazon to host his cloud application.

Now suppose he deploys the application in a nonvirtualized environment, which would essentially mean that each OS is physically consuming a single server (bare metal) and it cannot run another OS instance on the same server at the same time. This would mean that given Amazon had 10 servers and 10 users in total, including Salman, if he were to need another "instance" or a machine to scale his application if his user base grew, then he would need one physical server for every time he needed a new instance for scaling his application.

What if 5 of those 10 users were not really consuming much resources and their servers were sitting idle while the remaining 5 were humming at full capacity and needed more server power? Multiply this by a million times or more and you get a glimpse into the problem we would have if we just went with a bare metal, nonvirtualized cloud. It would simply be infeasible. This is the primary reason virtualization is important. Simple market economics are at work here: partitioning bare metal and enabling multiple OS instances to run on the same server at the same time to increase user density and hence making clouds commercially viable.

Serving the Whole World

Clouds come with the promise of delivering bottomless compute, storage, and networking resources on demand. This has enabled small teams to smoothly scale their applications running on the cloud from a few users to hundreds of millions of users. Let's consider the example of Snapchat.

Back in November 2013, Snapchat had 30 full-time employees, which included developers, managers, and business development staff. It was reportedly managing a throughput of 350 million photos through the app on daily basis. That is a tall order. If you compute just the data storage requirements for running such a massive operation, there is no way a team of 30 people—out of which probably not more than 3 or 4 would be handling the cloud infrastructure—would have managed to keep the application running at this scale 10 years ago. And Snapchat scaled very quickly, from a few thousand users to reportedly 50 million users by January 2014.

The cloud has been an enabler for a plethora of business, productivity, social, and whatnot verticals. The promise of availability of unlimited server resources when you need them is one of the cornerstones of cloud computing. For cloud providers, this means economy of scale, which translates into the requirement for building and operating massive data centers and hundreds of thousands of servers.

The Cloud Hypervisor

Hypervisors are the software, firmware, or hardware that manage the complete life cycle of a virtual machine (VM), including creating, monitoring usage, and deletion. In the following section, we will dive deeper into virtualization technology, including types, use cases, real-world examples, and benefits.

Type 1 and Type 2

Before we talk about the types of virtualizations, let's revisit the concept. Virtualization allows for packing multiple OS instances on the same hardware, running independently with different software stacks. Gerald J. Popek and Robert P. Goldberg, in their 1974 article "Formal Requirements for Virtualizable Third Generation Architectures" (*Communications of the ACM*, 1974), classified hypervisors into two main types. Figure 2.1 explains where two different types of virtualization fit within the whole hardware and software stack.

Type 1   Also called *native* or *bare metal* hypervisors, they run directly on the host's hardware and control it. Type 1 hypervisors also manage guest operating systems. Examples include Oracle VM Server, Citrix XenServer, and Microsoft Hyper-V.

Type 2   Also called *hosted* hypervisors, they run atop a host operating system already running on the hardware. Type 2 hypervisors constitute a distinct second layer of software atop host operating systems. They manage and run guest operating systems at the third layer from the hardware. Examples include VMware Workstation and Oracle VM VirtualBox.

FIGURE 2.1   Type 1 and Type 2 hypervisors

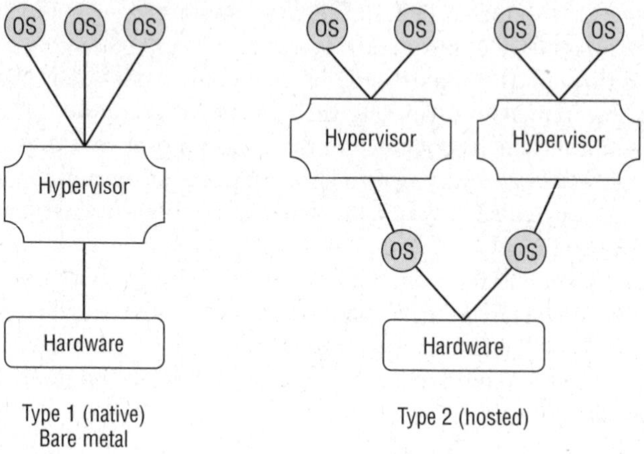

Type 1 (native)
Bare metal

Type 2 (hosted)

Use Cases and Examples

Hypervisors can be used in different roles, depending on their specific business requirements. Here we mention a few common and important use cases and examples:

Data Center Management   Organizations can use hypervisors to manage the virtual resources of a data center. This allows ease of usability by providing a one-stop platform (dashboard) for managing all the resources, diagnosing issues, and monitoring performance. Such a technology also allows organizations to create new private cloud environments.

Hosting and Service Providing   A hypervisor environment can be used to provision the infrastructure and resources for offering hosting and public cloud services. Customized cloud environments can be enabled that allow on-demand provisioning of resources, flexibility, and scalability. Moreover, they can provide multiple user interfaces, performance monitoring, accounting, and reporting for billing purposes.

High-Performance Computing and Science   Virtualized resources can be used to build and manage high-performance computing (HPC) and science cloud environments through the hypervisor technology. This enables flexible and elastic computing resources to solve engineering, analytics, manufacturing, and scientific problems. Hypervisors empower the users by providing support for heterogeneous execution environments, fast scalability, higher utilization, and lower costs.

Benefits of Hypervisors

There are several factors that can influence utilizing hypervisors to manage and run multiple incompatible and different operating systems on the same hardware. The guest operating systems in turn can provide varying provisioning services such as FTP/SFTP servers, email servers, secure shell connection servers, and more. Some of the benefits of using hypervisors are listed here:

Expanding Hardware Capabilities   A single host machine can do more simultaneous work. For example, you can launch new services that should be in a segregated environment and have different security requirements, such as an email server against a Secure Shell connection.

Costs   Because new hardware is not needed for launching a new operating system and services, costs can be curtailed and controlled. Moreover, this simplifies management through consolidation of *soft* servers.

Control Management   Cluster and data center management and installations can be controlled from one platform. A hypervisor, therefore, can act as a management console for various operating environments (i.e., the OS and its services).

Heterogeneous Environments   Hypervisors provide system administrators with the ability to run complex and operating-system-dependent applications on different hardware and operating environments.

Reliability and Independence   Environments managed via hypervisors offer greater reliability and independence because of two main reasons. First, a hypervisor provides a single point of management for all operating environments. Any faulty virtual environment can be easily replaced. Second, hypervisors offer independence from hardware requirements of different operating systems, thus neutralizing heterogeneity and incompatibility.

Hypervisor Security Concerns

One of the biggest concerns of using hypervisor technology is related to malware and rootkit auto-installation. An infected hypervisor environment can make such malicious software hard to detect. This is because the malware could access operations of the operating system that are managed through the hypervisor. An antivirus tool may also not be of much advantage because the malware runs below the entire operating system, as claimed by research at the University of Michigan: *SubVirt: Implementing malware with virtual machines* (April 2006).

However, IBM Linux Technology Center disputes such a claim and instead asserts that it is possible to detect the presence of a hypervisor-based rootkit:

    http://virtualization.info/en/news/2006/08/debunking-blue-pill-myth.html

Moreover, companies such as Microsoft research and develop tools that can provide protection against hypervisor-based rootkits.

Proprietary vs. Open Source

Earlier in this chapter we did an overview of Type 1 (bare metal) and Type 2 (VM) hypervisors. We also discussed how hypervisor technology became an enabler for large-scale data centers that originated from large enterprises, financial institutions, and such, becoming centralized and commoditized into public and private cloud offerings.

In the pre-cloud machine stack, we had silicon (bare metal—CPU, memory controllers, memory, etc.), BIOS (Basic Input/Output System), and operating system living on top of the machine as the interface between the bare metal and the end user.

Moore's Law, Increasing Performance, and Decreasing Enterprise Usage

Since the early '80s, Moore's law has been dictating the trend in performance increase of processors. As chip companies embarked on the race to fire up the clock and increase the number of transistors in processors in every release cycle, the raw performance of the processors has increased manifold and keeps on increasing. In addition to CPUs, we now have graphics processing units (GPUs) and field-programmable gate arrays (FPGAs) as coprocessors and accelerators for cloud applications ranging from scientific simulations to high-speed options pricing and high-frequency trading (HFT) within finance. The GPUs are massively parallel processors that have generally defied Moore's law because instead of increasing the clock of the processor, they have made processing cores lightweight and increased their count, making them ideal for parallel workloads. This massive increase in performance still needs to be matched with software that is most commonly used in enterprises, and this is where we realize the importance of hypervisors in increasing the density of users on a single server node.

Most enterprises have their own private data centers that are deployed in-house and host software applications in use across the enterprise. Intel holds a big chunk of the processors that go into the servers, which then get deployed in these enterprise data centers. For the sake of this real-world example, we will use the popular Intel Xeon series processor as a benchmark for available performance/CPU in a data center server. A third-generation Xeon supports at least four physical cores, which can then be extended with hyperthreading to at least eight. This gives plenty of raw computing performance for applications to consume. However, most of the applications that are used within any given enterprise cannot consume 100 percent or even 80 percent of the complete available raw performance. This, however, does not mean that all enterprise applications are "compute shy." There are compute workloads, especially when we deal with cleaning up, processing, and visualization of massive data streams generated by an enterprise, but these workloads would classify as an exception rather than the norm.

The majority of the applications' compute load would easily consume at best a quarter of the available raw compute power on a physical server. Now combine this with the fact that not every single enterprise worker would be connected to the data center at the same time; there will always be times of peak usage and times of low-density usage. This is where hypervisors come in. They map on the physical hardware resources available on a server, virtualize them, and create multiple instances of an OS on top of it, all emulating the same available hardware underneath.

These hypervisors have to map to every single element of the hardware they're running on. Mainly, this includes the following elements:

- Processors
- Memory (RAM)
- Networking elements (Ethernet adapter, Inifiband card, etc.)
- Storage (on-device connected storage and virtually mounted storage devices)

This list is not exhaustive because there are other elements that make up a server. A hypervisor's job would be to virtualize all of these resources transparently so the end consumer of the OS instance will use the OS without the need to perform any customizations. The hypervisor, in other words, will be the "factory" that fires up and winds down OS instances on demand.

In the following sections, we provide a quick overview of some of the popular proprietary and open-source hypervisors available.

Xen Cloud Platform (Open Source)

The Xen Project is perhaps one of the earliest and most popular open-source hypervisors available in the market. The project led to a much more enhanced enterprise version rolled out by Citrix, XenServer, which we will also touch upon. Xen is a Type 1 hypervisor and perhaps the only popular—and secure—bare metal hypervisor option available today. Some of the key features of Xen are discussed in the following sections.

Operating System Agnostic

Xen is compatible with most *nix operating systems, though the most popular deployment setup is to run Linux as the primary control stack, which administers instance creation, management, and recycling.

Device Driver Isolation

Ideally, no device driver should sit between the hypervisor and the hardware. Xen has implemented this isolation, which is one of the factors that make Xen secure. All device drivers run within the VM created by Xen, which means that in case any device driver goes "rogue," it will not threaten the actual hardware it's running on top of and the situation can be easily remedied by rebooting the VM. This would also mean that performance of device drivers within one VM would not impact the performance of device drivers running within other VMs on the same server.

Minimal Footprint

The whole Xen Project can be packaged into a 1 MB project. This is because of the fact that the Xen Project uses microkernel design with a limited memory footprint and limited user interface (UI) elements.

PV Support

The Xen hypervisor is capable of firing up paravirtual VM instances. This adds to the efficiency of VM instances initiated by Xen when compared with HVM-based instances. It also enables Xen to initiate PV instances on hardware that does not support virtualization extensions. Another option is to use fully virtualized hypervisor virtual machine (HVM) instances that utilize PV class drivers, often called PVHVM device drivers. This eliminates the emulation layer that pure HVM device drivers have to embed for networking, storage, and processor hardware. This in turn delivers PV-like performance for HVM instances.

KVM (Open Source)

Kernel-based Virtual Machine, or KVM, is another popular open-source hypervisor option. KVM is packaged with popular Linux distributions and can be configured to run on top of the Linux distribution currently installed on the server. KVM has deep integration and support for processors, networking, and storage hardware. It implements a modular approach with the primitive set of modules shipped with Linux distributions and an available additional set of modules that can be easily added on top of the vanilla deployment. KVM distributes these modules as KVM kernel modules—for example, the kvm-intel.ko or kvm-amd.ko modules for processor-specific support. KVM can be used to initiate and manage multiple OS instances, including popular Linux distributions as well as Microsoft Windows.

In 2008, Qumranet, the company behind KVM, was acquired by enterprise Linux distributor Red Hat. Since then, KVM is used for Red Hat Enterprise Linux (RHEL) enterprise virtualization server deployments.

OpenVZ (Open Source)

OpenVZ takes a different approach to virtualize the host server. It divides up the resources into "containers," much like what Docker is doing with application deployment virtualization. The containers are fluid in the sense that a complete pool of memory space is available for all containers, which means that a container may make use of the memory of another container as long as it's available.

OpenVZ does not implement native driver support for disk, processor, and networking devices but claims near native performance.

OpenVZ is popular among small and medium-level hosting providers who have deployed it to for virtual private server (VPS) offerings.

VirtualBox (Open Source)

VirtualBox is primarily used in the desktop virtualization market where it supports all the major server operating systems, including Sun Solaris, Mac OS X, Microsoft Windows, and Linux. VirtualBox was acquired by Sun Microsystems, which has continued development of the platform and kept it open source. In 2010, Sun became part of Oracle, and now VirtualBox is part of Oracle.

Citrix XenServer (Proprietary)

XenServer emerged from the Xen Project, which was open source. This is one of the primary reasons Citrix has kept the core XenServer offering free of charge. More advanced, feature-laden variants of XenServer are sold as regular commercial software with added functionality for better management, automation, and availability. Just like Xen Project, XenServer is tightly integrated into Linux itself, enabling native-like disk, network, and processor performance. Citrix XenServer ships in several editions with variants of the following functionality:

XenCenter Management Console　The management console is available in all editions, including the free core edition. The management console can be used to manage a virtual server.

High Availability (HA)　This feature is a must-have for enterprise virtual server deployments, especially in private cloud deployments.

Distributed Virtual Switch (DVS)　DVS provides network-switching flexibility when networking is implemented in a virtualized data center. It provides cloud network administrators with fine-grained control over switching stack layout. The granular control provides greater visibility into the network traffic pattern, and the Distributed Virtual Switch Controller (DVSC) can be used to fine-tune vSwitch settings or increase network security.

Power Management　Essential as well as elaborate power management functionality is available for administrators within the management console.

System Monitoring and Alerts　Administrators can configure event-based alerts.

Live Storage Migration　This feature is available in paid editions and lets users migrate their data into XenServer from another deployment without disrupting service.

VMware vSphere/ESXi (Proprietary)

VMware leads the overall server virtualization market with its enterprise-grade vSphere and ESXi server virtualization offerings. The vSphere and bundled ESXi are available in six variants, starting with one free edition and including five commercial editions. vSphere is a suite of components and modules that are collectively called the vSphere server.

　　VMware ESXi is a Type 1 hypervisor that ships with its own variant of Linux kernel module that is called the VMkernel and loads all other modules. Since it's a bare metal hypervisor, it does not require an OS on the host server and can support various guests, including all major OS offerings—Microsoft Windows, Mac OS X, and Linux variants. All versions, including the free version, come with a primitive set of functionality that includes a graphical management console and memory overcommitment functionality. Some of the unique features of vSphere ESXi are described in the following sections.

Memory Overcommitment

Memory overcommitment works the same way our banking system works. The central bank prints more money than it has physically available. Similarly, the ESXi engine would allocate more memory to each of the virtual machine you fire up than what is physically available on the server. This is a huge undertaking in terms of the risks involved. If the memory is not properly managed, one or more virtual machines may crash. This is based on the fact that most of the time, not all memory is being completely utilized by all the virtual machines running on a server.

Also, peak usage patterns indicate that whenever one or more virtual machines are completely utilizing their allocated memory, there would be virtual machines on the same server that are lightly loaded. This fact, coupled with smart memory sharing between virtual machines and data compression, enables the ESXi engine to allocate maybe up to 400 percent more memory than what is physically available.

 Real World Scenario

An Example of Memory Overcommitment

The ESXi engine may allocate 4 GB of memory to four virtual machines running on a server with only 12 GB of physically installed memory. Whenever an instance needs the additional "thinly created" memory, the ESXi engine shares available memory from other virtual machines with the virtual machine that needs more, giving the impression of boosted memory.

vSphere High Availability

HA is essential for any enterprise-grade application running in a virtualized server environment. It ensures that applications and their environment keep serving end users in case of both physical (hardware) and OS (software) failure. vSphere HA ensures that whenever a server goes down physically, all the virtual machines running on it are migrated to another available server without interruption. If the OS fails on one or more virtual machines running on a server, those virtual machines are restarted on the same server. This enabled offering HA to end user applications without the need to maintain dedicated failover servers because vSphere would utilize available resources on the current production servers for any failover migration needs.

vSphere Virtual Distributed Switch

Managing the network backbone for a medium- to large-scale data center offering a host of virtualized servers would not be feasible with traditional approaches to implementing and managing the network connections between the servers within a data center.

The vSphere Virtual distributed switch enables provisioning, administering, and monitoring virtual machines networks within a data center as well as across physically distributed data centers. The virtual distributed switch, or VDS, automates network configuration and deployment for a virtualized data center. The VDS can also connect with software-defined networking (SDN) configurations, which reduces operational efforts to plug a third-party SDN into vSphere.

The primary value add of VDS is its ability to treat the whole data center as a single resource pool and hence enable centralized network implementation, configuration, and management.

vSphere Storage vMotion

Even though migrating a virtual machine from one physical server to another is a pretty standard feature in every enterprise-grade hypervisor offering, the vMotion feature of vSphere can migrate a virtual machine while it's live, which would mean zero downtime when migrating virtual machines within a data center or even across data centers. Migration is OS agnostic and supports all major operating systems.

Microsoft Windows Server 2012 Hyper-V

Hyper-V is Microsoft's enterprise-grade hypervisor solution for the desktop and data center virtualization markets. Hyper-V currently supports Windows-based hosts and guests, and it can virtualize x86-based servers.

Hyper-V has a client-server deployment scheme, where guest nodes (physically on the same or different server) access applications deployed on the Hyper-V server node as if they are running natively on the guest nodes or virtual machines.

Consumer vs. Enterprise Use

Most of the hypervisor products, both open source and proprietary, target a niche set of verticals and can broadly be categorized as those targeting consumer use cases and those targeting large enterprise use cases. In the following sections, we'll detail some of the use cases for both consumers and enterprises.

Hypervisors for the Mobile Devices

This is currently not the biggest chunk of consumer use cases for hypervisors, but it is definitely one that will define the future of hypervisors getting into the hands of consumers—or IT workforce.

Bring your own device (BYOD) is now entrenched deeply into even the most standards-oriented enterprises, and the need for regaining control of enterprise IT is increasing. To provide a quick refresher, BYOD refers to the use of personal mobile devices for work. We all take our smartphones to work, and most of the time, they are not provided by our company; they are our personal phones. We access company apps, email, and sometimes sensitive data on our personal mobile devices. This is what BYOD means. A lot of solutions have sprung up to streamline the use of personal mobile devices for work within enterprises, but no single solution has succeeded in regaining the control that was a cornerstone of enterprise IT.

So how do hypervisors get into the enterprise IT equation? The answer lies in the very definition of what a hypervisor does—it abstracts physical hardware from software, making the hardware agile and hence liberating IT administrators from directly managing every single piece of hardware being used within an enterprise.

Mobile hypervisors aim to virtualize the mobile devices the same way traditional hypervisors have virtualized workstations and servers. With an "instance" of the mobile OS running on a personal mobile device of an IT worker, security risk can be minimized without compromising the level of service for all enterprise apps being consumed within an enterprise regardless of the device on which they are accessed.

VMware's yet-to-be-released mobile hypervisor was initially announced as a Type 1 (bare metal) hypervisor. This would mean that VMware would have to support all the mobile processors, or at least a set of the most popular mobile processors, networking chips, GSM processors, and a host of other components that make up a mobile device out of the box. This is a tall order given that the current mobile device, most of which are smartphones, is a mess to say the least. Mobile devices are refreshed several times a year, with each device often introducing a host of entirely new hardware components that power new features. The workstation and server markets are very different because new releases are announced at least a year in advance, giving software companies enough lead time to plan for supporting the new platforms.

A Type 1 hypervisor would itself yield enough technical challenges of its own, such as, for example, the support for non-x86-based ARM processors, to start with. With often little or no lead time, it would be difficult for hypervisor companies to support every new smartphone hardware refresh. Therefore, VMware abandoned its plan for building a Type 1 hypervisor very early on. Building a Type 2 hypervisor is relatively less challenging than building a Type 1 in the sense that the hypervisor can make use of the host OS's support for every smartphone hardware refresh. Because every major smartphone OS, including Apple's iOS, Google's Android, and Microsoft's Windows Phone, readily integrates support for every new ARM processor as well as the host of other components that go into the smartphone, it becomes much less risky for hypervisor providers to readily enable support for new hardware releases.

There are, however, other, smaller companies offering Type 1 hypervisors for mobile devices. Red Bend Software is one such provider; it offers VLX Type 1 mobile hypervisors for smartphone manufacturers. VLX puts itself between the processor and what it calls the high-level operating system (HLOS). It already has support for single- and multi-core variations based on ARM Cortex-A15 and Cortex-A17. This way, mobile device manufacturers can enable support for new hardware without the need to upgrade HLOS because VLX manages that by virtualizing the underlying processor.

Xen Project has also started support for the ARM virtualization extensions, which means that Xen-based hypervisors can also enable Type 1 hypervisors for mobile devices.

Hypervisors for Enterprise

In contrast to the hypervisor use cases for consumer-facing verticals, as in the case for mobile devices, the enterprise hypervisor is all about hardware *and* software consolidation. Medium and large enterprises would like to treat all their infrastructure as one large pool from which they can slice and dice "instances" of resources as and when required. Hypervisors virtualize the underlying compute processors, and hypervisor suites offer complete virtualization of small, medium, and large data centers, which includes virtualizing compute, networking, and storage devices across the data center. This consolidation creates what is called a *software-defined data center*, which comprises software-defined networking (SDN), software-defined storage (SDS), and Type 1 or Type 2 hypervisors.

This concept of consolidating enterprise IT with hypervisors as the primary enabling technology is not new. It has been borrowed from the world of consumer IT. Consider a multi-function printer; it has been a tremendous success because three high-frequency requirements (printer, photocopier, and fax) are consolidated into a single piece of hardware. Similarly, with smartphones, GSM phones and personal computers have been consolidated into a single mobile device. The success of smartphones can be gauged by the fact that their sales have now outpaced those of PCs.

At the core of the enterprise hypervisor use case is the ultimate software-defined data center (SDDC). In an SDDC, every single resource, including compute, storage, and networking, are not only defined in the software or virtualized but also consolidated into a single large resource pool where physical locations are also completely abstracted. The SDDC is powered by the software-defined infrastructure (SDI), which is further powered by the hypervisor, SDN, and SDS.

Workstation vs. Infrastructure

Another major division we can draw within the virtualization space in general and the hypervisor space in particular includes the most common use cases for hypervisor technology: virtualizing workstations and virtualizing infrastructure.

Workstation as a Service

This is where the roots of hypervisor technology lies—virtualizing enterprise IT workstations.

Virtual Desktop Infrastructure (VDI)

Even though VDI solutions have been around for over a decade now, real momentum was built around 2010 with the release of Windows 7, which is still the most popular OS for small, medium, and large enterprises. Before VDI, the most common and preferred OS deployment model was installation on every single workstation within an enterprise. Imagine large enterprises with tens of thousands of workstations. Deploying, configuring, and managing such large number of workstations required a mammoth IT department. Upgrading these workstations was another nightmare, and enabling support for updated enterprise apps would often require implementations spanning over several weeks.

With downsizing of IT departments across enterprises, a lazy model of individual workstation deployment would simply not work. This is where VDI comes in. It enables enterprises to consolidate workstations into a single data center where all the hardware resources and OS instances are managed, and workstations across the enterprise are connected to a single or multiple data centers, often spread over different physical locations for large enterprises.

Some of the key features of VDI are described in the sections that follow.

Rapid Deployment

With VDI, OS instances—for example, Windows 8—are available through "images," which are preconfigured and enterprise app ready. IT administrators can fire up a new OS instance for any given workstation with the image already available in the data center. This whole process of firing up and winding down OS instances takes no more than a minute, and it can be repeated for every workstation within the enterprise.

Centralized Management

Previously, with the individual deployment model, managing workstations (which included troubleshooting, upgrades, and configuration) would require significant human time. With the VDI model, a single OS image can be deployed on thousands of VMs and fired up for every single workstation within the enterprise. When updates are rolled out or modifications are made to configurations for specific enterprise apps, a single image can be updated and rolled out for every VM running without the need to manually touch the workstation. This tremendously increases IT administrator efficiency and productivity.

Upfront and Incremental Costs

Compared to rolling out individual workstations, the initial data center setup cost would be significantly more than it would cost to setting up individual workstations, but this cost balances out when workstations scale out because incremental costs would be minimal.

Infrastructure as a Service

With Desktop as a Service (DaaS), on-premises desktop machines connect to VMs running within the enterprise data center. In contrast to DaaS, the IaaS model is for enterprises as well as cloud providers to enable infrastructure resources on demand in-house as well as enable third-party developers to deploy their applications. IaaS is part of three key offerings of the cloud, the other two being Platform as a Service (PaaS) and Software as a Service (SaaS). In the IaaS model, hypervisors play the key role of virtualizing the compute, storage, and networking components of a data center and managing the complete life cycle of VMs (creation, management/monitoring, and deletion). Both Type 1 and Type hypervisors can be used to implement an IaaS solution depending on the end-user needs and business model.

There are three main verticals where IaaS is implemented, discussed in the following sections.

Public Cloud Providers

Cloud vendors like Amazon AWS, Google Cloud, and Microsoft Azure offer compute, storage, and networking instances as a service to third-party application developers to deploy and host their apps. Type 2 hypervisors are mainly used with these vendors because bare metal instances are either not available or cost much more than VMs fired up with Type 2 hypervisors. The underlying resources, which in the case of public cloud vendors are huge data centers spread across multiple continents, are completely virtualized and made available through pre-allocated chunks of resources that (in the case of Amazon AWS, for example) are called *instances*. These instances can be fired up and wound down on demand.

Enterprise Infrastructure

On-premises data centers deployment within an enterprise can be implemented as a private cloud offering for hosting applications being consumed across the enterprise. As already discussed in this and the previous chapter, most organizations now opt for a hybrid model where both private on-premises and public clouds are tapped into. In this model, usually sensitive data and applications consuming and operating on that data are hosted within the private cloud where data security can be properly managed. A public cloud is utilized as a spill-over strategy, where spikes in resource usage are compensated for by firing up instances on reserved public cloud instances. Technically, there is not much difference between private (enterprise infrastructure) and public (cloud) implementations with regard to hypervisors other than the difference in scale between public and private clouds. The hypervisors virtualize the underlying hardware and enable IaaS for end users.

Virtual Data Centers

Virtual data centers (VDCs) can be used to implement a hybrid cloud for an enterprise. A virtual data center abstracts the underlying data center resources and implements transparent switching between private and public clouds based on preset policies.

Some of the key benefits of implementing hypervisor-based IaaS are scalability, location abstraction, and failover support.

Scalability   Instances can be easily fired up and wound down based on demand, and because there's no per-instance configuration needed in most cases, the process can easily be replicated as more users connect to the enterprise apps and demand for resources increase.

Location Abstraction   The end user does not need to know where the physical servers are located. In the case of both private and public clouds, resources are abstracted from the physical location, which enables private/public cloud providers and administrators to manage current data centers and deploy new data centers without service disruption.

Failover Support   With infrastructure centrally managed, physical as well as software issues with one or more VMs can be easily fixed often without disrupting service. This feature was discussed in length at the beginning of this chapter.

Key Benefits of Implementing Hypervisors

Most of the benefits of implementing hypervisor-based infrastructure/data center virtualization and workstation virtualization have already been discussed at length in the previous sections. In the following sections we'll summarize the key benefits.

Shared Resources

Compute, storage, and networking resources within a data center are pooled together and treated as a single big resource pool. Hypervisors abstract these underlying hardware components and enable a centralized resource pool that can easily be shared across VMs on the same and also on different physical servers. As we discussed earlier, one example of shared resource utilization is the efficient failover support that hypervisors provide. Whenever a VM goes down, due to either physical server or OS failure, the VMs are migrated to another available server and restarted. If the OS failed, then the VM is restarted on the same physical server. Hypervisors treat all underlying hardware as a single resource pool.

Elasticity

Hypervisors enable creation, usage, and deletion of multiple instances of fine-grained compute resources on the same physical server. This enables cloud vendors and operators to utilize all physical servers in a data center as one single resource pool where compute, storage, and networking resources can be sliced and diced based on need and demand. We'll now take a more in-depth look at different aspects of elasticity enabled by hypervisors.

Time to Service/Mean Time to Implement

Compared to the old model of individual server hosting or workstation implementation, it takes no more than 1 minute in most cases to fire up a preconfigured VM and make it available for the end user. In the case of Workstation as a Service, a single OS image is used to fire up new VM for every new workstation that connects to the data center. Since a single server can host multiple VMs, the need to individually configure and manage OS instances is eliminated.

Resource Pooling

As already discussed, every physical component that makes up a server, including compute, storage, and networking components, are deeply virtualized. Servers within a single data center and between data centers are interconnected through virtualized network switches. This consolidation results in putting a complete infrastructure into a single resource pool.

Scalable

The promise of the cloud is infinite scalability. This is powered by complete data center virtualization with hypervisors abstracting every underlying hardware component. New tenants can be quickly added. With a public cloud, resources can always be scaled up to accommodate usage spikes and quickly scaled down when the usage normalizes again; tenants are billed for the exact resources they utilize.

Available

Because the complete infrastructure is treated as a single resource pool, the cloud implements true High Availability (HA). Hypervisors not only abstract the underlying data center resources, they also abstract the physical location, enabling availability regardless of the location from which a user connects. Physical agility can be controlled/limited in private cloud implementations where the enterprise has control over the physical servers.

Portable

A hypervisor offers abstraction of the OS from the server on which it runs. This would mean that you can take your VM from one server within a data center to another server within the same data center or to a server in a different data center by the same vendor.

Network and Application Isolation

Before hypervisors, building networked applications required choosing from various protocols and frameworks that often could not talk to each other. The Representational State Transfer (REST) standard emerged out of the need to standardize the implementation of networked applications. Because hypervisors virtualize the underlying networking components, applications need not be aware of the specific networking hardware or even physical addresses to implement and deliver networked applications. This network hardware isolation also enables smooth scaling and migration of applications across servers.

Figure 2.2 provides a quick example of how an application utilizes a backend RESTful API running on Amazon's cloud without being aware of the underlying network hardware.

In the figure, the sample application interacts with the backend REST API, which makes use of the underlying resources without being aware of the underlying network. All that the application may need to be aware of is the TCP/IP address of the instances it's running on.

An application may also be deployed across data centers spread in different physical locations without the need to modify any communication logic between different VMs running the application.

FIGURE 2.2   Cloud application stack

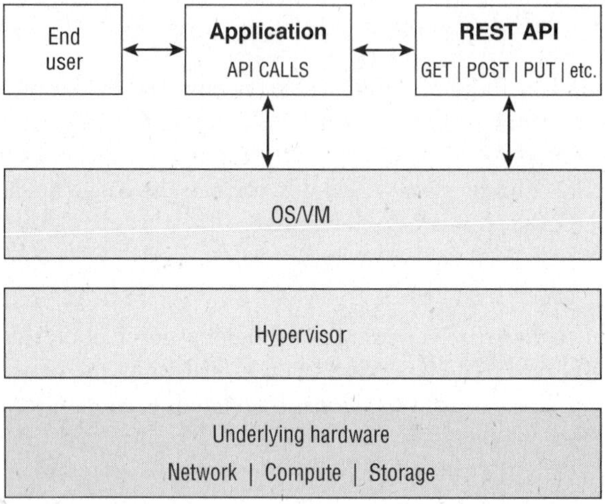

Foundations of Cloud Computing

In the following sections, we will discuss the primary components that make up a cloud. But before we discuss each of the components, let's take a look at the overall picture (Figure 2.3).

Infrastructure

Infrastructure is every piece of hardware an enterprise or a public cloud vendor deploys within a data center. As we discussed in the first chapter, the data center is where all the servers are housed and interconnected with a high-speed Ethernet or Infiniband (IB) network backbone. The data center is connected to the outside world (in the case of a public cloud) or within an enterprise through high-speed networking and/or the Internet. In the world of cloud computing, imagine the infrastructure as the ingredient that enables applications to be served to hundreds of millions of users across the globe.

The specs for the servers, storage devices, and networking components that make up the infrastructure do not need to be the same. Servers with varying configurations based on the target use cases can be deployed within the same data center. This is what enables complete abstraction of the underlying hardware from the end users who are cloud tenants. This isolation of the infrastructure from the end user also enables cloud providers to provide key features like scalability, HA, and effective failover support.

FIGURE 2.3   Cloud components

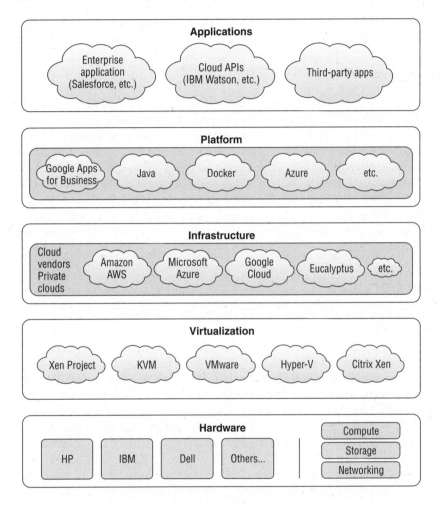

Resources can also be individually abstracted and offered as a separate service. For example, the object storage APIs that every public cloud provider offers is an abstraction built on top of the storage hardware. End users are charged only for the bandwidth and storage and not for any compute resources consumed in pulling the objects from the storage hardware.

Platform

On top of the raw infrastructure, there are Type 1 or Type 2 hypervisors running, which virtualize compute, storage, and networking components. These hypervisors are deployed on the hardware and enable complete life-cycle management of VMs, which run on top of them. A single physical server can accommodate multiple VMs. Each VM can run a different OS without affecting other VMs running on the same or different server. This is what becomes part of the platform.

All the major public cloud providers offer multiplatform support that includes support for all the major operating systems.

Applications

Applications are completely abstracted from the underlying cloud infrastructure on which they are deployed. The OS on which an application runs is itself abstracted from the underlying hardware by the hypervisor managing the VM life cycle. Some of the applications running on the VM are there to manage other consumer-facing applications. An example of this would be the object storage APIs implemented on top of the hypervisors. What hypervisors offer is storage virtualization. Storage API applications make use of this abstraction and implement functionality (APIs) that enable end users to consume the abstracted storage as a service. In the case of object storage APIs, the application would be responsible for treating units of storage as objects and exposing the functionality to push, pull, update, and delete an object or its metadata.

Enabling Services

Software as a Service (SaaS), Platform as a Service (PaaS), and Infrastructure as a Service (IaaS) are the primary enabling services for the cloud. The applications that run on top of the cloud are often distributed as SaaS solutions, where subscribers pay based on time or usage or a mixture of both.

With PaaS, cloud vendors as well as third-party developers provide vertical platforms as a service for end users. An example of this would be an enterprise-grade content management system (CMS) being offered as a service. This would mean that the application as well as the cloud VMs on which it runs and the networking, storage, and bandwidth are all accounted for and the end users would either pay per seat or based on a combination of time and usage.

An example of an IaaS would be private cloud implementations within an enterprise. The infrastructure is virtualized, consolidated into a single resource pool, and offered as a service.

Services that implement the key features of any cloud, like multi-tenancy, elasticity, abstraction, and federation, are all part of services that enable a true cloud.

Summary

Hypervisor technology is the key technology that has enabled cloud solutions. Hypervisors virtualize compute, storage, and networking hardware and consolidate all resources available within the data center into a single resource pool. This hardware abstraction can be implemented as a Type 1 (bare metal) or Type 2 (inside a host OS) hypervisor. There are a host of open-source and proprietary hypervisors available for consumer and enterprise use cases. Hypervisor technology enables the key features that define a cloud. These include scalability, availability, shared resources, location, and hardware isolation. Applications that run on the cloud are abstracted from the underlying physical hardware. This network and application isolation enables agility for the applications and their ability to be distributed across a single data center or across physically separated data centers.

The four key elements that make up the foundation of the cloud are the physical infrastructure, which is virtualized and offered as a service; the platform, which runs on top of the virtualized hardware; applications, which run on top of the platform, and the enabling services through which cloud resources are offered.

Chapter Essentials

Hypervisor   A hypervisor is the technology that sits in between the physical hardware and the OS. It virtualizes the compute, storage, and networking components. Hypervisors enable multiple VMs to run on a single physical server and to be created, configured, and destroyed through a centralized control panel. There are several open-source and proprietary hypervisor products available.

Type 1 Hypervisor   Type 1 or bare metal, hypervisors implement support for the hardware they run on because they directly run on the bare hardware without the need for any host OS.

Type 2 Hypervisor   These hypervisors need to be deployed on a host OS. Support for the hardware on which they run is managed through the host OS on which the hypervisor is installed. Both Type 1 and Type 2 hypervisors support running several guest OS instances.

Proprietary and Open-Source Hypervisors   There are a host of open-source and proprietary hypervisors available in the market. Some hypervisors started as an open-source project and later became part of a commercial solution, such as, for example, the Xen Project, from which came Citrix XenServer offerings.

Desktop Virtualization   Desktop virtualization or a VDI enables workstations within an enterprise to be virtualized inside a centralized data center and distribute resources based on demand. A single OS image can be used to spin up multiple VMs. Individual workstations connect to their respective VMs running inside the data center.

Infrastructure as a Service   All the servers inside a data center, along with the networking hardware that connects these servers, are completely virtualized and consolidated into a single resource pool. This virtualized infrastructure is then offered as a service inside the enterprise for applications to be deployed and delivered to end users or as a billable service in the case of public cloud offerings.

Chapter

3

Within the Cloud: Technical Concepts of Cloud Computing

TOPICS COVERED IN THIS CHAPTER INCLUDE:

✓ **Technical basics of cloud and scalable computing**

- Defining a data center

- Traditional vs. cloud hardware

- Determining cloud data center hardware and infrastructure

- Optimization and bottom line

✓ **The cloud infrastructure**

- Open source

- Proprietary

In this chapter, we dive right inside the cloud to explain concepts that you'll need in order to further understand the choices that have been made in cloud computing as well as their technical significance. For cloud technicians and administrators (or those who are preparing for or have passed the CompTIA Cloud+ exam), this serves as a review and reminder of the basic concepts behind cloud computing in general and gives a glimpse into its direction going forward.

The discussion of the technical concepts of cloud computing includes explanations of the hardware technology involved in the field, something that few cloud technicians take for granted. We compare cloud technology hardware to traditional non-cloud data center hardware and provide some insight on the hardware being used for cloud systems. Knowing about hardware technology will help technicians and executives to better select a proper cloud service provider for the needs of their organization by evaluating the methods and hardware that service providers use.

It's important for cloud technicians to understand the technical concepts behind cloud computing's enormous benefits and economies of scale in terms of how these benefits are achieved and implemented. Oftentimes we assume that a service carries over the benefit being highlighted, but this is often on a case-to-case basis that needs to be evaluated first. The concepts being discussed in this chapter will help technicians develop their own methods of evaluation.

Technical Basics of Cloud and Scalable Computing

When we hear the term *scalable computing*, we often associate it with technology being used for cloud computing, or even assume that it is a synonym for *cloud computing*, but that is just a misconception for us professionals in the cloud computing field. The truth is that cloud computing is just an application in the broader field of scalable computing. Scalable computing encompasses the hardware and software being used in different areas of the computer sciences, such as the design of chip-to-chip communication and the tools and interfaces being used in parallel computer systems. Just to be on the same page here, we are referring to our own area of scalable computing—that of cloud computing, *virtualization*, and *variable provisioning*.

In the following sections, we will discuss the data center, the hardware *infrastructure* that has become the backbone of modern business organizations, and how that definition has evolved into what we now know as the cloud data center. Then we shall look at a few software platforms that go hand in hand with the hardware to provide us with what we truly know as cloud computing.

Defining a Data Center

A data center, in the strictest sense, is simply a facility used to house technological equipment, usually computer systems and their components. This usually takes the form of computing and storage units as well as telecommunications equipment. Each data center is a little different based on the type of application it is used for. Large data centers cost upward of $100 million to build in the first place and somewhere between $10 million and $30 million to operate yearly.

There are many ways to quantify *total cost of ownership (TCO)* for data centers:

Per Kilowatt   Data centers are power hogs. And since they guzzle up electricity like a water tank with a hole, some would calculate TCO per kilowatt of power required.

Per Square Area   Another method for calculating TCO is the amount of area the data center occupies. This has something to do with the amount of cooling that data centers require because of the large heat output being generated by power-hungry equipment. It takes into consideration the amount of electricity consumed, the amount of cooling required, and the manpower to manage the entire area of the data center. This is expressed as cost per square foot or meter, depending on which measurement standard the organization follows.

Per Rack   Out of all the ways to compute for TCO, this one makes more sense to both IT professionals and facilities personnel because it is easier to quantify since parameters such as power, cooling, and displacement (required area) are pretty much standardized across open-frame *racks* or enclosures or cabinets as well as the IT equipment that goes in them. Therefore, it is more reasonable to use this method of physical quantification because all the quantifiable elements of all the rack components simply have to be added to get the cost per rack.

 The "per rack" notation is the most common way of referring to different aspects of the data center, such as heat generation, power consumption, computing power, and cost.

But of the total cost of ownership of a data center, approximately 50 percent goes to disaster prevention and recovery plans and their execution as well as hardware and software maintenance, which includes uninterruptible power supply and networking. The rest is spent on temperature control, utility bills, and various taxes and labor costs. In fact, approximately 40 percent of the overall TCO is spent on labor cost alone; data centers need 24-hour, round-the-clock monitoring to ensure 100 percent uptime and error control. When talking about TCO per rack, approximately half of its lifetime cost goes to capital expense, and the other half goes to operational expense, which is shown in Figure 3.1.

FIGURE 3.1   TCO distribution per rack

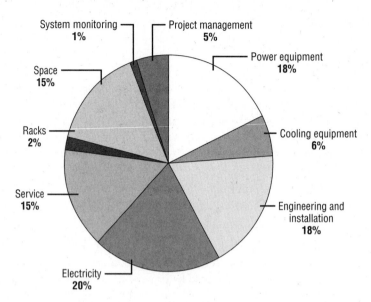

But the harsh reality being faced by organizations that own and run their own data centers is that things are further complicated by the need to maintain aging infrastructure and applications. For some older data centers, it is estimated that as much as 80 percent of the TOC is spent on maintenance. This is largely because of archaic applications and aging infrastructure that need to be maintained because they are still important for the organization's business processes.

It is not always an option to simply throw out your old data centers and move to the cloud. You must consider the nature of the applications and workloads that are the core functions of data centers:

- Traditional data centers run a multitude of applications and have a wide variety of workloads.

- Many of the applications running in data centers are specially designed to cater to a relatively few employees.

- Most applications being run on older data centers have already been phased out of the market but are still essential for the organization's core processes.

The nature of some of these applications means that it would not probably be cost effective to move to the cloud environment because replacing these core applications would require significant changes and interruptions in the normal business operations.

Hardware and Infrastructure

Traditional data center hardware is not that different from cloud data center hardware except for how they are configured in the underlying software and firmware. Non-cloud, or traditional, data centers often had multiple software platforms to support a diversified software ecosystem, which also affected the kind of hardware used. Cloud data centers are homogenous both in software and hardware, so optimization is simpler. Cloud data centers are designed and configured to cater to a virtually infinite number of users, while traditional data centers are meant to serve only the capacity of the organization and maybe some third parties such as partners and customers.

Since data centers are enormous investments for a company, meant to provide a significant return on investment (ROI) in the long term, great planning is required.

According to the white paper produced by Network System Architects (www.nsai.net/White_Paper-Planning_A_Data_Center.pdf), the following are key points to consider in the planning stages for a data center:

- Floor space
- Power requirements and conditioning, including backup and uninterruptible power supplies
- Heating, Ventilating, Air Conditioning (HVAC) and fire prevention systems
- Network connectivity and security
- Support and maintenance strategy
- Business continuity and disaster recovery
- Logical security

Floor Space Consideration

One important consideration is the building that the data center would be located in, especially the floor space. You must consider the overall weight of the data center, including all the equipment and even the flooring itself, especially if it is to be located in floors higher than the ground floor. The capacity rating of the building must be considered when the center needs to be placed above ground level, which is often the case in areas that are prone to flooding. The floor and floor tiles require special consideration because potentially heavy loads from equipment are concentrated in small floor areas. We are, of course, referring to the racks themselves. Each rack has a different rating according to its function. So let's consider one rated for 2,000 pounds. That means that each foot (caster) of the rack has a point load of 500 pounds, which needs to be carried by one or two square inches of floor space, and if tiles are used, we have to consider that one or two rack casters can occupy the same tile. So we must make sure that each tile is able to handle the weight that is placed upon it.

Raised flooring is often the choice of many designers because it gives the best flexibility in terms of network and electrical cabling and offers a cheaper alternative to open-air cooling because you would need to cool only the air beneath the floor and within the racks.

Power Considerations

Data centers by virtue of their purpose require a lot of power, which makes this an important consideration that must be addressed very early on. Power coming from the main electrical grid is not often stable and will fluctuate depending on the time of the day as the overall load changes dynamically. It is important to have *power conditioners*, which will ensure that the power supply is within an acceptable level.

Since uptime is important, uninterruptible power supplies (UPSs) and backup power generators are a must. UPSs are only there to sustain power before backup generators can go online, but they should still be able to provide sustained power in case the backups are running a little late. We do not need to stress how important backup generators are; they are a necessity for sustained uptime and disaster preparedness, so they must be able to provide more than enough power and provide it for extended periods. A good way to ensure uptime is through the use of a redundant power infrastructure, that is, to have two separate power infrastructures working together or alternately to power the data center. Figure 3.2 shows two separate power lines being connected to a cloud data center; this ensures that when one power provider goes down, the other can take over in powering the center.

FIGURE 3.2   Redundant power infrastructure

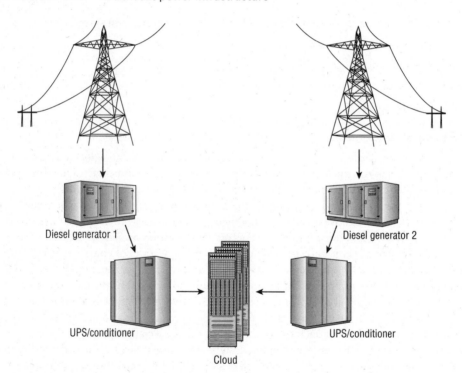

Heating, Ventilating, Air Conditioning (HVAC) and Fire Prevention Systems

Data centers are like raging fire pits. If you own a laptop, you know how hot it can get, and that machine has only one processor module. Now imagine that a single rack can contain 10 or more blade servers a little bit wider than a laptop, thrice as thick, and containing somewhere between 2 and 32 processors (stacking 16 server boards that have 2 processor sockets each). The heat generated would be tremendous, and so it follows that the cooling systems for the whole floor area and for each rack would have to be on par to keep the temperature at manageable levels, preventing overheating even in times of extreme processing load.

The industry ad hoc standard for calculating cooling requirements is to have one British thermal unit (BTU) of cooling for every three kilovolt-amps (kVA) power requirements. And cooling is usually described in tons, with one ton of air having 12,000 BTUs of cooling.

Another consideration is the equilibrium of the cooling for HVAC systems. The atmosphere within the center must maintain a good mixture of levels, keeping in mind operating temperature as well as operator comfort. Nicely cooled equipment is good, but the environment must be comfortable for the operators to work within the premises. Humidity levels must also be monitored as high levels would cause condensation and equipment corrosion while low levels facilitate occurrences of electrostatic discharge (ESD).

Network Connectivity and Security

All that super computing power would go to waste if you cannot direct it to your users. The main objective of a data center is to house computer equipment, and it needs network connectivity to have any purpose at all. The network must be well designed with future growth in mind, so an upgrade path must be considered in the design.

Data cables would consist of a mixture of fiber optics and Cat 5e or Cat 6 rated cables, but quality of connectivity will depend on the type of equipment being used, which also depends on the applications that the center needs to offer. The position and distribution of network equipment needs to be well thought out, especially in large data centers where the distances can easily go beyond recommended cable lengths for device interconnectivity. The data center's orientation to the building's telecommunications equipment should be considered, and any equipment meant for external communication should be placed as close to the Telco's closest ingress into the data center as possible to reduce latency.

But the main issues in planning network connectivity involve capacity and *redundancy*. Capacity is the total bandwidth in both directions of your data center, while redundancy relates to keeping the connection alive by selecting external connectivity providers that offer high redundancy or by employing multiple service providers. Table 3.1 shows different leased lines that are usually offered by network providers.

TABLE 3.1 Types of leased lines

Leased Line	Capacity
T1/DS-1	1.544 Mbps
T3/DS-3	44.75 Mbps
OC-3	155.52 Mbps

There are two ways to plan for redundancy, symmetrical and asymmetrical:

Symmetrical   Symmetrical network redundancy can be achieved by leasing, for example, two T3 lines from two separate providers.

Asymmetrical   Asymmetrical redundancy is by leasing a T3 line from one provider and a T1 line from another provider.

Network redundancy can be either active-active or active-passive.

Active-Active   Active-active means that both lines are working together simultaneously; this type of redundancy provides the greatest bandwidth because both lines are working at the same time.

Active-Passive   Active-passive redundancy, however, is what we consider backup redundancy. Only one line is really active at a time, and that is the main line, which has a bigger capacity. The other, lower-capacity line is used as backup in case the main line becomes unavailable. This scheme provides redundancy at a lower cost, at the expense of bandwidth.

Having an active-active network is beneficial for organizations that deal with high volumes of traffic from their customers. It does not simply offer high bandwidth, it's also a good way to maintain high availability. However, a cost-benefit ratio must be thoroughly analyzed to determine if this costly method is suitable.

Another redundancy measure aside from a redundant wide area network (WAN) is to be redundant at the edge of your network. It is always better to have two Internet routers meshed to your local area network (LAN) so that when one fails, there is still network connectivity between your data center and the outside.

Support and Maintenance Strategy

A high-tech installation such as a data center should be well maintained to keep it running in top condition even after many years of service. Our worst enemy would be software degradation. This is eventual failure of the various applications and OSs running in your servers. Due to processing, constant file transfers, data traffic, and other normal day-to-day processes, settings and file systems can get corrupted and cluttered. This leads to eventual slowdowns and even failures such as crashes and hangs. This can happen even when your hardware is kept in the best condition possible, so it is essential to have regular server maintenance (either automated or manual). This involves backing up critical data and cleaning or resetting various parameters and settings to make sure everything works as expected.

Eventually something will break down, so there has to be proper procedures to follow when it does. Backup systems have to be put in place to take over for whatever system broke down. A proper upgrade path also needs to be laid out. Which parts of the system need to be eventually upgraded or replaced with newer versions or standards has to be figured out beforehand. Upgrading has to be made easy; the center has to be laid out in a way that does not require a lot of teardown.

Business Continuity and Disaster Recovery

Disasters happen. They are out of our control, but their impact can be minimized through careful planning and preparation. This doesn't mean you have to have a bombproof building or one that could survive a catastrophic event; what it does means is that the most important commodity being housed in your data center should be well protected in the form of backups.

Backing Up on Tape   Tape backups are the cheapest and most common backup method used today. Since tape backups do not have the advantage of capacity, they are usually performed daily and then sent to a secure location offsite. This ensures that there are physical backups to use in case of disaster or accidental corruption or erasure.

Backing Up by Data Vaulting   Another method for performing backups is data vaulting. This involves a WAN link to a remote backup facility, which backs up data as frequently as desired, even up to the minute. This ensures almost real-time backup but is obviously more costly because the backup facility itself is a data center. There are, however, some third-party providers of backup services.

Physical Security

The *network operations center (NOC)* is your command center when it comes to the day-to-day operations of your data center. It can serve as the single point of monitoring, supervision, and maintenance for your network, software distributions and updates, and other essential processes. The NOC includes climate control systems and power and generator monitoring and can stand as the security control center for the data center facility.

The NOC will be the office of the operations staff, so make sure there are ample facilities and space for the consoles and monitoring equipment to be placed there. When interconnecting different data centers from different time zones, it is good practice to allow NOCs to be able to take control of data centers other than the ones they are originally set up for. This helps you to tap into your pool of technical experts from different locations to solve local problems. It also minimizes late-night shifts because NOCs from other time zones can take control during the late hours.

Here are a few things to keep in mind when designing security for the data center:

- All access points into the data center must be controlled by security access devices such as card readers, cipher locks, and biometric scanners. All access attempts must be logged, no exceptions, so this must be done automatically. If possible, a short video clip is automatically recorded with each access attempt and stored for a certain duration pending review.

- Avoid using exterior walls for the data center. The center must be a room within a room to prevent external accidents or intrusion. Windows especially should be avoided because they interfere with cooling.

- Video cameras and motion sensors must be installed and monitored around the facility, including on the raised flooring and dropped ceilings.

- Air ducts must be made inaccessible to humans to prevent physical intrusions.

Logical Security

Physical security is actually the least of your worries. Very few bad elements would go so far as to try to enter a data center because of the high risk of getting caught. The most valuable commodity is data, and it is not physical. System intrusions are common, and it is estimated that data center systems are besieged at least a hundred times a day. Most or all are unsuccessful attempts that the system handles by itself.

As for administering devices, multilevel authorization should exist, and engineers and operators should be given only minimal access, only that which is needed to complete their tasks. Access to the server console should be through a separate network that is available only via the local NOC. If a NOC from other time zones is given control at times, network connectivity should run to that specific location only and run parallel to the organization's internal backbone. Strong encryption is required at the very least.

Because the most logical point of entry of any attacker is the network, this is where security has to be at its finest. It should be applied in a tiered fashion:

Tier 1   This is your edge protection, the first line of defense, using hardware and software firewalls specifically calibrated for the center's needs. *Bastion hosts* belong here. A Bastion host is a special-purpose computer that is designed and configured to withstand attacks on the network.

Tier 2   This is the next layer, which separates publicly accessible devices such as DNS and web servers from the internal network. Typically, the devices used here are still firewalls, and in some cases both tier 1 and 2 layers reside in the same physical device. VPN tunneling for passing confidential data can be set up parallel to the firewall.

Tier 3   This is an additional layer that can be implemented when you need additional separation from the overall network for environments that store highly critical information, such as a database of classified files or bank records.

Traditional vs. Cloud Hardware

Traditional IT and cloud computing could not be more different in application and concept. They are not total opposites, and they actually have the same goal in mind, which is to get business processes done. But the approaches and concepts are very different. The key difference between cloud computing and traditional computing is *scalability*, which is to say that one is scalable and the other is not. Traditional computing, as we define it in the industry, is not scalable at all.

Traditional IT hardware infrastructure is built with capacities in mind. It answers questions such as how big or how many, so it aims for a certain number, a maximum capacity. So when you're building a traditional data center, the first on the list during design is the capacity of the system, its maximum. This means that you can use as little or as much as you want as long as it is within that capacity requirement. In this case, there is a very large chance that the system will be underused, and it's usually never used to its maximum potential, a huge waste in available resources. Or unforeseen growth might occur, rendering the data center inadequate so more money has to be spent on unplanned upgrades.

Cloud computing infrastructure, on the other hand, is built for scalability. Yes, it is true that when you're building a cloud data center, you will often choose the maximum capacity allowable by the budget, but that is where the similarity in capacity ends. Cloud data centers are designed with future upgrades in mind simply because demand will only grow and the data center has to scale for it. So in terms of a set initial capacity, traditional data centers and cloud data centers are quite similar, but only until customer demand requires additional capacity; it then becomes one of the biggest distinguishing points.

They also differ in how resources are being used. Traditional data centers are often meant for a single corporation with a capacity that is often way beyond the needs of the organization, but a cloud data center is often created for public use, with hundreds or thousands of customers using the resources at the same time. In this regard, cloud data centers often operate at close to maximum capacity at any given time, while a large portion of a traditional center's capacity will often be wasted.

There are many things that distinguish cloud computing from "simple" scalable, grid, or utility computing, but an easy way to determine whether cloud computing is being used is to think of two words: *scalability* and *virtualization*. If it is deployed with both of these present, chances are it is true cloud computing.

Consider the purpose of a data center. If it was made for traditional IT, it would likely be serving a multitude of applications across different departments, all of which are using just a tiny fraction of the center's overall capacity and power. It is estimated that most data centers are only utilized for 10 percent to 30 percent of their maximum potential. Of course, that is a general estimate. These numbers are totally dependent on the type of use that an organization has for its data centers; some, albeit only a few, are utilized at 90 percent capacity or more. But for cloud computing data centers, public or private, it is most likely that there are only a few dedicated cloud applications being run, and those are meant to perform multiple functions and are being used by a lot of people to which the servers have to allocate resources. This means that cloud data centers are often operating at optimum capacity.

Even with their major differences, however, in concept the general connectivity and components remain the same. You have your servers, which are essentially your computing units, and you have your storage units arranged in racks or cabinets. Everything is tied together with the core data center backbone and connected to the outside with various networking devices like switches and hubs. Figure 3.3 shows a simple design that is still the basic design used for both traditional and cloud data centers. Each organization or provider will have its own modifications to this simple design based on their needs, but again, the components remain the same, although some may be assigned with a slightly different purpose.

FIGURE 3.3   Data center schematic

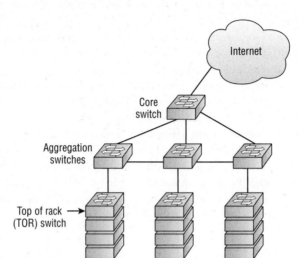

But ultimately, be it a cloud data center or a traditional one, there are three factors that determine its cost of development and ownership:

- Its capacity

- Its location

- Its application

In essence, the real difference between a traditional and a cloud data center is not in the individual technologies being used; technologies can be shared between the two and are mostly interchangeable, although some hardware technology is optimized for one or the other. The real difference is what the hardware is supposed to do and how it is configured to do it. So ultimately, cloud services will be considered the better option because they can give the same functionalities and services of the traditional data center yet offer it with far lower cost due to *economies of scale*. Table 3.2 shows a direct comparison between the characteristics of a traditional data center and a cloud data center.

TABLE 3.2   Traditional vs. cloud data center

Traditional Data Center	Cloud Data Center
Multiple supported applications and platforms	Few dedicated applications
Mixed hardware environment to support multiple applications and platforms	Homogeneous hardware environment and configuration

Traditional Data Center	Cloud Data Center
Multiple supported management tools	Few standard management tools
A lot of application updates and patching	Minimal required patching and updates
Multiple supported software and hardware architectures	Single cloud architecture
Complex workloads	Simple workloads

There is an inherent simplicity to the cloud architecture. It might look complicated on paper, but in essence its homogeneity and scale make it simpler if planned right. This means that it's easier to put in more of the same, and with multitenancy, a lot of people will be sharing in the expenses, which will make everything cheaper. It's simple and so it scales well.

Determining Cloud Data Center Hardware and Infrastructure

A cloud data center may not be as different in terms of the look of the infrastructure and the hardware used, but it is the architecture of the system, down to the software installed in the servers, that separates cloud computing from traditional on-premises data centers.

Cloud computing is defined by data centers, large data centers that made cloud computing viable in the first place. Before the advent of the modern, extremely large and modular data centers, which require little to no maintenance, selling or sharing computing resources with others would have been next to impossible.

While on-premises and cloud data centers serve similar purposes, there is a much larger audience for cloud computing data centers. They offer so much more to users and so therefore require substantial planning, especially for future trends and to keep up with technology and additional capacity.

The major selling points of cloud computing are also the main source of complexity when it comes to data center planning and design. Scalability, resiliency, availability, and security are all features that need to be incorporated into the design of your cloud data center in order to actually call it a cloud data center.

In the following sections, we will look into a few factors that should be considered when you're planning to set up your own cloud data center. These factors may also help in the selection of a proper colocation provider or a cloud service provider.

Designing for Cloud Functionality

The definition of cloud computing and the factors that make it what it is has been discussed and debated and run into the ground on the Internet for a decade now, not to mention in many parts of this book, so it would be redundant for us to discuss them in this chapter. Instead, we'll look at three of the most important aspects, which may not completely define cloud computing but are certainly three of the top factors that organizations look into when designing or simply considering cloud computing solutions: uptime, scalability, and security.

Uptime

For a cloud service, uptime is one of the most important features. For a customer, the promise of uptime is quite simple: they log on to the service they are paying for, and if they can access it, it is "up," and if they can't, it is "down." But for a service provider, it could be much trickier. Downtime can be the result of a larger problem like server or disk failure or even massive power outages with the backup generators failing as well. Some basic reasons for outages, such as power requirements and network downtime, can be attributed to larger planning issues, like the location of the data center itself.

As far as power facilities go, in many countries it might be impossible for data center owners to find more than one electrical power provider, so they would have to spend a lot more on uninterruptible power supplies, backup generators, and the fuel to power them. That goes the same for networking and finding a major leased line provider. It's true that in many countries there are often a few telecom companies operating, but chances are they are all leasing on the same backbone provider, which means that when the giant everyone is hanging on to takes a dive, everybody else falls with it. Without access to multiple line providers, an organization may be forced to spend millions to erect its own infrastructure or accept the fact that it would not be able to offer certain higher availability levels.

Uptime seems like such a given that people take it for granted, but they have no idea how much planning and effort it takes to deliver on that promise of a certain amount of uptime. That is where the cost for adding more "nines" into your uptime percentage comes in, as in 90 percent to 99.9999 percent. As a comparison, consider that 90 percent (one nine) would equal 36.5 days of downtime per year, 99 percent (two nines) is 3.65 downtime days, while 99.9999 percent (six nines) would mean only 31.5 seconds of downtime per year.

WARNING   Although uptime is an important factor and it's quite enticing to rack up those nines so you can have something to brag about to your friends, it is not always the best investment. It gets exponentially more costly as you add more nines. Besides, 3.65 days of downtime at 99 percent is negligible when spread over a year's period.

As the number of nines goes up, so do the costs in subscription. This takes into account the things mentioned earlier, like the costs of keeping infrastructure like power and network up against all foreseen and unforeseen events, cyberattacks, and the occasional hardware breakdown or malfunction.

Scalability

The word *scalability* is usually used to define cloud computing, and it is that single major aspect that cloud data centers are designed and built upon. It sounds wonderful and looks good on paper, but it can be a nightmare to implement and maintain. The idea of infinite scalability means that the service provider must constantly increase available computing capacity to be able to cope with any increase in demand from the customers. Most providers would need to add hundreds or even thousands of new servers daily to keep up and provision for future demand or replace older and failing servers.

When you offer the power of scalable resources to your customers, there is no real way of knowing how much a single user will be using. To safeguard against overprovisioning, many cloud service providers impose a limit on the number of virtual servers or resources that a single account can provision or use tiered accounts, with higher tiers being able to provision more but probably with added costs.

Security

One of the biggest hurdles to implementing cloud computing is the fear that it may be less secure than on-premises solutions, and some organizations are willing to spend just to achieve a better level of security. Cloud computing advocates would argue that this is not true, that security measures in terms of software and hardware are the same for both on-premises and cloud data centers. Yes, that would be true, but we should take in to consideration the difference in the nature of both solutions. On-premises or traditional data centers are designed and built to serve the organization and its stakeholders, while a cloud data center is designed to cater to a more or less worldwide customer base, meaning that its visibility is much wider compared to that of on-premises data centers. That fact alone means that cloud data centers are advertised more compared to their counterparts, and that means that more attackers are aware of them.

Some security experts would argue that invisibility or anonymity is not a security measure, but logically it is. No one can steal something if they don't know it exists, or at least there will be fewer attempts when only a few know about it. This apparent sense of invisibility of on-premises data centers stands as one the security advantages that wary organizations depend on.

 WARNING   Nondisclosure of sensitive items, though highlighted as a form of security for the most part, is not advisable as the only form of security measures. Hidden items are often the first things that attackers will look for.

Another security issue that people have with cloud computing in general is its public and third-party nature. The fact that people other than their own highly trusted personnel are handling their sensitive data is enough to make some CIOs cringe. There is really no assurance that people from third-party service providers can be trusted, and service-level agreements (SLAs) don't always mention anything about prosecution of personnel who mishandle sensitive data. The only option is for organizations to opt for a hybrid system where they keep their most sensitive data in their own on-premises data centers and relegate other data and services to third-party cloud service providers. This looks to be the best option for organizations with sensitive information on hand. They can keep a wary eye on critical data by using smaller on-premises data centers while offloading all other data and applications to the public cloud. They save money because they need to maintain only a small data center, so they still enjoy the cost effectiveness of cloud services. That is assuming that not all of their business revolves around sensitive data and applications.

Cloud Data Center Construction

Contrary to their major differences in application and architecture, on-premises and cloud data centers share the same planning and building considerations. You will need to plan for the issues discussed in the previous sections for on-premises data centers plus issues unique to cloud computing data centers because the latter are built and perform for a different scale of workloads compared to on-premises data centers. The issues that should be considered for cloud computing are described in the following sections.

Location

How location may be an issue might not be immediately obvious. You might ask, "Couldn't we just place the data center on our current building? We have some space." The answer would be no. As we mentioned, cloud data centers are created at an entirely different scale than on-premises data centers. Traditional data centers are often built on 5,000 square feet of floor space, but cloud data centers would require a lot more because they involve scalable resources that are virtually infinite in the perspective of the user. However, the hardware used to provide those resources is nowhere near infinite. That is why cloud service providers like Amazon, Google, and Rackspace are constantly building new data centers, adding more servers, and updating sometimes relatively new hardware.

Because cloud data centers have a global reach, somewhere in the future, cloud service adoption will become so prolific that so much hardware will be needed to keep up with cloud computing's promise of virtually infinite computing resources that a single 20,000-square-foot data center would not be enough for the customers of a single service provider. This means that hardware resources would have to be added regularly to keep up with customer demand. In contrast, on-premises data centers are built for a certain capacity and are rarely upgraded in capacity, just maintained and kept up-to-date.

Another consideration when choosing the location of the data center would be the temperature of the environment. The cost of cooling data centers takes up a large portions of the maintenance budget. So it would be in your best interest to select a location that has all the required facilities and can also be used for ambient cooling, at least for part of the year. The reason companies don't build their data centers in the Arctic and save almost 100 percent in cooling is that there is no infrastructure to speak off, no power or networking infrastructure. Plus, it's doubtful anyone would actually want to work in such locations unless they are paid handsomely.

The idea here is to strike a perfect balance of utility infrastructure availability, the likelihood of using alternative cooling methods, and an available workforce.

Homogeneous Hardware and Simple Workloads

Unlike traditional data centers, cloud data centers cater to only a few dedicated applications that run on the servers. This means that the architecture would be uniform, and so will software and the network that connects it all.

Traditional data centers housed a multitude of applications from just as many platforms, each with a different requirement, like the OS and the kind of processor that is used. That is why these data centers sometimes have different areas in which hardware is grouped together to be used for certain applications or operating systems. With cloud computing and standardization, a cloud data center can have a single, homogeneous hardware architecture, making it easy to connect all the components of the data center together and also making it cheaper because suppliers often give certain discounts when you buy in bulk. It also reduces maintenance costs since it would be easy to source spare parts and you would only need to train personnel for a single hardware architecture; there would be no need to hire experts with different hardware expertise. It certainly makes things simpler from a technical standpoint.

Moreover, compared to traditional data centers meant to cater to the different needs of different departments within an organization, cloud computing data centers are meant to serve many customers using one or a couple of applications. In essence, cloud data centers do only a few things but do them simultaneously and in bulk, which means processors and hard drives are doing the same things over and over. The workload is repetitive and simple, which allows operators and manufacturers to tune the hardware being used for a specific type of processing, making it much more efficient.

Higher Efficiency Requirement

As data centers become larger and larger, so does the power requirement by simple addition. More power means more heat, and more heat means more cooling. More of everything means more capital expenditure and more maintenance expenditure.

So because of cloud computing, data center hardware has been forced to evolve. It is becoming more efficient. For example, new server CPUs are clocked at speeds to that of previous generations, but they contain more cores and better pipelining and therefore can process more threads faster and yet produce less heat and consume less power. To put that in perspective, the 2006-released Intel Xeon 7150N "Tulsa" CPU built on a 65 nm process based on the old NetBurst architecture and running at 3.5 GHz was rated at 150 watts thermal design power (TDP) and cost $2,622 at that time, while the September 2013 Xeon E5-2697 V2 "Ivy Bridge-EP" with 12 cores and based on a 22 nm process running also at 2.7 GHz is rated at only 130 watts and costs similarly at around $2,614. It is simply amazing what a mere seven years can do in terms of hardware technology advancement.

With efficiency in mind, servers are now designed to be more energy and load aware and use minimal power when workloads are less, especially at idle. Older generations of servers still used above 60 percent of their rated power when idle, while newer servers are designed to use only about 25 percent to 50 percent of their total rated power consumption.

When considering equipment for efficiency, it is often a good idea to find out how efficient the individual parts are and how they actually perform in real-world applications. Sometimes manufacturers have methods of determining factors like efficiency that may not be compatible with the kinds of workloads you employ.

Hard disk drives, being the largest commodity in cloud computing, are also becoming more energy efficient. New improvements on earlier technology designs allow for saving energy during periods of inactivity, so as the idle time increases, so too will power savings, yet the drives can still quickly respond even after a long period of being idle. Manufacturers have their own power-saving features; for example, Seagate has PowerChoice technology, which was specifically developed for the enterprise and cloud computing. With PowerChoice, operators have more control over the hard drive's power consumption and functions and are able to create power modes.

In 2011, Ars Technica did some research to see if "green" hard drives are really that efficient. A 1 TB hard disk running at 3 Gbps will consume an average of 8.4 watts. So if you have a data center that runs a configuration with a total of 1,000 hard drives 24 hours a day, the total power consumption is 201.6 kilowatt hours (kWh). If you run that for a year, you have accumulated 73,584 kWh of power consumption. The average price per kWh in the United States is $0.135, so that means the energy cost for running 1,000 "green" hard drives for a whole year was $9,933.84. According to Seagate, PowerChoice technology can cut that energy consumption down to 39,735 kWh per year, bringing the energy cost to a mere $5,364.27, but that is just one of the benefits (others are increased capacity and performance). The savings that a technology like this can bring will only grow exponentially as the capacity of the data center expands.

Since there are efficiency requirements with all new data centers, there is a need to select hardware that is more efficient as well. It will not do to simply choose the "good enough" hardware. When you are building cloud data centers to cater to many customers, your goal is to achieve economies of scale. The more customers you think you will have, the cheaper it is to build the data center; because all these customers are carrying and sharing the costs, ROI would be quicker. Therefore, choosing the more expensive yet more efficient devices will not be a problem.

Security Promise

The future adoption of cloud computing by the masses will depend upon security. The need for physical security is of course a given, and system and network security must take precedence in this connected world. Service providers must promise that the security they offer is as good as or better than the security offered by on-premises data centers. They must also ensure that all employees are accountable for security failures, data loss, and data theft. Service providers must make sure their own employees and operators are not security threats themselves. There is no surefire way to do this except to have a good track record, so service providers should work at building up their reputation for security.

Optimization and the Bottom Line

For most modern businesses, IT is not just a business necessity; it is a critical piece of the business puzzle, and it has an important impact on the success of overall business operations and, of course, the bottom line. However, not everybody sees it that way. A lot of lower-level executives see IT only as a means to complete their tasks, and even those in IT sometimes think of themselves as support staff. They do not understand that even though they are not in the frontlines actively seeking customers and contracts and making money, the work they do affects everyone in the company. A good IT department keeps a company competitive, and since almost everyone makes use of IT, it has become a necessity to drive your organization.

IT is critical to business growth because it provides scalability and the ability to manage increasing complexity in an organization as well as the business model and its processes. But despite this, some professionals still struggle to grasp the importance of IT, thinking that it is a utility commodity such as electricity; it is important for everything to run smoothly, but it has no real impact on the business and provides only minimal competitive advantage. But studies show that companies can really benefit from intensive IT implementation and differentiate themselves from the competition. It would not be right to use examples like HP, Microsoft, and of course Google because they are actually IT companies. But this effect can be seen in companies like FedEx and Amazon. They have set themselves apart from the competition. FedEx uses IT for package tracking and customer satisfaction, and Amazon started out as a simple e-commerce portal that became so engrossed with IT that it is now a major IT service provider.

However, there is no systematic correlation between IT investment and the company's performance. It is entirely possible to spend a lot of economic resources in IT but see no significant improvements in operations or increase in operational capacity. That depends upon how the company leverages its IT resources. As demand for a company's IT resources increase, so does the demand for it to step up its game in terms of services and even contribute to operational optimization and the company's bottom line.

What exactly is a bottom line? If you are an executive concerned with the profit and expenditures of a company, then you know exactly what it is, but if you are an IT professional or even a rank-and-file employee, chances are you think it has something to do with profit margins.

Well, a bottom line is similar to a top line, and both describe the financial status of an organization. They are so named simply because of their positions on the income statement or profit/loss accounts. The top line is the total income/revenue or the total corporate sales or gross income generated by the business for a certain period, while the bottom line is the value after all the expenditures and liabilities have been subtracted from the top line. In other words, the bottom line is the total takeaway of the company, which means a big bottom line is good while a small one is bad. It's as simple as that.

When trying to increase the top line, a company needs to step up whatever activities it has for income generation, and this differs depending on the type of business. But increasing the bottom line would be similar for most companies. To increase the bottom line, an organization must decrease expenditure anywhere it can. And for organizations with a large IT department, especially one operating its own data center, one of the largest expenditures is data center maintenance. The total cost of ownership (TCO) of a data center often eats up a substantial chunk of a company's budget pie.

That is why most companies with an extensive IT budget have looked to their data centers for ways to cut costs and increase their bottom line. And the best way to do it without sacrificing IT functionality would be to go lean, cut off unnecessary operations, or change some process, that is, optimize the data center for the applications it is being used for so that it can produce more output in less time and with less power consumption. And sometimes even the opposite happens. You have to spend more to garner savings in the long run. We'll now look at same factors in data centers, cloud or otherwise, that can be used to optimize and cut costs.

In the following sections, we will discuss the importance of uptime and the realities of downtime and its associated costs. You will be surprised at how most of us could just downplay short downtimes when we should actually be worried about them.

The Cost of Data Center Downtime

As any output-oriented person will know, losing vital services that can hinder core business processes is costly, to both the top line and the bottom line. Imagine not being able to process hundreds of transactions simply because there is no power; millions in earnings would be lost in a short period. That affects the top line, and with costs remaining the same or even growing, the bottom line is heavily affected as well.

IT has become so ingrained into modern business that all industries—financial, banking, telecommunications, ISP, cloud services, and others—have relied on data centers, making them evolve into a monetized commodity and no longer just a support system for core business functions. The data center has become essential; many companies no longer use it to simply support the internal organization but have customers who pay premiums for access to a variety of IT applications and services.

Because of this reliance on IT systems, the connection between TCO and data center availability has become stronger than ever. A single downtime event has now the potential to severely impact the profitability of a company, or even worse its viability to future customers. Availability and uptime have become such a given and so essential to customers that downtime is now seen as almost unforgiveable. This is because, as mentioned earlier, they do not understand the complexity and work involved with keeping data centers online and available. Unfortunately, it seems that a lot of executive-level personnel do not understand this as well. They do not understand the frequency and cost of data center downtime, which severely impacts the way they view optimization efforts that can save money in the long run simply because of capital costs.

A study conducted by Emerson Network Power and Ponemon Institute in 2011 showed the differences in perception between C-suite or C-level executives and the rank-and-file IT staff. The study found that 71 percent of senior executives believe that their company's business model depends heavily on its data centers in order to generate revenue, while only 58 percent of the rank-and-file IT staff does. This shows a huge disconnect between how executives and the IT staff look at the value of the data center. Because of this trend, IT staff might view their responsibilities in a lesser light and might not perform as optimally as possible.

It is often a good idea to follow industry white papers and research just to keep up with technology trends. Who knows what precious little gems you might find.

The same study showed that 62 percent of senior-level respondents believed that unplanned outages happened only sparingly, while 41 percent of the rank and file agreed. This means that most IT staff members know that unplanned outages are happening frequently, even though they might not be severe and total ones. This data shows that C-level executives understand the economic importance of their company's data center operations, which is not surprising given that it is their core responsibility to understand all the resources and economic facets of their organization and put them to good use. However, it also indicates that these same executives are not as aware of the day-to-day operations of the data centers compared to those that are assigned with maintaining the organization's IT infrastructure. And as such, they are not aware of the frequency of downtime and other vulnerabilities of their IT infrastructure that may be contributing to these events. And because the rank-and-file IT staff may be unaware of the huge role of the data center in contributing to the organization's economic standing, they would probably not be proactive enough to report and recommend improvements in the infrastructure.

Downtime has associated costs no matter how short. They don't happen because someone just flipped the off switch for a second or two. A downtime always has a cause, and more often than not, this cause is a hole that needs to be patched up, which translates to spending money.

Quantifying Downtime Costs

According to the study, the average cost of downtime is $5,600 per minute, and based on an average reported downtime length of 90 minutes, the total is a whopping cost of $505,500 per downtime event. The calculated costs are a combination of many factors:

- Corruption and data loss
- Equipment damage
- Productivity loss
- Root-cause identification and recovery
- Legal repercussions
- Revenue loss dues to failed transactions
- Even long-term effects on reputation

Direct costs accounted for only about a third of the perceived costs; indirect costs and opportunity loss make up 62 percent of the reported costs. What's surprising is that about only $9,000 is attributed to equipment costs per downtime event, which means that intangible costs down the road far outweighs the cost of maintenance after a downtime event.

A typical data center in the United States experiences an average of two downtime events over the course of two years. So the costs incurred by downtime events can easily go beyond $1 million in less than two years. These downtime events are not even limited to total outages but include low-level factors and per-rack outages. For enterprises that depend solely on their data centers to deliver IT and networking services for revenue, like cloud service providers, telecommunications providers, and e-commerce organizations, the cost of a single downtime event can be more costly. The study showed it to be over $1 million per event, which is more than $11,000 per minute. The study mentions that the most recent downtime events of the 41 participating data centers totaled $20,735,602. That is such a substantial loss for an event that lasts for only an hour.

Infrastructure Vulnerability Cost

Downtime events occur for a reason, and most of them can be prevented. Catastrophic events are the least of a data center's worries. They are something that no one can really prepare for, only mitigate. The largest cause of data center downtime would be related to power. In fact, about 39 percent of the time the power infrastructure will be the cause of a costly downtime event. That is why it is important to nail down the power infrastructure during the planning process, which includes deciding on the location of data center itself and determining whether there are adequately reliable power utility companies serving in the area.

Of the data center failures related to power, UPS failures seem to be the costliest at around $687,700, and generator failure is a close second at $463,890. This proves to be the most costly reason for data center downtime. A power failure, especially in the UPS and backup generators, would mean total and catastrophic data center outage. Lights out! It would cause indirect costs (such as lost opportunities) to pile up on top of direct costs related to maintenance and repairs. The opportunity loss is a big one because it affects all stakeholders and not a just a portion of the customer base of the data center.

Most tier I and II data centers typically do not implement the technology to isolate a power system failure. So making investments to minimize the impact of a power failure to your data center is the most relevant course of action. There is no lean process improvement or cuts that can be done here, only capital expenditure on solutions like power redundancy, meaning backups, backups, and more backups. Implementing redundancy would mean that operators have the capacity to eliminate single points of failure in the facility's power infrastructure.

Equipment fails over time, but with a reasonable amount of redundancy, there should always be a backup that would kick in in times of need. The data center can run on its backups while the failed main module is being replaced, thus preventing a total catastrophic failure. Direct costs would still be incurred, of course, for repair and replacement of failed power modules or systems. One form of redundancy is having multiple power paths, but this would also mean multiple grid providers, which is a commodity not available in all areas.

Adding UPS systems for redundancy should be on top of the list of solutions. Long-term reliability of the UPS system should be the key element in determining what sort of UPS system to implement. By implementing input current tolerances, battery monitoring, and adequate service maintenance, you can ensure that the mean time between failures (MTBF) of a UPS unit can be maximized. Finally, integrating a comprehensive infrastructure monitoring tool can help operators isolate and rectify power infrastructure issues and prevent total catastrophic failure of a data center due to a power outage.

Real World Scenario

Amazon EC2 Outage

On June 29, 2012, users of the Internet had firsthand experience with downtime brought about by infrastructure vulnerability. By 11:21 p.m. EST, a large portion of the Internet was offline because of massive power outages brought on by a severe thunderstorm in North Virginia, where one of Amazon's biggest EC2 data centers is located. This affected only a single availability zone, but that zone contained widely popular media and social media sites, including Netflix, Instagram, and Pinterest. There were other sites affected as well, but the outage was immediately sensationalized because of the popularity of the afore-mentioned sites. Amazon reported to have resolved majority of the issues at 1:15 a.m., and all affected sites were brought back up a few hours later. Overall, the outage lasted less than 12 hours, but the amount of attention it garnered was staggering.

Since Amazon cloud services reach every corner of the Internet, when they fail, everyone feels it. But what about the promise of no downtime with cloud computing? Well, that promise is only a guarantee and needs to be explicitly applied to the uploaded application or website by the application or website provider. Amazon makes it easy for users to run their AWS workloads across availability zones and provides various redundancy measures. This simply means that the affected websites did not apply an important feature of cloud computing. And it shows that users are still not utilizing the cloud to its full potential.

Outages Caused Due to Environmental Reasons

Environmental issues are the leading causes of IT equipment failures. In fact, among the root causes of downtime found by the Emerson study, 15 percent of all the root causes can be attributed to an environmental variable like thermal issues and water incursion. Detection and recovery from these failures also incurred significant costs, at an average of more than $489,000 per incident. And when these environmental issues cause real equipment failure, it resulted in the highest overall cost, at more than $750,000, because expensive equipment has to be replaced in addition to the cost of man power and further downtime associated with the procedure.

The problem with environmental issues is that they can cause a chain reaction of IT equipment failures, which would require extensive efforts for detection and recovery of the issue that caused the outage, not to mention replacement of the equipment. The fact that cooling equipment does not even need to fail to cause an IT equipment failure is wor-risome. It shows a deeper problem within the cooling infrastructure itself. These isolated failures, which are typically caused by hotspots within the racks themselves, are often the result of inadequacies of the cooling infrastructure rather than a cooling equipment failure.

The failure was eventually going to happen; it was only a matter of time. And if this goes unaddressed, it will happen again in the same location, with the replacement equipment. This just further illustrates the importance of an optimized and well-designed cooling infrastructure.

 NOTE Even though environment- and cooling-related incidents are more isolated than power-related failures, an optimized cooling infrastructure with remote monitoring is still required to keep IT equipment performing at its optimum and to make use of it throughout its full, rated life span, therefore minimizing environment-related failures.

Fortunately all of this can be avoided by not skimping on the cooling infrastructure during design and construction, but if it is too late for that, upgrades or installation of a better system can help, although that may be a bit costly.

Here are some best practices and investments that can be applied to a data center with less-than-adequate cooling solutions:

- Bring precision cooling closer to the load through row-based precision cooling solutions to eliminate rack hotspots.

- Prevent water incursion by using refrigerant-based solutions rather than water-based ones.

- Install comprehensive remote monitoring facilities that have temperature triggers and thresholds to warn operators of possible cooling issues.

- Do regular preventive maintenance, and do not wait for something to fail before repair or replacement. This could mean the difference between catastrophic failure and no failure at all.

Though these are rather basic and common-sense solutions, you will be surprised how often they are put aside to cater to an executive's idea of saving money in the short term. Foresight is always more important than patching symptoms of current problems.

Data Center Monitoring and Maintenance

Data center monitoring has been mentioned quite a number of times in this chapter, and you might have an idea of how important it is even without us telling you.

As organizations go to the process of cutting costs and looking for ways to save money and increase the bottom line in the long run, data center optimization will be on the table, especially for those organizations that rely heavily on their IT for revenue. There will be constant upgrades and innovations in order to try to increase revenue growth, the top line, and companies might also be looking for ways to save money while upgrading, for that all-important bottom line.

But as new technologies are deployed to support newer services, complexity is introduced into the system, especially if it is being transitioned to newer technology. Cloud data centers are especially vulnerable to this complexity. Cloud data centers have a homogeneous hardware configuration, meaning all or most of their IT equipment is of one type, supporting a single or only a few platforms to keep things simple and easy to manage. But that will not be the case forever. Eventually new technology has to replace the old, yet the services being run on the older hardware still needs to be supported. Besides, you cannot change everything at once, so there will be a period of transition when there are multiple technologies and platforms running and supported. This introduces quite a bit of complexity into the operations in the data center. Putting, for example, upgraded cooling systems and a redundant power infrastructure in place also introduces complexity as people try to adjust to all the new equipment with different needs.

To manage this complex environment, most data center operators deploy a myriad of monitoring methods, like proprietary databases and custom-built software and even manual monitoring systems coupled with software like Microsoft Excel and Visio. These methods may work for some tasks, but they may not work for everything, plus they may not work together effectively, which may lead to some user error caused by manually configuring and calculating settings. For example, these tools may not work together to solve a complex issue like quickly isolating a network bottleneck due to misbehaving network equipment brought about by a power surge. With a mixture of systems and tools, you might not even be able to tell what resources you have in your data center.

A new class of software called data center infrastructure management (DCIM) software has been purposely built to help give operators the ability to run data center operations efficiently. DCIM software bridges information between organizational domains like Facilities, and IT incorporates it into data center operations in the network operations center (NOC), which allows for the optimum utilization of the data center. It can provide clear visibility of all data center resources together with their relationships and even physical connectivity in order to support monitoring and reporting of all related data center infrastructure. As far as optimization goes, this will increase data center computing efficiency and increase utilization as well as make operations workflow smoother in order to save time and therefore money for that company bottom line.

The beauty of a DCIM is that it does not really replace all those monitoring systems you have in place. It will merely act as a bridge and a single point of contact, complete with analytics functions and visualization of all that data so that it can be easily understood.

The Value of Energy Efficiency

We cannot talk about optimization and its importance to the bottom line if we do not touch on energy efficiency. This would be the most obvious area where C-suite executives look for way to save money, and everybody else would agree with them.

Since the data center became a standard for companies everywhere, energy efficiency has always been something that people have been striving for. In the past few years, it has become a nationally observed initiative and is no longer just an option or a luxury; industry-wide regulations targeting energy conservation have been made and implemented across the board. And it's no wonder; energy costs have only increased, even with so-called green energy being implemented every day. Energy costs are the second highest expense in data center operations next to labor costs. To give you perspective, a typical 1 megawatt data center is estimated to consume about 16 million kilowatt hours a year, which is roughly equivalent to the consumption of 1,400 average U.S. households per year.

In the planning stage, engineers typically look at the energy efficiency of each piece of IT equipment that goes into the data center. This might be an energy-saving measure, but it would not be enough. We always need to look at the bigger picture, and in this case we have to consider the end-to-end power efficiency of the entire data center system, from the power grid's point of entry into the facility to the equipment that uses this power. We have to look beyond energy-efficient servers and virtualization and start looking at our power infrastructure as well.

Consider that for each power conditioner and converter that electricity passes through, some electricity is lost. Each power module has its own efficiency rating, so only by adding the efficiency rating of all the modules that the power has to go through to get to the servers will we see the true energy efficiency of the entire data center system.

A 2008 study by the Eaton Corporation found that overall system power efficiency can be optimized by finding the total efficiency from end to end. The study showed that standard 480 V AC power distribution systems used in many data centers are inadequate when it comes to power efficiency. The study compared the newer, more-energy-efficient 400 V AC and 600 V AC power distribution systems. Eaton concluded that the 400 V AC variant would be more efficient and would save more money in the long run compared to the 600 V AC alternative. When you pair that with high-efficiency UPSs and servers, you can be sure that your data center is optimized for power efficiency.

But that study was done in 2008, and newer data centers have better alternatives for power efficiency that also conforms to state regulatory laws. Our conclusion here is that when calculating for efficiency and optimization, you have to see the whole picture and look from end to end, not just at the equipment you are familiar with. As cloud computing professionals, we must concern ourselves with efficiency and savings wherever we might get it.

The Cloud Infrastructure

Though cloud data centers and traditional data centers have similar hardware, their infrastructure design, or how everything is tied together, is different. In fact, depending on the purpose of the cloud data center, its infrastructure design may differ from another cloud data center. Again, all of this is down to what type of services are going to be offered or provided, and it all has to do with optimization.

Even with many differences in infrastructure design and components, cloud computing infrastructure has some common areas:

Distributed File Systems   Cloud computing often relies on distributed file systems, which are spread across multiple hard drives and machines or even across multiple data centers. They provide speed and reliability as well as data redundancy in case of failure. Data is never stored in just one place, so when a unit fails, another will simply take its place and carry the load or provide the required data. This offers high availability to the user, yet it's more expensive to implement compared to a solution that does not use data replication for redundancy.

Resource Provisioning and Virtualization   Resource provisioning and virtualization are key features of cloud computing, and the infrastructure must be able to reflect these two aspects. Though cloud computing data center hardware is homogeneous and used in a simple environment, the virtual environment makes up for that with its complexity. The cloud environment is a complex jumble that relies heavily on special algorithms that are used to allocate various resources like CPU, RAM, and hard drive capacity. Each of these resources is virtually provisioned to customers and users as virtual machines or virtual computers, with each having a set amount of computing resources.

When required, more computing power can be added to existing virtual machines, or more machines can be provisioned. Users only need to pay for what they provision; this is the *utility computing* aspect of cloud computing.

In the technological community, there have always been two opposing sides: open source and proprietary. The same goes for cloud computing infrastructure design, and we will explore both.

Open Source

In the world of computing, the term *open source* is often associated with the words *rebel* and *freedom fighter*. That was the sentiment decades ago. That is no longer the case for the majority, and *open source* doesn't really mean free anymore; it simply means freely accessible, but people have been making money out of open-source solutions for a long time. What really comes to mind when people use the term *open source* today is security and reliability, or the lack thereof. Which is more secure, more reliable, open-source or proprietary solutions? That entirely depends on what application you need.

Because cloud computing is the new global standard for delivering business applications and is meant to serve everyone, open-source solutions were not far behind. And now open source platforms have matured enough that cloud providers have become more confident in them and are deploying them for their customers.

But open source is not for everyone; it is for those that can embrace change, and lots of it. Open-source platforms and infrastructure tend to constantly evolve as more input is added from all the contributors and newer standards are drafted. This happens quicker as new technology perceived to increase workflow and provide other benefits is developed. So for companies that embrace fast-paced change and are able to keep up, open source is an appealing solution. But its ever-evolving nature can prove to be a challenge for cloud providers that may not have the expertise to manage complex technology.

There are a few open-source initiatives in the world of cloud computing, and they now have gotten a lot of backing, especially from open-source-embracing giants like Google and Facebook, who have worked closely with these initiatives to push for a powerful, ever-evolving technology within the reach of anyone willing to embrace it.

Open Compute Project

When hardware design and data center design move in harmony with each other, they improve efficiency and reduce power consumption. It is this goal that the Open Compute Project has dedicated itself to. In short, the Open Compute Project is a set of technologies that are designed to reduce energy consumption and cost and increase efficiency, reliability, and choice in the marketplace as well as simplify operations and maintenance. The key objective of the project is openness, and so the specifications and even mechanical designs, complete with drawings and 3D CAD files, for the components of a data center are being made open source so that everyone can benefit from them and add their own ideas and designs. The efficiency results achieved at facilities using Open Compute technologies are also freely available.

The Open Compute Project started with a small three-man team of Facebook engineers who worked on the simple question of how to scale Facebook's computing infrastructure in the most economical and efficient way possible. They worked out of an electronics lab in the basement of Facebook's Palo Alto headquarters in California. The small team designed their first data center from scratch, from the ground up, and in a few months started building another data center in Prineville, Oregon.

The project grew with the team building custom-designed servers, server racks, power supplies, and battery backup systems. Working with a blank slate meant the team had total control over every part of the system, from servers and the software to the whole data center itself. This meant they could use the most efficient hardware and remove any system that was perceived as inefficient. The resulting data center at Prineville uses 38 percent less energy and costs 24 percent less to do the same work as Facebook's existing data center facilities.

The team came up with some simple solutions to achieve this efficiency:

- Use a 480-volt electrical distribution system to reduce energy loss.
- Remove from servers certain parts that reduced efficiency.
- Reuse hot air from the racks in winter to both heat the offices and the air coming into the facility.
- Eliminate the need for a central uninterruptible power supply.

The Open Compute Project provides design and specifications for most aspects of the data center, including the design of the center itself. OCP's design for the data center is in tandem with OCP-designed servers and racks. The design also features an energy-efficient power infrastructure and cooling infrastructure. The designs can be found on OCP's website at www.opencompute.org/projects/.

The following specifications are provided by the Open Compute Project:

Storage   Called Open Vault, it is a cost-effective solution that was designed with a modular I/O topology and high disk densities by holding 30 drives in a 2U chassis and can operate with any host server.

Networking   The Open Compute Networking Project aims to create a fully open and disaggregated set of technologies that promotes rapid innovation.

Motherboard and Server   Open Compute motherboards and server designs are meant to have low capital and low operating costs by removing some traditional motherboard features that are usually unnecessary for servers.

Server Rack (Open Rack)   Open Rack is a server rack design standard that integrates the rack into the design of the data center. It uses a holistic design process that considers the interdependence of components from the power grid to individual gates on the chips.

Data Center   The design of Open Compute data centers is meant to leverage and maximize the mechanical performance and thermal and electrical efficiency of their other technologies.

OpenStack

OpenStack is an open-source cloud operating system that is able to control large pools of storage, networking, and computing resources available in a data center. All these resources are managed through a dashboard with powerful administrative controls, and users are empowered to provision resources through a web interface.

OpenStack is a joint initiative released in July 2010 by Rackspace, one of the biggest players in cloud computing, and NASA, which needs no introduction. The project was intended to help different organizations offer cloud computing services that run on standard hardware. The early code for the software was a combination of both NASA's Nebula cloud computing platform and Rackspace's Cloud Files platform. Nebula was designed to provide Infrastructure as a Service (IaaS) features, while the Cloud Files platform is predominantly storage oriented, and both come together to provide both services, which results in the foundation of the OpenStack system we have today.

The project, just like the Open Compute Project, aims to provide a robust cloud computing platform for both private and public clouds that is interoperable and without vendor lock-in. However, OpenStack is predominantly an IaaS platform, so it may not fit everyone's needs.

OpenStack itself is not a single software package. It is instead a conglomeration of smaller modules, individual projects that form the basic and advanced features that the platform provides. It is highly pluggable and can function without the other modules. This can also be a detriment because some modules will see better development than the others, but because it's open source, whoever needs one of those modules can simply spend some resources to develop for it and then share it with the rest of the community. Such is the beauty of open source.

We will look as these smaller modules in the following sections.

Compute Module (Nova)

Nova is a cloud computing fabric controller, the main portion of an IaaS platform that controls every aspect of the system. Nova is central to OpenStack's goal of providing cloud computing services on standard hardware because its architecture is designed to horizontally scale when running on standard hardware. It has no proprietary hardware or software requirements whatsoever, and it's even backward compatible with legacy hardware systems and integrates with third-party technologies, making it easy for organizations to jump on the cloud bandwagon without the need to retrofit existing data centers. As with all cloud platforms, it is designed to automate large pools of computing resources and work with a variety of virtualization technologies as well with bare metal machines (those with no OS) and high-performance computing (HPC) configurations, or, simply, supercomputers.

OpenStack Compute is often deployed using one of the many supported hypervisors in a virtualized environment. Popular choices for hypervisor application would be XenServer and KVM, which are also widely recommended for most use cases for cloud implementations. Hyper-V is supported for x86 to 64-bit versions of Windows servers as well as LXC for Linux.

Object Storage (Swift)

Swift is OpenStack's object storage facility, a redundant storage system. Data is written in multiple disk drives that are spread across the data center to ensure that they do not become unavailable at the same time, while the software ensures that that replication happens and data integrity is maintained across the storage cluster. If more storage is required, new servers have to simply be added since storage clusters scale horizontally.

In the event of a hard drive failure, OpenStack simply re-creates the contents of that failed drive into new locations within the cluster using backed-up or replicated data available from other active nodes. OpenStack uses software logic to ensure distributed replication across the cluster and different devices, and as such inexpensive standard hard drives and servers can be used.

Block Storage (Cinder)

Cinder is the module that allows OpenStack to provide persistent block-level storage devices to be used with OpenStack's compute instances. Cinder manages the creation of block devices and the processes of attaching and detaching them to and from the servers. These block volumes become integrated to Nova and appear on the dashboard, allowing users to provision and manage their own storage needs.

Block storage is essential for performance-dependent applications such as expandable file systems and database applications or to simply provide servers with access to raw block-level storage. Backup management is done through snapshots that can be used to restore or create new block storage volumes, a powerful functionality for backing up data on block storage volumes.

This is compatible with many storage platforms, including IBM storage, Linux LIO, Nexenta, Cloudbyte, Ceph, SolidFire, HP StoreVirtual and StoreServ 3Par families, local Linux server storage, and many more.

Networking (Neuron)

Neuron is OpenStack's network orchestration module, a system for managing networks and IP addresses. This is a relatively new addition to OpenStack and the first functioning software-defined networking (SDN) northbound API that allows an SDN controller to interface with higher-level management and orchestration systems. Neuron enables a high degree of cloud automation, multitenancy, massive scale, and, hence, added flexibility.

Neuron provides different networking models for a variety of applications, including flat networks or VLANs for separating traffic and servers. Its IP address management facility allows for dedicated static IP addresses or DHCP, and the use of floating IP addresses allows the rerouting of traffic to any computing resource, thereby allowing for the redirecting of traffic in the case of failure or required maintenance. Users will be able to provision their own networks, control all traffic, and have freedom in connecting their servers and other computing resources.

Dashboard (Horizon)

Horizon is the front-end interface that gives administrators and users a graphical interface to access in order to provision, set up, and automate cloud computing resources. The design of the interface allows for third-party products such as billing and other management and monitoring tools to be integrated into the interface. It is also customizable to reflect the brand of the service provider using it.

The dashboard is just the graphical way of interacting with OpenStack resources; however, developers are also able to do this through the native OpenStack API or the EC2 compatibility API. Figure 3.4 shows the Horizon dashboard used with Ubuntu.

FIGURE 3.4   Ubuntu Horizon dashboard

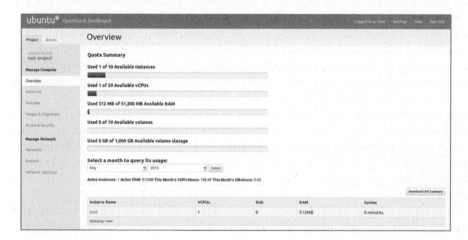

Other Modules

This sums up the major modules of OpenStack. There are still other modules that add value and ensure that OpenStack becomes a very enticing option for cloud computing providers. They are as follows:

Identity Service (Keystone)   The central directory and authentication system.

Image Service (Glance)   The module for registration and delivery for server and disk images, a part of OpenStack's backup system.

Telemetry (Ceilometer)   A single point of contact for billing and metering systems across current and future OpenStack components.

Orchestration (Heat)   A template-based system for orchestrating multiple composite cloud applications.

Proprietary

It seems that we have discussed so much about open-source solutions that it might sound like this book is pro open source. That is actually correct, but we realize that open source is not often the panacea or "cure-all" that others make it out to be. Because if that were truly the case, it would be the only type of product out there. It's not, though, simply because in some aspects proprietary products may be exactly what an organization needs. It has been this way since the beginning and will be for the foreseeable future. Open source is simply an alternative, and like all alternatives, there are pros and cons.

If you look around the Internet and read about open-source versus proprietary cloud infrastructure and providers, you will immediately see the great divide that the industry is currently in. The question is often in the selection of proprietary solutions versus the broadly accepted OpenStack solutions. The argument is always customer lock-in. But is this still an issue now? When an organization engages in cloud computing, it becomes a sort of marriage between the organization (the customer) and the cloud service provider, with the service-level agreement (SLA) serving as the prenuptial agreement. When both parties decide on a union and sign that contract, it becomes a till-death-do-us-part thing. It's a very significant commitment, and if the service is good enough and the price just right and if the provider honors the SLA, a customer will most often stay with the provider. So in most cases, lock-in is not going to be an issue.

This is not like buying a car, where you might want a different brand if ever you want a new car. Even if the customer comes up with a need that the service provider does not yet offer, it would still be reluctant to separate from the provider. Besides, most likely the provider will just develop that function and provide that service simply because it doesn't want to lose a customer.

There really is no reason to switch providers unless the new provider you are switching to is light years ahead in technology and is free or at least offers its services at incredibly cheaper rates than the current provider. The reality, though, is that providers are all neck and neck in terms of technology, and when one drops prices, others will follow suit within hours. Such is usually the case between Amazon, Google, Microsoft, and Rackspace. So now when you look at the cloud market ecosystem, you see service providers with very similar functions and offerings at very competitive prices. This ensures that the need to switch vendors periodically is really close to nonexistent.

A lot of service providers offer similar services that are sometimes customizable, and they often try to one-up the competition, so it would be a good idea to compare providers and make sure they know that this is exactly what you are doing.

Another argument is cloud interoperability, which is how separate clouds from different organizations can interact with each other to form larger clouds and a bigger ecosystem for collaboration. The question here is whether these organizations would really need or at all want to have this shared ecosystem. We imagine that would be quite bad for business if the organizations in question are profit-oriented ones. It might work for educational and research organizations, but these types of entities are historically known to embrace open-source solutions, so they would already be in the position to share and merge because most likely they will already be using a form of OpenStack. Profit-oriented organizations will be hard-pressed to collaborate with each other, and even when they want to collaborate with educational institutions and research organizations, they can simply create an interface between the two clouds. So this is another nonissue.

In the end, it all boils down to choice and adoption. Those companies that choose open source will see a wide adoption in the industry, and those companies that choose proprietary want none of that openness in the first place. So the final factor in the battle between open source and proprietary is simply the needs and desires of the organization. All organizations will think twice and really plan their move to the cloud, and their choice, open source or proprietary, will be based on their business needs and their stance regarding their future use of that infrastructure. It is not a battle of which is better; it's simply choice. If what an organization needs can't be provided by the open-source option, the proprietary infrastructure is best for them.

Summary

With technology moving quickly for business and consumer applications, it is becoming more evident that cloud computing is the direction the industry needs to take. But it must be noted that the cloud is a concept, or rather an application of a concept on distribution and usage of computing resources, and is not an entirely new and separate technology in need of its own unique constructs and infrastructure. Simply put, cloud computing is a better way of using finite resources. What that means is that it is not running on entirely different hardware compared to traditional on-premises enterprise computing; it's merely an evolution of it.

As for the data center that runs cloud or traditional IT, it can be interchangeable depending on the need. But the importance of good design cannot be stressed enough. We are talking about millions of dollars in cost, so efficiency and reliability should always be at the core of data center design no matter the purpose, be it cloud or on-premises.

Chapter Essentials

Key Differences between Traditional and Cloud-Based Hardware   The key difference here is configuration. What type of hardware devices and how they are connected to each other are essentially what makes the hardware infrastructure for these two concepts different. The cloud data center is designed to cater to thousands of users at once and will be configured for scalability, which means homogeneous hardware; this makes maintenance easier considering the scale of the facilities. Traditional on-premises data centers are designed to cater only to a single organization and its constituents, meaning that it is at a smaller scale, and the hardware configuration will vary depending on the requirements of the enterprise applications being supported. But both types of data center will make use of the same basic hardware, i.e., the same types of CPU, RAM, storage disks, and networking equipment like switches and hubs.

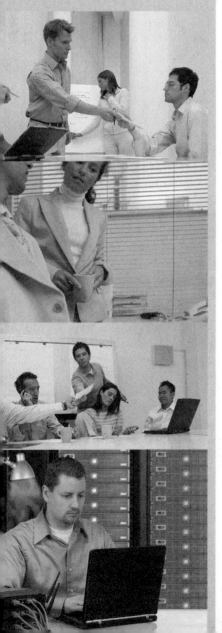

Chapter

4

Cloud Management

TOPICS COVERED IN THIS CHAPTER INCLUDE:

- ✓ Network and IP planning/documentation
- ✓ Configuration standardization and documentation
- ✓ Change management best practices
- ✓ Configuration management
- ✓ Capacity management
- ✓ Systems life cycle management
- ✓ Maintenance windows

Information technology just keeps on evolving. With cloud computing, it's taken to another level. And because of that, chief information officers (CIOs) and administrators are scratching their heads at the sheer enormity of the task that is cloud management.

Thankfully there are a lot of choices for services and applications that are meant to make things simpler and more streamlined, allowing administrators to simply sit back and let the system monitor the cloud infrastructure with minimum intervention required.

Cloud management does not start with the administration portion after deployment; it starts during the planning phase. All of the aspects of the cloud must be well thought out from a management perspective, from the proper operation of computing resources, updates, and upgrades to customer service and legal support.

Management is especially critical in enterprises where agility and efficiency are the main drivers because cloud technology is essential and key to addressing and achieving business objectives. This is because cloud computing is now considered a definite way to significantly drive business process efficiency, innovation, and differentiation of selling points. Proper management is therefore a pivotal requirement to achieve these benefits.

With today's highly competitive and connected world, customers are more vocal about their opinions than ever, leading companies to constantly innovate and deliver new ideas and services in order to stay in the game or ahead of the competition. In the past, enterprise IT has often been the bottleneck. It has greatly affected a company's agility because developers and QA engineers had to wait in line for IT administrators to go through their queue before development and testing platforms could be provisioned for them.

To address these concerns, most enterprises have turned to cloud computing and exploring its benefits in their own data centers using private clouds. For fast on-demand access and provisioning, smart resource allocation and scheduling, resource monitoring, and environment control, what we know as traditional IT must abandon its reactive ways, simply waiting for requests and orders, and be more predictive and proactive to the needs of the organization. This is especially true when it comes to data center and computing resource management.

Understanding Cloud Management Platforms

Cloud technology is proliferating at a high rate of speed, and a lot of organizations are diving into cloud computing because of the benefits. Most enterprises are at the very least implementing some type of on-premise private cloud, while a growing number are starting to use public cloud platforms from multiple vendors. Most organizations will probably be requiring services from multiple vendors simply because most vendors specialize in some service or another in order to differentiate themselves from each other. So when an enterprise needs Software as a Service (SaaS) technology for certain applications and also a platform for development, chances are they would need two separate providers for both services. This creates unnecessary complexity because those two cloud services are not meant to work with each other, even though in principle they should. This is a challenge for basic tasks like provisioning, orchestration, governance, and overall management. The situation in the industry right now is that there are a bunch of cloud computing silos being built separately by different providers. Most of them are innovative and will be needed by an enterprise or two. But the problem is that they are not made to coexist, and that's what the OpenStack open-source project aims to solve. For now, however, we have this fragmentation and we are left with a multi-cloud management challenge.

What we need is an innovative solution that is built on a layer above these standard separate silos, cloud platforms, or end points that have been implemented across the enterprise, a solution that can act as an abstraction layer so that you do not have to conform to the nuances of each cloud platform. That solution is the cloud management platform.

Management platforms are integrated products made up of several applications and tools that provide monitoring and management of private, public, and hybrid cloud environments. To be called a management platform, a product must at least integrate interfaces for self-service provisioning of computing resources like server and storage images and virtual machines, enable billing and metering, and provide workload and performance optimization to some extent. More advanced solutions may offer extended functionalities like better micromanagement and automation of computing resources and may have facilities to integrate with other cloud environments for collaborative work. It may also support advanced monitoring akin to that of the tools used by the service providers themselves to monitor and micromanage certain aspects of the infrastructure and environment. Figure 4.1 shows a basic overview of how a management platform can connect different implementations of cloud environments.

Cloud management platforms enable the deployment and management of enterprise-class services and applications across all cloud types. They serve to bridge different cloud platforms and act as a central focal point and management center to make different clouds from different vendors play nice with each other, to an extent. This kind of system really helps in solving the vendor lock-in debate between proprietary and open-source cloud platforms. It may not be a total answer and solution to the problem, but at least it helps somewhat. Management platforms are available as SaaS or as stand-alone on-premise software that enables you to control your cloud from within your own data center.

Management platforms then provide automation using a set of rules and policies as a blueprint to minimize the need for users and developers to know how to do what needs to be done for each separate cloud platform out there. They simply a set of tools and capabilities that the user can harness to be able to perform all cloud computing functions effectively and consistently across the multi-cloud environment. So instead of multiple silos or end points, the user is presented with a single plain field, minimizing the complexity to a bottom layer.

FIGURE 4.1   Cloud management platform

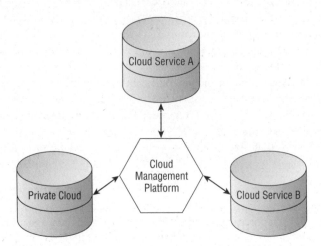

What It Means for Service Providers

Managing a small cloud for an organization would already be quite a handful; now imagine that cloud service providers are challenged with running and maintaining a massive, scaled-out infrastructure possibly made up of different remote locations while serving customers across the globe whose demands grow by the day. Ensuring the performance and availability of diverse, highly complex IT environments, meeting standards and compliance requirements in various SLAs, maintaining control, and securing the infrastructure are all common day-to-day problems being faced by service providers.

The pressure on cloud service providers goes beyond delivering stable and good performance for enterprises that are seeking to employ cloud computing to get an advantage over the competition. Cloud service providers are not simply here to make people happy. That is only part of the equation. They are here to make money. And so they are in an ongoing struggle to find, create, and deliver attractive solutions and better alternatives for on-premise IT or a similar or better level of service when on-premise approaches become impractical. If they fail in this regard, their business fails as well.

As a way to keep up with demand and attract new players to cloud computing, they could start with exceptional cloud management. Enterprises are all about control and information, for nobody likes to be blind to possible negative situations. Cloud management is therefore very important for the enterprise. It is at the forefront of the smooth cloud operations of any business.

Planning Your Cloud

Differentiation is at the core of being a cloud service provider. You do not simply want to be another fish in the bucket. You must stand out in order to compete, especially against the giants who already offer every known service. So when planning your business solutions, you must take into consideration a key question: What will you offer that will make customers choose you over the competition? It is a straightforward question that every business asks itself, but it is the answer that will truly set the business apart. Often the easiest way to differentiation is through fast and easy cloud migration and services that offer great customization for customers.

Because the cloud is on everybody's radar right now, cloud services and cloud projects have high visibility and inspire lofty expectations, as is fitting given its name. But so many planned objectives often fall short because of the disconnect between the business and IT, even though in this case, the business is IT itself. The common mistake of miscommunication between technical and executive staff is still pervasive, even though in this industry executives are technical, or at least they came from technical backgrounds. The fact remains that the viewpoint of executives is broad compared to the viewpoint of technical engineers. Oftentimes very optimistic time-to-market schedules exist and implementation is compromised, leading to the launch of a half-baked service, with features that should have been in the release being added over time.

Aside from that, organizations that embark on the journey of the cloud service provider without a comprehensive cloud service plan are often challenged to meet the demands and offer the potential value that customers are looking for. Remember that in business there is no such strategy as "if we serve it, they will buy it." But if those services are well thought out, architected to deliver business needs with more value, and designed to allow the end user to maximize their returns, they are sure to succeed. There must be a series of steps taken to properly plan for the cloud business. Even though this is supposed to be common knowledge and standard operating procedure by now, a lot of organizations still fail to do it properly or in a timely manner, perhaps because they are not exactly sure on how to go about it.

Cloud Service Solution Planning Workshop

The most straightforward way to plan—which may differ from a regular planning session where all the executives vote for which goals are the hardest to achieve and choose to implement those in the shortest time possible—is to have a planning workshop with representatives from all stakeholder groups. This planning session will take a workshop format, meaning everyone with any major role in the development and deployment of the services has to be present and participate with their ideas and plans. This would allow top executives and the technical team to see eye to eye so the technical people can better understand the business needs that drive the decisions and how important they are to the success of those decisions. It will also educate or at least remind the executives that not everything they want done can be done, at least not in the way that they expect it to. This would ensure that at the end of the workshop period of two to three weeks, the assembly will have reached some possible solutions that meet both administrative decisions and technical applicability according to the resources of the organization. It is also important to have a few cloud experts on hand to guide the workshop. It won't help at all if everyone present knows less than the next guy about cloud computing and its various ins and outs.

The experts, third-party or in-house, should be able to help with the overall flow of the workshop and especially help those present to formulate their own ideas, which can lead to solutions unique to the organization. The experts can help with the following tasks:

- Understand, and then refine the cloud objectives.
- Help analyze the current IT environment and infrastructure in both physical and virtual fields.
- Get a detailed gap analysis between the current and the desired IT states.
- Conduct a detailed review of and showcase the best-in-class cloud environment models as well as what the competition has to offer.
- Detail model use cases and various requirements for cloud deployment.
- Come up with a detailed road map arranged in phases and milestones for deployment.
- Create a risk and change management plan.

The duration and topics covered by the workshop will depend on what the body of attendees has come up with from the preceding list. Each one should be meticulously discussed, planned, and documented, so there should be no rush in finishing the workshop. A well-thought-out plan is the first step for smooth sailing. But the general length of the workshop for smaller projects with daily meetings would be two to three weeks.

The workshop should be focusing on the organization's strengths as well as finding solutions to patch up weaknesses. So at the end of the workshop, there should be a number of unique services that have been generated or simply newer takes of generic services with added value that are sure to draw in customers. And since these services are built around the organization's strengths, they are in a position to deliver with quality. This will help the organization understand the exact level of effort, commitment, risk, and business process changes that is necessary to plan, develop, deploy, and manage innovative cloud services that act as major differentiators of the organization to its competitors. The length of the workshop will depend on the scope of the objectives, with each workshop being tailored to address a combination of service planning and design.

Here is a sample workshop agenda:

- Introductions
- Review of the organization's cloud drivers
- Overview of the organization's current state in IT hosting as well as current and planned cloud initiatives
- Overview of planned solutions or vendors to contact, weighing of pros and cons
- Review of best-in-class cloud implementations and services and explanations of how those were achieved
- Current state of IT assessment
- Use case modeling for cloud services
- Determining deliverables, taking into account risk, change management, and organizational readiness

- Formal review (where all stakeholders must be present) of determined deliverables from previous session.

- Solution adoption plan (will take the longest because a plan to achieve each deliverable must be well organized; requires a dedicated group with representatives from each stakeholder group)

Workshop Attendees

When we say that everyone should attend the workshop, we obviously mean that everyone needs to be represented. For example, the CIO or CTO is often too busy to attend long workshops like this, so they should be represented by someone who shares their point of view and objectives, including the relationship of those objectives to the organization's business needs, directions, and initiatives as a whole as opposed to the departmental views of other stakeholders like technical IT and customer support. Figure 4.2 shows a simple diagram of the equal interaction of all stakeholders. All the views and ideas of each group must be given equal weight.

FIGURE 4.2   Workshop interaction chart

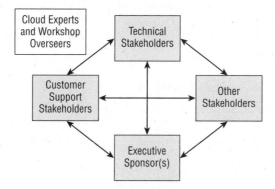

The workshop should be attended by the following people, without exception:

Executive Sponsor   The executive sponsor represents the CIO/CTO's broader views for the business objectives, initiatives, and future goals.

IT Staff   IT leaders and technical staff members can provide the assembly with a clear understanding of the organization's current state regarding the physical infrastructure as well as the virtual and cloud environments. They also shed light on the technical capabilities and knowledge of the general personnel as well as existing IT processes and procedures, roles, and tools in the following areas:

Discovery   Service design and assessment, architecture planning and design, capacity planning and evaluation, and service costs and pricing. The idea is to look for current hardware and software assets in the environment together with the relationships between them.

Provisioning   Cloud service catalog, hybrid cloud options, self-service portal, cloud and IT service management integration.

Management   Proactive monitoring and performance management, optimization.

Compliance   Cloud governance and compliance, service-level agreements (SLAs), licensing, and other legal management issues.

Cloud Computing Experts   Specialists who will guide the assembly to achieve the goals of the workshop, which may consist of a project manager or business service management architect, an IT service management specialist, a cloud service automation specialist, and a cloud service integration specialist.

Not all cloud projects are the same. Some enterprises want to start fresh with new software and hardware, and in some cases, even a totally new data center. Then there are enterprises that want to transform existing IT assets into a cloud environment. That is why it is important to plan the cloud deployment meticulously, and no two plans are ever exactly the same. The deployment plan must begin with the discovery and baselining of current IT assets.

Building Your Cloud

After extensive planning comes setup. This might just be the most significant part of the process because what good can a well-thought-out plan do if it is not implemented well. And given that the cloud is not about islands of automation of computing assets, but instead how the individual parts work together to deliver cloud computing benefits, there is a lot to do. Figure 4.3 shows how different parts of a cloud computing system interact with each other to deliver services to a user.

FIGURE 4.3   Basic cloud system diagram

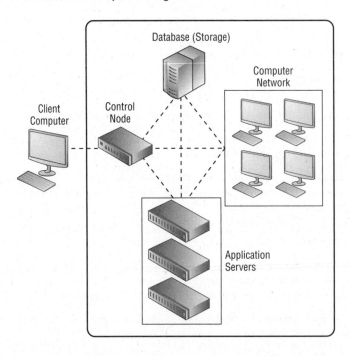

If you're starting fresh using new hardware and software or a new data center is required, see Chapter 3, "Within the Cloud: Technical Concepts of Cloud Computing." But if there is an existing hardware infrastructure, the problem here is how to transform that on-premise and fragmented environment into one single cloud environment. That should already be taken care of in the planning process during the discovery of existing IT assets.

Though the technical details might vary depending on the current infrastructure, the process can be broken down into a few steps.

Running Your Cloud

A lot of what goes into running and keeping your cloud online has to do with mitigation of technical problems before they can even happen. Operational intelligence is one way to deal with arising situations as they occur, so it should be a major part of any cloud management platform. Knowing exactly what might happen because of a given scenario is enough to raise flags when certain difficult situations might occur, and then operational intelligence allows you to detect and formulate solutions and workarounds in case specific unfavorable situations do occur. And when they do, you know exactly what to do to mitigate them in such a way that the customer will not even notice or to prevent them entirely from happening.

 Real World Scenario

Anticipating Unusually High Web Traffic

Michael Jackson died on June 25, 2009, almost taking the Internet with him. Actually, a lot of websites were bogged down and even crashed because of heavy traffic due to the buzz over the pop star's death. Administrators would argue that this was unforeseen, but it actually wasn't. Anyone who knew who Michael Jackson was and how famous should have known what kind of web traffic his death would generate and taken action immediately to prepare for it.

This is a good example of where operational intelligence would have come in handy. When a sudden spike in web traffic centered around certain keywords occurs, an organization's operational intelligence system should send out alarms, and operators knowing the cause of the alarms should quickly provision additional servers.

What This Means for Customers

Customers of cloud computing need to understand how exactly the end user will use the cloud; in other words, they need to understand the workflow as well as how the provider's underlying infrastructure performs and affects this experience if they will be buying into a cloud service that they will be patronizing for a long time. Cloud computing, despite its obvious merits and promises of being a cheaper alternative, is still a considerable investment on the part of the organization, so it is of the utmost importance that you as a customer know and judge for yourself that you are actually getting your money's worth.

Cloud management platforms (CMPs) are massive software suites that include management, automation, evaluation, provision, and orchestration solutions that are set up on top of a virtual infrastructure that may include other cloud environments. Cloud management solutions also allow customers to see exactly how their system is performing and how it affects their slice of the cloud as well as the performance of their own virtual cloud environment. These solutions provide real-time operational intelligence and allow for the following:

- Monitoring of system usage and performance, uptime, and various other metrics
- Fast root-cause analysis of system problems and failures through integrated active monitoring and report systems
- Generation of complex yet easy-to-read reports and graphs for various operational metrics like end-to-end throughput and response times, successful and failed transactions, and message queue lengths

Cloud management systems are able to harness generated machine data from the cloud infrastructure and applications in order to provide visibility and insight into operational capacity, problems, and outages and failures as well as performance and security issues.

The criteria for selecting a cloud management solution is plentiful and may differ depending on the organization. But here are a few key basic things to look out for:

Governance   This is one of the biggest aspects of your management platform because it gives you total control over your cloud environment. Access controls limit access to specific resources for certain users or user groups. Financial control allows you to set limits on the provisioning of resources to keep the operation within budget and prevent overspending. Security controls with key management and encryption would allow you to segregate roles and define access rights and privileges in order to impose a separation of roles.

Automation   Automation is one of the core features of cloud computing's value proposition. It allows for quick and reliable deployment of resources and for elasticity and scalability in ever-changing conditions. This helps to realize the reduced costs and agility being offered by cloud computing. Cloud management platform providers should be offering a myriad of tools for automation that more than meet the demands of a growing enterprise. If this has taken a backseat, take a step back from that provider.

Integration   Your cloud management platform should not integrate with just the largest and most prevalent cloud service providers; it should be able to integrate with the smaller ones as well. It is the smaller providers that are often more creative in their offerings and may offer more value in a specific area, so sometimes it's smart to work with a few different ones to leverage their strengths in different areas. This creates fragmentation, however, and it is the job of the cloud management platform to tie all of this together seamlessly.

Service-Level Agreements

The service-level agreement (SLA) is the most important document that exists between the service provider and the customer or user. It defines all of the levels of service that the provider is promising to provide to the customer in exchange for their compliance with some policies and, of course, for their hard-earned cash. The SLA will highlight the offered services in measurable terms like these:

- The percentage of uptime for a service
- The amount of user traffic that can be served at one time
- The data rate and bandwidth limitations
- Performance and capacity of resources
- The schedule of notifications for events like planned maintenance and outages
- Help desk response times and scope and limitations

The SLA serves as a binding contract that a customer can use for litigations whenever those promises are constantly missed. It provides assurance to the user that they will get their money's worth.

The SLA can be a good tool for evaluating a provider because you know exactly what you are getting. And if the provider cannot make good on its promises or deliver the expected level of service, the customer can look to the SLA to see what kind of compensation is offered. It is often in the form of refunds or discounts for the period in question.

Aside from the usual details like bandwidth, security, privacy, and availability, you should look at the provider's exit strategy. You must always avoid vendor lock-in because the business environment is constantly changing, so make sure the service provider offers a way for you to get out.

Also, see if the provider has other availability zones where you can offload some of your processes and even use as backups just in case your main availability zone fails. If the provider is just rebranding the bigger cloud providers, you have to ask if you have access to the availability zones of their larger partner. And as an added bonus, it would be good if the provider offers some form of help in the area of disaster recovery.

Policies and Procedures

Policies and procedures are the core elements of an organization; they are the epitome of the term *organize*. The hardware and software and their respective configurations are the tools that enable a business to drive the functionality they desire from their IT services. Policies and procedures enable the development, implementation, maintenance, and ongoing support for those functionalities.

Policies are the rules that everyone in the organization, including the users and administrators, abide by, and methodologies are the set procedures that these same individuals follow in going through their daily work routine. In the IT environment, the methodologies are the activities carried out based on the defined policies.

Policies govern how an organization will create its procedures and go about its work. For example, a Japanese company might value cleanliness and orderliness in the workplace, so they make it a policy that the workplace must clean, orderly, and clear from distractions. It follows that the procedures are built around this policy, so the company might implement a "no talking in the hallway" rule or require a specific uniform, or employees may be required to bow to any superior who happens to pass by, as is prevalent in Japanese custom. Maybe there is a prescribed time for employees to tidy up their own workspace so that everybody does it at the same time and no one leaves before 6 p.m. These procedures and methodologies are made with direct regard to the policies and morals the organization holds.

On the other side of the world, in the United States, policies and procedures may be entirely different. One policy, for example, might be to ensure that employees are happy as possible because studies have shown that a contented and happy employee is less likely to quit, taking valued skill sets with him. Distractions, decorations, and horsing around might be encouraged to foster creativity.

The same goes for an IT organization that may be thinking of deploying a cloud computing solution. For example, if the organization has a customer-focused policy, then it will follow that most of its procedures and methodologies will be centered around the happiness and satisfaction of the customer.

Planning the Documentation of the Network and IP

A network and IP planning document is rarely found, or sometimes even nonexistent, in most organizations. Network engineers and experts rely on theories and principles coupled with the simplicity of hardware setup, so most have not found the need for a formal document. What you will find will usually be just a few detailed network diagrams and a checklist of what to implement. The closest to a full document might be a few pages with lists and diagrams and notes on what and how everything will be set up. People have simply been winging it most of the time. But for a cloud infrastructure to be successful, there must be a proper network and IP planning document, if not simply for reference on future upgrades and changes.

Network and IP documentation is considered a good idea but not an absolute necessity, but we cannot stress enough how important it is, especially for service providers. Documentation can benefit the service providers too; documenting their customers' networks can make a world of difference when it comes to troubleshooting. It makes root-cause analysis easier when you can simply look at a diagram and a bunch of protocols being used and immediately discover a few suspects. These documents will also help the providers spot some inefficiencies and areas in a customer's network that need to be updated or upgraded, earning them some more positive points or even more revenue streams. Also, good network and IP planning documentation will prove that you are following good industry standards and practices and serve as a defense against network-related complaints and litigation.

When preparing the network and IP documentation, you should consider all communications occurring in and out of the network: between the data center or local network and its users, within the data center itself or within the network, and between the data center or network and other networks, clouds, or data centers. Detailed documentation of each type of communication and how they connect with each other, especially in terms of hardware mapping, will aid in root-cause analysis of network problems and help in making informed decisions in future network upgrades. The network is a combination of three domains, which are integrated differently depending on the customer's needs:

Core Network   The core network provides a high-speed packet-switching fabric for multiple access and edge network devices as well as high-speed communication within the local system.

Access Network   This is what most internal users will be on. It provides connectivity to shared enterprise servers and network-attached storage devices and any other IP or automation devices required by the system.

Edge Network   This provides connectivity to external users from different network types, most commonly the Internet. Wide area networks (WANs), backbones, and virtual private networks (VPNs) are other networks that can connect to the edge network.

Application-Optimized Traffic Flows

In the old client-server architecture of networking, traffic was in effect a single north-south direction scheme. Requests originated from a client system and went directly to an application server that responded directly to the client. But with the increasing use of cloud computing, interserver communication is now very common. In today's system, the client request is sent to an application, but the processing of the request results in information sharing between servers that exist on different machines and are distributed in different locations. And depending on the request, multiple servers might be processing the request at the same time.

Documenting how data flows through the network would help in root-cause analysis of network-related issues or conflicts. For example, a request might be approved, but it never gets carried out because somewhere along the line a server might have dropped it for some unknown reason. With proper data flow documentation, network engineers can follow the data to see where the request gets dropped and fix the problem quickly. Events such as these, that occur only intermittently and in very specific circumstances, are often the hardest to track and often left unfixed because there are only a few users. Sometimes the IT staff tells those users to simply change their settings, for example, instead of addressing the root cause of the issue.

Simplified Network Infrastructure

Cloud computing requires homogeneous hardware and infrastructure to provide scale and elasticity for rapid growth while also keeping down costs. Old network architecture that previously worked well for fragmented and oversubscribed tree structures and business process will have consistent scaling and performance issues. A simplified network infrastructure meets all the needs for scaling, performance, and cost effectiveness.

But during the upgrade process, the entire network will not be replaced at once; rather, there will be a series of upgrade and replacement scenarios. This obviously does not lead to a simple network infrastructure; that is why it would be wise to keep documentation detailing which nodes have been replaced and which have been retained. And even if the nodes that were not replaced scale very well or use the same hardware as the new infrastructure (which is to say that you are dealing with a uniform and simple network infrastructure), these nodes are still older than the rest of the network. Keeping tabs on them might prevent spending a lot of time looking for failing hardware because the older ones will be the first ones to be checked for inconsistencies and errors.

Standardizing Configuration and Documentation

For a cloud computing infrastructure, homogeneity cannot be stressed enough. All servers, network nodes, network-attached storage (NAS), automation devices, and the rest of the essential hardware must be configured in the same exact way—the same operating system, software, and firmware. Having different configurations will lead to incompatibilities and inconsistencies in performance as well as other unforeseen issues. In this way, we can immediately cross out incompatibility or configuration issues when problems arise.

This can be an issue in older systems when some parts are being upgraded and some are not because they are still "acceptable," leading to possible inconsistencies. It is always best to upgrade everything, even though this somewhat disagrees with the concept of modularity, where modules can be replaced without affecting the whole, but this is for the sake of configuration standardization. The system will still be operational 100 percent, but what we are trying to avoid are the "possible" problems that inconsistency fosters. As for the really quick development of software and hardware, that should not be much of a problem, even though right after you set up your brand-spanking-new data center with all the latest hardware, it could be considered second tier after a few months. The fact is that hardware just evolves and not by leaps and bounds, so your quad-core 3.5 GHz CPU from last year will still perform very much like the newer 4 GHz CPU that was just released. And with your configuration optimized for your current setup, there should be no worries about performance differences. That is the same reason there are still dual-core "business" PCs running Windows XP being sold today; the configuration is still powerful enough for office tasks.

A document establishing all configurations for various devices and software must be created to ensure that there is no second-guessing and miscommunication regarding device and software configuration so that decisions made by all administrators and technical personnel are based on the same exact document. The document must be updated regularly because configurations and settings change according to business needs, and there must always be a person assigned to the task. The same person should also enforce compliance across the environment, making use of model-driven management tools to discover and collect information about all relevant devices to ensure that they are configured correctly.

Implementing Change Management Best Practices

Change is inevitable; that much is certain. What is not certain are the changes themselves. It can be an exciting time for some, a chance for new opportunities and growth, while for others it can be a time of loss, threat, or disruption. The outcome rests mostly on the hands of the IT staff. We say mostly because not everything is certain, even in large systematic organizations. That is the reason companies that have been around for hundreds of years still go bankrupt. But the response to that change can be managed, and it can mean the difference between thriving and failing in the business environment. Change is inherent in any organization. All organizations must at some point undergo change in order to stay relevant or get ahead. Figure 4.4 is a simple visualization of what you can expect from change management that summarizes it quite efficiently.

FIGURE 4.4   Change management

There are two sources of change, external and internal.

External Sources   External sources include the changing state of the market, technology, trends, customer influence, and political and economic issues.

Internal Sources   Or change can come from within, such as for executive decisions in response to changing client needs, costs, human resource, or performance issues.

But in true essence, most if not all changes are due to external factors or sources or as a reaction thereof. Rarely will management decide something from out of nowhere without merit; all decisions are influenced by external factors in one way or another. There's a decision to downsize on costs? It's not simply your manager's initiative; it's because the market is predicted to go down, for example. But whether change is driven by external factors or not is not the issue. The issue is that no matter where it is coming from, it can affect a small portion of or the entire organization. You can never be fully prepared for change, but at least you can manage it.

In the IT environment, starting from the design to the implementation phase, we try to make changes in the least impactful ways possible. Change management is a collection of policies and procedures that are meant to minimize system downtime by ensuring that all changes are recorded, evaluated, planned, tested, documented, implemented, and finally reviewed using a controlled and consistent process. Regardless of the origin of the change, change management is the important process of taking a structured and planned approach to align the organization to whatever changes needs to happen. In essence, change management involves working with the stakeholders directly affected by the change and helping them to understand what it means for them, to handle the transition, and to overcome any challenges that result.

Though approaches to change management vary depending on the type of organization and the types of change vary, there are common factors that contribute to the success of change management, especially in the IT environment:

Planning   Develop a plan and documentation that clearly states the objectives of the change to be achieved and the means to achieve them.

Defined Governance   Establish appropriate management channels and organizational structures, responsibilities, and roles that engage and involve stakeholders into taking the initiative and controlling the change that affects them.

Committed Leadership   Leaders that show commitment and lead by example are required to drive the effort across the organization.

Well-Informed Stakeholders   Encourage stakeholder participation and commitment to the change plan and facilitate open and consultative communication to further the awareness and complete understanding of the required changes that permeate through the organization.

Organizational Alignment   The workforce needs to know exactly what they need to do to make a positive difference in support for the change.

Extensive change management planning must be in place to achieve a successful transition. Change management, therefore, has the following objectives:

- To maximize returns and business value through IT modification while reducing the disruption to the daily activities and avoiding unnecessary expense
- To evaluate both the benefits and the risks of the proposed change
- To plan, prioritize, test, implement, document, and review all proposed changes in a systematic and controlled fashion
- To be the guiding mechanism for configuration management by ensuring that all configuration changes in the IT environment are documented and updated to reflect in the configuration management system and the change document

The following sections describe a few concepts involving change management. They could be either the driver of change or a concept essential to the process of change management itself.

Request for Change

A request for change (RFC) should be submitted to initiate the change process. It can be submitted by anyone with a stake in the involved system, item, or service. For example, an administrator submits an RFC for changing the configuration of RAID storage devices in the name of reliability and stability. An IT executive may submit an RFC focused on increasing the profitability of a current service in order to compete with a close rival, or an end user may suggest a change of certain procedures to hasten the business process. All are valid sources for change.

Change Proposals

Change proposals are the big brothers of RFCs because they are reserved for changes that have a major organizational impact or financial implications. The main difference between an RFC and a change proposal is the scope and the level of detail that each one contains. The RFC is more detailed because it is concerned with smaller and more specific things like configuration changes or the removal or addition of hardware and software that will have some effect on certain portions of the organization but has minimal impact on the organization as a whole.

Change proposals are formal proposals meant to be read by top decision makers since the scope of the change is encompassing and will greatly affect the whole organization. It includes an overview of the changes, only detailing strategic benefits to the organization financially or technically, but it usually doesn't deal with details on how to implement changes; that will come after approval when the planning process commences.

Change Type

Each change is categorized into a change type depending on the amount of risk and urgency it carries. There are three types: normal changes, standard changes, and emergency changes.

Normal Changes   Normal changes are changes that can be easily evaluated by the defined change process in place.

Standard Changes   Standard changes are those that have been evaluated in the past, are recurring, or are made periodically. Their impact on the IT organization is already controlled and minimal. These types of changes are usually immediately approved or preauthorized.

Emergency Changes   Emergency changes are exactly that, urgent. This designation is used when a high level of urgency is required for the change to be implemented. However, the proper process must still be followed, albeit there is less time to do each task and usually a smaller group of people (top managers and decision makers, for instance) are involved with the evaluation process. In the event of an emergency change, there may not be enough time to assemble a full change advisory board (CAB), so an emergency change advisory board (ECAB) should be elected, whose members have the capacity and authority to quickly evaluate a change request.

Change Manager

The change manager is the person responsible for overseeing all the activities in the change management process. The change manager, therefore, has the final word in the approval or rejection of an RFC and also makes certain that all RFCs have followed the defined policies and procedures. The change manager is also in charge of properly selecting the most appropriate candidates to sit on the change advisory board, candidates who will provide all the necessary input to make an informed decision about whether to accept or reject a request for change.

Change Advisory Board

The change advisory board (CAB) is made up of stakeholders who provide input to the change manager regarding RFCs. This group is made up of representatives from all affected areas, including end users and customers, and as part of the evaluation process for each RFC should consider the following:

- The reason for the change
- The benefits and risks when implementing or not implementing the change
- The required resources for implementation
- The time table for the implementation
- The impact of the outage in terms of service levels and agreements to customers and planned compensation in case the outage is lengthy
- The back-out strategy plan in case of failure

Review and Closure

After the implementation of the change, it must go through a defined process of full review and closure. This is intended to verify that the process was successful by evaluating whether the objectives of the change were met, the affected stakeholders are satisfied, the benefits are fully realized, and any risk or side effect has been avoided or mitigated. This would include the evaluation of the resources used in the process, which includes the time and the overall cost of the change. This evaluation will ensure that future changes are successful and are also the basis for standard changes so that evaluation will no longer be needed and you can skip to implementation.

Documentation

Change initiatives sometimes fail because there was not enough strategic thought given toward the communication of the rationale and the impacts of the change to the stakeholders involved. To ensure that a change is understood by everyone affected and that the complexity and magnitude of the initiative is understood, the endeavor should be clearly documented. This includes the following:

- The reasons for undertaking the change in the first place, the business drivers, and the rationale
- The expected outcome for the objectives of the change
- The benefits and negative effects to the stakeholders, the organization, and any other entity that would be affected by it

Configuration Control

In a cloud computing environment, changes are often be caused by customer demand and technology. In any case, when there is a request for change, especially when it requires changing some infrastructure or virtual environment configurations, there will be some repercussions if the process is not done consistently and systematically. All configuration changes have to be evaluated first before being documented, tested, and then implemented. Of course they then have to be evaluated in terms of effectiveness.

The change manager should be responsible for documenting all changes that have to be made. The change manager must then make sure all configuration items were updated successfully and the specified objectives have been met.

Asset Accountability

One of the biggest drivers of change in cloud computing is the rapid change in technology. When new technology and processes become public, it may not be apparent whether they will catch on, but organizations often make an educated guesses. Sometimes the technology is replaced by something else. In this case, the organization either has to adapt or fail. There is only one option, therefore change is initiated.

When change affects the organization's assets, it must be tracked. All changes in configuration and even location must be documented by an officer who is accountable for the asset in question. To keep track of broad changes, asset managers can be assigned. The most logical candidates would be those already assigned to manage the assets. The managers of individual assets can report to a head asset accountability manager who then reports to the overall change manager.

Managing the Configuration

Change management is only one player in the arena. It offers great value to the IT organization, which in turn carries it over to its customers. But one problem when implementing change is how the assets that are being modified are to be classified and controlled. This is where configuration management comes in, by specializing in the management of IT assets and their configuration and relationships to other assets.

The purpose of configuration management is to ensure that the IT assets essential to service and function delivery are properly controlled and documented so that proper and accurate information regarding those assets is available whenever needed. Foremost among the controlled information is the configuration of and relationships between the assets, hence the name configuration management. It is an official process created by the *Information Technology Infrastructure Library (ITIL)* as an *IT Service Management (ITSM)* process to document and track the configuration information.

Configuration management is all about ensuring that IT assets are properly configured and has the following objectives:

- Identify configuration items (CIs)
- Control and protect the integrity of all configuration items
- Maintain a complete and accurate configuration management system by maintaining information on the states of all CIs
- Provide accurate and updated configuration information

With a configuration management process in place, you can ensure consistent and reliable performance throughout the IT infrastructure. It also helps to avoid incurring costs and risks from poorly managed IT assets that may lead to unexpected and extended outages and to avoid failure when it comes to compliance with both industry standards and the customer service-level agreements, all of which leads to fees or fines.

Here are some benefits of configuration management:

- Provides a clear understanding on the part of the technical staff of configurations and relationships of IT assets with other resources, which gives the team the necessary skills to troubleshoot problems and quickly identify root causes. This will also give them the proper tools to pinpoint possible issues, thereby preventing them.

- Serves as a good source for change management information that can be used to base future decisions on regarding the implementation and configuration of planned changes with current IT infrastructure and assets.

- Improves overall compliance with customers and legal, financial, and regulatory commissions, resulting in less administrative overhead.

- Provides realistic visibility of the cost and risks for delivering IT services.

- Provides insight into current baseline configurations compared to the original objective and requirements and the ability to track the difference.

- Ultimately reduces the time and cost associated with configuration discovery, and it certainly eliminates trial and error.

- Ensures compatibility across the whole IT environment.

Configuration management sounds simple, and in essence and principle it is, but in practice it is actually tricky and a bit tedious. It is not merely tracking IT assets and defining relationships between them, as you will soon find out.

Even at the beginning of the implementation process, configuration management is already present through definition, documentation, and tracking of IT assets that will be managed as configuration items (CIs). Careful selection of CIs is important in this early stage of implementation and could mean the difference between success and failure. Once a CI has been selected, there are various CI-related activities and processes:

- Each CI must have a unique identifier in order for all of its instances to be identified easily.

- CI changes must be done through change management processes.

- A configuration management system's database or the change management database (CMDB) should record all the attributes of the CI and be the authority on the documentation and tracking of them.

- CIs must contain an ownership attribute that will be used for asset accountability. It should clearly state who is in charge of particular CIs or assets and who will keeping all attributes and configurations current and be in charge of inventory, security, use, disposal, and financial reporting regarding the CI. The CI owner must be a member of the change advisory board.

The essence of configuration management is the trust it puts in the CMS and the owners of the CIs. That trust may also be a drawback, but it can be used as an indicator for the success of the configuration management process. It assumes that all information is accurate and updated and no longer needs to be investigated. If any change activity undermines the trust, then an investigation is necessary to rediscover CI attributes, relationships, and current statuses. In such a case, the value of control, cost and time savings are in fact lost, which configuration management was meant to achieve.

The following sections describe some main concepts you need to understand in order to fully grasp configuration management.

Configuration Management Database (CMDB)

As the name suggests, a configuration management database is the data repository used for configuration management in IT organizations. It is intended to hold configuration items (CIs) for various IT assets. For each CI, it includes information like settings, software and firmware versions, and the owners of the CI as well as the relationships it has with other assets around it, like upstream sources, downstream targets, and the various dependencies and interfaces. This can be broken down into three categories of data: technical, ownership, and relationship, which are all self-explanatory.

The CMDB is used to document and track the state of various IT assets arranged into configuration items. These are usually products, facilities, systems, individual devices like servers or a set of devices like a local area network or server farm, software, and even people. The CMDB can contain images that give insight into specific assets at a certain state. The images can then be used to restore or reconstruct assets to a specific state at any point of its existence. For example, if there was a change in network settings and it didn't work, the network could simply be restored based on the information contained in the CI for the network, taken from the CMDB. It can also be used for impact analysis and root-cause analysis.

The Information Technology Infrastructure Library (ITIL) framework describes the CMDB as an integral part of infrastructure operations and support and therefore the CMDB servers as the authorized and official configuration of the significant components of an IT environment. It helps the organization better understand the relationships. It is a fundamental component of ITIL's configuration management process, and its implementation involves the federation and inclusion of data from other sources, such as asset management, in a way in which the source may retain control of the data.

Managing Capacity

Capacity management is the process of ensuring that the current and future performance and capacity demands of customers and end users and other services are delivered with acceptable costs. Its main purpose is to ensure that there is enough IT capacity to meet customer demands and fulfill service-level agreements.

Capacity management is dependent on configuration management because it involves reliability and optimization, so the emphasis should be on meticulous detail and proper configuration. Starting from the design and planning phase, the capacity required to fulfill the service-level agreements must be taken into consideration and incorporated into configurations. When the required configurations are documented and designed, a baseline can be established to serve as the standard against which all capacity changes can be compared and monitored to understand current and future capacity requirements based on perceived trends.

The process involves the development of a capacity management plan that will highlight how to keep up with current demands and scale to future ones. The plan has the following objectives:

- Provide guidance and advice to IT personnel as well as to the rest of the organization on all performance- and capacity-related concerns.

- Evaluate the extent and impact of any changes on the capacity and performance of IT assets and services.

- Assist with the root-cause analysis and resolution of any capacity- and performance-related issues.

- Ensure that service meets or exceeds all the agreed-upon performance and capacity targets by managing them properly for both resources and services.

- Ensure that the current and future capacity and performance demands in relation to IT services are met within expected costs.

- Ensure that all planned performance and capacity optimizations and enhancements are implemented and executed properly.

During the development of the capacity management plan, all resources, including human resources, should be taken into consideration, especially the technical capabilities of the people implementing the changes. If these capabilities are lacking, sufficient measures have to be taken, such as further training or hiring external expert manpower as a temporary solution while the primary team is training (the latter depends on whether the budget allows the hiring of third-party consultants).

There are two important activities in capacity management that ensure that all service levels are adequately met:

Monitoring for Changes   Capacity management is still closely tied to change management, and in fact it ties into all of the IT service management processes discussed in this chapter. The capacity management team has to be ever wary and critical of any proposed changes because service delivery and customer satisfaction are its main goals and any change that causes major disruption should be reevaluated and its approach altered. The capacity manager or the stakeholder in charge of capacity management should be the most critical member of the change advisory board (CAB).

Capacity management should be closely aligned with configuration management because the capacity and performance of any IT asset depends mostly on its configuration. It will also help to better understand the interdependencies and relationships between assets, which might highlight possible optimization points within the system to increase capacity and performance.

Trending   Capacity is important, and it sometimes seems that demand is growing so rapidly that attempts to improve capacity can't keep up. You might think that blindly increasing capacity through upgrades is the way to go. But increasing capacity means change; it means additional costs and time, all of which will go to waste if the demand does not increase enough to even warrant that upgrade.

That is why analyzing the trends by using present and historical data can help with the optimization of capacity and performance. Following the trends and increasing capacity during periods of high demand and decreasing it during periods of low demand will ensure the ratio of proper service delivery and the cost associated with it.

Managing the Systems Life Cycle

Systems life cycle management is a collection of processes that are meant to aid in the development, control, coordination, management, delivery, and support of any configuration items, from their initial requirement inception until they reach the end of their life. There are two frameworks for life cycle management: there is the Information Technology Infrastructure Library (ITIL) framework and the Microsoft Operations Framework (MOF), which is based on the ITIL framework.

The ITIL framework emphasizes service delivery and is composed of five phases:

Service Strategy   This is essentially the service planning stage, where the organization focuses on the goal and how to get there. This is done through planning what types of services to offer, based on current trends and demands as well as from projected market shifts and business changes. This phase, of course, is aligned with the organization's mission and vision and its set policies and procedures.

Service Design   When the services to be offered have been formulated and the question of "what" has been answered, it is time to figure out the "how." In this phase, the services are designed based on current and projected future capacities, IT asset performance, resource availability, and manpower resources.

Service Transition   This phase bridges the gap between projects and operations effectively in the period between when the development phase is concluded and the service is implemented. It aims to improve the service by improving on changes that will be part of the live service. This stage brings together all the relevant assets and ensures that they are all integrated and tested together. It serves as the quality assurance phase, where we can make sure we have a quality product and impose control of the delivery of a new or revamped product or service. Diligence in this phase will ensure that there is less variation to the expected outcome of the service to be launched.

Service Operation   This phase takes over when the service has already been launched and there are customers and end users being supported. Operational teams must ensure that services and the infrastructure supporting them are based on robust end-to-end practices and procedures and support responsive and stable services. It serves as an ongoing support unit and strongly influences the perception of the service that is being provided.

A major part of this phase is the service desk, or customer support, which is directly responsible for problem or issue management and the fulfillment of customer requests and complaints, especially focusing on customer satisfaction. Specific to an IT environment, there are application management and technical support teams, while for the overall organization there is the administration support team.

Continual Service Improvement   As the name suggests, this is aimed at service improvement. It exists throughout the life cycle of the service and works with the other four phases to align the services available to the business needs of the organization (if internal) or the business needs of the customer. This phase actively seeks improvement opportunities and positive change.

The phases of the ITIL framework connect to each other with continual improvement serving as an overseer for quality, which becomes evident after multiple trips through a service's life cycle. With each iteration through the life cycle, positive changes and improvements are documented and then implemented based on the evaluation and feedback from previous stages. Further improvements to the processes and resources will enable the organization to implement its service offerings efficiently and effectively, which in turn provides value to the customers and the organization itself.

The Microsoft Operations Framework for life cycle management tries to simplify this process into four stages and can be applicable even to organizations that are not service oriented. The life cycle is made up of four actions: Plan, Deliver, Operate, Manage. So in application, there are three continual stages, to plan and develop, then deliver or launch, and then operate. Management encompasses the other three stage to ensure proper execution and continuous improvement.

Scheduling Maintenance Windows

When a cloud service is launched, there will be constant maintenance and improvements so that it will meet or exceed expectations and keep the customers happy. And because a customer will expect that the service will be online and meeting their needs, the service organization must enter into an agreement with the customer. Up-time ratings are defined by the number of nines used in the percentage, from one nine to as many as seven (90 percent to 99.99999 percent). Seven nines equal only 0.605 seconds of downtime per year. You might consider it overkill, but it is not entirely impossible with cloud computing, especially for service providers running a large network of distributed data centers. For example, they can simply mirror a service on separate hardware servers and do the maintenance there, and once it's completed, they can transfer all traffic into those new and updated services.

In traditional IT services where services and applications can reside only on specific hardware, maintenance windows are important, especially to the health of those servers. The service would have to be done offline so the technical team can conduct maintenance on either hardware or the applications and databases.

Server Upgrades and Patches

In an IT environment where services reside in specific hardware servers, maintenance is inevitable—upgrades, preventive maintenance, patches to security holes. It is important to schedule maintenance during times that would ensure the least disruption to productivity, such as during the night.

It is important for the maintenance window to be short to ensure that the service can resume quickly, and there should be a margin of error present in case the maintenance takes longer than expected.

If possible, maintenance should not be impromptu. What this means is that the technical team should have tried and tested specific maintenance operations or upgrade procedures on an exact replica of the actual server or environment. This is to ensure that any problems that might result will already be known and a solution found.

If you have played massively multiplayer games in the past decade, you will know that a lot of them have beta or test servers where patches, updates, and improvements are implemented first, and only after all the bugs are found and fixed will the update be implemented on the official servers. This also goes for most IT services across many organizations, but the test team would be selected from hardcore users instead of allowing the whole audience take part in the test.

Managing Cloud Workloads

Cloud computing is essentially the next step of grid and utility computing, where all resources are accessible through a virtual environment so they can be moved around and shared infinitely, at least in theory. Gone are the days of manual setup of any IT resource; we are now in the single-click era of computing. To this end, engineers have created ways to allow automated resource provisioning and deprovisioning as well as dynamic workload balancing between different virtual and physical servers to allow for massive scalability and almost zero downtime.

Not all workloads are suited for cloud computing, but most web applications are. And because of the prevalence of the Internet globally and the rapid advancement of mobile technology, web applications are now transitioning to cloud applications or scalable web apps. And it is this type of applications that will fully utilize the dynamic workload management for which cloud environments are built.

Managing Workloads Right on the Cloud

Web applications have the tendency to spike in traffic unpredictably, leading to exponential scale in the required resources, which in turn requires provisioning of multiple new virtual servers to cope with the traffic. If you are in a traditional IT infrastructure like an in-house data center, chances are you will face a "success disaster," meaning that you are getting a huge amount of traffic and audience but are unable to monetize on it. To illustrate, think of a coffee shop that sells extraordinary coffee and can serve only 30 customers an hour but actually gets 50 customers an hour. The queue just keeps on getting longer because they coffee shop employees can't serve fast enough. It is attracting more customers than it can serve, which to the casual observer would look like total success, but in truth the coffee shop is not seeing the profit that it should if it had a bigger area and more baristas.

This is the same for web applications. If you cannot serve all of your users, then you are missing out on potential profit. To be able to serve in such situations, your cloud infrastructure must be built for fast and predictive provisioning. Setting provisioning policies based on percentage of load will not be enough when a usage spike occurs. The traffic level would reach the threshold and pass it quickly, and your system would not be able to provision fast enough, leading to some users losing patience and leaving. The system should be able to calculate the rate of increase in traffic and accurately predict how long it would take for it to reach the threshold at that rate and then provision for additional load servers when it sees fit, even before the threshold is hit.

Intelligent workload management (IWM) is a new paradigm that came along with cloud computing and is made possible by dynamic infrastructure, virtualization, and identity management. IWM securely manages and optimizes computing resources across physical, virtual, and cloud environments in order to deliver business services for end customers in a software- and application-compliant manner. First, a workload is a specific request or processing request made by a user or an application that requires processing. An example would be mathematical calculations submitted by weather prediction software or a database process request.

IWM is a kind of systems process management where the workloads themselves know what they are, their priority, and where they belong. For example, in a hybrid cloud environment, a specific workload will be configured to detect its own security permissions and level of sensitivity so it knows whether to get processed on the private side or the public side of the cloud. In cloud computing, you can provision servers that specialize in specific types of processes, so when a specific workload is produced, both it and the system know at which server it should be processed.

Managing Risk

Risk is everywhere, and in a cloud computing environment, there are new types of risks that are unique to this kind of environment. And in relation to workload management, we must identify the possible risks that would occur. For example, in the event of a major *distributed denial of service (DDoS) attack*, dynamic and intelligent provisioning, the pay-per-use model, and virtually unlimited computing resources that are the major features of cloud computing can be the Achilles heel of the organization but not exactly pose any risk to the system itself. You might already have an idea what sort of risk this poses to the organization.

A major DDoS attack will quickly load up the servers with requests and perceived traffic, which would make the system provision more and more resources in order to cope. The problem here is that the attack will not exactly cripple the system; it will just keep on provisioning more resources. The result is a massive spike in cost due to the spike in resource provisioning. If this goes unnoticed, it could really rack up costs, so it is important to watch out and plan for potential risks in a system that seems foolproof because sometimes strengths can be turned into weakness.

All systems have vulnerabilities; the most secure ones are simply the ones that are best at hiding them. In this regard, the practice of vulnerability management should be considered. It is a security practice that has been specifically designed to proactively mitigate or totally prevent the exploitation of IT assets by external or internal threats. Vulnerabilities are first identified and classified, and then solutions are formulated. The solutions are then applied as patches on those vulnerabilities.

Because vulnerability management and other security measures are ongoing and we are unable to bring a system offline, properly scheduled server maintenance for patching should be considered. The fixes to vulnerabilities should also be well tested before application to prevent unexpected results, especially downtime.

Securing Data in the Cloud

Information has always been the biggest source of power in the history of man, and it is no surprise that people are always trying to steal it. To counter that, we are inventing new ways of keeping it safe. In the modern computer age, we became good at keeping data safe within our own cavernous data centers, away from prying eyes and sticky fingers. But the age of cloud computing threatens to destroy this security and expose our precious data by hiding it in public, in plain view of anyone who knows what to look for. That notion is indeed warranted, so we have to find new and unique ways for data management and security in the cloud.

Data becomes vulnerable in the cloud mostly during transport because it has to travel through public channels like the Internet. However, when it reaches its destination, which is most likely a remote cloud data center, then it is just as safe as if it were in the company's in-house data center, so the problem now is how to secure data for transport when it needs to be out of the firewall.

Transporting data via a *virtual private network (VPN)* is often the best way to make your transported data invisible because you are essentially making the public web your own private network. Of course, encryption has to be put in place, and the complexity of that encryption would depend on the governance requirements of the data being transported.

Some organizations will probably opt for a private cloud infrastructure so they can maintain control of their data while enjoying most of the functions of a cloud infrastructure, but not necessarily all of the benefits. A hybrid cloud can also be good choice, to have the best of both worlds. Sensitive data can be safe within the private cloud, while other data can come and go through the public cloud.

Managing Devices

The advance of personal computer and mobile technology means that most employees will prefer their own personal computers, in the form of laptops, tablets, and mobile phones, for office work rather than a company-issued device. And for the sake of data security and protection, there must be a way to manage and control these devices.

And as employees become increasingly mobile, the need to support the devices they use to connect with work increases drastically. Because of the mobile trend, there is a greater demand for remote access of confidential company data from mobile devices, opening a whole new level of benefits and risk. When the *bring your own device (BYOD)* wave started, it created nightmares for IT. New processes and software for mobile device management (MDM) and a new discipline called enterprise mobility management (EMM) were created, but they all proved to be tedious and inelegant solutions that turned IT into babysitters for devices simply because of the security risks they posed.

First, it important to understand what mobile device management and enterprise mobility management are.

Mobile Device Management   MDM basically refers to software solutions that are aimed at maintaining order amidst the chaos of device variety. It is often a clunky solution that has IT developing or sourcing different software for different device platforms and operating systems. Either the same exact MDM software has to be ported to different mobile platforms or different MDM software solutions already present for individual mobile platforms have to be modified to work together. Without cloud applications, an enterprise must resort to an installed MDM solution. As mentioned, this requires IT to babysit devices and answer a lot of individual requests for device diagnosis and installation, not to mention all the trouble it would cause when a device is stolen or lost. The potential damage to the organization would be tremendous.

Enterprise Mobility Management   EMM is a relatively new field in IT management that has been specifically created because of the wide use of mobile devices in the work environment. In short, because of the rapid increase of highly capable mobile devices, a business need for mobile management arose. The scope of this discipline includes security, application management, and financial management. This is a new discipline, so there are not so many practitioners and even fewer business entities implementing it. That is not to say that it is not a requirement; it is, especially if the organization has not yet embraced the cloud but needs to support mobile users. But the fact remains that it adds unnecessary strain to an organization's IT infrastructure and workforce simply to support employee convenience. MDM falls under EMM, but EMM is not a solution for workforce mobility and device management.

It is obvious by now that we are not advocates of MDM and EMM, and that is simply because they are unnecessary in cloud computing. Cloud computing allows the offloading of major computationally heavy processes from a connected device unto powerful servers optimized for such tasks; that is the nature of cloud applications. This is where it gets interesting. With cloud computing, we can make little distinction between a tablet, a mere media consumption device, and an actual business laptop. Security problems arise when data is traveling long distances in a public channel because it can be intercepted and then rest on a mobile device that could easily be lost or stolen.

The solution is simple: keep data confined within the virtual environment. We call this solution the virtual desktop. It is nothing new, but it is revolutionary, and before cloud computing technology got to where it is now, it was not a complete solution. We will explain more in the next section.

Virtualizing the Desktop

Desktop virtualization is one application that can be made available on the enterprise cloud. A virtual desktop environment can be accessed through any device with a proper screen, moderate to good computational performance, and Internet connectivity. The virtual desktop will wholly reside within the virtual cloud in private servers, so no sensitive data is ever passed to the devices except for control data and visual data, but for the user it would seem as if they are using a PC.

This is one of the most secure ways of implementing a "bring your own device" initiative within a company, and it leaves IT to focus on the more important tasks like big data analytics and better process management.

A virtual desktop is simply a virtual machine (VM) running in cloud servers and configured as a Windows PC. The VM will contain a Windows OS installation as well as emulate all the hardware functions of a PC. It is then controlled by client devices through a small application that allows it to connect and interact with the virtual machine. This is pretty much like Remote Desktop only you are not connected to actual hardware but to a VM. No data goes out of the VM unless it was meant to, such as when someone uploads something to the Internet through the VM. But essentially, it will act as an office PC, where all files are contained in a secure environment. This means that no sensitive data is ever sent to and saved on the client device, probably a tablet or smartphone.

Virtual Desktop Providers

Notable providers of virtual desktop services are VMware, Oracle, and OnLive. The apps for accessing the virtual desktops are usually provided free and can be downloaded from the Google Play Store and the Apple App Store for their respective mobile platforms. Users can even register for free accounts and have their own rudimentary virtual desktop provided with very limited resources. In the case of OnLive, they provide 2 GB of storage and some Microsoft Office applications such as Word and Excel for free accounts. Users who want more have to pay for regular subscription, as is the case for corporate customers.

Here is the answer to the problem of employees bringing their own devices to be used for work: no device management at all. What we now need to manage here is access security.

For example, how do we know that the one logging into the virtual machine is the actual employee and not his kid who happened to be playing with the device, or worse, a thief? There are a lot of creative ways to do this using a series of identification challenges or even biometrics. But one thing is for sure, the setting "keep logged in" should not be a feature.

Enterprise Cloud Solution

One solution is the enterprise cloud, which can link all devices of various kinds with a single enterprise platform. Email, applications, security, and file storage can be managed at the user level and not at the device level. IT does not have to worry about the security of a device at the other end because all the processing is being done right in the cloud; the device merely acts as a control unit for the application in the cloud

The enterprise cloud can become a closed environment where data is virtually passing from app to app without ever passing through a single external device. There will be no downloading of sensitive files that need to be processed by the employee. The employee will be directly manipulating it through his smartphone or tablet without ever touching the data, and there will be no data to transport because only control signals back and forth are being transported.

This will prove to be the safest and most secure way of working remotely. No data leaves the enterprise cloud, but the employees can work from anywhere.

Summary

The rapid evolution of business and technology creates complexity that needs to be managed, and it has become the job of CIOs to ensure that an organization does not get lost in the confusion. This requires equally complicated IT systems that tie up different portions of the organization, with each part seemingly appearing quite different to its counterparts, leading to confusion and maintenance problems. Thankfully, cloud computing has arrived to take the edge off a bit and make things in the world of IT and business a bit more coherent and simpler, not to mention more affordable.

At the forefront of this battle against complexity are cloud management platforms. They allow different cloud systems to be integrated and managed as a single coherent whole, making it possible for an organization to benefit from using different cloud systems from different service providers to fill their needs yet avoid the complexity that comes with it. The management platform is built on a layer above these separate silos as an umbrella that manages them all from a single point. For service providers, cloud management platforms allow integration of different geographical locations and different systems because of different product offerings. As a consumer, you can integrate all of your different cloud subscriptions and monitor and manage them from a single point.

The cloud is undoubtedly big business now, so service providers are quickly trying to monetize on this. The most straightforward way to do this is by creating solutions that appeal to a lot of businesses at an affordable price. Creating solutions and products takes a lot of planning, and that includes market analysis and knowledge of current business trends, especially in internal business processes that companies use. This is because cloud services are mostly enterprise-based solutions, which may also cater to small and medium-sized businesses (SMBs), and not simple consumer-grade products. Also, when a business needs to move into the cloud space, the staff is not always well versed in what it would entail to move to the cloud and has very little idea as to what solutions they actually require. So for both service providers looking to create solutions and organizations that want to know what solutions they need, the cloud service solution planning workshop is ideal. It involves getting all representatives of each stakeholder in the organization that will be affected by the change, such as those that will actually use the system or those that will create them. The seven steps to do this are mentioned under Cloud Service Solution Planning Workshop.

The workshop should focus on the organization's strengths and ensure that it has the capacity to implement and maintain solutions and, in the case of service providers, deliver them to customers in such a way that creates satisfaction with the product.

Planning is followed by the implementation phase. When building your cloud infrastructure, you should be mindful of the technologies used and how they interact with each other, ensure homogeneity within the system, and also make sure upgrades and maintenance can be handled easily.

Customers of cloud solutions should also consider cloud management platforms that would enable them to better control the solutions that they have adopted. This includes monitoring system performance metrics, which also helps with root-cause analysis and report generation. The CMP must cater to governance, automation, and integration in order to meet all of the organization's needs.

But how do we know you are getting what you pay for? Apart from the metrics, you must also have a clear understanding of what you get for the money you spend. This is the purpose of the service-level agreement (SLA). It will clearly show what the service provider is offering in terms of performance and the amount of resources that will be supplied to your organization. It will also show what penalties both sides may incur in failing to adhere to the promises held in the SLA. So essentially, the SLA is the promise the service provider makes for the type of service it is providing, and it also serves as an agreement for both parties on certain points.

Upon launching a cloud computing system, an organization must have set policies and procedures in place that will guide the operation and maintenance of the system. These policies and procedures will guide most of the actions of employees and management in relation to the cloud system.

Other documentation is required, such as network and IP planning documentation, which will highlight how the network infrastructure is built and will help immensely with maintenance and root-cause analysis. Through this documentation, the cloud system and applications can be optimized to better utilize the traffic flow of the system, dubbed as application-optimized traffic flow. And as we mentioned, cloud computing requires a homogeneous infrastructure, which helps to bring simplicity to a complicated system and helps with scalability and future maintenance and upgrades.

Together with documentation and set policies and procedures, standard configurations across the board are required for a cloud system, only differing in certain ways to cater to different user groups. Standard configurations can simply be loaded for certain user profiles instead of building resources such as virtual machines from the ground up. Change management is the best way to control configuration changes. The changes may come from external or internal sources, but with proper management, these sources can be controlled. External sources may be attributed to the market itself, which changes over time and influences how we configure our systems. While internal sources usually stem from reasons such as budget, infrastructure, and manpower, they may also be reactions to the external business climate. Changes, especially undocumented or improperly documented ones, are often the leading causes of business failure. Therefore, each change must be reviewed by experts, and the consequences must be evaluated before the change is implemented. A configuration management database is maintained to monitor all changes approved or otherwise as well as the previous state of the system prior to the change.

Capacity is also an important aspect of cloud computing. Despite claims of virtually unlimited resources, the reality is that resources are quite finite and must be managed accordingly. All resources should be allocated and used so none are idle or allocated but not used. Capacity can be managed in the form of horizontal and vertical infrastructure scalability, which means that resources can be added by simply adding more hardware or upgrading to more powerful ones.

The proper management of resources and configuration ties in to the system's overall life cycle management process, which is a collection of processes meant to aid in the development, control, management, coordination, delivery, and support of configuration items, from the initial ideas until the end of their life. Two standards for systems life cycle management are provided by ITIL and Microsoft (the Microsoft Operations Framework). The life cycle of the system includes the service strategy, the service design, the service transition, the service operation, and the continual improvement of the service. The cycle ensures that good solutions and systems that cater to actual business needs are designed, developed, deployed, and then continuously improved.

At the back of every good solution or service lies proper maintenance. The best-case scenario is that maintenance would not impact the system at all, but we usually settle for minimal impact or downtime. That is why maintenance has to be well thought out ahead of time. The maintenance process should adhere to strict time limits. Usually, new maintenance processes have to be worked on in a sandbox environment that mimics the actual production environment to test whether the new processes or upgrades work. Only routine maintenance that has been performed multiple times without problems should be done directly in the production environment.

Managing workloads within the cloud systems is also important. Workloads differ, even on the same system, and sometimes they can be erratic depending on conditions. Intelligent workload management (IWM) is a new approach in which, workloads are actually smart enough to know what their priority and resource needs are and can choose where they should be processed. The workload is automatically sent to specific servers, so there is no longer overhead as a result of job schedulers.

Finally, risk can be everywhere, and the sources can vary. Because it affects workload management and our system as a whole, risk has to be minimized. This includes securing processing servers from external attacks and securing data to prevent sensitive information from being stolen or corrupted. There are many security systems for managing risk and securing your infrastructure, and all of them use some sort of encryption as their primary defense. But awareness and best practices, especially in change management and policies, can go a long way in terms of lowering risk and increasing the security of a system.

Chapter Essentials

Network and IP Planning/Documentation	Network and IP planning and documentation is an essential step that most organizations skip because they feel that it is not important enough. But the essence of network planning is to have full control over the network and all of its nuances, from implementing proper homogeneity and configuration standardization to root-cause analysis of network problems. This will also help in planning upgrade paths.

Configuration Standardization and Documentation	Simplicity through homogeneity and standardization is one of the hallmarks of cloud computing. When every piece of hardware and every configuration are based on a well-defined standard, there is little room for error. An important note to consider here is timeliness of hardware upgrades and a proper upgrade path plan to ensure that configurations stay standard, homogeneity is not affected too much, and systems stay optimized. Formal documentation for different configurations for all system pieces must be kept on hand and updated. A configuration officer is often assigned to ensure this.

Change management best practices	Everything changes, and only the process of change is constant. There is no exception to that, so preparation for any sort of change is important. Change can be brought about by internal or external forces, but the most favorable change, and one over which we have absolute control, is internal change, meaning that we initiate the change ourselves as an act of innovation or part of a larger plan for growth. The opposite is change brought on by an external force, which almost always forces an organization to make unfavorable changes or ones that they are unprepared for. Change management minimizes the negative impacts of externally influenced changes and ensures the success of internal initiative changes. Changes can be initiated through requests or change proposals and can be categorized as normal, standard, or emergency. All changes should go through the change advisory board, and a change manager should oversee every aspect.

Configuration Management	Change brings about configuration changes as well, so configuration management is important. It ensures that all IT assets that are essential to service and function delivery are properly controlled and documented. ITIL and ITISM provide the standard for configuration management. The process involves the identifying configuration items (CIs), controlling and protecting them, and maintaining the configuration system, which includes the configuration management database (CMDB) to keep CIs accurate and updated.

Capacity Management   Capacity management is about the management of capacity for present and, especially, future demand. The aim is to strike a balance between scalability and usage, that is, between having too much unused capacity and not being able to scale with rapid spikes in demand. Capacity management relies on two activities, namely, change monitoring and trending. Change monitoring, as the name suggests, involves monitoring for changes that may affect the capacity of a system. For example, when hardware like storage and computing resources is upgraded, there will be some downtime, not of the whole system but some of its parts and resources, which will lessen the capacity of the entire system during the duration of the upgrade process. Capacity management takes this into consideration and ensures that capacity is available as expected through other means. Trending, on the other hand, looks at historical data and monitors current events to predict spikes or valleys in usage and ensure that there is always enough capacity, even when there is an extreme load on the system.

Systems Life Cycle Management   Life cycle management in cloud computing is tied to the life cycle of services rather than tangible products. The ITIL framework specifies five phases: service strategy or planning, service design, service transition, service operation, and continual service improvement. The phases are executed in sequence, except for continual improvement, which is part of all phases because the cycle goes back to the beginning, where lessons learned are applied to the next cycle.

Maintenance Windows   To a cloud computing provider, scheduling maintenance (and how long it will take) is important so that customers will not be burdened and their businesses interrupted. As a customer, you can actually set the dates for downtime in your SLA. Depending on the number of nines (99%, 99.9%, 99.99%, etc.) you specify, you can tell your provider which periods can be used as downtime for maintenance of the hardware where your system happens to reside.

Chapter

5

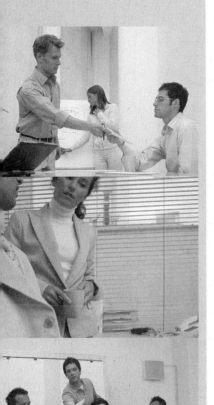

Diagnosis and Performance Monitoring

TOPICS COVERED IN THIS CHAPTER INCLUDE:

✓ Performance concepts

✓ Disk performance

✓ Disk tuning

✓ Disk latency

✓ Swap disk space

✓ I/O tuning

✓ Performance management and monitoring tools

✓ Hypervisor configuration best practices

✓ Impact of configuration changes to the virtual environment

✓ Common issues

In this chapter, we delve right into some technical applications that will be helpful for the Cloud+ certification exam as well as for solidifying your knowledge of concepts to help you in your daily routines. We cover performance concepts and the technology relating to the core functionalities that make up a virtualized environment, including the disks, hypervisor management, and common failure points in a distributed system.

Performance Concepts

At its core, cloud computing is a service meant to satisfy customers, and it just so happens that the service comes in the form of computing resources. Good performance—in terms of availability, reliability, and consistency—is essential for customer satisfaction. However, computers (just like other machines) tend to fail. Therefore, we must be prepared to deal with the anomalies that may eventually affect cloud systems and thus adversely affect their performance. The anomalies can be detected or, better yet, prevented through the use of best practices and the performance concepts of cloud computing. These best practices and concepts have been adapted from various computer engineering quality models.

The measurement of performance can be either quantitative or subjective. It is quantitative when we can numerically measure performance indicators using different tools and methods. A very good example is the measure of the performance of a processor either through its clock speed, measured in gigahertz, or via its throughput, or calculations per unit of time. More abstract measurements in performance may not always be apparent at first glance because they are not directly quantifiable. For example, an efficient database system would ensure the integrity of its contents and the automated backup system would ensure replication and, more important, the peace of mind of customers and administrators. Though there are some ways to measure the performance of the database and the replication system, there is no way to measure it in terms of the trust it may garner. That is the same concept as the satisfaction of users in relation to their mobile phones. For example, an iPhone 4 user might share the same amount of apparent satisfaction in terms of their device's performance and usability as a Galaxy S4 user, even though the latter is quantified as the faster and better-performing device in terms of hardware specification.

It should be noted here that setting expectation levels is an important concept in performance management. Moreover, the measures and standards that are used help determine realistic performance metrics. In order to achieve this, performance measures and standards should be measurable, understandable, verifiable, equitable, and achievable.

Following are some performance concepts and indicators that we use in the field in order to quantify the performance of our cloud computing systems. We use them as maintenance tools as well as root-cause analysis tools.

Input/Output Operations per Second (IOPS)

Because we are basically dealing with data and its inevitable storage, input/output operations per second (IOPS) is one of the top performance indicators that we consider in the industry. A computer system is not simply defined by its core processing components; that is, it's not defined by its individual parts but by the synergy of the whole. It won't do anyone any good to have powerful processors and lots of RAM if it takes too long to retrieve the data from storage and then takes as much time putting it there again. That, as we all know, is the proverbial bottleneck and would lower the system's overall throughput significantly. A computer system is like a chain; it is only as strong or, in this case, as fast as its slowest component. With that in mind, one of our main goals in performance monitoring should also include finding potential bottlenecks and actively eliminating them.

Storage systems, which usually employ devices with mechanical parts such as hard disk drives (HDDs), are by far the slowest components of any computer system. Motors and actuators simply cannot keep up with the speed of electrons. There are now better alternatives such as solid-state drives, but the technology is not yet mature enough to benefit from economies of scale. Because of this, IOPS remains one of the top performance indicators in any computer system, especially in cloud computing where data manipulation and storage is central to the paradigm. Figure 5.1 shows a screenshot of iostat, a common Linux tool.

FIGURE 5.1   iostat is a common Linux tool used to measure IOPS.

```
root@MACHINENAME:/home/deploy# iostat 1
Linux 2.6.24-28-server (MACHINENAME.forward.co.uk)        18/02/11
avg-cpu:  %user   %nice %system %iowait   %steal   %idle
          45.51    0.00    1.85    0.62     0.00    52.03

Device:           tps   Blk_read/s   Blk_wrtn/s   Blk_read   Blk_wrtn
cciss/c0d0       4.00        0.00        40.00          0         40
cciss/c0d1       4.00        0.00        64.00          0         64
cciss/c0d2      12.00        0.00       248.00          0        248
cciss/c0d3       0.00        0.00         0.00          0          0
cciss/c0d4      25.00        0.00       320.00          0        320
cciss/c0d5       0.00        0.00         0.00          0          0
cciss/c0d6      30.00        0.00       344.00          0        344
cciss/c0d7      42.00     3144.00         0.00       3144          0
```

IOPS is the most common measurement being used by the manufacturers themselves to benchmark different storage devices. Because the conditions of the benchmark testing are often standardized and testing is done in a controlled environment, the results do not always coincide with real-world use, and in most cases the IOPS numbers being advertised by the manufacturers are larger compared to what users get from their own tests. Again, this is due to the discrepancy in the applications and other hardware that make up the various computer systems of different users.

IOPS measurements vary greatly depending on the system configuration as well as other variables that the tester inputs into the testing software, including the ratio of read and write operations, the mixture of random or sequential access patterns, the size of data blocks, and the number of threads and the queue depth. The storage and device drivers and the applications running in the background as well as the overall health of the running operating system affect the results of IOPS measurement.

 Taking all performance variables into consideration, a real-world test can best be done when the system is working at near full capacity. This will show the real working measurement of IOPS for most users in the same situation. A lot of experts will disagree, saying, that this will not be the actual performance of the hardware, but it will be similar to the performance users will experience.

IOPS measurement is still broken down into different performance characteristics, that is, different aspects relating to the different ways that storage devices store and retrieve data: random and sequential read/write operations.

Sequential Operations   Sequential read or write operations access storage locations from a device in a contiguous manner and usually occur when large transfer sizes are involved. There are two measurements for sequential operations: sequential read IOPS and sequential write IOPS, which are the average number of sequential read and write I/O operations per second, respectively. On a hard disk drive and solid-state drive, these indicate the maximum sustained bandwidth capability of the storage device and are reported as megabytes per second (MBps) and calculated using the formula IOPS × transfer size = (mega)bytes per second.

Random Operations   Random read or write operations access storage locations from a device randomly or in a noncontiguous manner and are associated with operations on small data sizes. The two measurements are random read IOPS and random write IOPS, which indicate the average random read and write I/O operations per second, respectively. On hard drives and other electromechanical storage devices, this is usually dependent on the device's random seek time, and in an HDD, this depends primarily on the speed of its actuator arm and read/write head. But on a solid-state drive, these numbers depend on the device's controller and memory interface speeds, which are all electronic so in theory should be much faster compared to that of HDDs.

Read vs. Write Files

The file system performance, as we will discuss in the next section, has its dependencies on the hardware being used as well as the programming of the file system itself. Although the capabilities of file systems may vary, we use file systems that offer the best performance for our specific application set. For example, for a server cluster configuration, Lustre comes to mind. In this case, the IOPS performance of a given set of storage hardware will be the determining factor for performance, taking into account that we are already using the most suitable file system for our purpose.

File System Performance

Earlier we discussed the difference between read and write performance, and that essentially tells us how our file system will perform. Because cloud computing is a data-driven field, file system performance is one way to glimpse the overall performance of your cloud system. But first things first; the file system itself is only one part of the actual overall file "system." The overall file system includes the specific storage hardware used and the interfaces that connects all of them. If you have a powerful file system but have low-performance hardware, then that will be the bottleneck in the system. With that in mind, it is cheaper to change the file system than to change storage hardware, so you can upgrade and change as required by your applications; that is to say, different applications are optimized for or work better in some file systems and not others, so it is important to strike a balance for all the applications you are running.

Performance was also dependent on CPU power and amount of RAM decades ago, but those are still important factors when budget is concerned. Most modern multithreaded, multicore server CPUs will be beyond adequate for handling fully loaded database systems, but when on a budget we cannot always aim for the best. In this case, choosing the correct CPU and amount of RAM, factoring in the perfect file system for your purposes, and keeping scalability and future growth in mind will yield the best bang for the buck.

Let's get to the meat of the topic here. Let us reiterate that file system performance is dependent on how applications interact with the file system and how the file system communicates or interacts with the storage hardware as well as the hardware IOPS performance itself.

The first thing you can check, and of course optimize, in relation to your file system is how the different applications are interacting with it. If you are a developer of an applications, then chances are you know exactly how it interacts with the underlying file system. But if you are an administrator, then you might need to familiarize yourself with what type of I/O profile the application is presenting to the file system.

Our objectives in determining this I/O profile are as follows:

- Group small I/O operations into one big I/O operation in order to achieve minimize overhead whenever possible.
- Cache as much of the I/O data as possible and reduce the number of I/O calls.
- Reduce the number of I/O operation calls toward the underlying storage device. This will consequently lower additional system resource consumption by keeping the storage device idle most of the time.
- Optimize the seek algorithm to reduce the amount of time for disk seek.

With these objectives in mind, we can now begin to try to understand the characteristics of the I/O workload of our application, which will give us a clear idea of how we can tune our file system accordingly. In Table 5.1, you will find the different workload profiles that applications will fall into.

TABLE 5.1   Application Workload Profile

Characteristic	Value	Description
I/O size	Bytes/kilobytes	It is best if this value matches or is close to the file system's block size.
Access pattern	Sequential or random	The most common read or write access pattern used.
File access profile	Data or attribute	Determine if the app performs I/O operations on many small files.
Bandwidth	Mbps	The bandwidth requirement of the app.
Latency sensitivity	Milliseconds	Is the app sensitive to read or write latency?

I/O Size   The I/O size refers to the size of the files that are constantly being processed by the application into the disk. This plays a very large role in how the file system can be optimized. Part of the importance of the I/O size is that because of the inherent limitations of I/O devices, they are less efficient with small I/Os. That is why it is always a best practice to group small adjacent I/Os into a bigger I/O using a buffer so that there will be only one large operation, not multiple small ones that go through the same process, causing it to take longer and use more resources. Figure 5.2 shows a comparison between commonly used file systems as benchmarked by Vanninen and Wang from Clemson University in their paper "On Benchmarking Popular File Systems."

Access Pattern   The access pattern of an application has to do with how it seeks data in the storage media; it can read or write a file either sequentially or in random order. It is much easier to tune the file system if the application does a lot of sequential I/Os because these small I/Os can simply be grouped into a single large one. The third access pattern is called *strided access*, and it's typically used for scientific applications. However, this type can be largely considered as a type of sequential access with some characteristics of random access, such as caching.

File Access Profile   Applications can be either data or attribute intensive. Data-intensive ones shift a lot of data around but create or delete minimally. On the other end are attribute-intensive applications, which create and delete a lot of files yet read and write only a fraction of each. A good example of a data-intensive application that deals with large amounts of data (typically 100 MB or larger) is a big data application like *Apache Hadoop*, which utilizes a form of Google's *MapReduce* architecture and programming model. Attribute-intensive applications are those that check a lot of metadata and attributes to perform operations. Major examples are revision control systems such as *Git*, *SVN*, and *CVS*.

Bandwidth   Bandwidth refers to the amount of data that the application shifts around in the form of files. Bandwidth measures help in planning storage capacity as well as determining the proper caching characteristics of the file system. File caching helps in improving performance by keeping certain frequently accessed parts of various files in a small readily accessible memory (such as cache memory and random access memory). Bigger and faster cache memories of a file system ensure higher bandwidth.

Latency Sensitivity   Some applications are impacted negatively if a system takes too long to read or write, such as displaying some latency or synchronization error. Just as the CPU benefits from RAM rather than from actual storage, these applications can greatly benefit from well-thought-out caching algorithms, such as those in real-time applications like distributed multiplayer games and real-time distributed monitoring systems.

FIGURE 5.2   File system read/write performance

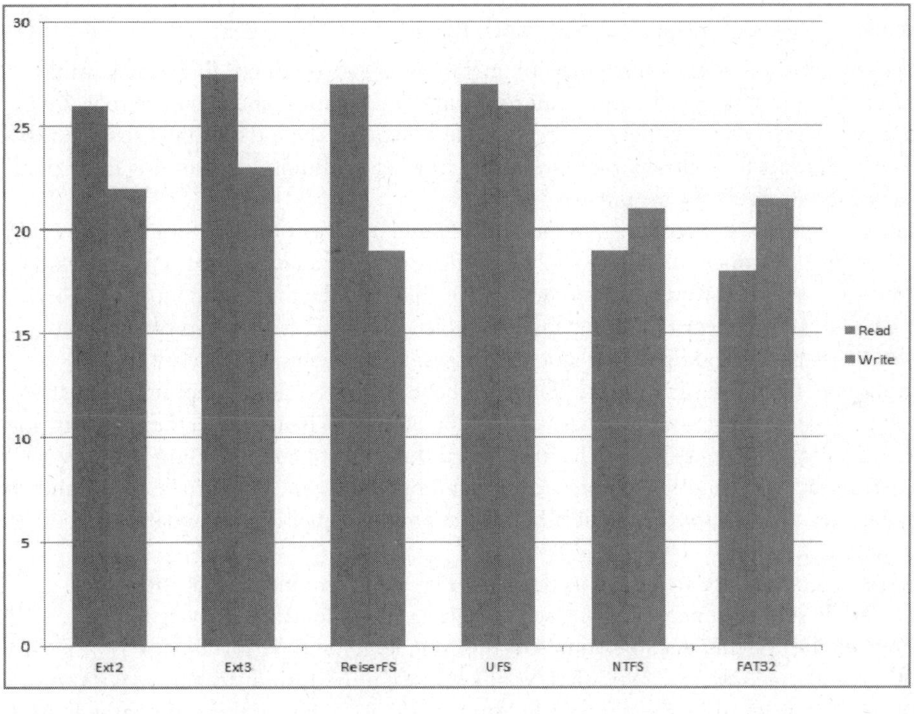

Metadata Performance

In most file systems, metadata is generated to provide information about specific files. For those unfamiliar, metadata is simply detailed information about a specific file, file attributes, or simply "data about data." It contains various kinds of information that may be unique to the file:

- File size
- Creation date
- Owner or creator
- Location on the storage medium
- File type or filename extension
- Dimensions for image files
- Compression algorithm
- Security and permissions
- Number of lines for documents and text files
- Location of image or video shot with a GPS-enabled device
- Encoding scheme of image, audio, or video file

Those are just some of the more common metadata fields you might find are viewable by the user. The file system will require more specific information about the file that it will not show to the user. File metadata is a type of file itself, and the file system keeps metadata with the file it points to or in separate directories or even mediums. The latter is more practical, especially for checking the integrity of files.

Metadata gives raw structure to storage capacity and consists of descriptions and pointers that link multiple sectors in a disk into coherent files and then identifies those files. Metadata is required for persistent storage, and to qualify for that use, the file system must be able to maintain its metadata integrity despite unpredictable system crashes such as ones caused by power interruptions and operating system failures. Such crashes often result in total information loss from volatile memory (RAM). The information that is kept in nonvolatile storage such as disks must always remain consistent enough to be usable in the deterministic reconstruction of a coherent state of the file system; there must be no dangling pointers or uninitialized spaces, no multiple pointers causing ambiguous ownership of resources, and no missing pointers to live resources. This requires the proper sequencing of updates in small on-disk metadata objects.

However, metadata updates, such as during file creation and block allocation, have always been the source of performance, security, integrity, and availability problems in most if not all file systems. As an example of the complexity and performance cost associated with metadata, look no further than your traditional old-fashioned library with thousands of books cataloged by the library's holdings database. The database at a large library is a small library in its own right. It is tedious to create, update, and manage the library database. Although searching takes just a few keystrokes, the time spent for search may depend on the size of the database and quality of the hardware. Once it's found, the librarian has information about the book such as author, publisher, publication date, and even edition. The database here is the metadata of the book. Managing and updating the database can be cumbersome and time consuming, just like maintaining file system metadata.

And because of the growing chasm between processing performance and disk access times, there is an obvious performance bottleneck. This growing disparity between processing and mechanical performance coupled with the increase of capacity of main storage actually means only one thing: the high-performance file systems such as those used in cloud computing systems should employ special *caching* algorithms or techniques in order to cover the performance gap created by disk access latencies.

Synchronous Metadata Update

Metadata is still basically a file in of itself, but it's handled a bit differently than other types of files. It is important to the file system, so it sometimes results in a bottleneck to the system, and that is why there is still active research going on dedicated to enhancing metadata performance. This performance is traditionally slow because metadata has to be written synchronously. This is called *synchronous* metadata update, and it happens because the file system resides partly on volatile buffers and persistent disks where the file system writes everything to disk as soon as a write command is received. File systems do not update everything synchronously because synchronous updates result in a slow file system, but metadata is still written in this way.

Metadata is written this way because many believed that file systems that employ synchronous metadata updates (like *BSD* and *FFS/UFS*) are safer compared to file systems that do not (like the *Linux ext2fs*) write metadata synchronously. Let's put that into perspective with an example.

You are working on a file in the UFS file system for 15 minutes and just recently executed a save buffer when the machine suddenly crashed. After bootup and the subsequent file system check, everything was gone; the autosave file, the backup file, everything either did not exist or was empty.

This was caused by synchronous metadata update. When the save buffer was executed, the file was written to the file system; the metadata got written to disk, and the data that was kept in memory was lost when the power was removed and the subsequent file system check made this file empty. The autosave file was then deleted even though the data had already been written on disk because it had no associated metadata. There was also no backup file written because it was a newly created file and the first save.

Soft Updates

A soft update is the alternative to sequence-dependent or synchronous updates and write-ahead logging. Write-ahead logging writes all modifications to a log before they are applied to the actual storage (on disk, such as in a database). Write-ahead caching ensures atomicity of operations, which essentially means that an update is either completely written or completely discarded (in case of a failure), thus ensuring system consistency. This method allows the safe use of write-back caching; that is, modifications to data in the cache are not copied to the cache until absolutely necessary. This enforces and tracks metadata update dependencies to ensure that the disk image remains in a consistent state. This method improves metadata performance by combining multiple updates into fewer background disk writes.

To maintain integrity despite unpredictable failures, sequencing constraints must be implemented when dirty blocks are moved into storage. To do this, the soft updates mechanism creates and maintains dependency information to keep track of sequencing requirements. This dependency information is associated with dirty in-memory copies of metadata. During metadata update, the in-memory copy of a certain block is modified normally and then its corresponding memory information is appropriately updated. So whenever these dirty in-memory blocks are flushed or saved to disk, the dependency information is consulted.

Dependency information is heavily maintained per field pointer to achieve fine granularity. When there are updates, both before and after versions are kept together with a list containing all other updates that specific updates depend on.

Caching

As has been mentioned, disk mechanical performance are leagues slower than digital processing performance, so they introduce some very large bottlenecks to the system, especially in the file system, which almost exclusively manages files and hence disk operations. If data is constantly updated on the disk whenever an application or a user accesses it, the system would spend its time waiting for the disk I/O to finish and would have less time to do anything else. Small and frequent writes to disk all carry overhead associated with seeking and allocation of segments, and because each operation has this overhead, it tends to pile up. In cloud computing circumstances where data is the main process driver, a lot of file system interaction and disk writing, and hence a lot of seeking and writing, are involved. In this case, caching is a good way to increase file system performance.

A cache is basically a part of memory where data that needs constant access is kept or data that is perceived to be needed soon is *prefetched* and kept; this is also a place where backlogged data for future writing is accumulated, in what is called a *write back*. In a write back, modified blocks are marked to be written into disk later, which enables batching I/O operations, saving on disk overhead. But the main problem is that when a crash occurs, all the data in the cache is wiped out so the longer write backs are postponed, increasing the risk involved for damage relating to a crash. The upside is increased speed.

Write backs should be done when the following actions occur:

- When a block, sector, or node is evicted
- When a file is closed so all data should be written immediately
- On an explicit or force flush of the cache
- When memory is running low to prevent a forced write back through memory reclamation, which is quite slow

> ### 🌐 Real World Scenario
>
> #### Cooperative Caching
>
> Processing performance increases more rapidly than disk performance, and that is one reason the file system should use caching to avoid frequent disk access. But another technology trend is also prompting the benefits of caching. Current and emerging high-speed low-latency switching networks enable the supply of file system blocks across network spaces much faster than standard Ethernet. This means that fetching data from remote memory is faster than ever, signaling a good performance boost for distributed file systems, NFS, and remote virtual machines that are at the core of cloud computing. Applications and file systems are now able to cache data using not just local memory and resources but that of networked resources as well. This prevents the issues that plague write backs if ever there are unexpected crashes.
>
> One example of a cooperative caching algorithm is Direct Client Cooperation. This is a simple approach that allows any active client to use another idle client's memory as a backing store. An active client with an overflowing cache can forward new cache entries to an idle machine. The active client can use this remote private cache for read requests and other caching applications until that idle client becomes active and needs its cache back, at which point it evicts the cooperative cache. This is a good method to use in a multitenant environment because not all virtual machines will be available all the time. This helps lighten the load for everyone and does not require the provisioning of more resources for a single instance.

Bandwidth

Aside from the performance of core low-level cloud technologies discussed previously, the most important aspect for a cloud system is the actual bandwidth available. It is a well-known fact that unpredictable network performance is a major factor that affects user satisfaction of cloud services. No matter the performance of the cloud system, if the receiving end is a bottleneck, the perception of overall performance will be low. If there is no network performance guarantee, there is also no application guarantee. But since the Internet is a collection of globally shared systems from multiple vendors and providers, network quality and hence bandwidth cannot be guaranteed.

Bandwidth and overall network performance are often the cause of major user complaints. It is not unusual for administrators and data center managers to be brooding over a collection of complaint tickets expressing user frustration because of application sluggishness and unavailability without a real concrete way of explaining what is wrong. The servers are performing at their peak, the network shows minimal congestion, storage systems all show green across the board, so there must be something else wrong. The only explanation is that it could be the WAN or external Internet end points at the user's end.

Turning our attention back to things that are under our control, what steps should we take to ensure network availability and bandwidth on our end? And between what ends (from the user's end or the provider's end) should we guarantee network and bandwidth performance? There are no standards for this at this time, but some cloud computing advocates are looking into these questions, so for now, to each his own. Ultimately, the decision for providing bandwidth performance lies with the provider, and the provider may guarantee this performance in and around only their own jurisdiction, which is to say their own networks and those in between data centers and availability zones.

Bandwidth and network performance should be a joint venture by different network providers because it cannot really be guaranteed by one single entity.

Throughput: Bandwidth Aggregation

Bandwidth is an important aspect of a network, especially one made for cloud computing applications. Bandwidth is directly related to network throughput, which is the rate of successful message deliveries over a given communications channel. But a single network connection has its limits. Take Ethernet, for example; its bandwidth increases by 10 orders magnitude every generation, so we get 10 Mbit/s, 100 Mbit/s, 1,000 Mbit/s, and 10,000 Mbit/s. When you reach the bandwidth ceiling of one generation, you simply move to the next generation for increased throughput. However, doing so can be cost prohibitive, especially for the latter generations. So if your need exceeds the limit for 1,000 Mbps, you can move your infrastructure to 10,000 Mbps, which would then cost a lot because you have to change a lot of elements in your infrastructure. A good way to circumvent this cost is by teaming or bonding, more officially known as link aggregation.

Bonding

Bonding, or NIC bonding, is a form of bandwidth aggregation where multiple smaller connections act as a single big connection. This requires multiple NICs working together in a single machine. This is applicable for personal computers, but servers, having multiple NIC slots, can make better use of bonding.

For bonding to work, there must be a server that breaks up data into multiple packets to send to a client. If there is a bonded connection between them, the packets are simultaneously sent over these different connections and then reassembled on the receiving end, which means they arrive more or less at the same time, or at least it takes less time for them to arrive through multiple connections as opposed to a single connection where they arrive almost in a serialized manner, even though in essence it is not actually serialized. That is the reason it takes longer to download large files; your machine will be waiting for all the packets to arrive and there is only so much bandwidth, so they have to come through one or a few at a time compared to having bonded links, which allows more packets to pass through at once. As an analogy, think of it as a highway: if you have four cars going to the same destination, approximately 10 minutes away, and they are traveling at the same speed on a single-lane road, they would arrive one after the other, with the fourth car possibly arriving at the 12-minute mark. If you have more cars, it would take more time for all of them to arrive. Now if you have four lanes, then all four cars would arrive at the same time, in exactly ten minutes, saving you two minutes. This value just scales up the more cars you have and the more lanes you have. This is bandwidth aggregation, and all of those links act as a single large one.

An example of bonding is PPP multilink, where the aggregate bandwidth is the sum of the individual physical connections. The Multilink Protocol (MP) is an extended version of Point-to-Point Protocol (PPP), which has the ability to bond multiple parallel connections together where the resulting virtual connection is equal to the sum of the individual bandwidth of each separate connection. Packets are broken up and then distributed over available links. This technology, however, needs compliant hardware or software at both ends of the link because these packets need to be recombined and properly sequenced, so this is doable only with a point-to-point connection from a client toward a directly connected server. This can be done even if the available links are not using the same bandwidth or connection speed, and it increases throughput dramatically and provides good redundancy and failover protection between the connected points.

Teaming

NIC teaming, or connection teaming, is different from bonding, contrary to most people's belief that they are synonymous, though they are both under the greater umbrella of link aggregation. Unlike PPP multilink, teaming links do not terminate as pairs of end points; instead, it is a form of bandwidth aggregation, which does not bond the different links but only makes them work together as a team.

Each link in a team is set up so all the links maintain individual TCP/IP sessions using standard protocols. Basically, you have two or more separate connections. Teaming is often used in a LAN environment with multiple client computers simultaneously connecting to the Internet through a common gateway. NIC teaming is implemented in the gateway, which is now referred to as the *connection teaming server*. The teaming server maintains multiple connections to the outside or to the Internet. It can have vastly different connection types, such as a DSL connection, a fiber channel, and a dial-up modem all working at the same time but not as a whole. The teaming server manages routing between the LAN and the Internet; it selects the best connection for the type of request or application that is being requested by the client computer. For example, one client opens an FTP link and downloads a large file. This connection uses the largest bandwidth link available, which is the fiber channel, but the client will not gain throughput like that of a bonded connection because it is just using a single connection. This act of downloading a large file would be enough to congest a single-link network, but a teaming connection allows for different connection channels for data to go through. So while one user takes up the fiber channel with their huge download, other users simply browsing the Web with minimal bandwidth requirements will be routed using the free links, the DSL and dial-up ones.

As an analogy, let us say you are moving to another apartment and have employed the help of three friends. You act as the teaming server by passing the packages to your friends for them to carry downstairs, deciding which box should be carried by whom based on its size and the size and availability of your friends. You take the large box and give it to the largest of your three friends, and while he is occupied with bringing it downstairs, you hand boxes to your two other friends and wait for their return. In this case of teaming, your three friends carry one load each based on their strengths; they are not necessarily combining into the Incredible Hulk who can carry all of your stuff at once. Though the bandwidth is not necessarily increased in theory, in practice you are still utilizing a bigger bandwidth limit due to the multiple sources of bandwidth and will greatly increase throughput. This is efficient for multiple requests and multiple users; it allows the server to avoid congestion in any single connection. What will not benefit from this scheme is the transfer of large files because only one connection can be utilized, even if it has the largest bandwidth in the group. It also greatly increases redundancy and failover protection.

In the same scenario, where your friends help you to move, they help carry your 100-inch TV and your large sofa together, which is now an act of bonding because they are a single element doing one large job.

Jumbo Frames

Networking technology has come a very long way, but some of the standards being used today are the same ones set in an era where everything was small and slow. We are referring to the default data payload size of the network data frame. The original 1518 byte maximum transmission unit (MTU) is a bit malnourished compared to today's gigabit standards. A small unit size was chosen because the speed and bandwidth capabilities of early networks and Ethernet were pretty small and large data packets pose large problems when communication errors occur, which meant that they had to be sent again, taking up valuable time and bandwidth. So they settled for a relatively small and manageable size. But this is largely no longer true because current technology can handle more than its share of large data packets.

Although the MTU was originally set for manageability, today it can sometimes be detrimental. The reason for this is that whenever a data frame arrives, the NIC issues an interrupt request (IRQ) to the CPU so that it can check out the new frame. The CPU then reads the frame and the TCP headers before actually processing the data contained in the frame. This is the associated CPU cycle overhead with each small frame received. Thankfully, CPU processing power has steadily increased, but that is still not a guarantee because DDoS attacks can use this process to overwhelm the CPU of servers. Because data centers always employ a form of bandwidth aggregation, attacks almost never generate enough requests to overwhelm a network, but instead they may overwhelm processors with the sheer number of IRQs generated by sending hundreds of thousands of small packets. Figure 5.3 shows the simple IRQ process being exploited by hackers to overwhelm the CPU.

A way around this issue is to use jumbo frames. As the name suggests, jumbo frames are frames with a larger size compared to the standard MTU. Sending data in jumbo frames means there are fewer frames sent through the network, resulting in fewer IRQs at the receiving end. This obviously generates big improvements in terms of bandwidth and CPU cycles. The maximum size of a jumbo frame is 9 KB, which means a jumbo frame is equivalent to six standard 1.5 KB frames, resulting in a net reduction of five frames, fewer CPU cycles used in both ends, and only one TCP/IP and Ethernet header. This results in a savings of 290 bytes sent over the network. It takes 80,000 standard frames to fill a Gigabit Ethernet pipe, and as you can imagine, that's a lot of interrupt requests that the CPU needs to process, which is an enormous overhead. In comparison, only 14,000 jumbo frames are needed to fill that pipe, resulting in a 4 Mbps reduction in bandwidth cost. The savings in bandwidth and CPU time cost can produce significant increases in network throughput and performance.

FIGURE 5.3 Data frame receiving process

Network Latency

Network latency, especially as it relates to cloud systems and applications, is not a simple thing to isolate and define. Before there was a real Internet, latency was simply measured as the number of hops between the user and the application and the inherent delays resulting from that travel from source to destination. In a proprietarily owned network like an enterprise network, network latency would remain constant because the number of nodes and traffic density within that network more or less remained constant. But with thousands of different networks making up the Internet, and adding to that the virtual networks and spaces that are inherent to cloud computing, network latency calculations are not simple, to say the least.

First and foremost, on the Internet, end points are not fixed as they can be in an enterprise or local network. Cloud application users can be anywhere in the world, and simply moving within a city block and switching to another cellular tower or Wi-Fi hotspot would change the paths on which the data travels, change the ISP, and essentially change the network from which the application is being accessed. With the flexibility, failover protection, and rapid allocation that the cloud offers, it may result in an application being transferred to a different availability zone or server, which again changes the path that data has to take in order to get to the user. That is the beauty of the cloud, but flexibility in this case has its price. The resulting latency can be unpredictable, even if an application is being accessed through a relatively fast ISP.

In a contained network, latency can be effectively measured, and it traditionally had three measures: round-trip time (RTT), jitter, and end point computational speed.

Round-trip time (RTT)   is the time it takes for a single trace packet to traverse a network from source to destination and back again, or the time it takes for a source client to hail a server and then receive a reply. RTT is depicted in Figure 5.4. This is quite useful in interactive applications like online gaming as well as for examining app-to-app situations such as measuring how fast two servers like a web server and a database server can interact with each other and exchange data.

FIGURE 5.4 Simple representation of round-trip time

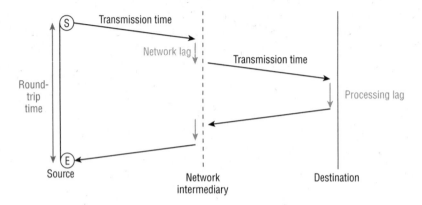

Jitter   Jitter is the variation in packet traversal or transmission delay that is caused by queuing and is the effect of contention or conflict and serialization (where data packets can travel only one after the other) that takes place anywhere on the network path between and within networks.

End Point Computational Speed   This simply refers to how fast the server, client, or whatever end points that are communicating can process data that has been received and how quickly they can send an appropriate reply. This is dictated by core computational elements of the device: the CPU, memory, and other core hardware and software.

Complexity can add to latency. The number-one source of latency is distributed computing. The nature of applications has changed, and now a lot of applications, especially those related to data analytics and big data, employ hundreds if not thousands of separate servers worldwide, which all have varying degrees of latency brought by the Internet connectivity and the networks between them. Depending on the time that these servers are running, the condition of network congestion in their respective areas could be good or bad as Internet traffic waxes and wanes as competition for bandwidth and infrastructure take place.

Virtualization is another source of complexity that adds to overall latency. Virtual networks and virtual desktops all mimic various hardware, including network interfaces, but they still have to be translated into hardware signals from the software virtualization. This adds another layer of processing latency on top of the network latency.

Hop Counts

Hop count is literally the number of hops that a data packet will take from one network node to the next until it reaches its destination. For example, if there are three routers between a data packet and its destination, the hop count would be exactly three counts. Of course, this is not as simple in today's complex web of networks. Back in the days of enterprise data centers and networks, the hop count could be determined easily. Now that the Internet is made up of varied networks owned by different entities with different settings and connections, the number of hops is not so easy to count.

The hop count is related to how many network nodes (like routers) the data goes through to reach its destination, but the shortest hop does not often correspond to a geographical shortest path. For example, the shortest path from London to Paris might go through Quebec, which does not make sense geographically but because of how networks on the Internet crisscross, it might just make sense in the number of hops.

A hop count can be measured through various networking tools and applications, with *traceroute* being the most common example.

Quality of Service (QoS)

Even with the cloud described with terms like *homogeneity* and *simplicity of service*, the truth is that everything relating to the cloud is one hot, piping jumble of complexity, maybe not in theory and concept but certainly in application and practice. The illustrations and explanations all look so simple, but the truth of the matter is that the age-old adage of "Better said than done" is quite applicable here. We have all the complexities coming from the extensibility and diversity of networks within the Internet, from the complexity of distributed computing and virtualization, and of course from having to please all of our customers who have zero tolerance for any sort of downtime or latency. Companies are pushed to create better Quality of Service (QoS) models or simply get creative creating their guarantees and service-level agreements (SLAs), getting "lawyery" for lack of a better term.

As part of the QoS promise, SLAs lay out what the service provider is offering the customer and what they are prepared to do in case they cannot deliver on this promise. But traditional SLAs do not usually differentiate between kinds of outages such as on a server, a NIC, an NFS, or even a security vulnerability or exploit. So they might be able to get away with a storage facility outage not being considered downtime because the rest of the service is still accessible.

But in a nutshell, QoS is the ability of a service provider to prioritize certain applications, users, and data flows and guarantee a certain level of performance in its applications and services. There are numerous QoS criteria, and they may vary depending on the application in question and include performance criteria like throughput, latency, delay, and others.

Multipathing

Multipathing is a technique that enables usage of more than one physical path to transfer data between a host and an external storage device. This is shown in Figure 5.5. In case of a failure of any element in the network—such as an adapter, switch, or cable—the network can switch to another physical path and avoid the failed component. This ensures uninterruptable, correct, and complete transfers with minimum failures.

Cloud computing relies on data and therefore large amounts of storage. Cloud computing providers often have large storage area networks with a massive number of storage servers. And there is a requirement that all users be able to access such resources quickly and consistently, so failover protection and redundancy are very important.

With data growing exponentially, especially with entertainment media going digital and high-definition videos becoming the norm, video streaming providers need powerful network interfaces to their storage in order to provide files quickly. Multipathing is an effective way of increasing the available bandwidth to Internet Small Computer System Interface (iSCSI) networks, much like bonding does for normal networks. In multipathing, multiple physical paths are used between hosts and data storage devices in case there is any link failure in the SAN network such as ones caused by faulty NICs, switch, or cables. The software can simply switch to another physical path, which circumvents the failed components. This is known as path failover.

FIGURE 5.5   A simple representation of the multipathing concept

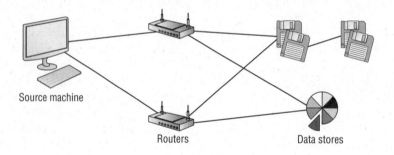

Load Balancing

Cloud computing services are used by thousands of users at once, enterprise customers as well as individual users. But the promise of virtually unlimited resources is still largely a fantasy, the ideal scenario. The truth is that resources are very, very finite and being shared by hundreds of thousands of people. The reason that everything—every server, every switch—doesn't just stop working that some ingenious resource management methods are used. Load balancing is one of these methods. A load balancer, usually just another server, assigns connections and requests to different servers, making sure that not one server is overloaded. This is essential in making things run smoothly.

Scaling: Vertical vs. Horizontal vs. Diagonal

Scalability is often one of the main aspects and reasons that companies are moving their infrastructures to the cloud. It makes sense because it is easier to scale and expand in a virtual environment when the number of servers you can deploy is no longer limited by the size of your racks or the size of your data center space or even your budget. Moving to virtual from physical makes a lot of economic sense, but it also makes sense from a design and development standpoint when considering infrastructure architecture. With the cloud, a moderate-sized organization is able to build a scalable infrastructure that would have otherwise been way beyond its means. Different types of scaling are described below and shown in Figure 5.6.

Vertical Scaling   Vertical scaling is the process of vertical growth; everything is grown bigger and faster, or simply more of something is added. In this case, adding more CPU cores or faster ones allows for faster processing, especially with batch jobs. Adding more memory allows for growing the cache and prefetching data, which further speeds up operations. Adding more disks and storage facilities helps with data retention, and faster disks with faster I/O time and fast seek and access times help with performance as well. Basically, vertical scaling means to grow bigger and go faster; it allows us to speed up individual applications. However, there are limits to this kind of scaling. Growth can cause diminishing returns, and there will come a time when adding more provides no more performance benefit, so we must find other ways of scaling and increasing throughput.

Horizontal Scaling   Horizontal scaling is sideways growth, so instead of creating faster and stronger infrastructure points, you are adding *more* infrastructure points. If increasing the processing powers of servers becomes cost prohibitive and the performance gains are no longer attractive enough to justify the costs, you can increase the number of servers. For example, you could take a web server that can serve 100 users at once and grow it vertically so that it will serve users faster, leading to better satisfaction and retention, but the fact still remains that only 100 people are being served. But by scaling horizontally, you add more servers. By adding another server, even one not as upgraded and beefed up as the first one, you can now serve 200 customers. That is actually doubling the throughput. It gives you the power to execute more concurrent workloads at the expense of added complexity because now you have to worry about two servers and 200 customers, but that could only be good for business.

Diagonal Scaling   Diagonal scaling is the combination of both vertical and horizontal scaling, and it is the result when both growth directions have already been taken. For example, if you have maxed out the performance upgrades to your server, then you can start multiplying your servers using the same specs and growing horizontally.

There has always been a debate about which type of scaling is best. Do you make your infrastructure more powerful to serve customers faster and have them finish quicker so that you accommodate more customers? Or do you scale horizontally with more servers to serve more customers even if it takes a bit longer for them to finish with their transactions?

Both horizontal and vertical scaling have their respective pros and cons and associated costs as well. It is like the hardware conundrum, where you cannot decide between buying the most powerful $10K machine or buying 10 slow machines at $1K each or whether to take the middle ground and buy four midrange machines at $2.5K each. The answer to that will depend entirely on your priorities and objectives and the types of applications being run.

FIGURE 5.6   Types of scaling

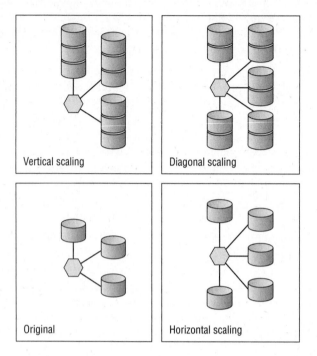

Disk Performance

The disk is currently the storage medium of choice for most enterprises and users because of its relatively cheap price, passable performance, and large capacity. But despite major leaps in capacity technology, disk performance is currently not where we want it to be, or where it should ideally be. This is because of the inherent limitations of mechanical moving parts. Mechanical parts simply cannot keep up with the performance of electronics. That is why solid-state drives are beginning to take over the market, but the technology is still new and it has a long way to go. So for now, we are stuck with the disk.

Since we are stuck with the disk, we might as well make the best of it and keep it performing at its peak. There are two categories associated with disk performance: access time and data transfer rate.

Access Time

Access time is the response time of the disk drive, which is the measure of time before the drive can actually transfer data. The factors controlling this facet of the drive are its various mechanical parts, such as the speed of the rotating spindle and the speed of the read/write head's actuator arm. All these individual measurable variables are added together to come up with a single value that evaluates the performance of the drive in terms of access time. This measure varies widely from manufacturer to manufacturer and per model; even dives of the same class and model may not perform at exactly the same level. Solid-state drives are not dependent on mechanical parts, so they do not have the same limitations and the access times are rather short and consistent. The two measurements that define access time are seek time and rotational latency.

Seek Time

The data on disk media is stored in segments called sectors, which are arranged one after the other linearly in circular tracks. The disk is in turn made up of multiple tracks arranged in concentric circles. Depending on the type of disk, some tracks are arranged in a spiral pattern, but the typical standard is a concentric pattern.

The seek time is the time it takes for the drive's disk head assembly to travel and position itself over the track where the data needs to be read or written. This is done through the actuator arm, which controls where the read/write head goes. The drive uses the actuator arm to move the head to the correct track where the sector containing the data is located. If the head is already on the correct track at the time a read or write command is issued, then the seek time would be zero. But if the head is currently on the outermost track and it needs data on the innermost track, the seek time is at the maximum.

A rotating disk drive's seek time is the average of all possible seek times, which is the sum of all possible seek times divided by the number of those seeks. But in application, the seek time is actually is actually determined by a statistical algorithm that is approximated as the seek time over a third of the total number of tracks.

The first hard drives had an immense seek time of 600 milliseconds (ms), but by the mid 1970s, this was cut down to 25 ms. In the 1980s, voice coil type actuation reduced seek times to around 20 ms. But that is the extent of the breakthrough because since then the improvements are at a snail's pace and average seek times today are still only a little bit below 20 ms, averaging in range from 10 ms to 18ms, depending on the quality of the HDD model.

Rotational Latency

Rotational latency is the delay caused by waiting for the rotating disk to bring the required sector under the read/write head. This is entirely dependent on the rotational speed of a disk through its spindle motor, which is measured in revolutions per minute (rpm). For most drives, the average rotational latency in milliseconds is half of the rotational period. On the other hand, the maximum rotational latency is the time that it takes to do a full rotation without taking into consideration any *spin-up* time. It is a simple matter to decrease the rotational latency by simply increasing the rotational speed of the disks, which also has the added benefit of increasing throughput, especially if the number of sectors per track is increased. Table 5.2 shows the common disk rotational speeds and the associated rotational latency of each.

TABLE 5.2 Spindle rpm and associated latency

Spindle rpm	Average Rotational Latency (ms)
4,200	7.14
5,400	5.56
7,200	4.17
10,000	3.00
15,000	2.00

Data Transfer Rate

Data transfer rate is the effective throughput of the disk drive; it covers both the internal and external data transfer rates. The internal transfer rate has to do with the speed at which the drive moves data between the disk's surface and the controller of the drive. The external data rate is the speed at which data is transferred between the drive's controller and the host system. Since a system is only as fast as its slowest component, the data transfer rate will be whichever is the slower of the two rates. The sustained throughput or sustained data transfer rate will also be either the sustained internal or the sustained external data rate, whichever is slower. The internal data transfer rate is determined by the sector overhead time, cylinder switch time, head switch time, and media rate.

Sector Overhead Time   This is the additional time the disk needs to process sector-related data, which is needed for the control structure of the drive and includes information used in drive management like locating and validating data in sectors and for various other support functions. This is similar to the processing of TCP/IP headers in a network frame.

Cylinder Switch Time   This is the time needed to switch between data surfaces and the read/write head because most typical HDDs have more than one disk and hence more actuators and heads corresponding to each surface. This typically takes 2 or 3 ms.

Head Switch Time   This is the time it takes to electrically switch from one read/write head to the next before reading can begin for multihead drives. This takes between 1 and 2 ms.

Media Rate   The media rate is the speed at which the head reads bits from the surface of the disk.

Choosing a storage device depends on particular use case. For example, consider choosing an instance of Amazon EC2 where various choices are available. The choice rests on factors such as data volume, data frequency or velocity, complexity of computation, and availability of processed data.

Amazon categorizes its EC2 instance types (http://aws.amazon.com/ec2/instance-types/) with various storage offerings into general purpose, compute optimized, memory optimized, and storage optimized. Amazon basically makes available two types of main storage devices: hard disk drives (HDDs) and solid-state drives (SSDs). These come with different performance levels and costs.

An HDD will be generally suitable for batch processing systems or systems that do not need to be used in real time. These include large databases (SQL or NoSQL), log storage, recorded audio, and video streaming. SSDs will be highly relevant for web servers serving millions of page hits per day. Moreover, data crunching systems, especially those involving GPUs, will definitely benefit from SSDs as compared to HDDs.

Disk Tuning

Disk tuning is the optimization of a disk's performance in relation to the system or platform that it has been installed on, taking into consideration the operating system and the file system being used.

The traditional approach to disk tuning is to use the advertised performance characteristics of the disk such as those discussed previously and then to create performance expectations. You can then benchmark the device and compare the actual performance to the modeled set of expectations.

Disk performance characteristics are largely consistent when you consider only the disk itself. What performance differences you do get from them is largely due to the kind of file system being used and how it manages the disks as well as I/O performance. Aside from the file system performance affecting disk performance, one very good way of maintaining disk performance is regular defragmentation. Fragmentation occurs simply because the processor and other electronic components of a computer system are leagues faster than the mechanical disk. To compensate, the disk will write to the free sector that is closest to its actuator and head; it will not seek out large empty portions to write large contiguous files into. Because of this, the disk eventually becomes fragmented, and parts of a single file are all over the place. Performance slows down because when a file is needed, the disk has to seek out those fragments and then piece them together, accumulating overhead because of all the disk seek and access being done to collect each fragment. The problem eventually exacerbates, and you are left with a system that crawls whenever an I/O operation is in progress.

Fragmentation typically occurs on logical drives, which are translated by the device drivers into the physical disk. In the case of virtual systems, as is very common in cloud computing, the logical volume, which is already a masking of the physical medium, is further masked by another application layer, the virtual disk. Virtual disks reside on logical disks as container files and as such are still prone to fragmentation in the logical drive level. Further, the virtual disk itself, perfectly emulating a physical disk, also gets fragmented. Now you have a double fragmentation scenario. The virtual disk is fragmented, the fragments are mapped onto the logical drives, which in turn are mapped on the physical drive. This would explain various performance issues in virtual machines.

Combating this is a simple process using a tool that comes mostly standard to any operating system, a disk defragmenter. Logical drives and especially virtual drives that move data heavily should be defragmented regularly. Depending on the disk usage, it should be done once a month or even once a week.

Swap Disk Space

Swap disk space, or *swap space*, is largely a Linux term that refers to a preconfigured space on the disk that stores data being frequently used by the main memory. On Windows this is called a page file, and the process is called paging. Swapping or paging is a memory management scheme in which snapshots of memory called pages are transferred to a specific location on disk. This is an important part of virtual memory implementation; it allows the system to use disk storage for data that does not fit into the main memory (RAM). This can be viewed as increasing RAM size because main memory can now accommodate more data by dumping older data into disk, virtually increasing capacity slightly.

It is typically the OS that sets a specific size for the swap file and then just increases that if there is need for more. The size is returned to the default value once this need has been fulfilled. However, the user is able to set a fixed amount, which cannot be changed by the OS even if it needs to.

I/O Tuning

Since we are on the topic of tuning disks, keep in mind that you cannot really alter how a disk operates and increase its mechanical performance. The best thing you can do is employ proper I/O tuning and some file system tuning.

As we have discussed many times, applications and many other processes are limited by disk input/output operations. And it is often the case that CPU activity is suspended until a specific I/O operation completes. If the application is often waiting for an I/O operation, it is said to be *I/O bound*. I/O tuning can help enhance performance if the applications are really working more on the disks and saving and modifying files, but it cannot do much for *CPU bound* applications.

The I/O requirements should be analyzed during the initial design phase for a system. You must find out what resources you require to get the desired performance. This is a top-down approach to I/O tuning. But if you already have a system in place, you must approach tuning from the bottom up. You can go do so by following recommended steps:

1. Determine the exact number of disks being utilized by the system.

2. Determine the specific number of disks being used by the application you are tuning for.

3. Determine the type of I/O operations being performed by your system.

4. Determine if those I/O operations are going through the file system or directly into devices.

5. Consider spreading objects over multiple disks through *striping.*

6. Determine through calculation the level of performance you can realistically expect from the system.

The first two steps are just to allow you to understand the extent of the tuning required. They will also help you identify hot disks in the system. Those are disks that are experiencing greater load compared to others. For example, in a 10-disk system, a single disk is experiencing 25 percent load instead of just 10 percent, which is a good indicator that the disk is hot.

Analyzing I/O Requirements

If you have a database application running on your cloud system, you should identify key points in its performance in order to understand which tuning characteristics to implement.

1. Calculate the required and expected throughput of your application so you can establish a baseline.

   You can do this by observing the number of reads and writes involved in each transaction or activity of your application and then identify the objects for which those operations are being performed. For example, in a single transaction your application might read from object A, then write to object B, and then do another write to object C. So a single transaction would yield three I/O operations: one read and two write operations.

2. Define the I/O performance (throughput) of your application or system by specifying the number of transactions per second (tps) required of the system.

   If the system is required to handle 100 tps to perform as expected, then based on the operations in step 1, the system has to support a total of 300 I/Os per second: 100 reads to object A, 100 writes to object B, and another 100 writes to object C.

3. Determine the number of disks required to achieve this level of performance.

   To do this, ascertain the performance of each disk in terms of the number of I/O operations it can perform per second. This is usually advertised by the manufacturer, but you can get a more accurate and actual reading by benchmarking it yourself. This will depend on three factors:

   - Disk speed.
   - Whether the operation is read or write. Performance varies depending on the model you have.
   - Whether the file system is being used or just the raw device.

4. Take note in a spread sheet how the disk performs in comparison to the reads and writes and use that to determine the number of disks required to achieve the performance.

   You can create a table similar to the one shown next to tabulate the disk performance and figure out how many disks are needed for the target performance.

Object	R/W Requirement	Disk R/W capability	Disks needed
A	100 reads	48 reads	2.02
B	100 writes	32 writes	3.04
C	100 writes	32 writes	3.04
			8.1 (9)

In our example tabulation, we need 8.1 disks to be able to support 100 transactions per second, but since we cannot come up with 1/10 of a disk, it's better to round up than down because it is the safer alternative in terms of performance. So we now have a clear understanding of our hardware requirement.

If you already have a system in place and it is not performing as expected, follow these steps to determine if the system is configured with enough hardware resources first before moving on to the next tuning methods.

Business Application for Disk Tuning

Disk tuning is important for one simple reason: the disk is the slowest part of the computer system. So in a lot of scenarios, the disk is the bottleneck, which means almost all I/O operations are bottlenecks. This is more strongly felt in systems that manage and manipulate a lot of data, like the ones being used by stock-trading organizations, for example. In the rapidly changing and volatile world of trading, the environment can change in an instant, which means new data keeps flooding in every minute. And for the system to analyze such large data sets, they would have to be quickly written into disk so that they can be processed and analyzed. This constant reading and writing will add latency to analysis programs, which may negatively affect the ability to arrive at timely decisions because the system is taking a long time to process analysis reports.

Performance Management and Monitoring Tools

It is important to note that storage is not the only thing that matters in a cloud system. Although it has a major influence on usage percentages, we still need to manage and monitor all aspects of the cloud system. Most major cloud computing system vendors offer management tools. But there are a lot of third-party management software programs that integrate with cloud platforms from most vendors.

Performance management software integrates information and workflow from across the whole system, including application data and statistics, network performance statistics, and storage and I/O statistics are specifically built and adapted to virtualized environments. Figure 5.7 and Figure 5.8 show the CopperEgg server monitoring tool. Figure 5.9 shows the metrics available with AWS CloudWatch. Figure 5.10 shows a report in the Nagios network visualization tool.

FIGURE 5.7   CopperEgg server monitoring tool

FIGURE 5.8   CopperEgg custom metrics

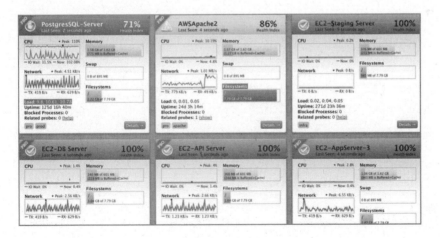

FIGURE 5.9   AWS CloudWatch metrics

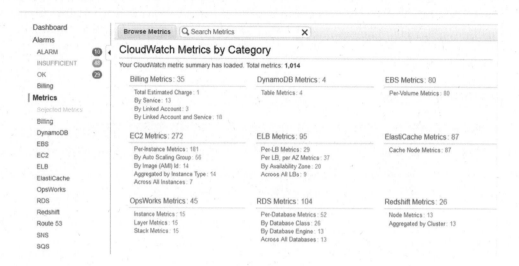

FIGURE 5.10   Nagios network visualization tool

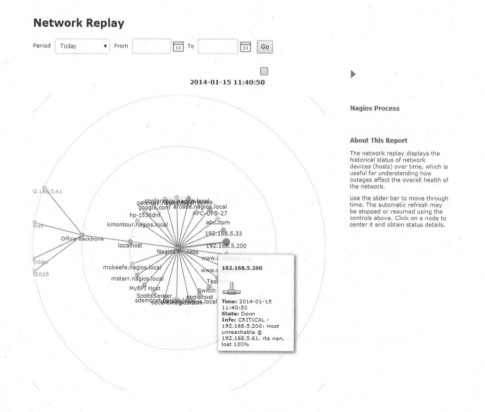

Monitoring tools such as CopperEgg provide comprehensive analysis of resources and applications, including traffic, and CPU and disk performance packaged in a neat and easy-to-understand UI. Often, the best monitoring software is not really the most detailed but software that can convey the message of system health easily to anyone reading it.

Since this is cloud computing we are talking about, you have the benefit of scalability. Your cloud system has the ability to automatically scale with traffic and performance requirements based on its usage, the extent of which is set by the administrator according to certain thresholds. For example, the administrator can set the system to create a new web server whenever the running one is experiencing 80 percent load traffic, giving ample capacity and buffer time to allow the new server to fully configure. When the new virtual server is ready to receive traffic, the system can automatically balance the load between all the running servers so that no one server is being taxed more than the others. All of these functions are accessible through the management interface being provided by your cloud service provider.

Hypervisor Configuration Best Practices

The *hypervisor* is at the heart of every cloud computing platform or system; it sets up the virtualization layer above it without the need for another OS, which is why it is also called a bare-metal system. So it follows that for a system to run at peak performance, the hypervisor should be one of the healthiest, if not *the* healthiest, of all of the system components. There is no single standard for how to configure all hypervisors because each one will have its own unique features. The provider of the hypervisor will have best practices for setting up and configuring specific hardware, so look to their documentation for specific needs.

But there are certain concepts that apply to allowing your virtualized system to perform better.

Memory Ballooning

Memory ballooning is a special feature implemented between the hypervisor and the *guest OS*, and it allows the hypervisor to reclaim memory from the guest OS or virtual machine. Yet it still allows the virtual machine to make intelligent decisions about which memory pages should be paged out in case it does not have the required free memory when the balloon driver is activated by the hypervisor.

In a virtual environment, there are three stacks of memory: the application virtual memory and guest "physical" memory as well as the actual physical memory of the host machine. Figure 5.11 illustrates the hierarchy of memory. The hypervisor is between the host and the guest OS. The guest OS or virtual machine behaves like an actual machine and is not aware of the hypervisor, sort of like the humans not being aware that they are in a virtual world in *The Matrix*. When the guest OS requires memory, the hypervisor provides it by mapping to the physical host memory.

FIGURE 5.11 Memory tiers in a virtualized system

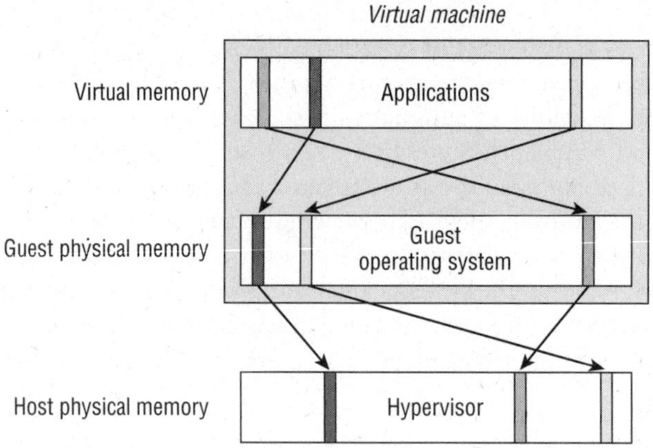

The host memory is finite, so it eventually runs out, but the guest OS has no idea of this, so the hypervisor has to collect memory back through the balloon driver, which collects the free memory from the guest OS. So, for example, if the guest OS has been allocated 4 GB of memory, after using most of it, it marks 2 GB as free. Since it does not know about the memory mapping to the host physical memory, the free memory remains in the guest OS. It is this free memory that the balloon driver collects. And as mentioned, if there is not enough free memory to give to the driver, the guest OS will decide which areas of memory have to be paged so that it can free memory to give to the balloon driver for remapping for other purposes.

I/O Throttling

Even with top-end hardware, and lots of it, computing resources are finite, so intelligent management is key for proper distribution and ensuring satisfaction. Aside from reclamation of memory through ballooning, you can implement I/O throttling to control access to your slowest resource, the disks.

I/O throttling is a function of the hypervisor that can be activated to set the maximum rate at which all guest OSs or virtual machines in the system are allowed to initiate I/O with real devices. This excludes the I/O operations that are initiated by the hypervisor itself.

The hypervisor converts the specified rate into a buffer time, the minimum time in which there must be no I/O operation occurring. So if an I/O request is received before the time in between I/O operations is past, that request is deferred or delayed.

In multitenant systems such as cloud computing systems where devices, channels, and control units are shared, throttling is an effective method for preventing one system from overutilizing shared resources.

CPU Wait Time

CPU wait time is the time the CPU is waiting for a certain process to finish instead of processing something else. This is usually because it is waiting for an important portion of a current process it is working on, such as waiting for synchronization or I/O operations to finish. This is why I/O operations must be kept at a manageable level.

Impact of Configuration Changes

Configuration management is an important aspect of any system, especially one where downtime is not tolerated. Configuration drift and unauthorized configuration changes are said to account for more than 70 percent of IT service outages. Improper configuration also contributes to performance issues and performance degradation and impacts IT productivity and budget as a result.

 Real World Scenario

Impacts of Unauthorized Changes

Change management is essential to foster a consistent and robust system, and the first step is to ensure that all configuration changes are known, planned, and approved.

What happens when this essential aspect is not addressed? Take, for example, a firmware development organization that develops firmware for automobile computers. The computers are connected to various sensors that provide them with information so that they can adjust various performance characteristics of the car in real time. The organization uses the C language and a compiler specifically configured for creating its firmware.

Now it just so happens that the company is pushing for new features that need new sets of code that have not been used before. Unfortunately, the new implementation does not compile with the current compiler configuration. Believing that the code is already perfect and that the problem lies with the compiler configuration not being compatible with the new code, the build engineer tweaks the compiler to allow it to finish building without notifying management. The code compiles and the firmware is delivered and functioning without a hitch. There are no problems until a new update is needed. Together with the older compilation, the newer code in the update compiles with the tweaked compiler, creating situations that cause the computer to malfunction.

It just so happened that the build engineer had already long ago left the company, so it takes a very long time for the developers to pinpoint the cause simply because the change the engineer made to the compiler was not documented.

Configuration tracking is an approach in which special software is employed to track the various settings and configuration used in the system that happen across virtual and physical environments. Understanding what sort of impact a certain change will bring is quite difficult sometimes, but it starts with authorization. If a change was not authorized, chances are it is an error or a breach may be occurring at that instance. But even though certain changes have been assessed and mandated, understanding the potential impact of those changes is still a constant challenge. It's this area of uncertainty where IT services sometimes lose control, and this breeds an environment that is vulnerable to security breaches, service infractions, or inability to comply as well as causing outages.

An organization must have a firm grasp of the configuration of its system and must balance dynamic business needs and initiatives without losing control. The formula for doing this is found in the section "Configuration Management" in Chapter 4, "Cloud Management."

Common Issues

In a system with hundreds of different components that range from physical hardware to various firmware and software applications that are essential to the system functioning properly, one of them is bound to eventually fail. Software is easy to fix through configuration or reinstallation, but hardware must always be totally replaced when it fails. Here are some common hardware failure issues.

Disk Failure   Disk failure is one of the most common types of failure you will see in a data center environment, especially one with vast storage area networks (SANs) used to keep up with customer database demand. This one is common because the HDD is composed of mechanical parts that are very small and moving at extremely high speeds. Because of the size of the mechanical components, they cannot be made to be absolutely durable, so a common failure point for any hard drive is its mechanical part. The electronic components like the controllers can fail as well.

A disk that is about to fail will often have various obvious symptoms like bad sectors despite proper file system management and maintenance and slower I/O speeds than expected, or it will shut down and then restart. A drive could fail and then after reboot run again for a while. This is a sure sign that the drive will totally fail in the near future. Constant backups and employing RAID configurations can mitigate the resulting impact, but they can never stop the inevitability of a disk failure.

HBA Failure   Host bus adapters are pretty much like network interface controllers; they are separate modules attached to the module slots of a computer system. The HBA serves to provide I/O processing as well as physical connectivity between a server and a storage device or cluster of devices. They serve to offload processing from the CPU so that it can concentrate on other matters.

This is a crucial point of failure because if a host bus adapter fails during important I/O operations, the data could be lost. Unfortunately, there is no exact way of telling when it fails because most electronic devices will just fail without warning. But some would exhibit signs such as intermittent disconnection with attached storage devices or I/O operations getting dropped or taking longer than normal.

Memory Failure   Main memory is one of the core components of a computer system. Everyone in IT knows that RAM performance is key to system performance and that memory failure is not an option, at all. Disks can be configured for backup and redundancy, but there are no such options for memory. A memory failure can cause an entire system to crash because the memory module that failed may contain important data that is being used by the system or its components. A computer will not even start when there is a defective memory module attached to it. So it is imperative to always check a system's memory, and signs of failure must detected ahead of time to prevent costly and untimely downtime.

NIC Failure   The network interface card (NIC) is a computer system's gateway to the network and beyond. It is the main communication interface and important for a distributed system that is supposed to be accessible from anywhere in the world. However, it is also fault tolerant. Losing a NIC would mean losing connectivity, but that does not involve system failure. There would be network downtime and the server might not be accessible, but it is an easily containable and preventable failure through the use of NIC teaming/bonding or link aggregation. It is certainly not as fatal as memory and CPU failure.

CPU Failure   The central processing unit (CPU) is the brain of the computer, hence the word *central*. CPU failure would mean utter and total failure. A CPU failure is one of the worst kinds of failure, in terms of cost and lost productivity, that can occur in your system. It ensures total shutdown of the system, and most operations will be nonrecoverable. The CPU is also one of the most expensive parts of the system and one of the hardest to replace in terms of installation. Unlike a NIC, HBA, or disk, which can all simply be plugged into the board or various sockets, the CPU must be completely removed and then replaced.

Summary

This chapter is all about performance of the infrastructure rather than the virtualized environment of cloud computing. We focused more on the concepts of how most of the hardware parts can perform and fail. The most prominent of these parts is the disk drive, which is incidentally also the largest bottleneck of the system. The speed and performance of the disk drive has hardly improved since the 1990s, but the capacity and affordability of the technology has improved by leaps and bounds. So it is this relatively weak performance that we examined. For a disk, its key performance indicators are its access time and the data transfer rate. The access time is the time it takes for the mechanical parts to position the read/write head on top of the track and sector that contains the data it is looking for. Taken into account are the spindle speed, which rotates the disk and is measured by revolutions per minute, and the actuator arm lateral movement speed, which brings the head over the correct track.

The file system also plays a major role in the performance of a storage system. It is important that the file system be configured specifically, tailor-made if you will, to your purpose, which is cloud and distributed computing. Common file systems used in this area are FFS and NFS. Most operating system users, especially Windows users, take the file system for granted because it is largely invisible to them, so it takes a back seat when enthusiast modders and gamers tweak their computer's performance. But for a service entity that deals almost exclusively in data, the file system is probably one of the most important factors in the service infrastructure. This is where most of the performance in the system can be attained or lost because cloud applications are mostly data related and data dependent. From the file system, you can control I/O operations and metadata operations, which helps to speed up various processes through proper tuning.

We also discussed various methods that help increase disk and memory performance, such as I/O tuning and disk swapping or paging.

Chapter Essentials

Performance Concepts   Although a multitenant cloud system is a diverse system with many capabilities, all of them are tied to data, which is in turn stored in disks. When talking about performance concepts, we often mean the criteria for which we judge a specific system or its constituents. In the case of cloud computing, it is usually the database and the storage system.

File system performance, I/O operations rate of processing, read and write operation speeds, and metadata performance are a few of these performance concepts that an IT professional, not just a cloud expert, should be familiar with.

Disk Performance   The disk is kind of like the bread and butter of the enterprise. Since disk performance has not really improved by leaps and bounds in the last decade, we are left with finding the right drives from the right manufacturers by taking advantage of every microsecond of performance we can. We are looking for great performance in access time and data transfer rate, which are characterized by the internal mechanical parts of the drive.

Disk Tuning   This is the optimization of a disk's performance in conjunction with other hardware and the software platform that is used to manage it. Obviously you cannot make a disk perform any better or faster than it's capable of, unlike processors, which can be overclocked. You can only make them perform at their best through proper configuration of settings and tuning the file system itself to work in the best way possible. You must take into account the actual performance of the disks being used, which is reduced to really just limiting I/O requests to the disks and doing batch file access and transfers because the disks are pretty much the biggest bottleneck in any system.

Swap Disk Space   The swap disk space is essentially a specially assigned portion of the disk that is being used as a place to temporarily store data from the main memory, known as pages, so that it can free up memory space for more urgent applications. This is process is widely known as paging and that space is called the page file. The size of the page file is ideally set to 1 percent to 5 percent of the total disk capacity, or it can simply mimic the size of the memory itself, so if the system has 8 GB of memory, then the swap disk space should also be 8 GB.

I/O Tuning   Moving away from the disks, because their performance is more or less consistent and hardware driven, we set our attentions to I/O operations, which by and large dictate the work that the disks do and to an extent the CPU wait times that we have to endure. I/O tuning involves working with the correct number of disks and memory as well as a lot of scheduling and prioritization. This includes setting buffer times between I/O calls to the disk. For this process, you must first test the actual performance of the disk in terms of read and write speeds and then factor that with the actual performance that is expected of the system, and that will determine the number of disks and the settings that will be put in place.

Performance Management and Monitoring Tools   In any cloud service model, there are monitoring tools that keep administrators informed about every aspect of the system, whether it is for IaaS, with monitoring CPU and memory and disk usage levels on the infrastructure, or for SaaS, with it statistics on user and traffic level as well as application and virtual environment health. Some solutions cover the entire cloud, from the hardware infrastructure down to the individual guest OSs running on the system.

Hypervisor Configuration Best Practices   The hypervisor is in many ways like an OS, but it is not as complex and simply serves as an abstraction layer between the underlying hardware infrastructure and the virtual environment. Since this layer serves to control both sides of the system, it is essential that all the settings here be just right. For example, the virtual machines that are running do not know they are virtual and assume that they are alone and that all computing resources they have are theirs alone, so they tend to go wild accessing them. It is the job of the hypervisor to, say, limit the number of I/O requests to the actual disk to prevent overusage by one particular guest OS.

Impact of Configuration Changes to the Virtual Environment   As discussed in the previous chapter, configuration management is important in keeping a system healthy and free of incompatibilities and security threats. But configuration changes have to be made eventually, and understanding the consequences that those changes will be bring is the challenging part. You also have to keep monitoring any changes being made to the system, in real time if possible, because unauthorized changes can lead to big problems such as vulnerabilities and even downtime. And in the event of downtime caused by an undocumented and unforeseen change, the root cause is often hard to track.

Common Issues   As a conglomeration of various complicated parts, the computer system or infrastructure is a well-oiled machine that works well when all the parts are working and comes to a dead stop when one fails, despite the concept of modularity. In this case, modularity is geared toward physical assembly and not functionality because most of these parts are codependent; without one, the whole does not work correctly or at all. That said, common failure points are the disks (because they feature a lot of moving parts), the NIC, HBA, memory, and of course, the CPU.

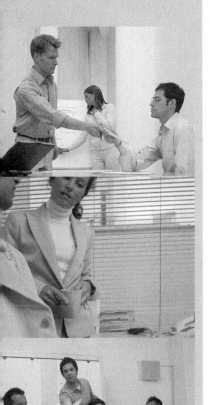

Chapter

6

Cloud Delivery and Hosting Models

TOPICS COVERED IN THIS CHAPTER INCLUDE:

✓ Private

✓ Public

✓ Hybrid

✓ Community

✓ On-premises vs. off-premises hosting

✓ Accountability and responsibility based on delivery models

✓ Security differences between models

✓ Functionality and performance validation based on chosen delivery model

✓ Orchestration platforms

In this chapter, we will discuss different delivery models for the cloud as well as their nuances. Just as with any other service or product, there is no single way to define how a cloud system delivers its services.

As discussed in previous chapters, what makes a cloud is the capability of the system to support its user base and provide vast amounts of computing resources at very reasonable prices. Of course, it has to be scalable and flexible.

Private

The private cloud deployment model is primarily the provisioning of private and unshared IT infrastructure and resources. If an organization already has some kind of data center set up in-house, this model will make a lot of sense because there is no additional capital expense to be rendered and no more installation required, simply reconfiguration of existing infrastructure. However, this doesn't bring in a lot of benefits in terms of cost efficiency, untapped scalability, and managed services, but it is highly effective for organizations having higher security, privacy, and regulatory concerns. A private cloud has two different classifications: full private cloud and semi-private cloud.

Full Private Cloud Deployment Model

As the name suggestions, a full private cloud is a type of cloud that is owned, deployed, and managed entirely by a single organization. It provides cloud-like functionality such as virtual machines, server virtualization, storage virtualization, and software delivery within an organization. This type of deployment is often more expensive than other deployment models and is restricted to a specific capacity. However, it also brings with it stronger security, privacy, and IT control. Take, for example, a private cloud deployed and used within a bank and its branches/offices; it provides banking software, computing resources, and storage just as a cloud would provide but also offers full private benefits such as invisibility from external sources.

The following kinds of organizations are suited for a full private cloud deployment:

- Banks that have an on-premises cloud computing infrastructure that delivers software, computing, storage, security, and backup
- Hospitals and health service providers, which have strict regulatory requirements and implement private cloud and virtualization solutions within their IT facilities
- Military services/armed forces that use secure and protected cloud computing technologies to automate their processes, store data, and share strategic knowledge
- Government institutions that require massive pools of dedicated computing

Semi-private Cloud Deployment Model

This deployment model is rather confusing because it is neither entirely public nor entirely private and yet it's not hybrid either. It is a type of cloud that is provisioned from a cloud service provider that offers an entirely dedicated cloud environment to a client, one that's separate from and not shared with other semi-private cloud customers. In short, it is a non-multitenant cloud service offered by a public cloud service provider that is delivered over public channels but contains all of the characteristics of a private cloud (including security and control) but is still considered to be off-premises. A dedicated server is a common example of a semi-private cloud that runs entirely for a single customer. It is not part of a public cloud environment, is accessed over a secure VPN or web connection, and provides enhanced levels of control of the cloud environment at the customer's side. Organizations looking to leverage the power of a secure and exclusive cloud in a cost-effective way are well suited for this type of cloud deployment model.

The following types of organizations are suited for a semi-private cloud deployment:

- Application developers (mobile/web/SaaS) that can utilize a dedicated server to develop, test, and deploy applications and services
- Banks that deploy and deliver external or partner banking applications through an external cloud
- E-commerce stores and web portals hosted and managed within a private cloud environment located on a provider's premises

Another, similar deployment is co-location, where the customer deploys and houses servers and other computing resources within the cloud service facility of a provider. The service provider maintains, manages, and operates the servers on the customer's behalf and delivers a cloud environment that can be accessed from anywhere over the public Internet. This is a good fit for organizations that are looking for a private cloud solution but have no means of housing a hardware infrastructure and do not want on-premises IT staff and other resources to operate the cloud environment.

Public

The public cloud deployment model is the most widely used and popular deployment model for cloud solutions. It is considered the true form of cloud computing or hosting. Public cloud environments are entirely owned, deployed, monitored, and managed by the cloud service provider. Public cloud customers can generally be any organization or entity that has some computing requirements. The customers can create and access cloud resources such as storage, computing, and software on a metered, pay-as-you-go billing scheme, and they can source virtual servers (from a single virtual server to thousands), cloud storage components, applications, and other resources instantly through a process called *provisioning*. The selling point for public cloud offerings is that customers do not need to spend much on up front capital costs, nor do they have to relinquish ongoing operational costs in order to create, access, and manage such resources. The cloud computing facility is shared by multiple users simultaneously. They each have their own share of computing resources, and their data and processes may intermingle in what appears to be separate machines with other customers' data and processes without them knowing it. This is called *virtualization*, which means that multiple customers are sharing or utilizing the same set of resources.

The following types of organizations are suited for the public cloud deployment model:

- General businesses (small and medium enterprises, or SMEs) using a public cloud to host their applications, back up data and files, and more

- Software developers and publishers that deliver their software on a Software as a Service (SaaS) platform

- IT service providers, managed service providers (MSPs), and value-added resellers (VARs) that use a public cloud to deliver IT solutions and services

Hybrid

The hybrid cloud deployment model enables organizations to keep their data secure and under their control in an on-premises or private cloud environment while also provisioning applications and shared storage from the public cloud. It is a combination of two or more cloud deployment models—specifically, using a private and public cloud. The hybrid cloud model is ideal for organizations that have some reservations about using the cloud but are still interested in gaining its benefits.

The following types of organizations are suited for a hybrid cloud deployment:

- SMEs having multiple IT resource requirements and using a public cloud to balance traffic/computational load from private to public cloud

- IT service providers using a combination of private and public cloud models to service their clients

- Application/software developers using a public cloud for testing, integration, and deployment

Community

A community cloud is a type of cloud computing deployment model that is used between a selective group of users or organizations. A community cloud is generally provisioned using public cloud technologies, but it can also be delivered using the private or even the hybrid model. The community cloud can consist of a number of individuals or organizations working on a joint project and/or collaborating knowledge and data among each other.

The following types of organizations are suited for the community cloud model:

- Scientific research organizations that use the community cloud to perform work on joint projects, research, and experiments

- Government organizations using SaaS application to perform business processes that are deployed and delivered through a community cloud

- Educational institutions sharing a community cloud to perform research and/or share knowledge

On-Premises vs. Off-Premises Hosting

The on-premises versus off-premises debate is nothing new. It existed even before the advent of real cloud computing. Way back in the 1961, John McCarthy of *artificial intelligence (AI)* and *Lisp* fame suggested during a speech given at MIT's centennial that utility computing would become an ideal business model. Following that notion, in the age of mainframes and large supercomputers, computing was mainly done online through early networking technologies. Companies bought computing time from mainframe providers, and users would sit behind extremely slow terminals for hours imputing data and creating reports. It was very labor intensive and costly. This went on for more than a decade until personal computers became powerful enough, with larger storage capacities and cheaper price points, to allow real on-premises computing. These PCs were still extremely slow and expensive compared to today's offerings, but they offered more value compared to the all-online utility computing alternative at that time. Remember your PCs from the '80s? They were essentially as powerful as modern calculators with the price point of high-end workstations. But at that time, they opened up a whole new world of personal computing possibilities, even though they were still considered underpowered at the same time.

As the advantages of computer technology in the '90s pushed businesses to adapt and change or be at a disadvantage, enterprise computing began to take hold. Data centers were being built across the industry to allow businesses to make use of computer technology for business operations. This was now the time of on-premises computing, where large data centers became the core drivers of business processes and where data and data security, as always, became a powerful weapon for large corporations. Then came the new millennium with its focus on online communication, global networking, and the Internet, which changed the landscape once again.

The cycle is now back to utility computing in the guise of cloud computing. But this time around, cloud computing looks to be a better option than just utility computing. It creates opportunities for business and allows smaller organizations to wield the same technological prowess as that of their larger counterparts. Small businesses with no capital to set up their own on-premises data centers can either rent an infrastructure where they can set up their own platforms or leverage already available ones and pay only for what they use. The barrier for entry is really low, which allows small businesses to play in the same field as the big boys.

But this is not exactly the same as when utility computing was apparently the only choice and then after a time on-premises became the only choice. Now both are legitimate choices, with their own pros and cons. One might argue that one of these is better than the other, but the truth is really more neutral: it's situational. We will shed light on the nuances of each one so you may determine for yourself which fits your own situation.

On-Premises Hosting

On-premises hosting of virtual environments essentially points to a private cloud solution. It is any cloud implementation that is set up within an organization's premises, literally within the same building or at least one owned or operated by the organization. This means that all hardware infrastructures as well as the software and configuration maintenance are operated entirely by the organization's own staff within company-owned premises.

This gives an organization total control over every aspect of the cloud environment, from physical and logical security to resource allocation and management. This is especially important for organizations hosting classified information or sensitive information such as financial records. You would never see the CIA, KGB, or any intelligence organization in the world outsource their database needs to a third-party provider. This is an extreme example, but you get the picture. On-premises hosting simply provides the best security options possible, that is, considering that the staff running the show is able to offer a high level of competence.

This option is really best suited for organizations with an existing data center that requires a high level of security, which they can provide themselves. However, for SMBs and startups, on-premises hosting would require a major capital expense. So unless your organization falls under the category mentioned at the beginning of this paragraph, your best bet would be a pure cloud environment. The only real advantages to an on-premises solution are security and total control over all aspects of the system.

Off-Premises Hosting

Only off-premises hosting can really offer the core principles of cloud computing. This is where you can reap the benefits of scalability, flexibility, and affordability as opposed to on-premises hosting. Off-premises hosting relies on third-party providers to serve the hardware infrastructure and resources the customer needs for its very own virtualized cloud infrastructure. This model liberates users from the need to maintain their own in-house infrastructure and the manpower necessary to keep it all together.

Listing all the benefits of off-premises hosting would be redundant because we would simply be reiterating the benefits of cloud computing in general, but here is a short, self-explanatory list:

- Global accessibility
- Scalability
- Built-in business continuity
- Consistency

Miscellaneous Factors to Consider When Choosing between On- or Off-Premises Hosting

Many people choosing between on- and off-premises hosting are focusing on raw face values and losing view of the bigger picture. They tend to look at the simple arithmetic involved of simply adding up-front costs and subscription fees, failing to see that there are actually other factors that may affect the performance and cost throughout their system's lifetime. Most of the factors that should also be considered (described in the following sections) will be pro off premises.

Power/Electricity Costs

This one should be obvious, but it is surprisingly always left out when considering costs associated with running an on-premises system. It is probably because the power bill does not come broken down into insightful tidbits, showing which items are consuming the most power. The bill just encompasses all the consumption of the office or building, so it would not be apparent to the decision makers how to factor the power consumption cost into the total cost of ownership (TCO).

Most computer components—and by extension, computer systems—now consume less power than their equivalents about a decade ago. But that does not mean their electrical consumption has to be ignored. Unlike a laptop or a PC, a solid server contains a mixture of multi-socketed processors, multiple sticks of memory, multiple sets of drives (often arranged in a RAID configuration), multiple NICs and other components required for such a class of computer, cooling systems, and two or more power supplies to power everything. That does not sound like an economical machine; in fact, it sounds like a power-guzzling beast. If we are to make a comparison to vehicles, consider a laptop as a Prius and that server as a Hummer. A server contains a lot of components that a regular PC does not need because the key definers of a server are power, uptime, and availability. That means this thing has to run 24/7.

Bandwidth Costs and Limitations

Off-premises or public cloud solutions can bring a lot of benefits, but just like the power required to run servers in-house, bandwidth issues may come around to haunt you if you do not do enough research.

When your servers are run in-house, you are limited only by your internal network infrastructure because switches and routers would be enough to handle bandwidth-heavy applications inside office walls. Cloud solutions make use of special techniques like teaming and bonding, discussed in the previous chapter, to handle the ever-increasing bandwidth requirements, but that doesn't change the fact that offloading heavy workloads to the cloud requires a wider pipe. Despite the technology being used by your cloud provider to handle bandwidth issues, and they have no trouble handling large file sizes on their end, the ultimate bottleneck would be the end-user Internet connection.

This issue will not matter much when all processes and data traversals occur within your virtualized environment; the problems arise when your actual workflow requires moving large data files to and from your cloud system. Multiply that by the number of people using the service and going about the same types of workflows in your office and you start to feel the strain in your bandwidth limitations. And then there are the latest trend ISPs are following, where they set bandwidth caps, and the speed gets ridiculously throttled after a set limit or exorbitant fees are added on top of your set monthly fee for the excess.

 Because your cloud service provider does not control any variables at your end, you end up having to look for solutions yourself. This is especially problematic in countries with very slow Internet speed standards or in areas with really bad ISPs, which means users really have no real choice.

There is also another caveat from the cloud provider's end: they impose a threshold on bandwidth consumption of data going out of the system. This means that aside from your constant struggles with your ISP for bandwidth on your end, you also have to wrestle with restrictions from your cloud provider. Again, this is not much of a problem if your workload does not involve moving large chunks of data to and from your cloud environment. Providers like Microsoft Azure offer 5 GB of outbound bandwidth, while cloud giant Amazon EC2 allows only 1 GB of outbound bandwidth. After those limits are reached, you might pay somewhere around $8 to $15 per gigabyte excess.

Another factor is the time it takes to move data between the cloud and local workstations. If your business relies heavily on moving large amounts of data every day, then off-premises hosting might not be for you. For example, for an animation studio or game development studio where heavy work is being done using 3D technologies, a cloud file-sharing service or even off-premises cluster-rendering service would not fit. That much data would be served better by in-house hardware.

Hardware Replacements and Upgrades

Hardware replacements and upgrades are not all that uncommon, and the costs are usually categorized as maintenance and upgrade costs. But sometimes, planners do not foresee what is going to happen in five years when the decision to move to a public or private cloud is being made. That entails capital expense and not necessarily upkeep.

The problem with having an on-premises solution is the inflexibility of the implementation. Compared to a public cloud provider that leverages economies of scale in order to grow its infrastructure, an organization dedicated to providing cloud services for itself does not have access to such economies of scale and will therefore be limited in the initial implementation or in adding additional capital for expansion and upgrades. On-premises solutions simply aren't as economical as off-premises or public offerings.

Scalability is another facet of cloud computing that is lost. On-premises solutions tend to be fixed because an organization is not as willing to shell out additional capital expenditure to increase the system's capacity, not unless the returns are really worth it. And organizations that opt for on-premises solutions are usually not ones that make a profit off of their cloud solution directly. They are in it for control and security of data mostly, so a large-capacity upgrade would not make sense economically but may still be very important to maintain operations. This is one of the biggest dilemmas after a few years of running on on-premises solutions.

Over- and Underutilization of Resources

In an on-premises solution, systems are created to exceed the capacity of their maximum usage scenario by a large margin. But during actual usage scenarios, usage almost never reaches that maximum capacity margin, let alone the actual capacity of the system. This leads to underutilization of the system's resources, causing most of them to be idle. This is equipment that has been paid for with a huge capital expense and it is not being used to its full potential. An organization has to consider its highest demand and configure the system for that and not its standard, everyday demand. However, this theoretical limit is seldom reached. In this case, it would be better to avail of the scalability and flexibility of real cloud services so you will pay only for the minimum usage and then occasionally pay more for those rare moments when usage levels peak.

The opposite scenario is overutilization, and it applies to off-premise cloud solutions. When we provision for new servers and more virtual resources, we tend to get so carried away by the prospect of virtually unlimited resources that we forget that there are still imposed limits to our subscriptions and corresponding payments. Sometimes we forget that these virtual machines and servers are semi-persistent, which means they stay on and keep using up resources in the system, and since they are easy to provision, we simply provision more in order to get a fresh environment, especially for testing purposes. But this can add up dramatically and translates to costs. The best solution would be proper management of resources using automatic *deprovisioning* of resources when they are no longer in use.

Automatic provisioning is good for keeping a website afloat despite spikes in traffic, but it has other uses too. In a non-cloud scenario, a server will eventually succumb to a DDoS attack because it cannot handle the sheer number of requests. But in a cloud environment with *auto-provisioning*, your system will keep adding more servers to handle the increasing load, so it will always be able to cope. In a legitimate traffic scenario, this would be good, but in a distributed denial of service (DDoS) attack, it is really bad because costs will skyrocket with false requests and there will be no real customer traffic and so no income—only additional costs. In cases like this, proper settings and attack detection systems are important. Your system should be able to distinguish between legitimate requests and attacks so that it can simply drop requests that aren't legitimate.

Comparing Total Cost of Ownership

On-premises hosting is generally not looked at as cloud computing, even though you might be running the same virtualized infrastructure and software in a real cloud environment. This is because a cloud is defined by its benefits and functions, not necessarily by the technology involved. This all sounds very ideological, but it really is technical. Let's say you generate your own electricity instead of using it from the grid; you are not availing of the electric utility grid even though you are using the same form of electricity. Or suppose you make your own burgers instead of buying them from Burger King.

What we are getting at is that even though what you end up with is the same, the way you get it may pose different advantages and disadvantages, depending on the circumstances. Generating your own power, for example, would require large up front costs compared to taking from the grid, but by making your own burgers, you have the advantage of knowing exactly what ingredients you use, which can result in a cheaper and healthier alternative. So it goes for on-premises and off-premises hosting. They might ultimately bring the same benefits, but a lot of factors will vary. Pricing and costs will be the definitive distinction, especially for SMBs and small office, home office (SOHO) businesses. Table 6.1 shows a rough comparison between costs for both hosting models. The values shown are not exact figures; they are rough estimates because a lot of these costs will vary. The table is a cost comparison for an SMB with 10 employees that must decide whether to host its application in-house or to avail of a real cloud solution.

TABLE 6.1 Cost comparison

Feature Up-Front Costs	On-Premises	Off-Premises	Description
Server hardware	$8,000	$0	Actual server hardware
Server software	$1,500	$0	Windows Server OS licensing, hypervisors, and cloud platform
Backup system	$2,000	$0	Backup solution and software
Miscellaneous equipment	$500	$0	UPS, networking equipment, server rack, and so on
Installation or migration	$3,000	$2000	Labor costs to set up the server and migrate the old system into the new server
Total Up-Front Cost	**$15,000**	**$2,000**	

Feature	On-Premises	Off-Premises	Description
Up-Front Costs			
Recurring Costs			
Maintenance and monitoring	$350	Included	Personnel expenses
Offsite/online backup	$50	Included	Disaster recovery solutions
Upkeep	$800	Included	Electricity and other utilities
Cloud hosting	$0	$1,000	Monthly subscription fee
Total Recurring Cost	**$1,200**	**$1,000**	
Unplanned repairs	$2,000 × 3	$0	May be caused by accidents and natural calamities and assuming it happens three times over the life of the system
TCO over expected life	$93,000	$60,000	Assuming a five-year life span

 Real World Scenario

Cloud Usage

Rackspace did a survey of 1,300 U.K. and U.S. companies together with the Manchester Business School regarding their cloud usage.

The study found that 88 percent of users of cloud computing have pointed to cost savings as the determining factor, and 56 percent of respondents agreed that cloud services have helped them boost profits. Additionally, 60 percent of respondents said cloud computing has reduced the need for their IT team to maintain infrastructure, giving them more time to focus on strategy and innovation. And indeed, 62 percent of the companies that have saved money are reinvesting those savings into the business to increase headcount, boost wages, and drive product innovation.

Table 6.1 clearly shows that over the expected life of the system, on-premises solutions tend to be more expensive. However, what we did not take into consideration here are some intangible factors such as security, control, and compliance, which may tip the scales toward on-premises solutions, especially if all three are required by the organization. If this is the case, then there won't even be a comparison at all.

Accountability and Responsibility Based on Delivery Models

Cloud computing changed how IT-based services are provided. It is a paradigm shift that brings various complications, raising questions about accountability and responsibility in the case of outages.

Traditional delivery of applications has been offered by vertically integrated organizations. Both hardware and software were already bundled together and purchased from a single supplier that was solely accountable for the product's performance. However, the cloud environment mixes things up because there are a lot of entities that have a stake in the system; there are infrastructure providers, simple cloud application providers and resellers, cloud environment providers, network providers, end-point ISPs, and many others. So when an outage occurs, who is to blame?

Private Cloud Accountability

For a private cloud or on-premises solution, responsibility and accountability reside with the organization itself, although it may extend to the equipment manufacturer or distributor in the case of hardware failure and software bugs. But for the most part, the maintenance and security of the system are the responsibilities of the IT department. This is simply because a private cloud or on-premise solution is, as we discussed earlier in the chapter, implemented behind the corporate firewall and maintained by the local IT department. It utilizes internal resources and is designed to offer benefits similar to those of the public cloud without relinquishing control of data and security as well as the recurring costs associated with public solutions.

Because the decision to implement a private cloud is usually influenced by the organization's need to maintain absolute control of the virtual environment, often due to business or even regulatory reasons, the organization itself remains responsible and accountable. That will not matter much, however, because users are often internal, part of the organization. But if there are external users, as is the case with most banking institutions, security concerns and outages should be shouldered by the organization, particularly by its IT department. This is really no different than other kinds of services.

However, if specific problems are the cause of security breaches, impairments, and outages, the responsibility can be passed on to the hardware manufacturer or software developer. For example, if a specific brand of NIC contains an inherent vulnerability that allows hackers to pass despite software-level restrictions and security measures, then the NIC manufacturer can be held accountable for releasing an inherently vulnerable product. The same goes for software, and that is why software is being patched periodically after various exploits and vulnerabilities are discovered by the developers themselves through extended testing or are found because of an attack. Whatever the case, the blame will initially be placed on the one running the show.

Individual hardware and software distributors for different parts used in the system assume responsibility and accountability by releasing regular software maintenance and updates because, technically, customers are still regularly paying licensing fees in some cases.

Public Cloud Accountability

Various entities are working to clarify and standardize many things about the cloud, and determining who is responsible when something goes wrong is one of them. But those standards are not in place yet, so we turn to the old-fashioned way, which is to dig a bit and try to evenly spread the blame. In a public cloud offering, data owners are ultimately accountable for maintaining control and security over their own information. However, the cloud introduces a shared level of responsibility between the data owner and the cloud service provider together with all other players in the system.

To understand better the complexity of the cloud, we must each look at the key roles of the players in the arena:

Infrastructure Suppliers   They develop the equipment and software used for IP networking in all cloud service and delivery models. They develop the hardware (such as the processors and memory), the servers themselves, NICs, storage devices, networking equipment, server software, *hypervisors*, and other essential parts of the system. Example players would be HP and Dell for full servers, Intel for some processors and storage devices as well, and Microsoft for operating systems such as Windows Server 2012.

IP Network Providers   These provide the networking infrastructure in and out of the cloud system and include most telecommunications companies and ISPs. They provide networking services to service providers and end users alike. You will know who they are depending on your region because they will be the ones providing you with telephone lines, cellular services, and Internet access (for example, AT&T in the United States and Vodafone in Europe). They need infrastructure suppliers to create their vast networks.

Cloud Service Providers   These entities own the computing equipment and infrastructure where cloud environments are set up. They buy equipment and services from the infrastructure suppliers and IP network providers. Notable ones are Amazon Web Services (AWS), Google Cloud, Microsoft Cloud, and Rackspace.

Cloud Consumers These are not really the end users as you might thing. They are also known as resellers; they buy services from cloud service providers through service models such as IaaS and SaaS and then push them to the end user in different flavors. The best example of this would be website owners that lease computing resources from cloud service providers in order to create virtual web servers that in turn serve the end users who visit the website. Well-known companies like Pinterest, Instagram, and Netflix rely on cloud service providers to keep their services running, in particular AWS.

End Users As the name suggests, end users are at the end point of the business hierarchy, the consumers. They can be individuals or other businesses or organizations who make use of the system and are not part of its distribution or upkeep. They make use of their own equipment and IP networks providers.

These are the key players, and each has its own responsibilities and accountability toward the system, which varies depending on the situation.

Responsibility for Service Impairments

Outages can be the result of vulnerabilities or imperfections in the software and applications, the hardware, the cloud environment itself, the network, and data. They can even be due to operational and service policies as well as natural disasters and human error. In the telecommunications sector, three traditional categories have been identified for outage accountability:

Product-Attributable Outages These are outages that result from hardware or software faults such as malfunctioning hardware and software bugs.

Customer- or Provider-Attributable Outages Includes downtime caused by scheduled maintenance and human errors. In the case of customers, their equipment or network could be the cause of an outage.

Externally Attributable Outages These outages are out of the control of operators and humans. Natural disasters and malicious acts fall into this category.

Accountability for problems with cloud servers is more complex, so these categories don't really apply. For example, accountability is usually now split between the cloud consumer and the service provider because the two of them are working together to deliver cloud services to end users. The service providers usually provide the virtual and hardware infrastructure while the cloud consumers make use of this infrastructure to run their applications, which end users ultimately use. We can break down accountability on a per-element basis, according to a portion of cloud services.

Accountability Categories

Cloud computing is all about interaction between many different layers of application, platform, infrastructure, and network. Different layers might be offered by different providers. Because multiple entities can be involved, the effects of problems with each layer may go well beyond the normal business domain of a provider. Thus, it can be difficult to determine exactly who is accountable during a failure or an outage. Here, we clearly distinguish among various layers:

Infrastructure Suppliers These are suppliers of computing, networking, storage, and other hardware and platform elements that will be used by the cloud service provider to form its infrastructure. They are responsible for ensuring that their products and equipment are reliable and robust.

Virtual Appliance Suppliers These suppliers provide the software-only appliances like hypervisors and server operating systems and are responsible for ensuring the stability and reliability of their software offering.

Network Service Provider The network service provider is responsible for availability and keeping the network running robustly at all times.

Cloud Service Provider The cloud service provider provides the cloud computing infrastructure and facilities and are therefore responsible for the robust and reliable delivery of cloud services.

Cloud Consumers Cloud consumers are usually companies that offer services using a third-party cloud infrastructure. They directly interface with the cloud service providers by making use of the infrastructure, so they are responsible for the proper provisioning, configuring, and operation of the cloud applications that they push to end users.

End Users End users represent the final destination of cloud services, where service impairments and outages may be attributed to operation, configuration, and failure of the end user device or equipment.

The different cloud service models will play a part in the determination of service outage responsibilities as well as the terms of agreement between the parties involved in the provision or reception of service. Also, a single organization may hold responsibilities in multiple categories, depending on the nature of their business. For example, a telecom giant like AT&T is a network service provider, a cloud service provider, and a cloud consumer all at the same time simply because it chooses to do business in all three categories.

Security Differences between Models

This is where most people believe the difference between the delivery models lie: security. The argument is that on-premises, private cloud solutions are more secure than their off-premises or public counterparts because of customization and control. This can be true in some unique circumstances, especially if the organization deals with sensitive information and uses proprietary safety mechanisms to protect that information.

Multitenancy Issues

Multitenancy has been considered an important factor in cloud computing scalability and savings. It allows multiple users (tenants) to make use of the same application and database instance but retain individual control of the application, and their data remains virtually separate from each other. Even though they are using the same application instance, to the user it seems like they are using their very own configurable instance of the application.

Multitenancy vs. Multi-instance

The term *multitenancy* is not the same as *multi-instance*, which means each user is given a separate instance of the application and database. Multitenancy allows for easier maintenance of applications because only a single application instance needs to be updated. In a multi-instance scenario, multiple instances of the same application with different configurations need to be updated.

Multitenancy, when implemented correctly, poses little danger to its tenants in terms of the separation of data unraveling, causing one tenant to end up with another tenant's data. The danger here is different. First and foremost is the security risk involved if an attack or breakdown should occur. In the event of an external attack, an attacker who manages to break into an instance of an application has the potential to access all of the data owned by all tenants using that application. The same goes for a fatal error where the database instance of an application simply unravels and all data is lost, which means that the data of no tenant currently using that application instance is safe. It's a one-for-all, all-for-one scenario, for both good and bad events.

Multitenant systems also tend to be a bit inflexible because of the way multitenancy has to be implemented. This includes the location of data, which cannot be altered at will because all of that segregation is done automatically by the system, so data may be scattered across different geographical locations. This poses big problems for organizations with strict compliance guidelines that need to be followed. For example, it is a compliance requirement for businesses in Europe to store data for specific people in the country in which they reside. For example, data for German people has to be placed in a storage location within Germany. So in this case, a multitenant system would cause the organization to fail to meet its compliance requirements and possibly face some kind of punishment.

This is also a problem for competitors, who for obvious reasons may not want to share space with each other. In a multitenant environment, Coca-Cola's data may reside in the same database instance as that of PepsiCo (the makers of Pepsi).

This problem does not occur in a private or on-premises solution. Even though multitenancy can be implemented in a private cloud, the previously mentioned problems do not manifest because those tenants are simply individual users of the organization, so if ever there is a successful attack, only one entity is affected. Regulations are easily dealt with as well because the owner of the private cloud has total control over where it places its data and how to go about it.

Data Segregation

Hand in hand with multitenancy, data segregation poses a unique problem for users of public cloud environments. As multitenants sharing the same software and database instance, all of their data is being stored in the same location, but through some clever data segregation techniques, it will appear to each tenant that their application is unique and separate. That does not, however, detract from the fact that data of one tenant is mingled with another's data. One issue here is if there is a mistake in multitenancy implementation where the wrong set of data is provided to the wrong requesting tenant, the possibility of inadvertently sharing sensitive information is tremendous.

Again, in a private cloud solution with only a single organization using the system, multitenancy and data segregation problems are nonissues.

Network Isolation

Network isolation is an essential component in a *multitenant* virtualized environment like the cloud because without it, tenants sharing the same physical infrastructure will unintentionally, or at times intentionally, be able to consume a large portion of the network and may be able to intrude on the networks and data of other tenants. It's essentially the same principle as in an apartment building: you do not rent a whole floor to a group of people and have them reside within the same four walls; instead, you subdivide and isolate the space physically using walls. In the case of a cloud environment, the networks and spaces are separated virtually. A proper network design that includes security and resource control will mitigate these issues.

There are two different types of network isolation that may be applicable in different scenarios:

Network Traffic Isolation   This method can be used to provide a first-level type of security and higher bandwidth for specific tenants or users to implement special chargeback policies and support tiered networks. This involves isolating special kinds of network traffic such as traffic for LAN-based backups, FTP transfers, and replication traffic.

The first aspect is the creation of individual segmented networks, which can be done physically or logically (virtually). When it's done physically, dedicated NICs will be assigned to specific applications. For logical isolation, applications such as VLANs are required, or you could create multiple logical listening end points to partition physical network resources. When it's done logically, each application will be using the same physical network resources, such as NICs, but it will see only resources and traffic assigned to it and not that of other applications.

To do this, a cloud provider must be able to understand how bandwidth is being consumed through monitoring and control of both physical and virtual network resources. Providers must be able to do the following:

- Identify possible bottlenecks to prevent network congestion in time and gather security data, which may help in preventing *denial of service (DoS) attacks*.

- Understand network-related traffic trends in order to properly charge network-related services.
- Establish proper service-level agreements (SLAs) and meet quality of service (QoS) promises and goals.

Network Security Isolation   This type of isolation can be built on top of network traffic isolation to ensure that database traffic is authenticated and secure for trusted clients. This can be implemented using encryption such as SSL/TLS and HTTPS and some other authentication protocol, such as allowing or denying database service access through validation rules.

Functionality and Performance Validation

Reliable performance will always be a requirement for a cloud environment. But aside from the specific performance metrics that were discussed in the previous chapter, such as disk and file system performance, performance of the system as a whole should also be validated. This means that all aspects must be taken into consideration, including end-to-end performance.

On-Premises Performance

Private cloud and on-premises solutions have a responsibility to internal customers. All performance is controlled internally, so there will be no problem regarding validation because performance will depend on the IT department and its competence. Still, benchmarking and testing have to be done in order to objectively conclude that a system is performing as expected according to specifications.

The methods used for validating and testing cloud performance do not stray too far from traditional software and system performance testing methods. The tools might differ because of different parameters, but the general process remains pretty close. The test team may get creative and test for other parameters, such the ability of the system to detect DoS attacks from legitimate massive traffic inflow.

Off-Premises Performance

Off-premises and public cloud solutions vary from their counterparts in one aspect, location. The cloud infrastructure, including hardware and the virtualized environment, may remain similar for on-premises and off-premises infrastructures, but a lot of other variables get introduced that affect the end user experience drastically. One is the public network between the cloud environment and the user. The Internet is a collection of networks owned and operated by different organizations, which means that there could be thousands of different configurations that may affect end-to-end performance. Even if the cloud environment is performing at peak conditions, the system between it and the user may be experiencing difficulties, and there may be a lot of *black holes* along the way.

But for these external systems, the responsibility of performance validation already falls to the service provider, so the users simply have to access the service provider's data sheets regarding benchmarks. Still, some types of tests are hard to replicate or perform. For example, for cloud applications with fluctuating or unpredictable user traffic, there is no definite way of predicting traffic surge, so systems may be tested on threshold levels or whatever settings have been put up in order to cope with such situations. If the regular traffic is between 1,000 and 2,000 users using the application concurrently, then a threshold of 3,000 may be set so that the system will automatically provision new instances to handle more users and initiate *load balancing*.

Types of Testing

As mentioned earlier, the testing methods are similar to software and system testing methods, so they will be familiar to most:

Stress Testing   This type of test will determine the ability of the system to maintain performance beyond an identified breaking point. This is usually done by simulating peak loads and creating scenarios with extreme circumstances. A stress test will test the cloud application's or system's ability to scale with load and traffic.

Load Testing   Often load and stress testing are grouped together because of their similarities. Load testing simply determines if a system can handle its advertised loads effectively. Going beyond that is already the realm of stress testing.

Performance Testing   This involves benchmarking the system's various performance characteristics (some aspects of performance testing are discussed in Chapter 5). It enables the tester to find bottlenecks and areas where performance enhancements are still possible.

Functional Testing   Functional testing, as the name suggests, is simply testing the various functions of the cloud application or system to make sure they work as advertised and according to the specifications.

Latency Testing   This is one of the more unique types of testing performed on cloud and network systems. The idea here is to test the response of the system from a user's perspective. It doesn't necessarily test latency between the system's various components, although that is certainly included, but latency between the system and the user. Latency testing takes into consideration a lot of external variables that may differ from user to user because the networks between them and the cloud environment would be entirely different. So this test can be done more effectively on the user's end than on the provider's end.

Orchestration Platforms

Orchestration is traditionally described as the automated management of complex computer systems, which includes automatic arrangement and coordination of applications, middleware, and resources. This applies to any and all fields of IT, but the popularity of cloud computing within this decade has made it an ad hoc cloud-related term. It almost seems to be tailor-made for cloud computing. It somewhat suggests a level of autonomy and even some intelligence because of its effects, but that is largely just an association because, technically, it is simply automation done right using elements of control theory.

For our purposes, it is the ability of an organization to automate the processes of managing the cloud environment and any underlying infrastructure. It is used to simplify and accelerate the delivery of cloud services. The delivery of cloud computing solutions goes through a series of intense and complex IT and system orchestration processes at a very granular level. Orchestration is the key driver behind cloud computing technology because it enables IT and other computing resources to be created and provisioned automatically. A key example is how users access software services by provisioning virtual machines or servers in order to deliver websites and other cloud applications.

With literally no installation and complexity at the user end, cloud applications can be used from a standard web browser and the cloud orchestration platform automatically connects the user to the server infrastructure hosting the application for seamless connectivity and control. The API calls, port selection, and all other aspects of connectivity are managed by the primary or host software and installed and deployed at the software server or the web server end, not at the user end.

The following IT resources can be orchestrated using the cloud:

Computing Power   Virtual computer and servers can instantly be provisioned and are available for use by the end users. Users just need to sign up for the service and select a type of server/computer to use, and they are instantly provided with an interface to connect to it and install the operating system and other related applications. In most cases, service providers provide templates of virtual or cloud servers that include a predefined specification, an operating system, and possibly business or workflow applications.

Orchestration is typically achieved through virtual machine creation software such as a hypervisor. KVM, Oracle Virtual Box, and Microsoft Hyper-V are popular virtual machine software packages. For enterprise orchestration and automation solutions, most popular vendors such as Microsoft and VMware provide server or enterprise cloud automation and management software. Multiple virtual computers and virtual servers can be provisioned in very little time, and with just a few key strokes multiple virtual machine instances can be created.

Cloud Storage   As with other compute resources, cloud storage is supported by orchestration. Typically, to provision cloud storage, you make use of storage management software that controls the entire storage infrastructure, which is usually already a part of the cloud management platform. The capacity of the virtual drives is not derived from a single drive and not even from a single location or cluster but may be a composite of storage devices from different availability zones and countries.

The cloud storage supports or works on hardware abstraction. For instance, if a single availability zone or even data center has a measly total of 1,000 terabytes and a user simply needs to provision a 100 GB virtual drive, the orchestration platform will not take all of that 100 GB from that single zone, even though it has more than enough resources for it. It will take from different zones and centers allocated for the user. However, for the end user, it will show up as a single virtual storage capacity or drive with 100 GB available storage, and the user will have no idea where the actual data will be stored physically.

The multitenant architecture of the cloud separates the storage drives or allocated storage areas of each user from each other. This is usually done through the management software or virtualization management software that creates a logical boundary between each storage instance. It decides where each data object will be kept and stored, how it will be accessed and managed, and how other administrative processes that ensure the cloud storage performs as expected are performed. For security reasons, the data is usually encrypted by default when stored.

Software   Software orchestration is perhaps the most common form of orchestration on the cloud. It is performed by the core cloud software itself. In fact, orchestration is a key implementation of SaaS offerings. SaaS orchestration manages how each software instance will be accessed, creation and assignment of APIs, allocation of server resources, network connectivity, and port access. This enables software to be accessed by multiple users simultaneously, each having a separate interface and without interfering with the work and data of other users. This is the core function of multitenancy.

Network   Network resources serve as the backbone of any IT solution. Its importance has become much more prevalent in recent times, specifically with cloud solutions that heavily depend on the underlying network infrastructure to deliver IT solutions and services to end users globally. Network orchestration involves a substantial amount of work that needs to be organized and aligned to ensure availability of network services to all nodes, software, and requesting services. Network orchestration usually happens in real time, so the changes are applied and take affect instantly. These changes may be on an individual node or the entire network. Network orchestration also helps in reinstating a network when problems disrupt normal network operations.

Summary

In this chapter, you learned about the different delivery and hosting models of cloud computing. Some people may initially confuse delivery with the service models such as SaaS and IaaS, which is understandable because service and delivery are usually tied together. But these topics are covered in Chapter 12.

We reviewed the three main delivery models—private, public, and hybrid—and also the community delivery model. In a private cloud, service is dedicated to a single entity or organization, yet its deployment may be both on-premises or off-premises, as is the case of co-location and private cloud hosting services. Co-location and private cloud hosting offers the same control as on-premises solutions, but the performance and security may be different because both hosting models have to be accessed via the public Internet. Even using VPN and other tunneling protocols, running through public infrastructure may still pose a certain level of security risk as compared to running everything on-premises.

Public clouds, on the other hand, are always hosted off premises because, as the name suggests, they are open to the general public. In this model, a cloud service provider provides the infrastructure as well as the virtualized environments, complete with orchestration and other platform-specific functions, while at the same time employing multitenancy to maximize the use of resources. However, this poses some valid security concerns, especially if the multitenancy has not been implemented properly. This might lead to users unexpectedly having access to the networks and data of other users. To mitigate this problem, network isolation and user isolation are applied so that each user will see only their own network and data, as if they are the only ones using the system. This offers economy of scale for the provider and allows the provider to constantly add hardware infrastructure for added resources in order to cope with customer demand. It also allows scaling, a major selling point of cloud computing. Compliance issues are among the concerns about this model since some countries have special compliance requirements (for example, data belonging to a certain country and its people must stay within the borders of that country). There is no single way to isolate data for each user because it would mean reimplementation of the cloud platforms. Organizations with similar compliance requirements have to resort to private or hybrid solutions, which offer a little bit of both worlds.

The hybrid cloud model is essentially a combination of both private and public cloud solutions. As long as there is one aspect of the organization's system that is being conducted in a private cloud environment and another in a public cloud environment, the system can be called a hybrid. A good example for this is a company that deals with a lot of customers with sensitive financial information and data that has to be kept under close surveillance; the company places the data in-house in an on-premises private cloud while the user portals and other publicly accessible applications are being offered through a public cloud service.

A community model is more of an application of one or more of the delivery and hosting models. It is essentially a cloud that is being shared by different organizations to facilitate faster communication and sharing of data and resources. Oftentimes, this is done through a public cloud service, but if the collaboration is secretive, such as classified research of company secrets, then the cloud can be a private one owned by one of the collaborators, probably the biggest one. As with any system, this can be implemented using a hybrid cloud, with sensitive information kept in a private cloud and the interface between community members accessed through a public cloud or application.

Chapter Essentials

Private Cloud   The private cloud is a type of cloud deployment model that is dedicated to serving a single entity or organization. It does not fully realize all of the benefits of true public computing but also does not fall into the same traps. This model is appropriate for those that can afford and really require the added security and those that have special compliance requirements. However, a private cloud solution is not necessarily on premises. A private cloud can also be an off-premise solution, such as co-location services and solutions sold by private cloud vendors, such as a private cloud infrastructure delivered through public networks.

Public Cloud   A public cloud is any cloud service with an infrastructure that is offered to the general public that shares its resources. A public cloud is what experts consider to be the true cloud, with all of its theoretical benefits and features such as affordability, flexibility, and scalability. This is mainly because of the multitenant model, which allows the service provider to maximize hardware infrastructure resources and achieve savings through economies of scale, which in turn allows the service provider to keep on adding resources to support scalability and the growth of the customers. The public cloud will always be an off-premises solution.

Hybrid Cloud   A hybrid cloud is the combination of both public and private clouds, though it does not necessarily mean the best of both worlds, or the worst of both, because benefits will vary depending on how the hybrid solution is implemented. Essentially, a part of the system will be public in nature and procured from a service provider, such the website and all of its application. But the other part, the part that requires more security and probably needs to comply with some special regulations, such as customer data, would have to be kept in a private on-premises cloud. Banks use this model all the time; the public interface is through a public cloud, but all customer data remains in-house.

Community   A community cloud is a mere application of cloud computing and not so much an independent cloud computing model. It is essentially an implementation where a community of entities or organizations makes use of the same cloud environment to facilitate better communication and sharing of resources and data. The implementation can be private (where one of the community members shares the use of its private cloud), public (where the community makes use of the same public cloud service), or a little bit of both.

On-Premises vs. Off-Premises Hosting   Some people confuse on-premises and off-premises hosting as private or public cloud services, respectively, because they associate *private* with *in-house* and *public* as the opposite. In fact, private clouds can be hosted both on premises and off premises as in a private cloud Infrastructure as a Service (IaaS) solution or a co-location service. Public clouds, on the other hand, are always off premises because the real benefits of cloud computing can be achieved only through public subscriptions and multitenancy. On-premises hosting is considered more secure yet more expensive in terms of capital expenditures, while off-premises hosting is considered to have more benefits like flexibility, scalability, and affordability, but it takes a perceived hit on security and control.

Accountability and Responsibility Based on Delivery Models   The cloud adds another layer of complexity to the delivery of IT services because so many entities are involved. With this complexity, who is to blame when something goes wrong? For example, if your provider experiences downtime, it may not be their fault. It may be due to some inherent problems in the design of a hardware component they use. However, in this case, they must still answer to their customers, while the manufacturer/distributor of the faulty hardware will have to answer to the provider.

Security Differences between Models   Security is the main reason there are different delivery models for cloud computing. Even though the public option provides the best overall benefits, some organizations simply cannot afford the loss of control that comes with not knowing the full extent of the security procedures and protocols being implemented. But for a relatively small organization without resources or security expertise, the public option is the most viable course. And security in public clouds cannot be considered as anywhere near lackluster; in fact, public cloud providers have much to lose if they fail in security, so they really cannot afford to skimp in that area.

Functionality and Performance Validation   Performance is the most important aspect for any system or application because it has an impact on whether it is worth its asking price. A lot of the validation and testing techniques are the same as that of software and systems testing, but with a unique twist that specifically applies to a cloud environment. However, the overall principle, and possibly the processes, remains the same. This includes stress, functionality, latency, load, and performance testing.

Orchestration Platforms   Orchestration platforms are complete cloud solutions because they contain all the software required for the automated provisioning and virtualization of a converged infrastructure. It is about aligning business with technology, providing the necessary tools for "conducting an orchestra" of tools, software resources, people, policies, and business goals—in short, the whole package.

Chapter

7

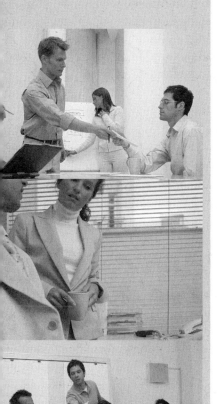

Practical Cloud Knowledge: Install, Configure, and Manage

TOPICS COVERED IN THIS CHAPTER INCLUDE:

- ✓ Creating, importing, and exporting template and virtual machines
- ✓ Install guest tools
- ✓ Snapshots and cloning
- ✓ Image backups vs. file backups
- ✓ Virtual disks
- ✓ Virtual switches
- ✓ VLAN
- ✓ VSAN
- ✓ Establishing migration requirements
- ✓ Storage migration
- ✓ Online vs. offline migrations
- ✓ Physical to virtual (P2V)
- ✓ Virtual to virtual (V2V)
- ✓ Virtual to physical (V2P)

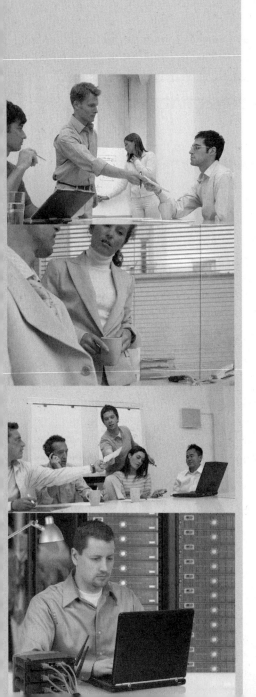

- ✓ **Maintenance scheduling**

- ✓ **Virtual network components**

- ✓ **Shared memory**

- ✓ **Virtual CPU**

- ✓ **Storage virtualization**

In the previous chapters, we focused on discussing theories and principles and briefly touched on some technical aspects with regard to performance of some parts of a cloud system. In this chapter, we will get our hands a little more dirty, so to speak, as we delve a bit deeper into the technical details on how to configure and manage a cloud system.

Setting Up the Cloud

For a cloud service provider, cloud environment setup can be complex and is usually a massive undertaking performed by teams of experts with years of experience and training. Configuring the hardware infrastructure and hypervisor as well as other support systems can take time and patience and a detailed plan laid out by the designers and architects. This must all be done so the end user can begin in as few steps as possible.

For an end user, setting up a cloud environment and some virtual machines (VMs) is as easy as creating an account because after account creation, everything the user has signed up for has already been set up. It's a no-brainer system meant for ease and speed of use in order to increase throughput and productivity.

Creating, Importing, and Exporting Templates and Virtual Machines

A major contributor to the success of a major IT implementation such as a cloud system is proper and detailed configuration management. It is important that all aspects of the system, including end user instances, are well maintained in terms of configuration. It simply will not do when a successfully running virtual server cannot be replicated properly because when a new instance has been provisioned, it does not have the exact same configuration as the successful one, probably a default configuration. This adversely affects both scalability and flexibility of the system to cope with changing environmental factors.

It is for this reason that virtual machines have configuration templates that can be exported and imported for better configuration control and to serve as backup as well. The virtual machines or templates can be moved between data centers, or *availability zones*, meaning to a totally different implementation or different virtual environment.

First, you should know what a virtual machine template is because it is at the core of cloud computing. A virtual machine template is a library resource that consists of a guest operating system profile, a hardware profile, and one or more virtual storage devices, which, when combined, create a full virtual machine, containing the same parts as that of a tangible physical machine. End users who must do self-servicing in terms of provisioning must use specially assigned templates when creating these virtual machines. Usually, users can request a template of a specific configuration if they want to customize their virtual machines.

The exact steps for creating, importing, or exporting templates may be a bit different depending on the cloud platform being used, but the process flow remains largely the same for most systems.

WARNING   Creating a virtual machine template out of an existing virtual machine will destroy the source because the Microsoft Virtual Machine Manager's (VMM's) Sysprep.exe process will strip, so to speak, the virtual machine of its computer identity. Therefore, it is advisable to clone the source virtual machine first unless it is no longer required and thus can be retired.

Creating Virtual Machine Templates

A virtual machine template can be created from an existing virtual machine or from a virtual hard disk, so it is important that the virtual machine be already configured properly since all of its settings will be carried over to the template. Exercise 7.1 walks you through creating a template from a virtual machine, and Exercise 7.2 will show you how to create one from a virtual disk.

EXERCISE 7.1

Creating a Template from a Virtual Machine in Microsoft VMM

This exercise sheds light on how to create VM templates in *Microsoft Virtual Machine Manager* using an already existing virtual machine. First, the following conditions must be met:

- Since this is about VMM, the virtual machine must already be managed by VMM and not another distribution of hypervisor from a different vendor.

- The virtual machine must be running a guest OS of Windows Server 2000, 2003, or 2003 R2.

- The source virtual machine must have Virtual Machine Additions installed on its virtual hard drive containing the operating system.

- The source virtual machine must already be deployed on a *virtual machine host* and run by the *virtual server*.

Here are the steps:

1. You can click the Create VM Template icon to launch the creation wizard shown in the following illustration, or alternatively go the Library view ➢ Actions pane ➢ New Template.

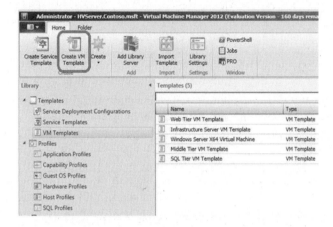

2. Complete the wizard by filling in all the required information.

3. To select the source virtual machine, simply select any existing virtual machine located on a host and then click the Select button.

4. In the Select Library Resource dialog box, select the virtual machine that you have previously selected and then click the OK button.

5. In VHD Containing OS dialog, select the virtual disk that contains the system files.

6. You then need to configure the template's identity. Enter the template name and description and then specify an owner for the template. You can also configure hardware settings if required.

Note that if the template will be used for virtual machine self-service, the specified owner of the template will be the only one who can create, see, and manage the virtual machines created from the template. However, all VMM administrators will still be able to use the template.

EXERCISE 7.2

Creating a Template from Virtual Disks

Creating templates from virtual disks is a bit different than creating them using virtual machines because the disks remain intact and usable. Before creating the template, you must first prepare the source virtual disk.

1. You prepare the virtual disk for duplication by running Sysprep on the VHD (.vhd) file to remove the computer identity information from the virtual hard disk. You then install Virtual Machine Additions on the VHD file.

2. Add the source virtual disk (.vhd) file to the library by copying the file to a library share on a library server and then refreshing that library share.

3. After adding the VHD file to the library, follow the steps in Exercise 7.1, except this time select the virtual hard disk you just added to the library.

4. You can then configure the template identity and the other hardware configurations if required.

Importing and Exporting Service Templates

Importing and exporting service templates gives you the ability to back up and share service templates between different environments, providing you are using the same hypervisor or that the different virtual machine managers are still compatible with each other.

When you export templates, all the important settings and configurations, such as hardware settings, tier definitions, application installation settings, and network configurations, are saved to an *XML file*. The export can even include sensitive data such as passwords and product keys and global and application settings that have been marked as secure, which are then encrypted upon export. When sensitive data is exported, an encryption password is also provided because when service templates are imported and the optional sensitive data is included in the import, the generated encryption password is required.

In addition to the templates, physical resources such as virtual hard disks, scripts, and full application packages that are associated with the XML file and service templates can be exported. And upon importing the service template, the virtual machine monitor validates the physical and logical resources that are being referenced by the service template within the current environment, which also allows you to include or update references to missing resources such as virtual hard disks and logical networks. Upon export, it is best to store the files in a library share to ensure that all administrators have access to the service template files for later importing.

Exercise 7.3 shows you how to export service templates in VMM, and in Exercise 7.4, you will import service templates in VMM.

EXERCISE 7.3

Exporting Service Templates in Microsoft VMM

As mentioned, exporting of service templates will allow us to use them at a later date or at a different deployment without having to manually reconfigure everything. Follow these steps to export your service templates:

1. From the VMM console, open the Library workspace. This is the same one you saw in the illustration in Exercise 7.1.

2. Find and expand the Templates node from the library pane on the left and select Service Templates. On the Template pane on the right, select the service template you wish to export and then click the Export button.

   From the Export Template Resources dialog box, you can export other physical resources associated with the service template.

3. In the Physical Resources column, click None.

   This is because you want to individually select the resources in the Select Resources dialog.

4. Select the resources and then accept your selection.

   You can also export sensitive information such as passwords and product keys and other settings.

5. Select the Export Any Sensitive Template Settings check box.

6. Configure the encryption option for the sensitive settings.

7. Select the Encrypt Template Settings check box and enter an encryption password.

If the sensitive template settings are not included during export, an administrator can simply update the template later or provide these settings manually during template import.

EXERCISE 7.4

Importing Service Templates in Microsoft VMM

When you already have service templates exported or ready, any administrator or user that has been marked as an owner can import them and all associated resources.

1. Follow the first two steps for exporting templates (Exercise 7.3), and in the Library pane, expand the Templates node and choose Service Templates.

   On the Home tab to the right, there is an Import group where there is a button labeled Import Template.

2. Click Import Template, which will then bring up the Import Package Wizard.

3. On the wizard's select page, do the following:

    a. Find the location of the package to import by clicking Browse in Package Path.

    b. Select the XML file you need.

    There is an Import Sensitive Template Settings check box that you may select if you need to do so; otherwise, the references can be updated later during the actual import.

4. After making your selections, click Next, and if the Import Sensitive Template Settings box was selected, a Password dialog box opens.

5. Enter the encryption password used during export of the template and click OK.

6. When the Configure References page appears, enter a name for the service template in the Name box. Note that if the reason for the import is restoration of the template, then the name should probably be kept the same.

7. There is a Release box that also needs to be filled in, so put in the release value for the template. Again, if you're doing a restoration, it would be easier to track if the release value remains the same.

8. If you did not select Import Sensitive Template Settings earlier, this would be the time to review the list of logical and physical resource references in the service template and determine any missing resources.

    Missing resources will show up in the resource list as having a current mapping value of None. The most common missing resources are virtual disks and logical networks. Upon update, Current Mapping Value displays the current resource.

9. When you're finished, click Next.

10. On the summary page, review your settings and selections and then click Import.

    You can then verify if the import was successful.

11. Go to the Jobs workspace and check for a "job completed successfully" status, or alternatively, go to the Library workspace, expand the Templates pane, and check if the name of the recently imported template is there with a Status value of OK.

Installing Guest Tools

Guest tools are a relatively new kind of software that emerged in the wake of virtualization and cloud computing. The name comes from the term *guest operating system*, implying that the operating system does not actually run the show but is simply a guest in the system. They are designed to be installed inside virtual machines after the guest operating system has been installed. These tools are installed on guest OSs to expand their capabilities, such as being able to share input devices and folders with the host easily and provide virtual device drivers, better automation, and overall virtual machine performance gain.

The guest tools vary according to the cloud platform and service being used. For example, we have VirtualBox Guest Additions, which can be installed on most guest operating systems such as Windows and Linux using Oracle's VM VirtualBox.

Guest tools extend the functionality of your virtual machines but must be installed in a special way because VMs will be typically dissociated from the host machine, meaning they cannot access some of the host's accessories or peripheral devices out of the box until guest tools are installed because they believe themselves to be a real machine independent of a host. Some VMs have this functionality already, depending on the virtualization software you are using, but it would be safer to assume that they don't.

The most common method of installing guest tools is through the use of virtual CD-ROM drives. That is why most guest tools are distributed in the form of an ISO (.iso) file. Virtual drives can be created and attached to the virtual machine through the virtualization manager you are using.

Installing guest tools is easier on some host systems than it is on others. For example, using VMware Tools in VMware Server and Workstation using a Windows host is as simple as going to the VM menu, clicking Install VMware Tools, and then following the instructions in the installation wizard on the guest OS that pops up. This goes the same for VirtualBox. However, for both systems, the installation of the guest tools in a Linux host is more technical and requires more steps. But if you are familiar with the process, it may take less than 10 minutes.

Snapshots and Cloning

Creating virtual machines from scratch would be quite tedious. That is why it is always best to create them from prepared templates, unless of course you are aiming for a configuration that has not yet been made into a template. But sometimes we just need a fast way to create a virtual machine and be able to revert to a previous state for testing purposes quickly and easily. This is where snapshots and cloning of virtual machines come in.

Snapshots   As many of you may have already guessed, even though you might be not entirely in the cloud computing field but are veterans in the general computing field, a snapshot is essentially a photo, a record of a specific state. In this case, a snapshot is a record of a state of a virtual machine. The reason we take snapshots and not just create virtual machines from a template is that even though we might have the entire configuration and installed applications all set in a template, some forms of optimizations cannot be captured in templates. It is therefore important to take a snapshot of the VM after doing a lot of work to achieve the state it is in. If something goes wrong later, having a snapshot makes it really easy to revert to that state of a virtual machine. This is handy not only for when something goes wrong but also for comparing the performance of the VM before and after certain alterations are made.

In Exercise 7.5, you'll create a snapshot.

EXERCISE 7.5

Creating Snapshots

It is easy to create a snapshot because it is one of the major functions that every hypervisor must support. To take a snapshot, follow these steps:

1. Just go to the VM menu for your hypervisor and find your way to Snapshot Or Take Snapshot.

2. A pop-up window or dialog box should appear in which you can enter a name for the snapshot and input details for the description parameter.

3. To make identification easier and avoid confusion at a later date, you should describe what the snapshot is about and what it is used for.

   In Hyper-V, the snapshots will be given a default name by the system. Once the process of taking a snapshot has begun, it will take a while to complete, as indicated by a progress bar. It's not exactly like taking a picture. You can actually continue working on the virtual machine you are taking a snapshot of, in theory, but in practice the VM becomes really slow and unresponsive. So it is better to leave it alone until the process has completed. The files are created in the directory where the files of the virtual machines are stored. Again, this may differ depending on the hypervisor being used. For VMware Workstation and other VMware hypervisor products, these files are located in the directory where the VMDK files for each virtual machine are stored.

Snapshot Manager   Snapshots allow you to create separate states with your virtual machine, creating different branches in which you can move between. This allows the user to work with snapshots.

Clones   Clones are pretty much related to snapshots, but as the name suggests they are a complete copy of the original virtual machine. You can actually clone a snapshot of a virtual machine, which is like just simply duplicating the snapshot, and you can even clone a current state of a virtual machine, which essentially creates a snapshot of that state. To understand this, you have to know the difference between a linked clone and a full clone.

Linked Clone   A linked clone only stores modifications, which means that if something goes wrong with the virtual machine, such as it being corrupted, the linked clone befalls the same fate; that is, it gets corrupted as well. But this method also has a huge benefit, which is the fact that a linked clone requires very minimal disk space, so is very efficient in this aspect. This is because only modifications are stored in the clone, which also leads to a very quick process during clone creation.

The linked clone uses the same virtual disks as the parent as well as all of the installed applications and files that were available to the parent when the snapshot for the clone was taken. Any changes made to the disk of the parent do not affect the linked clone, and in turn any changes made on the clone do not affect the parent. However, the clone is still linked to the parent, so if the parent is taken down, the clone will not work.

Linked Clone Usage Scenario

Because a linked clone can be created swiftly, it is very useful in development scenarios such as bug fixing. Take the scenario of a test engineer finding a difficult-to-replicate bug using a virtual machine. The development engineer can quickly create multiple linked clones of that virtual machine to ensure that there are working virtual machines exhibiting the current state. Then he can proceed to work fixing the bug on the clones and have multiple machines handy for multiple solutions. In the meantime, the test engineer may continue working on the parent virtual machine without affecting the clones.

Full Clone   This is a full copy of a virtual machine. Every aspect of a virtual machine, including all of the contents in its virtual drives, are copied over to the clone, so this means that it requires the same amount of disk space, more or less, as the original virtual machine and the cloning process is quite long.

The main benefit of this is that it creates a fully independent virtual machine, which offers a lot of flexibility, especially for testing applications and new configurations and creating comparisons between performances.

Exercise 7.6 walks you through creating a new clones.

EXERCISE 7.6

Creating Clones

Though quite similar in purpose, a clone and a snapshot are different in a major way. As stated, a snapshot is merely a picture of a virtual machine's specific state, meaning that you are still dealing with the same single virtual machine. Depending on your application, that may pose some limitations. A full clone, on the other hand, is an entirely separate virtual machine independent of the original virtual machine, so what happens to one does not necessarily happen to the other, unless you are using a linked clone. So when you have created a new clone, you can also start taking snapshots of that new virtual machine.

1. First, you have to determine your reason for making a clone.

   If it is just for personal convenience and you do not need it to do something entirely different and function independently, then a linked clone would be the best option because it takes very little space and can be created quickly. However, if you need the clone to function independently from its parent, then you would need a full clone. With a full clone, you can make it into a parent and create additional linked or full clones from it, create and revert to snapshots, and perform other activities that can be performed only on fully independent virtual machines. Also, creating templates destroys a virtual machine, so you need to clone a virtual machine before making it into a template or make the template from the clone.

2. Clones can be created in different ways, but with all methods, you need to shut down the virtual machine before proceeding.

   The reason for this requirement is that the virtual machine files cannot be modified during the cloning process.

   Another reason has to do with process and file ownership in operating system file systems such as those used by Windows and Linux, which do not allow multiple processes to modify the same files at the same time. So if a virtual machine is using its files and resources, the hypervisor cannot work on those files to create the clone.

   There are specific configurations for which the requirement of shutting down virtual machines is no longer enforced, such as when you are using VMware Virtual Machine File System while at the same time using VMware ESXi as a *bare metal hypervisor*.

   In VMware Workstation and ESXi, the most straightforward method is choosing the Manage option from the VM menu and then selecting the Clone option in order to start the wizard.

   In the first step, the wizard asks what the source of the clone will be. The source can be a snapshot of a virtual machine state if there are any, or you can base it on the current state, which will create a snapshot.

3. Select the source.

4. Select either a full or linked clone, the differences of which we discussed previously.

   But just to reiterate, when selecting a full clone, you have to make sure that there is enough disk space because the full clone will take up approximately the same disk space used by the source virtual machine on the host computer. This includes all of the files in the virtual disks, so if the source virtual machine takes up 50 gigabytes of space on the host machine, you will need at least that much extra space on the host as well.

5. Verify that there is ample disk space, and then the cloning process can begin.

6. Name the clone and decide where it should be stored on the host computer.

   After completion, the clone with the assigned name should appear on the console and in the library as an independent virtual machine because that is what it actually is.

The other way of creating clones is through the snapshot manager of your hypervisor. Simply select the snapshot you want and the click Clone.

Image Backups vs. File Backups

The need for backups is a given for any computer system, cloud systems especially because they literally exist because of data. Therefore, making backups of data is one of the most important processes in IT and should be a big part of an organization's plan as well as budget.

Losing data is the worst-case scenario for any system, especially one being used for business, so a backup schedule that is close to real time as possible is important. Performing backups every few seconds would be unrealistic because that would require massive amounts of storage as well as computing power because of the overhead, not to mention the costs. Planning the backup methods and technology is part of the business impact analysis and business continuity planning. During those phases, the recovery time objective (RTO) and recovery point objective (RPO) must be established based on the kind of processes and workflows the system will handle.

Recovery Point Objective   The RPO is the maximum acceptable amount of data loss allowed measured in time. It is simply the age of the data in backup storage that is required to resume the normal operations of the system after a failure. For example, if the RPO for a given system is determined to be 15 minutes, then a backup must be taken every 15 minutes to ensure that if there just happens to be failure resulting in data loss, the amount of data lost is only a maximum of 15 minutes' worth. So if a system generates 5 MB of data per minute, it is acceptable for it to lose a maximum of 75 MB of data.

Recovery Time Objective   On the other hand, RTO is the amount of time allowed for the system to be down or the time before the system can fully function again. It is the time span between the failure and recovery. Usually, there are multiple RTOs being defined because different forms of failure have different recovery times, depending on the severity of the failure. For sure, major failure caused by infrastructure failure or disasters take longer to recover from compared to simple software crashes or failing hard disks.

These items have to be considered when choosing the correct type of backup. And along with the different technology used for backup, discussed in Chapter 8, "Hardware Management," administrators can fully control the backup and recovery plan of the organization and aim for the most performance- and cost-efficient solution for the system in question.

Currently there are two types of backups. Each has its merits and also some downsides, and we will next discuss both in detail.

File Backups

File backups, or file-based backups, are the traditional kind of backups, the kind most of us might be used to doing. The process simply involves creating a duplicate of a file or a whole folder and then placing it in a separate location or a storage medium that can be easily accessed to restore it when needed. This method of backup is selective and usually employed for personal files such as videos and MP3 files or really important files that are few in number, such as photographs, word processor documents, and spreadsheets.

The primary purpose of file backups is to make it easy to recover these important files no matter what happens to your primary hard disks or computer. Because file backups are selective, they have the added benefit of being faster and much smaller in terms of used disk space compared to image backups.

Image Backups

The other kind of backup is an image backup, which by definition is an actual bit-to-bit copy of each sector of the entire hard drive, hence the name. It is basically a backup copy of the whole hard drive stored as an image file, which includes all the unnecessary files such as temporary files, caches, junk files, and even malware and viruses.

The basic idea of an image backup is simply to copy each bit on your hard drive into another drive without regard for files, folders, or any other related concept. Having a backup image is a true 100 percent backup and can be considered a snapshot of the exact state of the hard drive at the time the backup was performed.

The real payoff for having an image backup comes when real catastrophe strikes and your main hard drive is totally lost. In this scenario, you can easily restore to whatever state you have in your image backup. This includes all installations, settings, and optimizations. There is no need to reinstall or format anything, which saves a great deal of time. In this scenario, an image backup was the perfect choice. For organizations running large data centers that store large amounts of data, with various hard drives being used to store data only, image backups are not just ideal, they should be mandatory. All of the data from customers and other sources can be considered important, so a selective backup like file backup is not ideal because you will back up everything anyway. Also in this case, cost is likely not a concern.

Image backups are more suitable for catastrophes or to back up machine configuration and installation tools, especially when there are a lot of machines to be configured in the same exact way, as in an organization with many employees. It would be tedious to manually install the OS and other required applications and then configure each application for each machine or PC. Multiply that by hundreds and the IT department would have an almost insurmountable task ahead of them. With disk images of the ideal machine, they can work with batches of PCs at the same time with minimal supervision; intervention is just needed for the beginning and end of the procedure.

There are also major downsides of using image backups:

- For one, they require large amounts of disk space because you are actually making a copy of the entire disk.
- There is also the factor of time. It takes a long time to do the backup, and it requires large amounts of bandwidth if you plan to back up to the cloud.
- The resulting image is considered a single file located on a disk or spanning several disks, the latter more likely because of the file's size. One drawback to this is if just one of those fragments gets damaged or corrupted, then you are left with one big corrupted and unusable file and no backup at all. There are ways to prevent this, but it is still a possible scenario.

- One major drawback is that malicious software and viruses get backed up as well. This means that if files and application installations from the source have been infected without your knowledge, the infection gets backed up as well.

WARNING If the source disk has been infected with damaging malware and viruses right before backup without the knowledge of the administrator, the infected portions of the disk get backed up as well. That means you have an infected backup image. Then if your original source gets corrupted and destroyed by an infection a short while after backup, you can only turn to your infected backup image and there would be little chance to save the system.

Selecting the Backup Method

It goes without saying that no one method is good for every scenario. But the differences between the methods should be enough to give you a good idea of which method to use based on your organization and the types of workflows you are using. For example, if your organization works on specific files such as 3D and CAD files and multiple employees need to access and edit the same files, the best backup method would be the selective file backup because you will not need to back up whole computers, just the important files people are working on. The scenario could be that a few folders are automatically backed up to the cloud or to multiple external local drives just to make sure there are multiple copies. The backup procedure would be quick since only a few files or folders need to be periodically backed up when there are actual changes. An organization such as this would be considered small to medium and will not have that many computers to install and reinstall applications for, so total image backups for fresh installations are not required but may come in handy.

If an organization deals with massive amounts of data that fill up drives easily, then total image backups are a must. This type of data is often important, so selective backups do not apply because all of the data needs to backed up. Magnetic tape backup is the most favored form because of its relative durability and low price point compared to using disk drive backups. But backup centers that utilize hard disks are also quite common because of the ease of restoring data.

Virtual Network Interface Card

A virtual network interface card (virtual NIC), like all concepts described with the word *virtual*, is an abstract nontangible construct that is created to emulate the functions of a physical network interface card. Like the real deal, it requires both high sustained throughput and low latency.

The virtual NIC appears to the guest OS or virtual machine as a full-pledged PCI Ethernet controller complete with its own unique MAC address because, as you know, the virtual machine actually believes itself to be a real physical machine. The virtual NIC can be connected in two ways: it can be either bridged to a real physical network through a real physical NIC or connected as is to a virtual network created on the host. In both cases, it is powered through a net driver installed on the host OS through the hypervisor or as a separate plug-in.

A virtual NIC is implemented via a combination of code within the virtual machine itself and the underlying hypervisor. All the communications, the IRQs, and the virtual I/O ports as well as the virtual DMA transfers between the VM's memory and the adapter are semantically equivalent to that of a real network adapter.

Virtual Network

At a basic conceptual level, a virtual network and a real physical network are not that different. The reason for this is that a virtualized network is made so that it acts as a real network and the virtual machines or guest operating systems believe it to be a real network, so all of the interfaces and protocols being used are the same or made to act very similarly with minor differences. For example, instead of data going directly out of the virtual NIC to a virtual router and then to the outside network, it actually goes through the hypervisor interface, which manages everything in the virtualized environment, before it is passed to the physical NIC for actual delivery. A virtual network is simply made to mimic an actual network.

In most networking scenarios, for a machine to connect to a network, it needs a network interface card (NIC), which enables it to interface with a network via a switch or router that at the same time connects multiple machines and networks to form a larger network. A virtualized network is made up of the same hardware, and the virtual machine must also have a network interface controller, in this case a virtual one, in order for the guest OS to communicate with a virtual switch or router. So in the strictest sense, everything is the same except the fact that the other is made entirely in virtual space.

A virtual network also consists of multiple virtual machines that can send and receive data to and from one another. Each of those virtual machines represents an actual computer in the network, and the virtual switch or router can connect these computers to each other and other virtual networks as well as with the physical network.

Connecting a virtual NIC to a virtual network is the most straightforward method and does not require an Ethernet interface on the host. This can be done by creating on the host a virtual network that functions even if the host itself is not connected to any type of network at all. The virtual network, as well as all the connected virtual machines, is running within the host privately. If desired, the host can perform *IP masquerading* or routing to connect the virtual network to an external network, even to a non-Ethernet one.

IP Address

The IP address is, and always should be, unique for each NIC or device, and that remains true for virtual NICs. It is important to make the distinction that the VM is a totally separate computer even though it is residing on the host computer, and as such it cannot simply communicate using the host's network adapter unless it's configured as bridged, meaning the virtual NIC is bridged with the physical network adapter of the host. Another way is to connect the VM in a virtual network with its own virtual gateway connection to an external physical network. Or the entire ecosystem of virtual devices and networks could exist privately within the host as a local network without connection to outside networks.

Default Gateway

The default gateway is the virtual network's connection to the outside and other networks, be it virtual or otherwise. In typical networking, the default gateway is often a network router that sets the path and routes all packets in and out of the network. This router forwards traffic to remote subnets on behalf of a host.

In order for your virtual network to connect to the Internet, the easiest and most straightforward way is to have the virtual NIC running in bridged mode so that it is connected to your physical NIC, allowing it to connect to all networks that the host is connected to.

If you are connecting different virtual networks together, there are various methods that you can use:

- The virtual machines themselves can be tricked to blindly route packets to all available virtual subnets by making the default gateway IP address the same as the address of the virtual machine. This will trick the virtual machine into sending the packet to itself since it has been configured as the default gateway. It then sends the packet to the default route of 0.0.0.0/0, allowing all hosts (VMs) on the subnet to receive it. All the virtual machines that receive the packet will inspect it and either forward or accept it, depending on whether they are the recipient or not.

- You can create a virtual machine that will act as the routing mechanism for the various subnetworks.

- You can use an external physical router.

Netmask

The implementation for subnetting is the same as in regular networking. You still apply the netmask through four octets, which determine the number of subnets in the network and the subnet to which a specific computer belongs.

Bridging

Bridging refers to the connection being made by the virtual NIC to the physical NIC in order for that particular virtual machine to appear as a unique machine on the host's network along with other physical machines. It is analogous to a physical Ethernet switch that is used to connect multiple network interfaces, both virtual and physical, on a single machine while at the same time they share the same subnet. It is the easiest way to give a virtual machine access to other machines on the host's physical network and not just the virtual network. A dedicated IP must be allocated to the virtual machine to be connected in bridged mode to give it its unique identity.

The following are the requirements for connecting a virtual machine in bridged mode:

- A dedicated IP address for each virtual machine to be connected in bridged mode is essential for the virtual machine to have its own identity on the network; it cannot share the IP address of the host. This doesn't necessarily mean that it must have a static IP address; it means that there should be an empty IP slot within the subnet for the DHCP server to assign one to the VM.

- There must be a connected host network interface controller. To be in bridged mode, a host must have a NIC and a physical network to attach it to. Otherwise, what would be the point of bridging?

- The bridge driver enables the virtual NIC to communicate with the host's NIC and allows for the bridging to occur. For VMware products, this is called the VMware Bridge protocol, while for Microsoft's virtualization solutions, it is called the Virtual PC Network Filer driver. Both should be enabled through the host computer's network settings for the associated network adapter.

- The host's Ethernet adapter has to be set to promiscuous mode to enable all traffic to enter instead of just discarding those that are not meant for its own MAC address. This allows traffic meant for the bridged NIC to be received and routed to the bridge.

Virtual machines with virtual network interface controllers do not directly interact with the outside physical network for obvious reasons. All data and signals go through *virtualization intermediaries (VIs)*, which are special programs that handle communication between the virtual machines and the host. The VI can be either a part of the hypervisor or the host itself.

The virtualization intermediaries are used for safely sharing I/O, meaning that multiple operating systems may share the same PCI device through the virtualization intermediary. The virtualization intermediary can perform this by multiplexing the I/O flows from each operating system and performing the PCI I/O transactions in behalf of the participating OSs. The VI also performs as a communication medium for all the OSs running on the same hypervisor. This is assuming that the PCI device being used is of the modern PCIe (PCI Express) variety, which supports multiple-Mac addresses to allow for a unique MAC address for each OS, and has state-of-the art IP stack accelerators and functions like transmit and receive queue pairs.

Virtual Disks

Along with all things virtual, a virtual disk is simply a software implementation—in this case, a file that presents itself to the user and the guest operating system as a hard disk drive. To the user and the virtual machine, the virtual disk behaves and looks like a real disk drive. The virtual disk resides in a single physical hard drive or, in the case of large cloud computing implementations, is striped across multiple physical drives and possibly across multiple availability zones, complete with backups.

To a virtual machine, a virtual disk is as important as a physical disk to a physical computer. Without it, the machine cannot boot nor do anything because there is no place to install an operating system. Take note that a virtual machine is often called a guest operating system, so without a drive to install that OS, there is no virtual machine, just a bunch of settings ready for prime time.

A virtual disk can be created from scratch as a single file on the physical hard drive as part of the process for creating a virtual machine, or it can be part of a virtual machine template or even separately created inside a storage repository. There are different file types used for virtual disks, and it varies depending on the virtualization software provider. Microsoft uses VHD, Oracle uses VDI, and VMware uses VMDK.

The beauty of a virtual disk is that it can be manipulated in many ways that a physical disk cannot. For example, it can be easily copied and backed up because it is made as a single file. It can even be made into a dynamically sized drive, where the capacity can increase or decrease depending on the usage requirements. That last part is obviously impossible for a physical drive because it is already constrained to its maximum storage capacity. But there are of course downsides to the virtual disk. Among other limitations, the virtual disk capacity is limited by that of the host's capacity, as will be discussed in the next section.

Limits

Despite the flexibility of virtual disks, they are not without limitation. For example, dynamic capacity is a great feature that optimizes the virtual disk capacity by keeping it to its actual size requirement rather than allocating a fixed amount of space that may never be used or may not be enough, leading to the creation of another virtual disk in order to cope with the capacity requirements. The obvious limitation of dynamic capacity is the actual capacity of the host's physical hard drive, which contains other files as well. This is less of a problem in enterprise solutions that employ large data centers dedicated to storage capacity where they can simply stripe the virtual disk file across multiple physical drives.

A big problem that can be encountered when employing virtual disks, especially in older systems, is the file system limitation. Since the virtual disk must be a single contiguous file, it is not advisable to be used in systems that employ FAT/FAT32 or similar file systems that cannot support files larger than 4 gigabytes. It is still possible, providing the file size limit is not violated, so using dynamically sized virtual disks would not be appropriate. However, multiple instances of smaller-capacity virtual disks can be used. It is advisable to use NTFS and similar file systems so that all the benefits of the virtual disk can be enjoyed.

There are two kinds of virtual drives, the fixed disk and the dynamic disk. The fixed disk is obviously fixed in size, and the capacity is specified during creation, and the dynamic disk expands with use. The fixed disk is in every way similar to the physical drive, even in performance. However, the dynamic disk is slower than the fixed disk and has a substantially higher chance for data fragmentation. A dynamic disk contains a lock allocation table that expands along with the contents of the disk, so a fully expanded dynamic virtual disk will be a bit larger compared to a fixed virtual disk with the same usable capacity.

Virtual Switches

Virtual networking components are not easy to comprehend without an actual background in and understanding of networking in general first. So let's do a little review. First of all, networking is just a connection between shared resources, systems, and services, which are usually connected through wired or wireless medium. This is the same theory applied to the virtual or logical environment. But there is a catch. You must be able to tell the difference between a virtual and physical adapter and how they can be linked together through the virtual switching fabric being implemented by your virtualization provider. There are minor differences on how each provider implements switching and networking features, so it will be up to you to learn the nuances of your chosen provider's virtual network implementation solution.

Virtual switches are the key components of a virtual network implementation, which allows you to create multiple switches that can number up to the hundreds, again depending on your chosen virtualization solution. In theory and practice, virtual switches are similar to physical switches, but in some notable ways they are very different. This is mainly because developers can be more creative with virtual switches because they are all implemented via software, and the possibilities, as you may know, are quite numerous to say the least.

Similarities to Physical Switches

Most implementations of virtual switches work in the same way as modern Ethernet switches. A virtual switch relays packets and maintains a MAC port forwarding table. It can perform the same functions as a physical switch:

- Forwards frames to one or many ports for transmission
- Checks each frame's MAC destination upon arrival
- Avoids unnecessary forwarding, unlike hubs, which just forward everything

Differences between Physical Switches and Virtual Switches

Since virtual switches are essentially programs, they can be configured for functions that are not being used in physical switches. For example, some virtual switch implementations have built-in shortcuts to certain functions that require a lot of tinkering for physical switches, such as learning multicast group membership or automatically switching ports to mirror mode when sensing that a virtual NIC's promiscuous bit is set.

Another major difference, at least in some implementations such as VMware's, is that virtual switches cannot be cascaded within the same host. The virtual switch can provide all of the ports required. That is why, unlike a physical switch with a very limited number of ports, it does not need to be cascaded. This has added benefits:

- Bad virtual switch connections are avoided.
- Virtual switches do not share network adaptors because only one is required per host, so there is no way to create loopback that would cause leakage between virtual switches.

Each virtual switch's forwarding table does not contain any entries that point to a port on another virtual switch, and there is actually no mechanism to do this. So every destination that the virtual switch can look up matches only ports on itself, as the originator of the frame. This is called virtual switch isolation, and it is quite unlikely that an attacker can circumvent this.

Virtual Local Area Networks

Virtual local area networks (VLANs) are often confused with virtual networks because of the name, but they refer to different concepts. This confusion is quite common because not all professionals who work in the field of computers actually deal with networks; many are experts in subfields other than networking. The *virtual* in both *virtual local area networks* and *virtual networks* means artificial and intangible, but when taken as a whole, the terms stand for different things, though both are concerned with networking. Virtual networks are essentially the software counterparts of physical networks, but the virtual local area network is only the virtual interpretation of a LAN to an extent. It is a way to further segregate or divide a network or multiple networks into subgroups that in many ways act as an actual local area network and communicate as if they were attached to the same network node. The virtual or logical counterpart of an actual local area network would still be a virtual network, though VLANS are referred to as such because they are meant to act in many ways similar to a local area network. More about VLANs in the next section.

Since virtual switches are not entirely different from physical switches, it would stand that configuring them for VLANs would be the same exact thing. That's not exactly true, though; virtual switches are only secondary to physical switches and should be configured based on the physical switch configuration.

Interface Configuration

The VLAN interface is a logical interface that is associated with an existing VLAN and defined at the switch. The interface can route traffic and serve as a hop junction for routing protocols, so it has its own IP address, which is at the same subnet as that of the VLAN it is associated with. It is not a port on the switch but exists in software, hence logical. The interface provides the Layer 3 processing for all packets coming from all the switch ports that are associated with the specific VLAN and also serves as the routing mechanism toward other Layer 3 interfaces, eliminating the need for a physical router. This is also known as the switched virtual interface (SVI) or the management interface.

To create the interface, log on to your virtualization manager's network configuration menu or command line and input the commands. The configuration process differs depending on the software and operating system used, so consult your data sheets. You can input the name of the VLAN as well as the associated IP address of the interface. Remember that it has to be in the same subnet or the virtual machines connected to it will not be able to reach it.

Configuring Virtual Machines for Several VLANs

When configuring a virtual switch for internal VLANs within the virtual environment, all the settings can be done with the virtual switch and virtual machines without regard for external physical switches because you will not be connecting them to external interfaces anyway. But if you are to configure virtual machines as part of several VLANs, there are two easy ways to do this.

Simple Single VLAN

The first way is with a simple virtual network scenario. Say you have some virtual machines in a network connected to a virtual switch that you need to connect to a VLAN that includes physical machines and an external network. In this case, you can use a single physical NIC on the host, and you should not overthink the architecture of this simple network. Think of the virtual switch as a simple pass-through, a simple linking mechanism that connects the physical NIC to the virtual NICs in the virtual machines and is configured as an external type of virtual switch. The host's NIC is then connected to the port assigned to the specific VLAN that the virtual network needs to be a part of, and that's it. There is no special configuration; it is as if you just plugged your machine to a switch port assigned it to a specific VLAN.

Multiple VLAN Using Multiple NICs with Virtual Switch Binding

In a more complicated networking scenario, we have two sets of virtual networks, each connected to an external-type virtual switch. This is the same method as the previous one only multiplied. Because only one external-type virtual switch can bind with a physical NIC, the host must have two NICs installed and two different ports on the physical switch configured for each VLAN and then connected to the appropriate NICs on the host via cables.

If you want to add more VLAN segments, then more NICs will be required on the host. But this time we can change the settings a bit by setting the VLAN configuration and assignment of the VLAN ID on the virtual switch and then setting the ports on the physical switch as trunk ports, which are not tied to specific VLANs. This means that you can plug any of the NICs to any port because they are configured as trunks and will not do VLAN tagging; this will be done by the virtual switches. However, this presents an obvious limitation, which can be solved by the method described in the next section.

VLAN ID Setting on VM

The method described in the preceding section has a major limitation in regard to the number of NICs and VLANs, but this next one can address this problem properly. You can create as many VLANs as you want using only a single virtual switch, which also means only one NIC on the host and one port on the physical switch will be required. The configuration for the VLAN and assignment of the VLAN ID will be transferred to the virtual machines themselves, so now they will associate themselves with a specific VLAN, and you would not need to do anything on the virtual switch. Simply set the physical switch's port to trunk mode. You can configure the VLAN IDs on the virtual machine's virtual NIC console.

Assigning IDs

Based on the preceding scenarios, there are several ways for assigning the VLAN ID in order to create a VLAN or assign a device to it.

- You can assign the VLAN ID to the ports of the physical switch, which converts them all to access ports. Any device attached to those ports automatically becomes part of that specific VLAN.

  With this method, you need another group of virtual machines to be part of a different VLAN segment; then they would need to be connected to a different virtual switch, which would also require an additional physical NIC on the host because an external-type virtual switch binds to a host NIC in a one-to-one manner.

- Another way to assign a VLAN ID is to assign it to the virtual switch.

  This is similar to the preceding method, where the ID is configured on the physical switch, but this requires the port on the physical switch to be configured in trunk mode to allow all traffic for all VLANs to pass through, giving the job of packet segregation to the virtual switch. That virtual switch is now dedicated to that specific VLAN, and all virtual machines attached to it belong to that VLAN segment.

- The third method is to assign the VLAN IDs in the virtual machines themselves by configuring their virtual NICs.

In this way, each VM already knows which VLAN it is assigned to and will accept all communication meant for it and drop the rest. No further configuration has to be done on the virtual switch, and only one virtual switch is required even though we can have multiple VLANs active at the virtual machine level. A port on the physical switch needs to be configured as trunk for this to work.

Binding Interfaces

As mentioned in the section "Interface Configuration" earlier in this chapter, in order for a connected machine to be able to ping the switch or communicate at all, there must be an existing VLAN interface on the switch to allow routing of correct packets with VLAN tags associated with them.

Once the logical or VLAN interface has been created, it is bound to the VLAN ID in order to associate the IP address of the interface with a specific VLAN. Again, the commands and where you input them might be different depending on your network solution provider, so consult the technical documentation for your specific network equipment.

Virtual Storage Area Network

A virtual storage area network (VSAN) is based on the same concept as the VLAN. The physical counterpart, the SAN, is a dedicated network that interconnects different hosts and storage devices with the primary goal of exchanging SCSI traffic. It's basically a network to consolidate all storage devices into a network in and of itself. Physical connections are of course used here together with a set of protocols that handle routing, traffic, naming, and zoning.

In concept, a VSAN is very much like a VLAN in that it creates additional segmentation and isolation from a larger network. For example, in a single SAN with 10 storage servers, you can create any number of VSANs that connect different servers virtually isolated from the others in order to fulfill a specific purpose. Usually it is to give specific users access to only a specific portion instead of the whole SAN.

The main purpose of a VSAN is to achieve greater security and stability within Fibre Channel fabrics by creating isolation among physically connected devices. You can create multiple logical SANs over the same common fabric. And although a VSAN has all of the properties of a SAN, it has some added advantages:

- The same topology can be shared by multiple VSANs.
- VSAN scalability can be increased by using the same Fibre Channel ID on another host in a different VSAN.

- Every instance of a VSAN is running all of the required protocols, such as FSPF, zoning, and a domain manager.
- Fabric-related settings or configurations in one VSAN do not affect other VSANs.
- Traffic disruptions and other errors in one VSAN are contained there and will not affect other VSANs.

The VSAN identifier is automatically assigned when you are creating a VSAN through the console. Just remember that VSAN 1 is the default ID and that it is used for testing, management, and communications purposes and should not be used as a production environment VSAN. This is because it has some features that when configured can interfere with normal traffic flows in a VSAN. So make sure that upon creation, you specify an ID from the user-defined space, which is VSAN 2, 4093. VSAN 4094 is also reserved as the isolated VSAN.

VSAN ID vs. VSAN Name

Take note that a VSAN ID is not the VSAN name. The VSAN name must be unique for each VSAN. The VSAN ID serves to associate the VSAN with its name and will be used for configuration and traffic routing, while the VSAN name is mostly useful only to the user for more humanly understandable identification and easier management. By default, the VSAN name is the word *VSAN* concatenated with four digits, which represent the ID. For example, the default name for VSAN 2 is VSAN0002.

Virtual Resource Migration

Assuming that you have now chosen your cloud service provider or have constructed your own private cloud, you are now ready to migrate all resources and enjoy the benefits of the cloud. But before that, along with your research for what sort of cloud service your organization needs, you should have already planned what resources and services to migrate and how it should be done in order to minimize downtime and ensure that everything goes without a hitch. The following sections shed some light on this somewhat arbitrary process. We say *arbitrary* because there are no standards set in stone and people usually have to learn as they go along or from the mistakes and success of others.

Establishing Migration Requirements

When you planned on moving some or all of your business processes to the cloud, you considered the full extent of the endeavor and had embarked on research and studies before actually committing to a service or starting construction of your own cloud. This is being said in past tense because, up until this point, you should already have a good idea about the cloud, its surrounding technologies, and the benefits it will bring to your organization. No one moves to the cloud because the other guys are doing it; it is done because of the benefits. Let us then explore a bit on the requirements for a smooth migration of services and data.

To establish business requirements, you must hold stakeholder meetings if you have not already. Have your stakeholders list what they want and what they do not want during the migration phase. The business stakeholders will probably list near-impossible things like zero downtime or no disruption, but that is the purpose of the meetings, so that the business folks and the technical folks will see eye to eye regarding what is wanted and what is possible, easy, or ideal. Of course, everyone wants zero disruption, which is not entirely impossible, but it will take a lot to accomplish—in short, a lot of planning and effort.

Data and application migration used to be purely technical issues that the IT department had to handle, but that is no longer the case with the advent of the pay-as-you-go cloud computing model. No longer is the migration process in the hands of the organization's IT department; it's now in the hands of your third-party service provider. The beauty of this is that the service provider has already made a business out of migration and they already have set guidelines and best practices that you can apply based on your own migration requirements. The least you would need to do now is have the business and IT managers be present along with some engineers in order to smooth out the migration details with the provider.

Even with that already taken care of, you still need to establish your requirements so that the provider has something to work with and then tailor their migration solution to your specific needs and requirements. The answers to the following questions might be enough information for the provider, but the more detailed information you can provide, the better.

- Why are we migrating data and applications in the first place? The answer to this is straightforward because this is the driving force for "cloudifying" your processes anyway.
- Which data needs to be migrated, and which data needs to stay in-house? This has a lot to do with the control and security of your data. The best people to answer these questions are your business and technical managers.
- When should the migration take place? The best time is often on a weekend or at night when very few people are working. But this entirely depends on the type of organization because some are global and because of time differences, the current system may not be in use in one place but very active in another. Also, some systems such as online retail and some services have to be accessible for 24 hours and seven days a week, so a migration will be tricky and downtime will be inevitable.

When migration is completed, the old system can be decommissioned and all operations transferred to the new system in a way that minimizes or totally removes downtime. And once all business operations are on the new cloud system, you can focus your efforts in keeping things running through constant maintenance and process improvement.

Migrating Storage

When it comes to actual migration, there are quite a few ways that data can be migrated, and your service provider might offer you the method best suited to your exact situation. This can vary depending on your current infrastructure, such as available bandwidth and location. For example, if bandwidth and connection speed allow it, the migration can be done over the network via the Internet. But if this would take a very long time and would not be feasible, it would be faster to mail in all the data that needs to be migrated via physical storage media.

Online vs. Offline Migrations

In this day and age a lot of activities are being done online, even data and application migration. But online migration is dependent on one factor: bandwidth. If an organization's current infrastructure does not allow for such a large amount of data to be transferred within a specified time period, then online migration is simply not feasible. Most of the time, network providers would charge extra if data transfers go over the bandwidth utilization limit allotted for the subscriber, but maybe with some negotiation a deal can be made that a specific amount of data be allowed with an agreed-upon amount of payment. Online migration is the fastest and most hassle-free method for migration if the infrastructure can handle it. But if there really is no other way, then offline migrations would be appropriate.

Offline migration would be a hassle, but it could also become the cheaper alternative. What this requires is that all of the data and applications that need to be migrated be consolidated into physical storage media such as hard disks and then shipped to the service provider so that they can upload it to their servers. The problem with this is bookkeeping, keeping track and organizing the data that needs to be placed in hard disks and then making sure that at the other end the correct data will be uploaded to the proper places. This requires the team doing the data consolidation be present at the other end to ensure the correctness of the migration. Together with the hardware and the manpower required for such an endeavor, the cost would be a bit more than online migration if your infrastructure already allows for it. But if there really is no choice, this might be the better method compared to upgrading your slow network infrastructure and paying overcharges on your data subscriptions. Besides, it will not take millions, probably a few thousand US dollars depending on the location of the service provider. If that happens to be in the same city or state, then the cost would probably be only for gas and lunch money.

Physical to Virtual

Physical to virtual (P2V) migration is the process of decoupling a physical machine's software component, which includes the operating system, data, and applications, and then putting all of that into a virtual machine guest that is hosted on another physical machine. It's like moving from a house into an apartment building. We liken physical computers to houses because they are buildings separate from each other, while we liken the virtual environment to an apartment building because you have multiple full living spaces in a single large building. Both are physical, yet the apartment simulates the multitenancy found in public cloud platforms or simply the basic fact that multiple virtual machines live in the same host machine.

There are a few methods to do this. The first and most basic one is manual migration:

1. Someone has to literally install all of the required applications into the virtual machine.

2. Configure the applications exactly like the original.

3. Copy all of the files from the physical machine to the virtual machine.

A more reliable method would be using a semi-automated or automated tool that is provided by your service provider or hypervisor vendor.

Semi-automated Tools   A semi-automated tool would require some human intervention with settings and the conversion itself, with the end result usually being a virtual machine file or template that is ready to be created into a virtual machine. Here are a few examples of semi-automated P2V solutions:

- VMware vCenter Converter
- Microsoft System Center Virtual Machine Manager
- Sysinternals Disk2vhd

Fully automated Tools   With fully automated P2V converters, the conversion could happen online, and the end result is usually an already fully usable and running virtual machine. Here are some examples of fully automated P2V solutions:

- vContinuum by InImage Systems
- Symantes System Recovery
- Leostream
- Quest vConverter

Virtual to Virtual

Virtual to virtual (V2V) migration can be considered interhost migration because there would be no other explanation for moving a virtual machine into another virtual machine. Otherwise it would simply be cloning and not actual migration. In any case, this type of migration would simply involve cloning a virtual machine and then activating that clone on a different environment or host, and then the original can be retired.

Virtual to Physical

Virtual to physical (V2P) migration is the opposite of P2V. A virtual machine, presumably a server, is migrated into a physical server, possibly so that it can serve using a more powerful configuration than a virtual machine can offer. The process for doing this differs for Windows and Linux guest operating systems and should be provided by your service provider or infrastructure provider.

Scheduling Maintenance

Maintenance is one of the best ways of preventing future problems; that is why it is better known as preventive maintenance. However, no matter how important maintenance may be, it often has a direct effect on the system, such as requiring total shutdown to the public or client base or severely affecting performance because portions of the system have to be taken down.

There really is no easy way to prevent downtime, so it's best to schedule it in such a way that the overall effect is minimally felt by the community. The schedule would vary depending on the nature of the system and who it serves. Sometimes the weekend or nighttime is best if the system is directly tied to a business that operates within regular office hours. If the system is tied to leisure use or gaming, which are usually not allowed at work, then it would be best to do maintenance during peak office hours.

But on cloud and virtualized systems, there are ways to do maintenance in the background without the users ever noticing. Because everything exists in a virtual space, you can simply move around the environments into other hosts with little effect to the users and then do maintenance on the hosts from which you just migrated.

Reasons for Maintenance

It might be obvious to us why we do routing maintenance, but sometimes these reasons are lost to us, especially if the activity becomes too routine and we forget its importance. Reminders are often a good thing.

Performance Issues   Virtual environments create a lot of metadata that the hypervisor needs to sort out and use, and this is the same for storage servers. Programs run on guest operating systems and sometimes encounter errors. Even RAM gets cluttered up by being provisioned and reprovisioned to different virtual machines, not to mention all the caches and shared storage being used. Sometimes these things just need to be flushed so that the system can start anew, free of the clutter that once hindered it. This is the same reason we occasionally have to clear the temporary Internet files, cookies, and caches of our browsers or why we periodically have to restart computers that have been running for a long time.

Testing   To test new features for a service, we have to use a production-like environment invisible to the general client base. There is no problem system-testing new features in a mostly simulated and controlled environment, but it's totally different when it's done in a real production one. And in order for any installation of these features to take place, the system may just have to be shut down for a short duration, which includes testing the system on the production environment.

Upgrading   Despite cloud systems being modular and the ability to add and remove stuff without really shutting down the whole system, there are certain upgrades that really do require everything to stop. For example, if the hypervisor is being changed to a different one or has a major update, it might need to be shut down first, which means that the virtual environment will be unavailable for the duration of the upgrade. Also, if the system is moving to a new infrastructure and the old one is being retired, it might also require shutdown for migration. But this can be done by sections, slowly, so downtime can be lessened.

Utilization   Overutilization can cause adverse effects to a system. If the resources are being exhausted or approaching their limits, it might cause inconsistencies in files such as metadata and configuration files due to there not being enough resources to go around. In these cases, some portions really have to be shut down and rebooted. Scalability mitigates this, but in reality that benefit is only ideal and in practice. Especially in a pay-to-use model where a client might not be financially capable of scaling yet, some utilization may have to be dropped in order to stay within profitable margins.

Virtual Components of the Cloud

We have already discussed most of these components in the preceding sections and even in the preceding chapters, so the following sections will count as a recap and summary of sorts.

Virtualization is the key to cloud computing despite most people saying that its heart lies in the benefits and the functionalities. For us, the heart of any service or technology is the infrastructure that supports it, for good reason. Without it, the functionalities cannot be offered and the benefits cannot be achieved.

Virtual Network Components

Just as virtualization is at the heart of cloud computing, networking is the basis for delivery. Without it, there is no way to deliver the benefits and functionalities.

Virtual NIC   The virtual NIC is the logical equivalent of a physical network adapter and was specifically designed to mimic and emulate its functions and inner workings. It allows the virtual machine to be connected to a virtual network or to an external physical network by binding to a physical NIC or connecting to a virtual switch bound to a physical NIC.

This is one of the most essential components in a virtualized system because it allows communication between virtual components and the physical network, allowing the virtual machines to truly become part of the infrastructure.

Virtual HBA   When every facet of the data center (such as storage, servers, and storage area networks) goes virtual due to cloud computing, so too must the interfaces that connect them. The virtual host bus adapter is the logical equivalent of a host bus adapter used for input/output processing and communication between servers and storage devices. Like the physical HBA, the virtual one relieves the VM processor of I/O processing and facilitates high-speed I/O communication between it and all connected logical unit numbers (LUNs) and SANs.

With the virtualization of the HBA, it becomes easier to isolate parts of the network and facilitate better management and traffic efficiency, preventing unwanted overall downtime through virtual SANs.

Cloud Virtual Router   The cloud virtual router is the logical counterpart of a physical router in the same vein as virtual machines, virtual NICs, and virtual switches. It serves the same purpose in the virtual network as that of the physical one in the physical network. It is used for routing, but its main draw is easier administration of security such as firewalls and of network policies and using a familiar technology. But when we say virtual router, it could mean different things to different people because the concept has been around for a time. Even before proliferation of cloud computing, it has been used to mean a software implementation for allowing a host computer to act as a router through its regular NIC or wireless NIC.

The term *virtual router* still mostly refers to the software implementation described earlier; that is why we may specify that we mean cloud virtual routers, those that exist in hypervisors and used in virtualized environments to connect multiple virtual machines together. Virtual routers also serve to lessen the clutter that making a single host run hundreds of virtual machines creates. When there are so many virtual machines and virtual networks present, a routing virtual switch often is not up to the task because it really is not meant for that job. The switch keeps tabs on the MAC address of each NIC connected on its ports and is usually suitable for local networks with devices directly connected to it, but a router not only routes packets, it also ensures that they reach their destination using the shortest path possible and is responsible for connecting different networks together because of this capability. So when we have multiple networks within the virtual environment, the only logical way of connecting them to each other and to the outside network is through virtual routers that act as gateways between each virtual network.

Shared Memory

Cloud computing architecture demands that multiple machines and multiple availability zones can act together as one, able to consolidate resources into a large pool. Storage area networks, or SANs, do this for disk storage, but there is currently no SAN equivalent for main memory. That means that memory still resides in each individual physical machine or server, so there is a need for all of these machines to be able to pull their collective memory capacity into a pool and then be able to reallocate it to individual virtual machines that need it. This is quite important because a virtual machine can exist even when its individual pieces are scattered in different machines geographically. This is one way of implementing shared memory, specifically known as distributed memory, for redistribution, but it is not yet implemented, so currently virtual machines reside in a single host machine where they get their processing power (virtual CPU) and memory (virtual RAM), while the file that makes up the virtual hard disk can be striped across multiple machines or even SANs. Although, that would cause a bit of latency depending on the system, but it can and has been done.

A shared and distributed memory view does not distinguish from local or remote data, which can cause performance degradation, especially if the memory is allocated from geographically separated nodes. This actually is counterintuitive to the goal of main memory, which is to be a quick and physically near or close to the CPU (module). But the concept is in line with the goals of cloud computing and would especially help scientific research that needs supercomputing levels of power.

But current implementations of cloud shared memory allows for only a type of shared cache that exists between virtual machines.

Virtual CPU

The virtual CPU (vCPU) is the logical counterpart of the physical CPU and is meant to work as such. Each virtual machine is allocated one vCPU by default but may be assigned more CPUs or cores depending on the guest operating system and the number of CPUs the host contains. The virtual CPU does not directly correspond to a physical core or CPU but is represented as time shares on the physical CPU's resource stack; it is not a one-to-one assignment.

In a Type 2 hypervisor, this allows for more virtual machines to run on a single host without affecting the host's performance adversely up to a saturation point where there are too many timeshares that need to be accommodated, leading to various performance hits for all VMs as well as the host. But in a Type 1 hypervisor, the bare metal one that takes the place of an OS that runs the host machine, all of the CPU's processing power can be allocated to virtual machine vCPUs because the host does not actually require CPU time on its own because it is not running any sort of OS or software except the hypervisor itself.

As mentioned, the number of vCPUs that can be assigned to a virtual machine depends on the type of guest OS that is being run and the underlying hypervisor. Different hypervisors from different providers also have different limitations. This can also differ according to the subscription level that you are using. Higher subscription levels usually allow for more powerful virtual machines with more processors or computing power, more RAM, and more storage, which of course comes at increased costs. This is quite expected of the grid computing model that cloud computing uses; you pay for what you use, so if you use more, you have to pay more.

Storage Virtualization

We have discussed in the previous sections how virtual disks work and some details regarding virtualization. To recap, storage virtualization is creating a logical equivalent of storage devices within a virtualized environment. So we are effectively creating a simulation of separate storage devices, which in application are just single file formats located on the physical storage medium of the host. But for the virtual machine using it and to the user, it all appears in the same way that a physical storage medium would in a typical operating system.

Shared Storage

Cloud computing is a multitenant solution and is all about pooling resources and smart reallocation to those that need it. CPU time, main memory (RAM), network bandwidth, and of course storage are all gathered into a large share pool and allocated and reallocated, processes we refer to as provisioning and deprovisioning. So in essence, all tenants or users of the same infrastructure share computing resources with each other unknowingly because of abstraction. Each user sees only the part of the infrastructure and resources allocated to him, so it would appear to each one that they are the only users of the system.

So like all shared computing resources, shared storage is simply a large pool of storage capacity that is collected from all connected devices within the infrastructure that provide storage, such as host servers, SANs, and NAS.

Clustered Storage

Clustered storage, or grid storage, is a relatively new paradigm in storage technology that pushes the efficiency and scalability of storage area networks (SANs) to new and higher levels. It is based on concepts used in clustered computing, making use of large storage farms that are linked in a grid fashion through horizontal scaling with more storage servers rather than vertically using servers with more storage capacity.

Clustered storage systems are made up of smaller network-connected storage systems with administrative functions that manage individual disks to act as a collective whole. To a user client or a server making use of the clustered storage, the abstract collection appears as a single large pool of storage capacity. There may be more control because clients can be allowed to access smaller portions of the pool such as a single SAN or even micromanage single servers or disks. These storage clusters can be made available to the whole network for use, and each client is able to create a logical volume (like a virtual disk) on demand. The beauty of clustered storage is the modularity and failure tolerance; you can add and remove resources without affecting the whole pool. And because the smaller clusters that make up the whole can be located in different geographical areas, outages can be isolated to certain locations and clusters without adversely affecting the whole. Clustered storage would be highly available and fault tolerant.

But common clustered storage offerings available in the market today are still using legacy architectures. This older clustering technology requires a master controller that coordinates tasks among the different nodes in the cluster. This introduces a possible bottleneck and a single point of failure for the whole system, and it may also limit scalability because adding more servers also means that more nodes are now contending with the master controller's resources, which will eventually impede the performance of the whole system, a point where diminishing returns occur.

The newer clustering technology removes the central master by essentially creating multiple masters that control smaller portions of the cluster. These masters act as peers that, when combined with a distributed file system, are able to work in parallel with each other to enable sharing, selection, and aggregation of storage resources, which are likely to be distributed in different administrative domains. This method allows us to horizontally scale almost infinitely by simply adding new master controllers when more capacity is added and eliminating the single point of failure.

Clustered storage is the best approach to delivering cloud computing benefits of scaling as storage technology becomes cheaper and it becomes easier to add more resources into the pool.

Managing large pools of resources has historically been a complicated and expensive process, and often single points of failure can bring an entire system down, requiring more time and expense to get it back up. The answer to this problem is distributed storage clustering, which brings the following benefits:

- Easy management through multiple master controllers
- Failure tolerance because failure in some areas cannot take down the whole grid
- Scalability of capacity, performance, and availability through small and modular increments
- Higher utilization rates due to better administration
- Lower hardware cost because upgrades can be done in small batches at a time compared to building new data centers every time a new pool of resources is required

N_Port ID Virtualization

N_Port ID Virtualization (NPIV) is a new Fibre Channel facility that allows multiple worldwide names for ports and nodes to be assigned to a single N_Port, which can be a physical Fibre Channel host bus adapter (HBA) in a server or a target port on a storage array. This is in the context of storage area networks (SANs), logical unit numbers (LUNs), and virtual machines.

Normally, an N_Port will have a single N_Port_ID associated with it. This is not the same as the World Wide Port Name (WWPN), but their relationship is typically one-to-one, which means that every N_Port can have only one N_Port_ID and one WWPN. What NPIV does is allow one N_Port to have multiple IDs and hence multiple WWPNs as well.

To get an idea of why this is useful, consider a virtualized environment where you have multiple virtual machines and a LUN or a SAN that you want to be available to only specific virtual machines through a Fibre Channel. If you didn't use NPIV, the N_Port on the host would have only a single WWPN and ID. LUNs then would have to be zoned and presented to this single WWPN assigned to the single N_Port, but because all the virtual machines would be sharing this single N_Port, the same ID, and the same WWPN, all of them would be able to access the LUN when you want only a few specific ones to have access to it.

Using NPIV, you can now assign multiple N_Port_IDs and multiple WWPNs to the single physical N_Port you have on the host. When you register additional WWPNs, each virtual machine can have its own WWPN, so when you build SAN zones and present LUNs to virtual machines using the specific WWPN assigned to those VMSs, the LUNs will be accessible to only those specific VMs and not the others.

Summary

We started the chapter with some tutorials about basic cloud setup, such as creating and importing/exporting virtual machine templates and service templates. These are basic necessities for starting your cloud infrastructure; taking care of them also makes future deployments and provisioning of instances and resources easier to manage in the future. Installing guest tools on your VM or guest OS will increase its capabilities, such as being able to make use of hardware graphical acceleration or be seamlessly integrated into your desktop environment if you are using Type 2 hypervisors.

Knowing how to create clones and snapshots of virtual machine states will help in the fast creation and backup of VMs. A snapshot and a clone have similar uses, but they have fundamental differences. A clone is a full independent copy of a virtual machine from its settings to the contents of its hard drive, while a snapshot is essentially just a save of a specific state of a virtual machine and so is coupled to that specific virtual machine. The snapshot can be used to quickly jump between states of a VM and will be very useful in a test environment to help determine the difference between the states from before and after an error. Each snapshot is dependent on the original VM and will work for only that VM. A clone is an independent VM from its parent and can be used in any way after creation; it is simply a good way of replicating a VM in its specific state. It is also useful for testing purposes, especially for testing software installations and deployments so that you can work on a full environment without compromising the original VM in case something goes wrong.

You also learned in this chapter the various parts of a virtualized environment. The first one would be the virtual disk. It is simply a representation of a hard disk that the VM uses to store its files. On the networking side there is the virtual switch, which is in every way equivalent in function to the physical switch with the added bonus of having a lot more ports, which means that an entire virtual network can be supported by a single virtual switch bound to a physical NIC.

VLAN is not the actual virtual representation of a LAN as in connecting some VMs in a networking using a vSwitch. Rather, it is a concept of further subdividing a portion of a larger network so that those specific nodes can act as if they are connected locally even though they may span different geographical locations and different segments of a larger network. This means that they are able to communicate easily without the need for further authentication or encryption because they are treated as local connections and not as outside connections as they most probably are. A counterpart to the VLAN is the virtual storage network (VSAN). In the same vein, a VSAN is a way to further subdivide a large SAN into smaller ones. For example, you can subdivide a SAN with 10 servers into any combination into 5 VSANs composed of 2 servers each.

Once the infrastructure and environment has been set up, what comes next is data and process migration. Cloud technology allows easy data and process migration, and all of this can be done by the provider, allowing the local technical department to deal with other important issues.

Prior to everything, the migration requirements have to be established. The management, the IT department, and the provider all have to see eye to eye about what the customer wants and what is technically possible, not to mention the level of downtime allowed and the proper scheduling of the migration. The migration can be done either online or offline. If the current network infrastructure of an organization allows for a lot of data to be uploaded at an acceptable rate, then online migration is the best method, but if there is too much data and not enough time, offline migration is the best option. In offline migration, physical drives containing the data to be migrated have to be shipped or delivered to the provider's location to be uploaded there. On the other hand, if you are migrating your system from a virtual one to a physical one such as when virtualized servers can no longer really keep up with server requirements, even with more instances, then that would be a virtual to physical migration.

After all the migration, business operations can finally proceed using the new system. Now the focus shifts to maintenance of the new system and keeping all processes going at top condition, even perhaps to create better ones. This requires regular maintenance of servers, even virtual ones. Maintenance often means downtime, so it has to be scheduled accordingly. Fortunately, in virtualized environments, this does not have to be the case. It can mean running at lesser capacity because of the reduced number of servers, but there does not have to be real downtime where the service is not accessible at all.

Finally, you learned about virtual network components: the virtual switch, virtual HBA, and virtual router. These are the virtual analogues to the physical switch, router, and HBA, and they do exactly the same things with a few improvements, such as more ports, prevention of loopbacks, and other security features. We also dug further into the virtual CPU, which is just a time slice representation rather than actual CPU control. This means that there is no guarantee of CPU usage, but each vCPU is given a time allocation on the physical CPU. Finally, we discussed storage virtualization, how storage can be pooled so that it can be shared and how the capacity can be further increased through the use of clustered storage.

Chapter Essentials

Creating, Importing, and Exporting Templates and Virtual Machines   The creation of virtual machines is central to a virtualized environment. We went into some detail on how to create virtual machines from scratch, how to clone virtual machines, and how to take snapshots, which also act as clones. Virtual machine templates are important because they help to lessen the time to create multiple virtual machines of the same type.

Installing Guest Tools   Guest tools are applications that you install on the guest operating systems to allow the virtual machine to support additional functions, such as making better use of the GPU, allowing for shared storage, or dragging and dropping in the case of Type 2 hypervisors. The functions being provided by the guest tools depend entirely on the virtualization provider.

Snapshots and Cloning   Creating snapshots and cloning are good ways of creating backups of a virtual machine. Snapshots take a sort of photograph of the current state of the machine that you can restore at a later date. This is very convenient for reverting to a previous working state, especially if some settings that caused some undesired effects in the machine have been changed. Cloning, on the other hand, creates a full copy of the virtual machine as well as all of its files and settings. Unlike the snapshot, which is still connected to the original virtual machine, the clone is fully independent and can be deployed any time, even in a totally different virtual environment or host from that of the original.

Image Backups vs. File Backups   The two types of backups are image and file backups. File backups are selective in nature, meaning that backups are made of select files that are deemed important while other files are not backed up. The backups are in the form of copies of the file itself and not some interpretation of it, so it is a one-to-one copy. The backups are often stored in media or in places separate from the original location, such as an external disk or tape backup or even flash memory and optical media. Since only selected files are backed up, the resulting backup repository is relatively small compared to that of a total backup.

Image backup is a total and all-encompassing kind of backup. The method involves creating a disk image from the disk that needs to be backed up. Everything is captured by the backup, including unnecessary files such as temporary files, cache content, recycle bin contents, and even all of the viruses and malware if any. It is a total backup but with many drawbacks. One is that it takes up so much space, and then it takes time to create, so it can be done only periodically, like once a day. This means that you could lose all of your work if you are only halfway through the day and something bad happens. You would then have to revert to yesterday's backup, whereas for file backups, only the modified files need to be backed up again.

Virtual Disks   Virtual disks are the logical counterparts of physical hard disks. They are used in the same way as the physical ones, and for the guest operating system they would appear as physical disks. The virtual disks are created by the hypervisor as a single file located on the host's hard drive and as such can be ported or even copied.

Virtual Switches   Virtual switches are the logical counterparts of physical switches with some differences that are due mainly to enable enhanced security. For example, virtual switches are logically isolated from each other, they cannot be cascaded, and there is no mechanism for a virtual switch to map a port that connects to another virtual switch; it can only map ports unto itself. This keeps each switch isolated from other switches and prevents bad connections that attackers can exploit. There is also no need to cascade switches because a virtual switch can have as many ports as required, as opposed to the limited number of ports physical switches have. Only one virtual switch can be attached to a physical NIC.

VLAN   A virtual local area network, contrary to what the name might imply in the context of virtualization and cloud computing, is not the local area network formed when you connect virtual machines in the same host together. That is still referred to as a virtual network. A VLAN is actually a further subdivision of a larger network that is meant to work as if the nodes are connected locally even though they might be located in different geographic areas, as in different countries. For example, an organization has a global network across its various offices using the Internet or WANs, but all the regional managers want to be able to communicate with each other as if they were in a single office LAN. This is possible with a VLAN. Another example is a large building network. All of the computers are connected to the same large network, but it can be subdivided by floors or departments, which is all done via software and settings of the computers and the routers and switches in the network, without really altering the physical connections in the network. With a VLAN, you can connect virtual machines and physical computers together.

VSAN A virtual storage area network is similar to a VLAN. It is meant to further subdivide a storage area network into smaller parts that can be made available to different users. It is mostly meant for micromanaging the SAN.

Establishing Migration Requirements Migration can become a tricky endeavor, and sometimes a portion of data is lost in the process, as well as applications and systems no longer working correctly or as expected, even losing performance. Some will attribute this degradation to the cloud environment, when really the problem is with a botched migration.

It is very important that the migration goes off perfectly, so requirements have to be established by the business beforehand. Because your service provider will be the one to usually handle all migration, we now have this saying that migration is no longer a technical issue but a business one. It is the business side of the organization that will make use of the system and not the technical IT department, so the migration has to be in the hands of a business user or manager with the support of a technical manager.

Storage Migration Storage migration is simply transferring the data contents of a repository into a newer or more technologically advanced one, assuming that it is an upgrade and not a downgrade.

Online vs. Offline Migrations Online migrations are done through the Internet by streaming all of the data and the applications from the old system or repository right into the new one. This usually happens automatically and is done via replication, so there is often perceived disruption to the normal operations of the system. The only major requirement for this is that the current networking infrastructure of the organization supports the large amount of bandwidth that is needed to transfer large amounts of data. Most of the time the network provider will require an extra charge for the bandwidth used.

On the other hand, offline migrations are done when online migration is not feasible to do in a timely manner. The organization has to resort to saving all of the data, which needs to be migrated, into multiple storage devices and then shipping them to the new service provider so that the data can be uploaded into the system. Business managers and technical managers or representatives have to be around to oversee the migration at the other end just to ensure that everything is placed where it is supposed to be.

Physical to Virtual (P2V) Physical to virtual migration involves converting the software side of a physical machine into files that can be migrated into a virtual machine.

This includes the operating system, all the applications, and data in the physical machine. Sometimes it is just the data that needs to be migrated to a virtual machine, so the process only needs some form of replication or copying. But if a whole physical machine needs to be converted to a virtual machine, special software is required. The tools are often provided by the service provider.

Virtual to Virtual (V2V)   Virtual to virtual migration is often done when a host needs to be shut down for some reason, such as maintenance or retirement. The virtual machines are often cloned and then deployed to the new host while the original virtual machines are still running on the old host so that there will be little to no disruption of services.

Virtual to Physical (V2P)   This is the opposite of P2V and is often done when a virtual machine server needs to be able to produce more power in order to serve better. That is the current limitation of virtual machines; they cannot scale too much vertically, only horizontally. So when raw power is required, the best option is to convert the virtual machine into an actual physical server so all the applications and data have to be migrated there. The tools and procedures on how to convert a virtual machine into a physical one is provided by the service provider.

Maintenance Scheduling   Maintenance is important for any system because it ensures that the system will be performing in top condition for the duration of its lifetime. But it also means that there will be possible disruptions as the system itself or at least parts of it are taken down so that maintenance can be done. This will have an effect on the system's performance, making it slow and run at reduced capacity because of the missing parts. Because of this possible disruption, the maintenance schedule has to be set accordingly, and it has to be performed within the shortest time possible.

Reasons for Maintenance   The main reason for maintenance is to keep the system running at top condition and to prevent possible downtime and errors from happening in the future. But maintenance is not only about keeping everything together; upgrades, new feature releases, and testing all count under maintenance.

Virtual Network Components   The cloud environment is defined by its virtual components, all of which are logical representations of physical devices and constructs. These components are the virtual CPU, virtual disk, virtual NIC, virtual switch and router, virtual memory, virtual HBA, and many more.

Shared Memory   Shared memory by definition is a pool of memory that can be allocated to any client that needs it. Unfortunately, in current implementations it is not yet possible to literally share this resource into a pool so all guest operating systems would still get their much-needed memory from the host machine.

Virtual CPU   The virtual CPU is the logical counterpart of the physical CPU, and rather than being able to directly control the host's CPU, this virtual CPU is simply a representation of timeshares that are allocated to it from the host's overall CPU time by the hypervisor. Together with graphics processing, this is the biggest unscalable factor for virtual machines. When more power is required by a virtual server and the problem cannot be remedied by more virtual servers, the only option would be to convert that virtual machine into an actual server so that it can have access to a powerful CPU, or a whole set of them.

Storage Virtualization   Storage virtualization is essentially creating virtual disks from a large-capacity pool that is a conglomeration of the storage capacity of all the hosts, servers, and SANs in the system. A single file format is created that the virtual machine can see as an actual disk. All of the files, operating system, and applications of a virtual machine are located in this single virtualized storage. It makes a virtual machine very portable because you only have to copy or transfer this virtual disk file to other environments in order to have the same virtual machine, provided you have configured for the new virtual machine to have the same settings as the old one.

Chapter

8

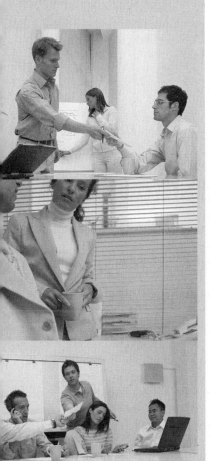

Hardware Management

TOPICS COVERED IN THIS CHAPTER INCLUDE:

✓ Cloud hardware resources

✓ BIOS/firmware configuration

✓ Minimum memory capacity and configuration

✓ Number of CPUs

✓ Number of cores

✓ NICs quantity, speeds, and configurations

✓ Internal hardware compatibility

✓ HBAs

✓ Storage media

✓ Proper allocation of hardware resources (host)

✓ Proper virtual resource allocation (tenant/client)

✓ Cloud storage options

✓ Management differences between public, private, and hybrid clouds

✓ Tiering

✓ RAID levels

✓ File system types

Chapter 7, "Practical Cloud Knowledge: Install, Configure, and Manage Virtual Machines and Devices," touched on a lot of technical details about the cloud and related technologies. We will be going in the same direction here in this chapter as we visit, or rather revisit, a lot of the technologies and terms you have encountered in previous chapters and go into a bit more detail.

Cloud Hardware Resources

In earlier chapters, we discussed how cloud hardware technology isn't exactly different from any other enterprise and consumer technology, and for the most part, the cloud paradigm actually changed computer hardware technology for everyone. Computer hardware technology (CPU, disk, and networking) is progressing to fill the need for better *cluster* and *distributed computing*. The difference between enterprise and cloud technology is not in the hardware or even the software, because both paradigms are able to make use of the same technology and even apply virtualization. The real difference is through implementation, so it is worth our while to familiarize ourselves with the different hardware resources and configurations used in implementing cloud technologies.

In the following sections, we will discuss in detail some of the configurations that are being used for cloud infrastructures and virtualized environments.

BIOS/Firmware Configurations

The pre-boot sequence and BIOS configurations remain important aspects of many application configuration requirements as well as other requirements and settings that need to be controlled by IT administrators. But for most, moving to the cloud means losing control of this important aspect. This is because it happens before the operating system loads inside a virtual machine.

With pre-cloud computing enterprise installations, application developers and system administrators had unrestricted access to the system's pre-boot sequence for easing asset management, recovering from failure, or even fine-tuning system performance and compatibility. Cloud computing Infrastructure as a Service (IaaS) and other solutions should be the same and offer access to BIOS capabilities to allow further tweaking and customization of virtual machine performance and compatibilities.

By allowing for BIOS-level access, service providers are able to make their virtual machines feel and look more like their bare metal counterparts. This gives IT admins more control, and they are able to feel more at home as well as get all of the benefits that cloud computing offers.

To date, only ProfitBricks, a relative newcomer to the cloud scene, has announced explicit user-end BIOS configuration support. The larger providers like Amazon, Microsoft, Oracle, and Google do not explicitly allow (as a feature) users to directly configure BIOS settings for the infrastructure or for individual VMs, but they may support this through other methods, such as special configuration requests, internal script programs, and other specialized tools.

Minimum Memory Capacity and Configuration

Virtual machines may not really be as fast as their equivalent hardware with the same specs, but numbers are still important. When you're creating virtual machines, the minimum memory capacity should be above that of the requirements of the OS and the required applications combined. In a cloud environment, you can provision for additional resources, but, for example, provisioning for additional resources like memory to hundreds or thousands of virtual machines because of miscalculation of memory requirements would become a costly mistake.

This doesn't mean that virtual machines are inefficient; on the contrary, they are cost effective in terms of the ratio of computing power to cost. The message here is that too much of something won't necessarily make things better. After a certain point, you will usually get diminishing returns, especially in a service environment where every move costs money. You really need to plan every move so that you reap the actual benefits instead of additional costs.

Number of CPUs

Depending on the function of a virtual machine, whether it is meant to be a server or a simple personal computer, the number of required virtual CPUs (vCPUs) will differ. The number of vCPUs will depend on the number of logical cores on the host machine and the type of guest operating system (non-server OSs will be able to support fewer CPUs) installed on the virtual machine. The number of logical cores is double that of physical cores installed if hyperthreading is enabled. But this will entirely be up to the provider if its platform can support the number of CPUs that your virtual machines require. It also requires support for virtual *symmetric multiprocessing (SMP)* on the guest operating system. Figure 8.1 shows how virtual SMP factors into the virtualized environment.

Since vCPUs are simply representations of time slices in the host's physical and logical CPUs, a virtual machine cannot have more virtual CPUs than the number of logical cores that the host has. Again, this really depends on the maximum number of vCPUs that your provider can license to you. For example, VMware vSphere imposes the following limits per license:

Standard   A maximum of eight vCPUs and 24 GB of memory per VM

Enterprise   Eight vCPUs and 32 GB of memory per VM

Enterprise Plus   32 vCPUs and 48 GB of memory per VM

FIGURE 8.1 Virtual environment with SMP

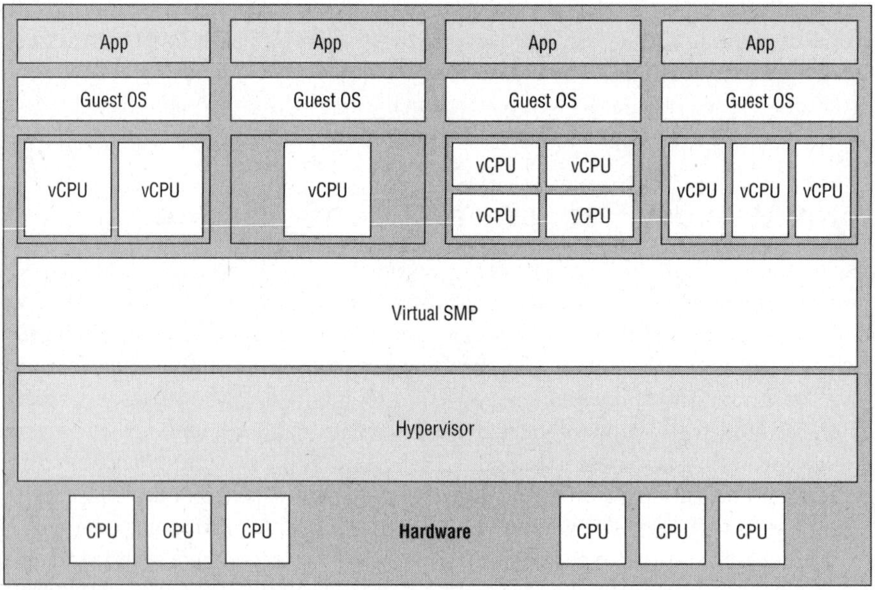

This actually means that you may have to purchase additional licenses if you require more memory per VM, but a maximum of 64 vCPUs seems to be the current technical limitation for ESX 5.5 hypervisor. Sun VirtualBox 3.0 supports up to 32 vCPUs per VM, while the relatively new Microsoft Hyper-V still only supports a maximum of 4.

Because of performance and service tiers, you must consider the needs of your organization, which will be reflected by the specs of your virtual machines. It's okay to start small as long as it is enough for your workloads. Cloud flexibility and scalability will always allow you to grow with your needs. Most providers offer *auto-provisioning*, which allows you to scale resources automatically according to load.

Number of Cores

Multicore virtual CPU support allows you to control the number of cores per virtual CPU or virtual socket in a virtual machine. This is quite useful because not all guest operating systems support multiple sockets or vCPUs, so using multicore vCPUs can allow a virtual machine to utilize more of the host's CPU cores and increase overall virtual machine performance.

Again, a virtual machine cannot have more virtual CPUs than the number of logical CPUs in the host, which is simply the number of physical CPU cores present, or twice that if hyperthreading is enabled. So if a host has 8 CPUs with four cores each, then it has 32 logical CPUs without hyperthreading and 64 logical CPUs if hyperthreading is enabled.

Let us assume that a virtual machine with a guest operating system capable of 4 virtual CPUs or sockets is used. It can be configured in the following ways:

- 4 virtual CPU/sockets with 1 core per CPU/socket
- 2 virtual CPU with 2 cores per CPU
- 1 virtual CPU with 4 cores

NIC Quantity, Speeds, and Configurations

A host to a virtual environment needs to have multiple channels for data traffic, and the only way to provide them is via network interface cards. NICs are also required for connecting each virtual machine to the network because a VM's vNIC needs to be bound to physical NIC in some networking configurations. But theoretically, you can make do with a single NIC on the host and share that among all the virtual machines residing in that host. However, saying that configuration is not recommended would be a gross understatement. It would work, but network performance would be severely limited.

In network virtualization, we can typically assign a single NIC to a vSwitch or vRouter to act as a gateway to the virtual network through that single physical NIC. But taking into consideration all the performance, security, and failure precautions, we need multiple NICs in a single bare metal host. To facilitate proper networking, we need a large bandwidth path between the host and the network core. That means NIC teaming and *bandwidth aggregation*, which already requires at least two physical NICs. Long story short, we need a lot of NICs in our host, but the question of how many really depends on the performance requirements, the workflow, and the technical and physical limitations of the host hardware as well as the hypervisor that needs to run it all.

So when the host's hardware is planned, all the performance requirements have to be established and it has to be fitted to the budget. This includes the number of physical processor sockets, memory sockets and memory capacity, and of course the number of slots available for NICs on the motherboard and its extensions. The hypervisor maximums also have to be taken into consideration, though this maximum is often larger than what is possible for the hardware configuration. For example, VMware ESX hypervisor can support as many as 32 e1000 1 Gigabit Ethernet ports on Intel PCI-x, but most high-end server motherboards may only be able to support up to eight physical NICs aside from the built-in internal NICs because of PCI port limitations. This requires more hardware to be put together before that limitation is reached.

Internal Hardware Compatibility

When you're building or choosing the host hardware, the mix-and-match method is not going to cut it. Extensive research must be made regarding full hardware compatibility when you're building a host from scratch. For example, every part of the host server (such as processor or NIC) has to be server grade and not consumer grade. There are often server versions of consumer-grade computer parts, which are optimized for workflows typically found in a server. This is basic knowledge, but even though some of these parts are server grade and designed to work with any other brand and module out there, that does not always mean they actually do. There are often inconsistencies in compatibility, where one part works well with a certain model from a certain manufacturer but not with another. Sometimes this problem does not manifest itself until later, so firmware or driver patches have to be made to make the parts fully compatible and remove any bugs. This is where research comes in, because these things are not advertised or not really generally known. We have to learn from the mistakes, experiences, and observations of others.

Even prebuilt systems such as ones being sold by Dell and HP sometimes come with a little conflict between the individual parts, which has to be addressed by patches or fixed in later models.

Storage Media

We have entered the era of big and even bigger data in terms of scale and analytics. We are being flooded by a lot of unstructured data as well, mostly from the high growth of digital archives for compliance-related data (which is mandated by government and standardization entities), multimedia files (such as video, audio, and digital images), some fixed content, and the ever-growing data related to social networking.

It is difficult to predict and define what capabilities and benefits we get from cloud storage technology as it continues to evolve. But the benefits of cloud storage is already obvious in two areas: storing archival data and storing unstructured data.

A lot of archival and compliance data is unstructured because of the lack of a proper and universal naming conventions and tagging and indexing schemes. Therefore, unstructured data is stored as files and not as blocks, so capacity more than management is required for this type of data.

For decades, economic factors have been major influences on storage initiatives and storage infrastructures that organizations consider and deploy. Now, cloud computing provides the flexibility and potential cost savings, with both public and private clouds, for storing massive amounts of data.

Let's look at a few types of storage media being used in cloud computing.

Tape

Tape storage has traditionally been the go-to media for storing large archival and backup data, mainly because of economy, with the relatively low cost per gigabyte of capacity. But it has always been viewed by many as an outdated medium; you have probably seen it being used in movies to indicate to viewers that they are watching a scene that occurs in the '60s or '70s. It would probably surprise a lot of people to know that tape storage technology has continued to evolve. We just don't hear about it a lot, especially if we don't work in large archival data centers. It certainly isn't advertised in the mass consumer market.

But tape media has continually evolved to keep up with the archival needs of large corporations. We already have enterprise-class *tape robotics*, which allow tape drives to be rapidly changed and selected, and the Linear Tape File System (LTFS), which allows us to search and index files in a tape drive.

Though tape storage might have taken a backseat to faster and more easily accessible disk arrays, it is still being used as a cheap archival storage system. Now, with the continuously increasing demands for high-capacity, low-cost media with a long storage life, tape storage is gaining wide use in cloud computing systems.

In the age of cloud computing and big data, the challenge is to contribute to the retention and analysis of immense and diverse data. In the area of analysis, the demand is for significantly enhanced I/O performance because of the need for fast processing. Disks and SSDs can serve well for this purpose. But in the area of retention, there is an incomparably greater quantity of data that needs to be stored than in the past, and it is important to archive it at low cost for a very long time. We refer to low cost not only for initial investments but also in terms of operations management and energy costs. This is where tape storage shines.

Tape media is very cheap for the storage density it provides; it costs less to maintain because minimal energy is expended while it's idle, so heat is not an issue, which also helps in its reliability and lifespan.

Solid-State Drives

The solid-state drive (SSD) is a relatively new storage technology, having more in common with flash drives than disks drives. It is basically a high-capacity flash-based storage device. Because there are no moving mechanical parts, failure is less likely compared to disks. However, capacity is not yet where it should be, but it's steadily increasing. SSDs were initially more expensive compared to disks, but that gap is slowly getting smaller. There will come a time when SSDs offer more capacity at a lower costs than disk drives.

SSDs are currently the fastest storage media available and are being used in cloud computing and big data, especially for systems that deal with dynamic data and need to move it around frequently for analysis and other processes.

Disk

Disk storage is the most common storage media being used in the world today; it provides a combination of performance, capacity, and affordability. It is getting cheaper to manufacture large-capacity disks as the technology matures. The problem with it is actually reliability; there is only so much we can do to make it durable because moving parts will always wear down and break faster than nonmoving ones. It also requires relatively more energy to run a single disk than it does to run a SSD or tape drive. A SSD requires only a little power to run, and although it's also mechanical, a tape drive can simply stop running when it's not in use, compared to a disk, which continues to spin even when idle. This means that a disk storage array actually needs sufficient cooling to maintain performance and avoid failure.

Proper Allocation of Hardware Resources (Host)

Cloud computing promises virtually unlimited resources, but this is only due to smart provisioning, scalability, and the ease of simply adding additional hosts and storage arrays to increase capacity. But the truth is, actual resources are very limited, and that is why they should be allocated properly.

Providers are offering varied service portfolios that differ in resource configurations and additional services. So a comprehensive solution for optimizing resource allocation should be fundamental for any service provider. And because you will be paying for every move you make if you are at the customer end of a cloud service, it also makes sense to have your own resource allocation policies and rules.

The following sections provide some insight into proper resource allocation, but because there are no set standards as of yet, they will fall under the category of advice and as such may not be suitable for all organizations or situations (although there is now research being done in this area).

Memory

Memory is required by all applications and is one of the most important resources a computer needs. It is one of the most limited resources in the data center because hardware technology still has limitations on how many memory sticks can be accommodated and even the maximum amount of memory the hardware or OS can handle.

As a rule of thumb, if you are a customer, allocating memory should be based on the workload that the VM will undertake. If the VM is a simple PC used for code development or testing, then it will not need much memory, perhaps 1 or 2 gigabytes will suffice. But if you are provisioning a virtual server or something similar that handles heavy workloads, it makes sense to provision it with lots of memory.

This seems to be straightforward, and you would think people would understand it at the onset, but it may surprise you that many do not see the importance of being lean. Most users who self-provision VMs like to put in the highest specs they can come up with simply because they like looking at large numbers. Usually this is due to ignorance, not knowing that each VM instance may add up to overall costs, and the assumption that there are enough resources to go around. Proper education and constant reminders, as well as properly laid out policies, are the easiest solutions to this problem.

But on the part of the host, memory really is not reserved for each VM, even though an amount is specified for each one. Memory is dynamically allocated to each VM that requires it, and the amount that each VM is supposed to have is just the limit that can be allocated. On-demand resource allocation is key to efficiency in terms of smartly allocating a very important in-demand and finite resource.

Memory is treated as a large pool, and bits and pieces of it are allocated to VMs that require it. If this were not the case and VMs were given the slice that they initially wanted, the resource pool would be drained quickly and most of the resource slices allocated would be idle. That is why there is a need for smart allocation with constant checks of idle resources so they can be put back in the pool to be reallocated to those that need it.

Dynamic memory can be allocated through a technique called swapping, which involves transferring data present in idle memory into caches and other forms of storage for later retrieval while the idle memory is sent back to the pool. When low memory is detected in the host, swapping is enabled, and the hypervisor "steals" idle memory that has been allocated to virtual machines and moves it to a virtual-machine-based swap file, which then frees up host physical memory. But this has huge performance impact on the virtual machine, so it should be used as a last resort.

Another memory allocation technique is called transparent page sharing (TPS). A host runs multiple virtual machines that share the same profile, such as the same OS, same hardware specs, and the same workflows. Because of these similarities, there is a fair amount of identical memory pages that can be shared by multiple virtual machines so that each of them does not have to keep a copy; they could just access the same page while the hypervisor reclaims the other identical pages. The performance of this method is determined by the page scan rate and opportunities for shared pages.

Central Processing Unit (CPU)

The CPU, or in this case the vCPU, is at the heart of the VM instance and can be considered another core resource. Relying on knowing the exact number of vCPUs required for your VM's workload is not a straightforward approach, and there really is no way to be exact. You need to determine the amount of CPU time required by a virtual machine, let's say a web server, to provide satisfactory response times for the end user of the application. This amount totally depends on the workload that needs to be processed by the web server. But since workloads and traffic on the Internet significantly differ from time to time, you cannot simply determine the resource requirement at the peak rate because that amount of resources will be underused during off-peak times.

The amount of CPU resource that should be allocated to a virtual machine must depend on two factors: the achievable performance with a given resource allocation and the associated resource cost to the user. This amount of resource can be determined by creating an allocation model that establishes the relationship between the amount of CPU resource and its corresponding level of performance, such as comparing the response time to the amount of CPU resource. This model will then be used to determine the amount of resource to be allocated to a VM based on the desired performance level. However, it cannot be entirely accurate because of the complexity brought by multiple layers from the hypervisor, the guest OS, and the subsequent running applications, so there has to be additional checking. There must be a feedback loop wherein the allocation is fine-tuned based on the performance feedback of the virtual machine, so any inaccuracies in the model can be compensated by feedback and adjustment cycles. For example, if a virtual server is supposed to cater to a thousand users at once, and based on the model, the appropriate amount of computing resource is given to it. If feedback then indicates that it is not performing satisfactorily, additional resources have to be allocated; less resources should be allocated if the server is performing above expectations. This sort of dynamic allocation allows us to provision lean machines that work satisfactorily as intended, not allocating too much or too little.

Storage and Network Allocation

Storage is easier to allocate because it is the most abundant and easy to scale out of all the resources, but you still have to be smart and lean with allocation since it is still finite. During provisioning of a VM instance, you can choose to create a static or dynamic virtual disk. A static disk's size is no longer expandable, while a dynamic disk will scale along with the growth of content on the VM. Most providers will set limits in the number of vCPUs available for each virtual machine for each product set offering. If the customer wants more-powerful virtual machines, they have to avail of more-expensive offerings or pay for extra resources used.

Network bandwidth allocation is a different matter because unlike CPU, memory, and storage, it is not proportionally shared according to payment, nor does any provider offer minimum guarantees on network bandwidth. This resource is difficult to share because the network allocation for internal virtual machines depends on its connections from outside networks, which are out of the provider's control. And as part of the quality of service agreement, the service provider has to offer fast and satisfactory access to the virtual machines and the cloud, which means full access of the network. But in the cloud computing paradigm we should be able to proportionately share this resource.

First you need to fulfill some requirements.

Guaranteeing Minimum Bandwidth   One is that you should be able to provide each tenant or client with a minimum guarantee for network bandwidth that they can expect for each VM they have without regard for the other tenants' network utilization. This is the minimum guarantee.

Providing High Utilization Performance   Another requirement to be met is to be able to provide high utilization performance, which is providing more network bandwidth to applications with high utilization in terms of bandwidth when other tenants are actually using less. This will significantly improve the performance of applications that experience a dynamic traffic flow, which may increase or decrease dramatically rather quickly.

There are two ways to tackle this problem, but there are trade-offs. If you follow a minimum guarantee path, you cannot provide proportionality because every VM, client, or tenant will be allocated bandwidth whether they are using it or not. This leads some bandwidth being underutilized. However, if you implement proportionality in allocation, you may not be able to guarantee minimum network performance at all times because you will need to use a first-come, first-served model. Tenants who have been network-idle and have not been allocated minimum bandwidth will experience little or no connectivity, at least for a short time until proportional resource allocation has finally run its course. There are downsides to everything, so you just have to find the proper balance. A hybrid approach might work, making the client decide whether to opt for proportional or minimum guarantee depending on their needs, which will then be reflected in the service-level agreement (SLA).

Entitlement/Quotas (Shares)

For a host or service provider, the most obvious resource management measure related to tenants is the imposition of quotas, which should be a clearly defined line stating how large a share each one is entitled to. This makes it easy to actually determine the actual tenant capacity of the infrastructure in terms of license or service tiers. So even without the use of advanced resource sharing algorithms in the hypervisor, you get a clear picture of the full extent of the number of tenants that can be supported satisfactorily.

Let us go back to our comparison of a multitenant cloud environment and an apartment building. Just like an apartment building, a cloud service will have entitlements that can be likened to rooms, which differ in size and amenities, so the owner (service provider) knows exactly how many rooms there are and hence the total capacity of the building (in the case of the cloud environment, the capacity of the infrastructure). Because resources in a cloud environment are dynamically allocated to each tenant's entitlement requirements, the overall capacity would vary, but at least you have a good estimate of how many more license entitlements can be given before you would need to expand the infrastructure again to support more tenants.

This is why many service providers offer different choices for licensing their services and they vary in price and resource entitlement. It depends solely on the type of cloud service being delivered. This is usually the case for SaaS and IaaS vendors, and hypervisor solutions sold by companies like VMware and Microsoft are geared toward creating such environments.

Specific limits must then be established for specific service tiers or entitlements.

Hard Limit   A hard limit is a limit that cannot be circumvented in any way. It is a hard-coded limit that is always imposed until the provider says otherwise. For example, there used to be a 32 GB hard limit for supported host memory in the VMware ESXi 5.1 free version. Anything more than 32 GB of memory will be ignored because of the imposed hard limit.

Soft Limit   A soft limit is something that is not absolute; you can actually go over a soft limit, but there are usually fines, penalties, or extra charges imposed. The most common resource with this sort of limit is bandwidth. When you have exceeded your soft limit for bandwidth, you will be charged for every additional resource used.

Reservations

Resource allocation in cloud computing, as we have discussed, is usually not defined because there are many algorithms that can be used to dynamically allocate unused (though previously reserved) resources when they are required. For memory, the usual process is called ballooning, which is basically a set amount of RAM that has to be retrieved from various guest OSs without their actual consent.

Licensing

Licensing in cloud computing is similar to enterprise licensing. Customers have to pay for a set of features and products, and it is the primary source of business revenue for cloud operators. For example, VMware provides a free version of its hypervisor, which is good enough in a very basic sense but would never be enough in a production environment. In turn, those that license the cloud software infrastructure from VMware create the actual cloud environment together with the hardware infrastructure, so they could bring an actual multitenant cloud to customers who license and use the resources, services, and infrastructure being provided.

Resource Pooling

Computer resources can be divided into three categories: compute, networks, and storage. We treat the resources we have in a cloud infrastructure as resource pools. We view resources as a sum, or a single large pool, such as when we say that a host has 128 gigabytes of RAM or that a storage cluster's capacity is 1 petabyte or that a system has 128 teraflops of computing power. This simply makes it easier to distribute and collect the resources if we view it as a single pool, and it's also easier to manage.

The idea here is that resources can be dynamically allocated from these large resource pools while idle resources previously allocated to tenants can be reclaimed and returned to the pool. Tenants can dynamically scale with the workloads they have as long as the pool has contents. The management of the resources would be abstracted from the tenants, who would simply perceive the pool to be limitless.

Proper Virtual Resource Allocation (Tenant/Client)

For the host, resource allocation is all about proper management, allocation, and recollection to keep the resource pools filled. At the other side of the equation is the tenant. Abstracted from what the underlying hypervisor is doing, the tenant view on resource allocation is about scalability to keep up with workloads while keeping things lean in order to keep costs down.

Virtual CPU

The vCPU is often the most controlled among the resources because it is the most finite and most expensive. Service providers often impose hard limits for the deployment for each VM instance since this is the only resource that cannot be literally divided among users. As previously discussed, each VM instance is given only a certain amount of CPU time based on the vCPU allocated for it.

The amount of vCPU that can be assigned to a VM usually depends on the service tier or package that you have licensed. For example, most service providers would probably allow a single dual-core vCPU for their cheapest standard package and more than eight vCPUs for their most-expensive package. So it goes without saying that you should choose the service package most suitable to your workflows; do not go lower or higher. Lower-cost packages would not offer enough performance and capacity, while higher-cost ones might not offer enough benefits because some of the resources are underutilized.

Memory

As with every virtual resource, virtual memory limits will be imposed for every service package. The cheaper the package, the less available memory provided. The usual scheme for memory allocation is like that for vCPU, where you have to specify the amount of memory for each instance.

In recent years, some service providers have begun offering virtual memory as resource pools that tenants can make use of in any way they want. This allows for great flexibility because you can allocate more memory to specific instances and less to others, so you can produce very lean virtual machines.

Storage and Network Allocation

Just like physical computers, virtual machines are created for different purposes. Some are created for computation, others are for storage (such as database servers), and others are meant to serve applications through a network. The latter requires more bandwidth than compute or memory resources. This has to be considered when selecting the service package to use. You also need to consider whether the service provider can actually provide enough network resources for high-networking-demand applications.

As for storage, we have what we call storage tiering, which we discuss later in this chapter. Tiering is mostly related to backups and allows you to select the best storage resource for your application in terms of performance, availability, and cost. But if you are just in need of storage capacity, the continuing advancement in disk technology has ensured that this resource is abundant and cheap. Even in the cheaper packages, storage capacity is ample. Besides, if you need more than what is provided in your service package, you could always use more; you just have to pay extra.

Entitlement/Quotas (Shares)

Entitlement and quotas come predefined in the service package. This is standard in order to prevent overutilization from a single source, even if that source can afford it.

These limits are set as hard or soft limits. For example, if you allocated a static hard drive of 100 GB for your VM instance, then you are stuck with that amount for that specific drive. There is no way to increase unless you have a spare virtual drive. That is a hard limit.

A soft limit, on the other hand, is one that is more flexible, though it is still considered a limit. A good example is your bandwidth quota. Your network connection will not be cut off if you reach it, but there are always consequences if you go beyond the soft limit. Usually you would incur additional costs, which may be higher per gigabyte than the standard rate of your package, or your bandwidth and network performance might be intentionally reduced. The hard and soft limits of the service package should be highlighted so that the customer is able to incorporate them into their planning, and automatic notifications should be set up so that there will be a notification whenever you are nearing these limits.

Dynamic Resource Allocation

Dynamic resource allocation is there simply to make our lives easier. Instead of the administrator manually evaluating the resource utilization of virtual machines and then assigning more resources where it's deemed necessary, specialized monitoring algorithms in the hypervisor react to different situations and allocate or remove resources dynamically based on the business logic or settings that are present for each scenario. These settings could include the amount of traffic, process utilization, and even cost-to-performance ratios. With dynamic allocation, precious time is saved by the administrator, not to mention that a human operator may not be fast enough to manually cope with dynamic workloads.

Resource Pooling

In a tenant's view, resource pools are hierarchical abstractions of virtual resources that can be arranged according to importance or weight. Pools are hierarchical, so there can be parent and child pools. The parent represents a higher order of virtual machines that have priority and access to more resources. By using pools that pertain to certain people or departments, administrators can flexibly allocate resources to these entities and even implement isolation, delegation, and access control.

Physical Resource Redirection and Mapping to Virtual Resources

Virtual machines sometimes require connection with outside physical world resources such as thumb drives and external hard drives. This would require the virtual machine to access a physical port located on the host computer to connect with the device.

Serial Ports

A virtual serial port must be set up between the virtual machine and the host computer. The virtual machine can then capture data directly from the host's serial port. There aren't a lot of devices that require a serial port nowadays, but an oscilloscope and other such sensing instruments come to mind. These devices can be connected to the host's serial port while data is being captured by the virtual machine.

USB and Parallel Port Mapping

Much like the serial connection of the VM and host through a virtual serial port, we are able to connect the VM to the host's various USB ports and parallel ports. This is called USB pass-through and parallel port mapping. Parallel ports are still used for devices like printers and scanners.

Management Differences between Public, Private, and Hybrid Clouds

Managing pools of resources for distribution may differ depending on the workflows and processes being used by the organization, as it should because efficiency is an important factor for proper delivery of cloud services. Different types of cloud computing require different management styles and processes in order to be successful. Policies and management processes applied to a public SaaS cloud will not be efficient when used for a private IaaS one.

The management tools and software an organization uses may be the same exact ones, depending on the organization's choices, but they must differ in how they are configured and how policies are shaped. In the following sections, we will take a look at why.

Public Cloud Management

Customers of public cloud services have the added advantage of offloading technical management processes to the service provider. That is part of the service provider's business model, so it should already have been considered and planned for. As a user of a paid service, making wise use of resources to avoid unnecessary expense is always top priority, and therefore proper and stringent management of these resources has to be imposed. The best way to do this is by restricting the provisioning of instances and resources per user according to their needs. There would always be exceptions, so management policies should reflect this also.

A service provider selling cloud services such as SaaS and IaaS has to adhere to strict and direct management policies to avoid problems such as overdrafting of resources toward one group or toward certain customers (those who can afford to avail more than they actually need), leaving other customers no slice of the resource pie. Sure, everyone is paying for what they use, but no one should be allowed to monopolize resources simply because they can afford it. The service provider has signed contracts with each and every one of its customers to deliver the service they need, so everyone should be provided with what they require, even if it means having to deny others extra services they may want. Of course, there should be enough resources to go around; if not, it negates the benefit of scalability. But there will certainly be occasions such as these, call them worst-case scenarios, that will test the limits of the service provider's infrastructure. It is just good management to be prepared for them.

As a manager or administrator of a public cloud, delivering services through the pay-per-use model, you must maintain significant economies of scale on your side, which in turn allows you to deliver scalability and flexibility to your customers. As we have established, this requires tight management protocols and best practices. Sometimes trial and error is required, because we cannot really foresee all the different situations that may arise. Sometimes we have to learn from our mistakes or the mistakes of others, especially in terms of security, which can sometimes look very similar to a chess game between security professionals and hackers.

Managing a public cloud means having the flexibility to cope with different customer demands and tailoring your services to what your customers need in a way that draws them and locks them in, not through vendor lock-in but through loyalty and satisfaction.

Private Cloud Management

A key difference between a public and a private cloud is who is managing what. For a public cloud, the provider is often managing resources on the back end to make it as painless as possible for the users, but for a private cloud, it is often the organization or the users themselves who manage the cloud environment or infrastructure. This in and of itself will cause there to be a lot of differences in management style and policies.

Because of the feeling of ownership a private cloud brings, policies for its usage will often be less strict and more forgiving. This is especially true if the organization is implementing a private cloud using its own infrastructure. There may be no service tiering or payment for additional instances or resources, giving users more leeway when it comes to provisioning and using those resources.

The management style will often be lax, allowing users to do as they please most of the time and imposing only certain best practices, such as "deprovisioning" of resources and instances that are no longer in use. However, if the private cloud is a service from a third-party provider, there will still be fees and subscriptions imposed, making computing resources valuable commodities that should be used with care and planning. In this case, the management style would be similar to that for public clouds.

Hybrid Cloud Management

Hybrid clouds are a mixture of the two previous types, so therefore, they also require a mixture of both management styles. The management for the public cloud portion should be stringent, with emphasis on proper usage and limitations, while for the private side, which is usually deployed in-house, the management policies can be more open.

Management Styles and Policies

There are no management styles and policies set in stone for cloud computing yet, though there are organizations and people trying to standardize the field. But since the standards are not yet in place, each organization must find the management style and policies that would best suit its situation. An organization must assess its capabilities and then match that with its needs. For example, if your organization requires a lot of computing power for your virtual machine instances and also requires that your users are able to provision as much as they need, then it seems obvious that the management style should be less strict. If you impose thriftiness here, it might just have a negative impact on the workflow and the quality of the results. It would also mean that you are better off getting or deploying a private cloud in the first place.

Tiering

We discussed the different disk types and the benefits of each earlier in this chapter, and now you understand that storing specific types of data onto the appropriate kinds of disks can increase performance as well as decrease costs for storage. This flexibility in storing data is another reason cloud computing should be considered by most organizations, especially data-driven ones.

Tiering refers to a storage infrastructure that has a simple two-tier architecture, such as one consisting of both SCSI disks and tape drives. It can also refer to a more-complex architecture, where there are three, four, or more tiers, each tier differing in performance and purpose.

By using tiered storage, an organization can control exactly where their data is going to be stored based on the performance, cost, availability, and recovery requirements of a specific application. For instance, if you have data that needs to be recovered quickly, such as transaction and user records, you would want them to be stored in fast disks or SSDs, while data required for compliance and regulatory purposes may be stored in slower and cheaper tape storage. This helps an organization plan its data and information life cycle management properly, and proper data management helps to reduce costs and increase overall efficiency.

Organizations can establish their data storage tiering requirements by determining functional differences in data such as restoration and replication needs. The general rule of thumb is that dynamic data, which is often mission critical and required by applications and users quickly and frequently, is stored in lower-tier storage for increased performance and nonessential data, such as long-term backups, can be stored in slower, higher-level tiers.

The different tiers are determined by the kind of access, performance and reliability associated with the kind of data you are storing. Time and money can be saved by implementing or making use of a tiered data storage infrastructure.

Performance Levels of Each Tier

Organizations have to define each type of data and then determine how each is classified. The criteria can be in the form of questions, such as, How critical is the data for the daily business processes of the organization? How long is the data going to be archived (days, months, or even years)? How frequently will the data change and how quickly will it need to be restored? The answer to these questions and many more will determine which tier is appropriate.

Tier 0   Tier 0 data is defined as data that is mission-critical, frequently accessed, or recently accessed or that requires high levels of security. This data requires very high I/O activity and low latency and a mix of reads and writes. It should be stored in high-performance and highly available storage systems such as disks or SSDs in a RAID configuration with parity. Tier 1 storage systems must have the best performance, reliability, and manageability, yet they need less capacity, which translates to being the most expensive storage systems.

Tier 0 storage would be appropriate for online look-up tables, VM/VDI (virtual machine) files, indices, databases, and log or journal files.

Tier 1   Tier 1 data includes data generated by major business applications such as customer relationship management (CRM) and enterprise resource planning (ERP) software as well as email and other documentation data. This type of data has a higher ratio of storage to I/O activity and has only moderate I/O activity with a mixture of reads and writes as well as some random and sequential access and writes. This tier hovers between performance and cost and should be used for data that does not require absolute microsecond response times yet still need to be reasonably fast and adequate for its purpose. Cheaper alternatives to Tier 1 systems can be used, such as less-expensive disks that perform relatively well and can be set up as RAID.

Appropriate data for tier 1 systems is similar to that of tier 0 systems—such as database tables, VM/VDI files, and web user files—but may be considered less critical in nature.

Tier 2   Tier 2 data is still important, but it may not be required in daily business processes, such as financial and transactional data and other machine-generated data. Tier 2 systems focus on high storage capacity at low cost with occasional quick random access to data. The data is important, but it doesn't require high performance and high availability, so it doesn't need to be placed in either tier 1 or tier 0 storage. High-capacity disks which offer more storage than performance may be used.

Online video archives, images, snapshots, and day-to-day backups are good candidates for tier 2 storage.

Tier 3   Tier 3 data is data that we consider appropriate for long-term backup, such as old financial and historical records, compliance requirements, and data such as older email conversations that may need to be kept for long periods of time. This is high-volume data that requires infrequent access with high storage capacity at very low cost. Various tape and virtual tape solutions are the most suitable media for this tier.

Tier 3 data includes offline master backups, gold copies, and long-time retention backups.

Policies

A multitiered storage system can provide a quick and automated way for organizations to move data between expensive high-performance systems to lower-performing ones through the implementation of policies that define what sort of data will fit into each tier. For example, most financial data would fall into the tier 2 category, but if it becomes more than a year old, it could be moved to the tier 3 category and become historical data. The same goes for database records, which lose their importance as they get older and turn into historical data for long-term backup.

Using policies with tiered storage provides a service delivery organization with the best solution to managing data while saving time and money to meet service-level agreements (SLAs) with the most efficiency and the lowest possible cost.

RAID Levels

Redundant Array of Independent Disks (RAID) is a disk storage virtualization technology used to combine multiple disk drives into a logical unit. The purpose is to introduce data redundancy and improve performance. The key goals of RAID are reliability, availability, performance, and capacity.

RAID has different levels, which allows data distribution in several different ways. Each level represents a different and specific balance of redundancy and required performance. RAID levels range from 0 to 6. RAID 1 and above provide the capability to recover from unrecoverable sector errors as well as whole disk failure.

There are a total of seven RAID levels. However, many non-standard proprietary levels have also evolved. We will discuss only the standard levels of RAID.

RAID-0   This level offers performance enhancement through I/O parallelism across multiple drives. There is no data redundancy and fault tolerance with RAID-0. It has no error detection mechanism and therefore failure of one disk can cause loss of all data on the array.

RAID-1   This level offers mirroring without parity checks or striping. RAID-1 implements mirroring by writing data identically to two or more drives. The mirrored data can then be read by any of the drives containing the requested data. Read operations can be fast because data can be read from the drive with lower seek and rotational latencies. However, performance of write operations can be degraded because data must be written on multiple drives. Moreover, the slowest drive determines the write speed. As long as at least one of the drives from the array is functioning, the array continues to function.

RAID-2   Level 2 comprises bit-level striping using dedicated Hamming-code parity. Data is striped and disk spindle rotation is synchronized such that each sequential bit is on a different drive. This technique enables write and read parallelism by striping input and output data, respectively. Hamming-code parity is stored on a dedicated parity drive. RAID-2 is not used in commercial systems, but it sets a precedence for RAID-3 and onward.

RAID-3   Level 3 uses byte-level striping with dedicated parity. As with RAID-2, disk spindle rotation is synchronized and the data is striped to place each sequential byte on a different drive. Parity is calculated in bytes and stored on a dedicated parity drive. RAID 3 is not commonly employed.

RAID-4   Level-4 uses block-level striping with dedicated parity. RAID-4 has been replaced with a proprietary implementation called RAID-DP. RAID-DP stands for RAID-Double Parity and uses two parity disks (redundancy of parity).

RAID-5   This level uses block-level striping with distributed parity. Parity information is distributed among drives to minimize the loss of all parity information in case the parity disk fails. RAID-5 requires that all drives but one must be present to operate. In case a single drive fails, subsequent read requests can be served by calculating from distributed parity. This way no data is lost, but the read performance is substantially degraded until the failed drive is replaced. RAID-5 requires at least three disk drives. However, it comes with some complications: it requires long array rebuild times, and there is a higher chance of failure during rebuild.

RAID-6   Level 6 uses block-level striping with double distributed parity. An upgrade from the distributed parity of RAID-5, double parity provides fault tolerance of up to two failed drives. This enables the creation of larger RAID arrays, especially for systems with high-availability requirements. If drives are used from multiple different manufacturers, it is possible to minimize chances of problems associated with RAID-5. With larger drive capacities and larger array size, it is important to choose RAID-6.

RAID systems are suitable for use with tier 0 and 1 systems because it adds more flexibility and redundancy. In fact, most tier 0 and 1 systems already utilize one or more of the RAID levels in various storage clusters.

File Systems

File systems are a critical part of the overall system. They are used to manage stored data and control how it is retrieved. A file system maintains segregation of different files and manages information about where different fragments of the same file are placed. Sophisticated file systems that offer high availability, reliability, redundancy (in an event of failure), and capacity are even more relevant for cloud computing applications.

The type of file system that will be used has to complement the different technologies used in the different storage tiers. Some of them are more suited to tape storage, for example, while some excel when used with the much faster SSD.

EXT   EXT stands for Extended File System. It was the first file system that was specifically created for the Linux kernel. It was inspired by the Unix File System (UFS) and its idea of metadata structure. EXT has gone through several revisions, the latest being EXT4. Table 8.1 presents some stats and figures for EXT evolution.

TABLE 8.1   EXT revisions

EXT revision	Introduced	File allocation	Max volume size	Max file size	Filename length
EXT2	January 1993	Bitmap (free space), table (metadata)	32 TB	2 TB	255 bytes
EXT3 (unlike EXT2, offers journaling)	November 2001	Bitmap (free space), table (metadata)	32 TB	2 TB	255 bytes
EXT4 (unlike EXT3, offers: extents for up to 128 MB of contiguous space, enhanced subdirectory limits, delayed allocation to prevent fragmentation)	October 2008	Extents/bitmap	1 EB	16 TB (4 KB block system)	255 bytes

VMFS   VMFS stands for Virtual Machine File System. VMFS is cluster file system developed by VMware for use with its ESX Server and vSphere (a server virtualization suite). VMFS was initially developed to store virtual machine disk images and snapshots. In VMFS, multiple servers can read/write the same file system simultaneously, while individual virtual machine files are locked. The size of VMFS volumes can be logically and nondestructively increased (nondestructive to written data). The volume size can be increased by spanning multiple volumes together. The features are as follows:

- Optimizes virtual machine I/O with adjustable volume, disk, file, and block size.
- Allows simultaneous access by multiple ESX servers by implementing per-file locking.
- Adds or deletes hosts without disrupting other hosts.

- Distributed journaling enables recovering of virtual machines in the event of server failure.
- Uses large block sizes for virtual disk I/O and sub-block allocator for files and directories.
- VMFS3 enables connecting up to 32 hosts.
- Single volume supports up to 64 TB.
- Enhanced VMFS performance with volume, device, object, and buffer caching.

Summary

The chapter is called "Hardware Management," and we went into detail about how BIOS and firmware configuration can be used to sort out incompatibilities and even increase performance through various tweaks. For now, most service providers do not explicitly offer end-users direct BIOS configuration capabilities, but users can make special requests to the service provider or make changes through special configurations.

Memory is an important resource because it can allow for more workload to be handled by the virtual machine. But control in allocating memory should be exercised because excess allocation can add up, especially if there are multiple instances. Imagine allocating an extra gigabyte of memory to each of 100 virtual machines, which would be a crazy amount. In this situation, lean really is mean.

In addition to memory, virtual machines need compute resource. The vCPU resource is the heart of the VM, but it is the only resource that does not explicitly belong to the VM because it is only a representation of time slices that are allocated to each instance. The allocation of CPU time is proportional to the number of vCPUs and cores that are assigned to a virtual machine. This has to be scaled with the type of workload that a VM is subjected to. If it is a mere database server, it might not need much computing power, but if it is a server used for analytics, it might benefit from more vCPUs with multiple cores. Hyperthreading doubles the number of cores that the host has.

If the workload is more network hungry than storage or compute hungry, you need a good interface with the network, and a single NIC will usually not be enough. The host can use a single NIC for multiple virtual machines by attaching that NIC to a virtual switch component, but the network will be shared among those VMs and is really just useful for workloads that do not demand much network traffic. If the workload is network intensive, the ideal setup would be a single physical NIC per virtual machine, which would ensure that the VM has the whole pipe to work with.

When you're selecting host hardware, compatibility has to be taken into consideration. Although most hardware modules are made to be swappable and interchangeable, incompatibilities will still occur because of the different manufacturing processes and configurations of the modules. To avoid downtime and performance degradation, it is important that no inconsistencies and incompatibilities occur between host hardware resources.

Another choice you have it what kind of storage media to use: tape, disk, or SSD. Tape is the cheapest, with the most capacity but the worst performance. Hard disks are between tape and SSDs when it comes to performance and capacity, while SSDs have less capacity but offer the best performance.

With all of these resources at your disposal, if you are the host, you have to be able to allocate them properly lest you have shortages and be unable to meet your service-level agreements. You can allocate each virtual resource differently; you can even set up various algorithms for proper allocation. The most visible of these measures are the different service packages that we make available to our customers. Service packages also effectively allow us to estimate the total tenant capacity of the infrastructure.

Conversely, if you are the customer, your view of proper resource allocation is no longer on how you can extend your finite resources but how to effectively make do with what you have and maintain peak performance while lowering costs. The best way to achieve this is to have a lean approach, which is to allocate only enough resources for satisfactory performance of virtual machines.

You learned in this chapter how different the management approach is for a public and private cloud. Public clouds are managed with economies of scale and cost efficiency in mind, while management of private clouds is geared more toward proper resource allocation and authorization.

Finally, we covered the different tier levels for storage configuration, how each one is used, and what technology is attached to each. We then explained how RAID levels differ from each other and the nuances of each level.

Chapter Essentials

BIOS/Firmware Configuration   BIOS configuration is a good way to improve virtual machine performance by tweaking various settings that would be available in a physical computer. The difference is that a VM has no proper BIOS that can be set up; this has to be explicitly made available by the service provider.

Minimum Memory Capacity and Configuration   Each VM instance should be allocated the memory it requires, not less or more. The problem with allocating too much memory is that not all of it will be utilized, removing it from the resource pool when it could have been allocated to another VM. Memory also incurs more costs; multiply the memory by the number of VMs, and it could become a staggering amount.

Number of CPUs   The number of CPUs that can be allocated to a VM instance depends on the service package in use. Lesser packages allow for only a single CPU for each VM, which may not be enough for the type of workload necessary for that VM. In such cases, a higher-level service package should be availed.

Number of Cores   The number of cores that a host contains is doubled if hyperthreading is enabled. This means that if a host has 4 physical CPUs with 4 cores each, totaling to 16 logical CPUs, it can support virtual machines, which can have up to 16 single-core vCPUs.

If hyperthreading is enabled, this doubles the number of logical CPUs in the host for a total of 32 logical CPUs, so in turn it can support virtual machines with 32 single core vCPUs.

NICs Quantity, Speeds, and Configurations   The network must be free for network-intensive applications and workflows, so if a virtual machine with this type of workflow has to share the host's NIC with other VMs, the performance of the virtual machine would be severely impacted. A one-to-one ratio of VMs and NICs should be considered for such situations.

Internal Hardware Compatibility   All the hardware in a cloud data center must be compatible. It's true that incompatibility still exists because of programming and manufacturing processes, even if it is not intentional. Therefore, research must be done to ensure that the different hardware modules to be used are 100 percent compatible without issues and bugs that may impact performance and availability later.

Storage Media   We are actively using three types of storage media. Tape is the cheapest, with the largest capacity but weakest performance. Disk provides a mixture of both performance and capacity, while SSDs are the best performers, but with the least amount of capacity and also the most expensive.

Proper Allocation of Hardware Resources (Host)   For a host, resource allocation is all about fancy algorithms for allocation and reclamation of resources. We have to make sure that idle resources are put to good use and that they are immediately returned when they are needed by the idle VMs who previously possessed them. We also have to make sure that metering and dynamic resource allocation is satisfactory.

Proper Virtual Resource Allocation (Tenant/Client)   Client allocation of resources is geared toward satisfactory performance of virtual machines. Resource allocation must be lean to minimize costs.

Management Differences between Public, Private, and Hybrid Clouds   Managing a public cloud is a serious affair, and proper management of resources is important in serving all tenants and meeting all service-level agreements. For tenants of a public cloud, lean management of resources would be the most efficient approach. In a private cloud, management can be more relaxed; limits for resource use and allocation can be more lax and users can be allowed to provision as much as they want because resources are plenty. However, this does not mean that cleanup and reclamation of resources are not required.

Tiering   Different tiers provide businesses with different ways to approach their backup storage needs, which depend on workflow and type of backups. For example, you can use tape storage for data that belong to the tier 3 category because it is only required as long-term backups. High-performance storage such as SSD must be used for critical and dynamic data that changes rapidly, which is considered tier 0 data.

RAID Levels   With the RAID method of storage, data is striped in multiple identical disks. When one or two disks fail, the data is not actually lost because it is still available in other drives. Each RAID level also features some unique features used for security and recovery. RAID can be expensive because multiple disks must be used and will contain more or less the same data.

Chapter

9

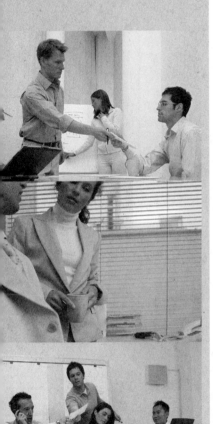

Storage Provisioning and Networking

TOPICS COVERED IN THIS CHAPTER INCLUDE:

- ✓ Cloud storage concepts
- ✓ Understanding SAN and NAS
- ✓ Cloud vs. SAN
- ✓ Cloud provisioning: migration and security
- ✓ Storage provisioning
- ✓ Network provisioning and optimization
- ✓ Cloud storage technologies
- ✓ Data replication
- ✓ Amazon EBS and S3
- ✓ OpenStack Swift
- ✓ Apache HDFS
- ✓ Case study: loading and processing archived data
- ✓ Choosing a storage technology
- ✓ Cloud storage gateway
- ✓ Cloud security, privacy, and legal issues

Storage provisioning is the process of optimizing the performance of a distributed data store, such as a data center, storage area network (SAN), or network-attached storage (NAS). The main idea is to assign and manage storage in terms of server disk space. Networking is critical because it forms the communication backbone of such a distributed data store.

Storage provisioning is an important task and requires steps that should be taken to ensure a well-configured network of storage drives. Storage provisioning is required to make certain that the data storage and recovery routes are made available when needed. As a contingency plan, alternate routes should be in place that can keep the data store functional in the event of partial failure. A good architecture would inherently include future expansion prospects. Like any other piece of equipment, the entire data store must be tested against data extraction and storage tests before it is put under production load.

Recently, the industry has seen a rapid shift from on-premises storage facilities to viable cloud-based alternatives. Enterprises are adopting the cloud for services, solutions, and transformation of those services. The shift is displacing existing technologies and bringing new technologies to the business environment.

In this chapter we will cover topics related to cloud storage, storage provisioning, and networking. We begin by describing cloud storage concepts that are essential for developing an understanding of the various cloud technologies described in this chapter. We then compare SANs with virtualized cloud storage. You shall see what is meant by cloud provisioning, and we'll explain a number of cloud storage technologies, including Amazon's cloud storage products. The chapter also focuses on the role and importance of a cloud storage gateway and its applicability to cloud-oriented enterprise IT environments. We'll also briefly cover important security and privacy issues associated with the cloud.

Cloud Storage Concepts

Before we dig a bit deeper into storage provisioning and popular cloud storage technologies, let us take a look at few important concepts. These concepts are essential in understanding how technologies work and the advantages and limitation of each technology.

Object Storage

Object-based storage devices (OSDs) manage data and its corresponding metadata by changing it to flexible-sized data containers called objects (Figure 9.1). Each object contains data, corresponding metadata (attributes describing the data), and a globally unique identifier (called the object ID). This object ID is used to refer and uniquely identify each object to differentiate it from the others, thus providing a security control mechanism that provides per-object and per-command access control.

FIGURE 9.1   File hierarchy and object store

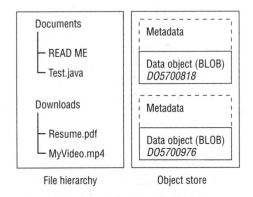

Object-based storage is different than other storage architectures such as file systems and block storage. A file system manages data in a file hierarchy, whereas block storage treats data as blocks within disk sectors and tracks. Object storage abstracts lower layers of storage from applications. Low-level storage management functions such as constructing and managing logical volumes, RAID configuration for disk failure, and disk defragmentation and compression need not be performed actively.

Object-based storage enables capabilities not offered by other storage architectures. An object store can be implemented at multiple levels: the device level, the system level, and the interface level. This enables multiple features:

- Namespaces can be declared across multiple machines, thus enabling hardware-level abstraction.

- Interfaces can be directly programmed by the application to span across multiple disk drives, thus enabling unified access to data across multiple nodes.

- Data can be distributed and replicated at the granularity level of the object (which can range from few KBs to GBs).

Metadata

Metadata, or descriptive metadata to distinguish from structural metadata, refers to *data about data* or *attributes describing the data*. Metadata can also be thought of meta-content that provides information about one or more aspects of data, such as the following:

- Purpose of the data

- Time stamp (time and date) of creation

- Means (tools) by which the data was created
- Author
- Text encoding used (ASCII, UTF-8, UTF-16, etc.)

Data/Blob

The word *data* is the plural of *datum*, a past participle form of the Latin word *dare*, which means "to give." In computer science, data refers to pieces of information, such as anything that is based on numbers, words, images, audio, and video.

A *binary large object (blob)* is basically an amorphous collection of binary data stored as a single unit in a file system or, more commonly, in a database management system (DBMS). Blobs are generally used to store nontextual data including images, audio, and video. Blobs may also be used to store executable code.

Extended Metadata

Extended or additional metadata is the metadata that is derived from application-specific or user-specific information about the access and usage of data. The purpose is to build sophisticated and personalized indexing schemes.

Furthermore, additional metadata is used to support data management policies, such as a policy to migrate data objects from one storage tier to another. This is especially relevant for load balancing during peak performance hours.

Replicas

A *replica* represents an exact mirror image reproduction of an original item. In computer science, a soft-copy replica might be indistinguishable from its original due to the lack of hard effects created during the hard-copy process and the surrounding environment.

A soft-copy replica of an item creates a symbolic link (also called symlink or soft link) to another file or directory. It is just an additional reference to an already existing file. Hard-copying an item creates an identical copy of the item in storage media. The newly created item can be considered a clone. The two items—the actual and the copy—are indistinguishable, and each has an individual presence on the storage media. This is opposed to soft-copying, where an item may have two or more references.

Policies and Access Control

Policies in computer systems are used to define networking rules, data storage, data security, data archiving, data deletion, access control, and a multitude of other activities related to computer systems.

Access control policy defines selective restriction of physical or virtual access to one or more computer resources in order to establish physical and information security. The act of accessing may entail consuming or using a resource. Authorization is the act of granting physical or virtual access permissions to a person for consuming or using one or more computer resources.

Understanding SAN and NAS

A SAN is a dedicated network that provides access to consolidated, block-level data storage. SANs are primarily used to make storage devices, such as disk arrays and tape libraries. NAS, on the other hand, is file-level data storage that is connected to a network of heterogeneous computer systems. NAS is often manufactured as a computer appliance and used for specialized purposes. NAS is often compared to SAN because of its ability to behave as both data storage and a file server (see Figure 9.2).

To conceptualize this, think of SAN storage appearing as a local disk on a computer to which a SAN is attached. This enables the host computer to fully control the SAN storage (disk/volume management). NAS only appears as a file server providing block storage capability and thus allows only a limited number of nonadministrative operations from the host machine.

FIGURE 9.2   SAN vs. NAS

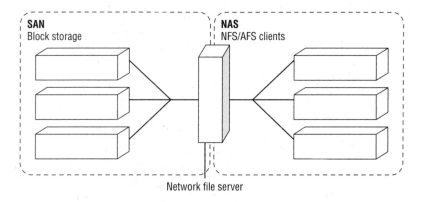

Network file server

Both of these systems were designed as high-speed on-premises solutions. However, as services and applications move into the cloud, the requirement or need for an on-premises data center diminishes almost completely. Locating storage close to the services that consume data from those storage sources is far better, both technically and administratively, than having to maintain two separate environments.

One of the basic intentions of the cloud was to make different hardware components act and behave as a large but single entity. The applications and services running on top of such a platform should be unconcerned about their physical location as well as the physical location of the data and other applications and services they are accessing or using.

However, to take complete advantage of the cloud platform and bypass network latency and performance lag, both logic and data should be placed in a consolidated cloud environment. If applications and services are running in the cloud, then data sources should be placed near those applications and services. This essentially translates to cloud-based storage, which eliminates unnecessary problems with the overall system infrastructure.

Cloud vs. SAN Storage

The primary purpose of SANs is to make storage devices, typically disk arrays, accessible to servers throughout the network such that these devices appear as if they are locally attached to the operating system. A SAN does not provide file abstraction, only block-level operations. However, file systems that are built on top of a SAN do provide file-level access and are called SAN file systems (Figure 9.3).

FIGURE 9.3 How a SAN works

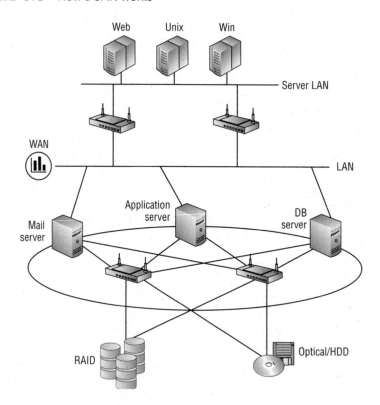

This scheme comes with some particular benefits. Because the SAN disks appear as local devices, servers can boot directly from SAN storage. This allows quick replacement of faulty servers and fast reconfiguration of the replacement server to acquire the *logical unit*

number (LUN) of the faulty server. Another advantage is the effective disaster recovery process through storage replication, where SAN can span a distant location containing a secondary storage array.

A SAN utilizes a high-speed network, such as Fibre Channel (FC) through host bus adapter (HBA), to connect computer data storage. FC technology commonly supports operating rates of 2, 4, 8, or 16 gigabits per second (Gbps). It uses Fibre Channel Protocol (FCP) as the transport protocol that transports Small Computer System Interface (SCSI) commands over FC networks.

A SAN makes available several devices and ports, but restricts access for each connected system to a subset of devices/ports. Smaller subsets restrict interference, add security, and simplify management. This is called FC zoning, and it can be done only in switched fabric networks. However, FC can also be used over Ethernet (called FCoE); FC frames are encapsulated over Ethernet networks, such as 10 Gigabit Ethernet (GigE), while preserving the FCP protocol. Zoning differs from zoning in a virtual SAN (VSAN) in the sense that a device or port can be part of multiple zones but only one VSAN. A VSAN is in fact a separate network (think of VLAN).

There are a couple of types of zoning: soft and hard. Soft zoning restricts a machine to see only the devices that it is allowed to see. However, any machine can contact any other device using the device address. This helps in establishing security through obscurity. On the other hand, hard zoning restricts communication physically across the network fabric, which ensures security.

In an FC setup, devices are identified using a unique identifier called the World Wide Number (WWN) or World Wide ID (WWID). Access to a device can also be restricted using its WWN in a SAN environment. This is called name zoning and is more secure than using port zoning. The port to which the host is connected can be moved while preserving the access, whereas in port zoning, the access can be gained inadvertently to any resources the previous host had access to.

Cloud Storage

As most other things in the cloud, storage is based on a highly virtualized infrastructure and inherits the same characteristics as cloud computing in terms of agility, scalability, elasticity, and multitenancy. It can be made available in both onsite and offsite configurations.

The biggest advantage of cloud storage is that it acts as a single entity despite the fact that the infrastructure would most likely be geographically scattered. This makes many distributed storage services behave and act as one, which is obviously advantageous in terms of visibility (of data), transfer of data sources, and troubleshooting. Cloud storage is agnostic when it comes to where the data is actually located. The administrator does not have to worry about setting up a block or file storage configuration to determine where the data actually resides (as in the case of a SAN).

Cloud storage provides high fault tolerance through redundancy and distribution of data. Although SAN also provides redundancy, it is actually set up using techniques such as Redundant Array of Independent Disks (RAID). Even though RAID has been used widely, it does come with a few difficulties. Failures are common among drives and are statistically correlated. Unrecoverable read errors are among the most common problems and emanate due to sector read failures. RAID-6, with a double protection scheme, addresses this issue but pays the penalty in very high disk I/O (writing) time.

Moreover, due to nonatomicity of data and therefore inconsistency arising from random system crashes, parity and data are left in an inconsistent state.

Cloud storage uses version copies, which makes it highly durable. Atomicity of operations in the cloud environment ensures that the data is in one consistent state (before committing the transaction) or another (after successfully committing the transaction). Moreover, in the event of failures, a cloud system is guaranteed to reach a consistent state eventually (called *eventual consistency*) with regard to the data replicas. Eventual consistency informally guarantees that if no new updates are made to a given data item (which is replicated to various locations), eventually all access to that item will return the last updated value. This is because the data item will eventually be "updated" at every location with the latest value.

Advantages of Cloud Storage

Cloud storage also offers a number of advantages over an onsite data store setup such as a SAN. For instance, companies using the cloud storage services need to pay only for the storage they actually use. This not only means a lower operating expense, it also avoids capital expenditure and maintenance costs.

Moreover, storage availability and data protection are intrinsic to object storage architecture. Cloud storage also provides users with a broad range of applications and resources as part of the service provider's infrastructure.

However, not all is well in the world of cloud storage. If care is not taken for a few but important factors, cloud storage could become a great concern, especially for organizations for which data translates to money. These concerns include attack surface area, supplier stability, accessibility, security, and privacy and are addressed in detail in the section "Cloud Security and Privacy" later in this chapter.

Cloud Provisioning

For companies making the transition, there are some big business and administrative questions to answer. Companies are not only thinking about the costs and flexibility of technological operations, they're also thinking of tactical advantages like automated provisioning (of virtual resources and services) and encrypted storage.

This administrative and technological conundrum of the extent and procedures of transition is what cloud provisioning entails. Companies need to decide what part of their infrastructure goes into the cloud as a part of their cloud computing strategy. They also need to see whether to have segregation between a privately deployed cloud infrastructure and the public cloud.

Typically, such a process involves first selecting the applications and services that will reside in the public cloud and those that will remain on premises behind a firewall or in the private cloud. This decision varies from company to company because there are many factors to consider, including and not limited to core intellectual property, data, the size of the data, and the client base.

Cloud provisioning also includes processes for interfacing with the cloud applications and services. The cloud provisioning team needs to see the compatibility of applications and services and make a decision of how much of the core software infrastructure they need to re-architect in order to make a fruitful transition. It also entails auditing and monitoring who accesses and utilizes the cloud resources. This process is similar to auditing access privileges in an internal or VPN network of a company.

Migrating Software Infrastructure to the Cloud

The most common reference to cloud provisioning is when a company seeks to transition some or all of its existing software infrastructure to the cloud without having to significantly rearchitect or reengineer the applications and services.

Earlier we discussed advantages like automated provisioning, which is quite simply an advantage because of the ease, predictability, and speed of preparing a resource for internal or external use.

The resources that could be provisioned include a virtual data center (Infrastructure as a Service), a virtual machine (VM) with or without a software stack (Platform as a Service), or hosted applications and services (Software as a Service). The advantages do not stop here. Other advantages include what can be done with the infrastructure. Availability can be enhanced and latency can be controlled by provisioning multiple instances of a service. Speed of access can be improved by using solid-state drives (SSDs) offered by the cloud provider. Redundancy can be added by provisioning a service across multiple data centers.

Provisioning represents a delivery stage, and such a delivery system comes with challenges. One of the key challenges is the integrity of the system, including data and processes. Integrity is the key element of whatever is delivered, and this must be checked before delivery and deployment. Businesses can use VM images to migrate some of their components to the cloud. Master images can contain business applications and processes, configurations, and, in some cases, even metadata. These master images need to be protected and should be deployed intact and in a secure manner.

Cloud Provisioning Security Concerns

One of the critical problems during provisioning and deprovisioning is the reliance on hypervisors and ensuring process isolation at every stage. After a VM or service is provisioned, it has to be protected and kept isolated from other tenants and services. Multitenancy is a critical security concern and is usually controlled and managed by the service provider.

However, even though a tenant may have on-demand access to security controls such as virtual firewalls, authentication services, and logging, things could change swiftly if the underlying implementation is patched or updated (by the service provider).

Moreover, as you reprovision the VM in an updated infrastructure, the security configuration data might become operationally incorrect. To curtail such problems, configuration management and version control systems might also need updating.

The biggest concern of all is the unintended interactions and information transfer when on-demand security controls are integrated with a customer application. What is possible is that if machine IDs and IP addresses are recycled, it might become possible for a user/organization to unintentionally and inadvertently gain access to an information resource that is not theirs. Allocation and deallocation of VMs, IP addresses, machine IDs, information resources, and other such elements is the essential concern here.

Cloud service providers usually ensure this by allocating and deallocating IDs, IP addresses, and other such elements using algorithms that make sure that such elements are not repeated for a reasonably long time or until the previous NAT entry has been discarded. The system makes sure that even if an IP address does get reallocated to some other user, the NAT table does not have any information regarding the relationship between the IP and its previous host. This enables rewiring the IP-host relationship from scratch.

Another cause of concern regarding multitenancy could be the data leaks, such as stack overflows, that could possibly result from processing of data. There are multiple techniques available to isolate a user's data from data belonging to other users. One of the solutions is to assign a unique ID (based on the object being accessed) to each individual request, thus identifying each data item separately. Isolation can be mutually reinforced at multiple levels, such as at the physical disk level, the VM, disk partitioning mechanisms, and file system permissions.

Cloud storage often uses centralized facilities, which can be a potential target for criminals or hackers. The threat can be mitigated by applying the appropriate security controls (access controls, firewalls, and anomaly detection proxies). We will explore more on this in the section "Cloud Security and Privacy" later in this chapter.

Complex hardware and software implementations form the storage systems. The potential is always present for catastrophic failure that might either destroy the data or even worse expose the data from one customer to another, which is a breach of security.

To mitigate the consequences of such a failure, cloud service providers continuously back up data for disaster recovery or retention purposes. Usually these backup data stores are kept at an off-site and offline facility. The idea is that data should not just exist in one place where it becomes vulnerable to operational failures that make it inconsistent and faulty.

Although providers act within the bounds of their contract and preserve the confidentiality of these data copies, they are subject to error. They are also subject to jurisdictional laws, which vary greatly from country to country and region to region. It is advisable to be one step ahead and be cautious and vigilant about your data. We will discuss jurisdictional laws later in this chapter.

Storage Provisioning

To use disk volumes for storing data, you must create a LUN, which can be mapped to any host, cluster, or data center (Figure 9.4). Once mapped, a volume can be mounted on a VM and used for storing data.

FIGURE 9.4   LUN network mapping

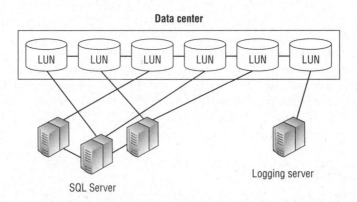

Though a disk volume may be mounted to only one host at a time, it can be shared between a number of hosts or VMs. This is termed as *network sharing* or *sharing a resource*. A disk volume can be remotely but transparently accessed from another computer using network sharing techniques.

In a SAN, devices requesting I/O operations are initiators and devices performing these operations are targets. FC zoning, as explained earlier, is implemented at the hardware level and configured on a per-target and initiator basis. In a SAN, access must be granted to appropriate storage devices (or logical units, as they are referred to in this context). LUN zoning provides a method of configuring initiator-target relationship.

LUN masking can enable you to further constrain the access to ensure that only devices authorized to access a specific initiator (a server host) may access the corresponding port. This method subdivides access to a given port. In such a case, several LUNs can be accessed through the same port, but server masks limit each server's access to only allowed LUNs. LUN masking is typically conducted at the switch or HBA level.

A usual big future challenge is to add more capacity to SANs. One way is to add more physical devices. This of course means that the system has to have empty and open slots and the cabling necessary for installation. The key challenge here is the change in configuration and incurred downtime, or at least some interruption of service.

Another option is to add an additional node. In this case too, installation and configuration require planning. The biggest advantage of this approach is to provide higher availability, failover, and an opportunity to scale up not only capacity but also performance. The key challenge here is to balance performance and capacity. Adding only capacity may create performance bottlenecks.

Data deduplication is another technique for eliminating duplicate copies of data using data compression. This technique is applied to improve storage utilization and reduce network data transfer latencies. Unique chunks of data or byte patterns are identified and stored during a process of analysis. Subsequent chunks of data are compared to the stored chunks. Whenever a match is found, the redundant chunk is replaced with a reference that points to the stored chunk. This technique reduces the amount of data stored considerably for systems where the same byte pattern for a considerable chunk size of data might occur multiple times. Examples include machine-generated log data from network hardware. The technique is different from standard file compression tools that do string matching inside individual files. Deduplication techniques focus on chunks of data such as entire files or collection of files to find identical copies and store only one copy.

A much-overlooked approach to adding more capacity is to "manage" the data. A large chunk of data is not accessed on a regular basis and is a good candidate for archival. Moreover, careful planning for redundancy level and data backups is useful in reclaiming large amounts of space. The key challenge here is to find which data can be archived and compressed without being required and decompressed regularly.

Network Configurations

Network Address Translation (NAT) is a network protocol that allows multiple internal devices (inside a private or local network) to connect to an external network (such as the Internet) using the same public IPv4 address. The idea is to modify the IP header as the packet leaves or arrives at the border gateway or router. IP-masquerading through NAT was originally designed to conserve IPv4 addresses and delay exhaustion. The technique makes sure hosts that do not require support for inbound connections do not consume public IPv4 addresses.

Many different configurations can be created with NAT; some of the more common ones are described in Table 9.1.

TABLE 9.1 NAT configurations

Configuration	Features
One-to-one NAT	Internal address (iAddr:iPort) is mapped to an external address (eAddr:ePort).
	Internal host can send packets to external host using iAddr:iPort.
	External host can send packets to internal host using eAddr:ePort.
Address restricted NAT	Internal address (iAddr:iPort) is mapped to an external address (eAddr:ePort).
	Internal host can send packets to external host (hAddr:any) using iAddr:iPort.
	External host (hAddr:any) can send packets to internal host using eAddr:ePort, if and only if the internal host previously sent a packet to hAddr:any. *Any* means this scheme is not port bound.

Configuration	Features
Port restricted NAT	Internal address (iAddr:iPort) is mapped to an external address (eAddr:ePort).
	Internal host can send packets to external host (hAddr:hPort) using iAddr:iPort.
	External host (hAddr:hPort) can send packets to internal host using eAddr:ePort, if and only if the internal host previously sent a packet to hAddr:hPort.
Symmetric NAT	Each request from the same iAddr:iPort to a specific destination IP address and port is mapped to a unique eAddr:ePort.
	External host can send packets to an internal host, if and only if the internal host previously sent a packet to the external host (hAddr:hPort).

Port Address Translation (PAT), a port-based variant of NAT, allows many internal hosts to share a single external IPv4 address. The main idea is to use ports to distinguish between, and correctly route, traffic of various internal hosts.

Generally, cloud service providers implement NAT-ing as part of the service package. However, there could be cases where organizations need to provision Internet connectivity for the instances within their virtual private cloud (VPC). For such scenarios, cloud service providers allow using a NAT instance to enable outbound traffic to the Internet, but they prevent inbound traffic by unknown hosts from the Internet using any one of the aforementioned NAT configurations. The selection of configuration varies depending on the particularities of the business use case and an application's network behavior (some are network intensive and some just follow a symmetric pattern).

Dividing a Physical Network into Smaller Logical Networks

To logically divide a single physical network into two or more smaller logical networks (called subnetworks or subnets), we use subnetting. In large organizations, it is necessary to allocate address space efficiently; that is, the static IP addresses should be used only for machines or hosts that have to be made externally or publicly accessible. It also helps in network management because different subnets can be administered by different groups having varying needs. And it helps in enhancing routing efficiency.

The division is expressed in *Classless Inter-Domain Routing (CIDR)* notation: the address prefix of the network followed by the bit length of the network address space. For example, 192.168.1.0/24 depicts that the network starts at the given address and has 24 bits (3 octets) allocated for the network prefix and the remaining 8 bits (1 octet) are allocated for the subnet address space.

In a cloud setup, a NAT instance can act as a bridge between the private subnet and the public subnet within the VPC. The NAT instance can send traffic to the Internet gateway for the VPC, where the traffic is attributed to the IP address of the NAT. The response is then collected by the NAT instance and forwarded to the relevant instance in the private subnet. This is accomplished by implementing PAT-ing.

Another important concept is related to supernetting (also known as prefix/route aggregation or route summarization). A supernetwork, or supernet, is created from the combination of two or more networks with a common CIDR prefix. The new routing prefix aggregates prefixes of the constituent networks. Any prefixes that do not lie in the same routing path are not considered.

Consider a large company that has 100 routers in 25 districts. That means a total of 2,500 different networks and quite a large combined routing table. One way is to proceed with this routing table, but this is inefficient in terms of memory storage of route information and the processing overhead associated with matching routes. Another more efficient way is to use supernets instead.

For example, consider a company has these four networks:

192.168.98.0

192.168.99.0

192.168.100.0

192.168.101.0

First, the addresses are converted to binary and aligned. The common bits are located and redefined as the aggregated or summarized route with the remaining bits defined as the uncommon address space. In this case, 192.168.96.0/21 depicts a supernet of the previously mentioned four IPv4 addresses with 192.168.96.0 as the first 21 common bits. The more networks there are to aggregate, the fewer the common bits. For example, if we had been using only the first two networks in the preceding list, the summarized route or supernet would have been 192.168.98.0/23.

Avoiding Topological Fragmentation

Within the Internet, supernetting can serve as a preventive strategy to avoid topological fragmentation of the IPv4 address space. It accomplishes this by using a hierarchical allocation system that delegates control of address space segments to regional network service providers. This also facilitates regional route aggregation.

Table 9.2 shows the OSI model. Whereas subnets are layer 3 constructs, VLANs are layer 2 constructs that partition the network to create multiple distinct broadcast domains so that communication between domains takes place through defined routes. VLANs help in traffic control, provide the flexibility to adapt to changes in the network, and allow for simplified administration.

TABLE 9.2   The OSI model—network layers

Layer (Higher Is More Abstract)	Name	Protocols/Examples
7	Application	DHCP, FTP, HTTP, LDAP, SSH, Telnet
6	Presentation	Telnet

Layer (Higher Is More Abstract)	Name	Protocols/Examples
5	Session	SDP, SOCKS, NetBIOS
4	Transport	TCP, UDP
3	Network	IPv4/IPv6 (Subnets are constructed from IP addresses.), ICMP, ARP, IPSec
2	Data-Link	Ethernet (VLANs are constructed over Ethernet.), PPP
1	Physical	DSL, ISDN, USB, IRDA

A VLAN has the same attributes as the physical LAN, but the advantage is that it allows for end stations to be grouped across network switches. Organizations utilize the VLANs to avoid the trouble of going through physical allocation and reallocation of devices and connections in an internal network.

Organizations also partition a local network into distinctive segments to maintain segregation, a high level of security, proxy enabling, and great flexibility. For example, a production network has distinct availability requirements that are different than those of a guest network, and Quality of Service (QoS) schemes can optimize traffic on links for real-time traffic (VoIP) or low-latency requirements (SAN).

Network Optimization

Network optimization typically refers to the processes and tools that help a network administrator operate an enterprise network at peak efficiency. This includes keeping the physical infrastructure, such as routers and switches, up-to-date with latest security patches. One important task is to resolve data flow bottlenecks. Network optimization helps administrators maintain service-level agreements (SLAs).

There are two critical parts of network optimization: network planning and network operations, as described in the following sections.

Network Planning

Network planning involves designing the network according to the requirements of the business or enterprise, such as, for instance, LAN deployments for office spaces, MAN deployments to connect multiple offices over the same citywide area, and WAN deployments for connecting countrywide or continent-wide regions. The administrator has to think about effective VPN-enabled connectivity across the board for each type of deployment.

Typically, enterprises lease common carrier circuits to connect MANs instead of laying out their own cables (which can be expensive). MANs can also be connected via wireless technologies such as radio or infrared (IR).

Network Operations

Network operations involve handling bandwidth requirements and limiting latency as well as handling compression, caching, and load balancing. Generally, companies assign bandwidth quotas to user groups. To load balance Internet usage, multiple Internet connectivity providers are contracted. For instance, a large enterprise might have a high-capacity link for its production systems and a general usage network link for office usage.

Latency requirements and caching levels are defined on per-application or -system basis. This is mostly done by keeping in perspective the usage expected for each production-level application or system, such as the amount of clients (incoming), amount of queries (incoming), amount of responses (outgoing), expected response time per query, typical user operations (e.g., 8 of 10 are read), nature of operations (read or write), most used application, least used application, and so on.

Cloud Storage Technology

Cloud storage is a model of networked storage for enterprise-level systems. Data is usually distributed over a large number of virtualized storage resources. A typical data center would host large chunks of data from various sources. This is not true in all cases, but very large quantities of data (usually hundreds of petabytes) might physically span not only across multiple servers in the same data center but also across multiple geographical locations.

In order for their customers to use cloud storage services for accessing data, companies operating in the data center marketplace offer web services, content management systems (CMSs), APIs, desktop software, and cloud storage gateways (cloud storage gateways are discussed later in this chapter).

Cloud storage provides all the cloud features such as scalability, agility, elasticity, and multitenancy. Perhaps the greatest feature is the federated data storage, where multiple virtualized data storage resources appear and behave as a single unit. This is further supported by fault tolerance and durability through redundant replicas.

However, redundancy does come at a cost. Most of the data storage systems use the primary storage location to read and write data transactions. The data replicas are only guaranteed to be eventually consistent. I/O operations (including cross-network) are still expensive, and pushing each singleton update would overload the data and network buffers throughout the route, thus rendering the system useless. This might even cause a chain reaction and cause disruption of services throughout the platform. I/O write updates (data manipulation) are carried to replicas in batches of designated sizes to minimize network costs and prevent possible service disruption.

Data Replication

Different techniques are used to achieve eventual consistency, and we will discuss these shortly one by one.

To understand fault tolerance, you must first understand the correct behavior of a replicated resource, linearizability, and sequential consistency of operations. Correct behavior is desirable to ensure fault tolerance. The correctness refers to the freshness of data and timely delivery. Imagine a scenario where a web service offers flight information data to two clients and upon two requests of exactly the same kind, but separated by a few seconds, the data displayed to the two clients is different. This is incorrect behavior.

There are two main kinds of correctness criteria for replicated data. Most strictly correct systems are linearizable. Consider a scenario where two clients perform read and write operations on a single system simultaneously. The correctness criteria in such a scenario would be defined as virtual interleaving of operations of the two clients. Thus, a replicated service is said to be linearizable if for any execution there is some interleaving that specifies the following two conditions:

- The execution meets the specification of a nonreplicated service.
- The execution meets the real-time order of operations in the real execution.

However, there is a problem with the linearizability criteria: it is impractical for real-world scenarios, where it is impossible for all the clients to receive exactly the same piece of information because clocks cannot always be synchronized to have absolutely no time lag. Clock synchronization is one of the hardest problems in distributed computing. We will not go into the details of clock synchronization because it is beyond the scope of this chapter. You may think of it as a process whereby clocks share their time among a number of geographically distributed machines in order to adjust the machines' internal clocks to the exact relative time that is expected. The need to synchronize results emanates from the problem of establishing coordination among distant systems.

Since we cannot always ensure practicality of linearizability, a weaker correctness condition is used. Sequential consistency replaces the notion of real time and replaces it with the order of operations. A replicated service becomes sequentially consistent if for any execution there is some interleaving that matches following conditions:

- The execution meets the specification of a nonreplicated service.
- The execution order of operations matches the program order of operations in which each client executed them.

 There is no notion of "real time" in sequential consistency, nor is there any condition of maintaining the total order of events. The only requirement is to have an order of events at each client that matches the program order.

Further, there are two kinds of replication: passive and active.

Passive Replication In the passive replication model, the primary storage takes the responsibility of immediately serving the client and recording any updates. The system would then perform lazy updates to the backup storage. If the primary node fails, one of the backups would take over from the last consistent state of data.

Active Replication The active replication scheme depends on the nodes updating each other almost instantly as the record update is being processed. This makes such a model a completely decentralized one where the system does not have any hierarchical structure (i.e., no predefined primary or backups) but rather a collaborative system. The advantage of such a system is that this could support models with high-frequency transaction requirements.

However, such systems are operated only for specialized purposes in controlled environments such as a stock exchange or in mission-critical environments such as a launch sequence of a space rocket.

Amazon Elastic Block Store (EBS)

The Elastic Block Store (EBS) (`http://aws.amazon.com/ebs/`) is Amazon's block-level storage technology for data volumes in use with Amazon Elastic Compute Cloud (EC2). These volumes are networked together and are independent of the lifetime of an instance. EBS is multipurpose storage that provides a user with the capability to use it as a database or a file system, or even as block-level storage for deploying their own virtual cloud. EBS provides high availability and high reliability and can be plugged dynamically to a running EC2 instance.

Features

Amazon EBS offers many features with regard to provisioning, usage and performance. A few relevant ones are listed here:

- Volumes behave like raw, unformatted block devices with a block device interface. Users can use the block storage like a disk volume or create a file system on top of the EBS.

- The latest (December 2013) EBS technology allows provisioning storage volume of sizes ranging from 1 GB to 1 TB. These volumes can then be mounted as drives in EC2 instances. The biggest advantage of such a system is the ability to add or remove volumes at will.

- Provisioned I/O operations per second (IOPS) (`http://aws.amazon.com/ebs/piops/`) provides the capability to provision specific levels of I/O performance. This is particularly important for high-transaction systems such as databases. The user can specify an IOPS rate during provisioning of volumes.

- Snapshots provide backup capability as well as the ability to use a snapshot as a starting point for new Amazon EBS volumes. Snapshots can also be used to instantiate more volumes and can be copied across AWS (geographical) regions. This helps in future expansion of data stores, migration, and disaster recovery.

- EBS volumes are placed in specific Availability Zones. Amazon EC2 is divided into regions and Availability Zones. Each region is a separate geographic area and has multiple, isolated locations known as Availability Zones. Each volume is automatically replicated within the same Availability Zone. This serves as a backup to the primary instance in the event of data loss due to hardware failure.

- In order to monitor performance, Amazon provides CloudWatch (http://aws .amazon.com/cloudwatch/) for EBS volumes. Performance metrics such as bandwidth, throughput, latency, queue depth, and more give users insight into how the volumes are being used. AWS CloudWatch is accessible via the AWS Management Console or the CloudWatch API.

Usage and Performance

Amazon EBS volumes are bound to a particular Availability Zone with sizes anywhere between 1 GB and 1 TB. A volume can be attached to any Amazon EC2 instance in the same Availability Zone. A volume appears as a mounted device similar to a local disk volume. The user can then choose format the volume with any file system (OS dependent).

It must be noted that the volume can be attached to only one instance at a time. However, many volumes can be attached to one instance. This feature can essentially be exploited to partition data across multiple volumes for increased I/O and throughput performance. A high-frequency transactional database can particularly benefit from such a setup.

The EBS volumes are persistent in storing updates to the data kept in the volumes. If an instance crashes, the instance can be immediately replaced with a new instance and the volume can be attached to the new instance. The only restriction is that the instance and volume must both be in the same Availability Zone.

In order to increase size of the boot partitions, EBS volumes can be declared as boot partitions for EC2 instances. The size of the boot partition can be increased up to 1 TB. This would essentially mean that the user can bundle the instance and data altogether in one instance.

The EBS volumes come in two configurations, standard and provisioned IOPS:

Standard IOPS   The standard configuration delivers approximately 100 IOPS with a best-effort ability to boost to hundreds of IOPS. Standard volumes are generally well suited for boot partitions.

Provisioned IOPS   Provisioned IOPS configuration is designed to deliver high performance for I/O-intensive workloads such as databases. An IOPS rate is selected by the user during provisioning. Amazon currently supports up to 4,000 IOPS per provisioned IOPS volume.

To utilize the full potential of provisioned IOPS volumes, EBS-optimized instances can be launched that deliver dedicated throughput performance between the instance and the volume of anywhere between 500 Mbps and 1,000 Mbps. Amazon claims that such a setup is "designed to deliver within 10% of the provisioned IOPS performance 99.9% of the time."

Durability and Snapshots

Amazon EBS volumes are designed to be highly available and reliable. Amazon EBS volume data is replicated across multiple servers in an Availability Zone to prevent the loss of data from the failure of any single component. The durability of your volume depends both on the size of your volume and the percentage of the data that has changed since your last snapshot. As an example, volumes that operate with 20 GB or less of modified data since their most recent Amazon EBS snapshot can expect an annual failure rate (AFR) of between 0.1 percent and 0.5 percent (failure refers to a complete loss of the volume). This compares with commodity hard disks that will typically fail with an AFR of around 4 percent (as found by independent studies from Google, Carnegie Mellon University, and University of Wisconsin at Madison), making EBS volumes 10 times more reliable than typical commodity disk drives.

Replicating data across multiple volumes within the same Availability Zone provides only a certain amount of durability. That is where point-in-time consistent snapshots of the volumes play a part. Snapshots are stored in Amazon Simple Storage Serve (S3) cloud storage for a nominal fee. The S3 automatically replicates the data volumes across multiple Availability Zones. Taking regular snapshots is a convenient and cost-effective way to increase the long-term durability of data. In the event of a volume failure, these snapshots will allow the user to re-create the volume from the last available snapshot, thus minimizing the absolute data loss.

Amazon Simple Storage Service (S3)

Amazon S3 (`http://aws.amazon.com/s3/`) is web-scale storage, which makes it easy for the developers to store and retrieve data at any time and from anywhere on the Web. S3 provides a simple web services interface used for storing and retrieving vast amounts of data. It is highly scalable, reliable, secure, and fast and is based on an inexpensive infrastructure. Amazon uses S3 to run its network of websites.

Features

Amazon built S3 with a minimal feature set to have a generic base design. This enables it to support various different objectives and otherwise conflicting requirements:

- S3 can store an unlimited number of objects. These objects can be acted upon (read, write, delete). Each object is stored in a bucket and assigned a unique key (required to act upon the object). An object can contain data of anywhere between 1 byte and 5 TB.

- A bucket is stored in one of the several geographical regions. A region can be chosen by the user for minimizing latency and costs and to conform to the address regulatory requirements.

- Objects in a region stay in that region until explicitly transferred by the user. This makes it easier for users to conform their services to international regulatory laws that govern legal issues regarding IT (information technology), information, and data.

- Unauthorized access is blocked by standard authentication mechanisms. Objects can also be made public or private. Moreover, rights can be granted to specific users.

- Options for secure data upload and download is provided. Encryption of data is also provided as an additional option.

- S3 uses standard REST and SOAP interfaces to work with any web services development toolkit.

- S3 is built for flexibility. Users can add protocol or functional layers. HTTP is offered as the default download protocol. BitTorrent protocol interface is provided as an option to lower costs and enable high-scale distribution.

- S3 also provides functionality to simplify management of data. For example, the Amazon S3 Management Console (http://console.aws.amazon.com/s3) provides options for segregating data by buckets, monitoring and controlling spending, and automatically archiving data to low-cost storage.

Data Management

Amazon S3 offers data life cycle management, which refers to how the data is managed from creation to deletion (if and when it is no longer needed). The life cycle management handles storage capacity and automatic archival and sets up scheduled deletions.

One of the biggest advantages of S3 is the ability to dynamically increase or decrease capacity as required. This eliminates the need for capacity planning in advance, especially in circumstances where it is difficult to predetermine the quantity of data inflow. Moreover, this mitigates underutilization of storage resources, thus also cutting operational costs.

Amazon S3 also takes care of automatic and transparent migration of data from old to new hardware, thus eliminating the need to perform this tedious, risky, and costly process.

The S3 also provides programmatic options for setting up recurring deletions, including high-volume deletions of objects in a single request. Objects can be standard, RSS, and archived.

Data Durability and Reliability

To ensure durability, S3 redundantly stores data on multiple devices in multiple facilities. For detecting corrupt data packets, S3 calculates checksums on all network traffic when retrieving or storing data. To avoid tedious data verification and repair, S3 performs data integrity tests regularly and automatically handles manual repairs if required.

Versioning systems are used to store, retrieve, and restore objects according to a saved previous version. This way, unintended user actions and application failures can be conveniently reversed. The API provides the ability to retrieve an older version of an object by specifying a version in the request. By default a request would retrieve the latest saved version of the object.

Amazon claims that the S3 system is designed for 99.999999999 percent durability and 99.99 percent availability of objects over a given year. Amazon further claims that the system is able to sustain concurrent loss of data in two facilities.

Within Amazon S3, users get a couple of options for archival and low-cost storage. One is a cheaper version of S3 offering lower redundancy, which is called Reduced Redundancy Storage (RRS). The other is the Amazon Glacier, extremely low-cost storage for data archival. Amazon recommends Glacier for data that is infrequently accessed and for which retrieval is not time critical.

OpenStack Swift

OpenStack is an open-source initiative to produce ubiquitous cloud computing platforms for public and private clouds that are simple to implement and massively scalable and support many features. OpenStack was founded by Rackspace Hosting and NASA. The reasons for the open-source initiative are to provide direct cloud computing toward a standardized domain and to prevent proprietary/vendor lock-in for cloud customers.

OpenStack supports both object and block storage options. Like Amazon's storage offerings, it provides a fully distributed storage platform that is accessible via an API and can be directly integrated into applications or used for backup and archival. Moreover, redundancy and scalability are ensured through the use of clusters of standardized servers.

The OpenStack object storage system (Swift) is mainly a distributed storage system for static data such as VM snapshots, backup, and archival. It is much akin to Amazon's S3 storage technology. Objects are written to multiple drives across the data center. OpenStack software takes care of data replication and integrity across the cluster. This means that in the event of a drive failure, the OpenStack software is responsible for replicating data to a healthy drive (self-healing).

Features

The Swift object store provides the following features:

- Objects of up to 5 GB in size can be stored.
- A proxy server handles all the requests from the other server. For each request, it looks up the location of the account, container, and object and then routes the request accordingly. Failures are also handled by the proxy server.
- A container server is responsible for keeping track of listings of objects. It does not know where objects are located but instead what objects are in a specific container.
- An account server is similar to a container server but keeps track of listings of container rather than objects.
- An authorization server contains and authorizes the cloud storage.
- Swift crawls through the saved data and replaces a bad file or object with the correct replica (self-healing).
- Statistics of objects are made available through tracking containers.

Hadoop Distributed File System (HDFS)

The Hadoop Distributed File System (HDFS) is part of the Apache Hadoop Core Project:

```
http://hadoop.apache.org/core/
```

```
http://hadoop.apache.org/docs/r0.18.3/hdfs_design.html
```

It is a distributed file system designed to run on commodity hardware. HDFS displays many similarities with existing distributed file systems, some of which have been mentioned already. It is highly fault-tolerant because of configurable degree of data replication. Further it can fit well into a low-cost system design as it can be deployed on low-cost hardware. HDFS provides the ability to handle very large data sets (in terms of tens or hundreds of TB) and provides high throughput access to application data.

Features

HDFS was built with the following goals in mind:

- HDFS is tuned to support large files. A typical large file on HDFS could very well be in the range of a few hundred GB to a few TB in size. Since one file will be distributed across the cluster in the shape of multiple smaller files, HDFS should first scale to hundreds of nodes and should provide high aggregate data bandwidth.

- HDFS acknowledges that failures are the norm rather than the exception. A typical production-level HDFS cluster may consist of hundreds of machines, each storing part of the data. Given that there are a number of components, each with a probability of failure, it is always likely that one or more of HDFS components are nonfunctional at any given time. HDFS implements automatic detection of failures and quick and automatic recovery from those failures to support overall infrastructure.

- The system is designed to be a high-throughput batch-processing system rather than providing low-latency interactive usage. However, varying implementations of HDFS exist (such as Hadoop Online Prototype) that provide the ability to implement interactive consumption of processed data in real time.

- HDFS employs a simple coherency model whereby appending writes to a file are dropped in favor of a write-once strategy. Thus, once a file is created, written to HDFS, and closed, it need not be changed. Such a model proves to be extremely efficient in providing high-throughput access because it avoids all the tedious tasks of serialization/deserialization, file-hold locking mechanisms, and repeated verification of the continuously growing file.

- Moving the computation to the data is often considered to be more efficient than moving the data it operates on. This is especially true for very large data sets. HDFS provides interfaces for applications to migrate themselves closer to the data.

- Since the HDFS is based on highly portable Java language technology, the system itself is also portable from one platform to another.

- HDFS has highly scalable master/slave architecture. An HDFS consists of a NameNode, which is a master node that manages the file system namespace and governs access to files by clients. The NameNode is also the repository for all HDFS metadata. The user data does not flow through the NameNode. Instead, there are DataNodes that manage storage attached to the nodes. HDFS exposes a file system with behavior similar to the local system. Underneath, a file is internally split into one or more blocks, and these blocks are stored across a set of DataNodes. The algorithm makes sure that the data is kept in a manner that distributes load evenly across the cluster. The NameNode executes file system namespace operations like opening, closing, and renaming files and directories. The NameNode also determines mapping of blocks to DataNodes. DataNodes perform block creation, deletion, and replication as directed by the NameNode. The DataNodes serve read and write requests from clients.

▪ HDFS is built using the Java language. Any machine that supports Java can run the NameNode and DataNodes. One of the major advantages of Java is that the HDFS can be deployed over commodity hardware running the GNU/Linux operating system (OS).

▪ HDFS exposes a typical hierarchical file system namespace. Directories and files can be created and removed. Users can move directories and files from one path to the other. Directories and files can also be renamed. User quotas, access permissions, and hard and soft links are not yet supported by the HDFS. Users can implement these features or use the underlying OS. The NameNode maintains the file system namespace, recording changes to its properties. Users can specify replication factors using a configuration file on the NameNode, which determines the number of replicas.

Architecture

Figure 9.5 shows the architectural overview of the HDFS system, including the NameNode and DataNodes. The clients can execute read and write operations, and it is up to the NameNode to maintain the replicas, including when and where to place new replicas. The NameNode also receives a heartbeat and *block report* from each DataNode in the cluster. A block report contains a list of all blocks stored on a DataNode. The purpose of the heartbeat is to check if the DataNode is still alive and functioning properly. A faulty node is immediately blacklisted. The purpose of the block report is to make the NameNode aware of what replicas are located on which DataNodes. It also helps the NameNode in making future decisions about where to put new replicas.

Data Replication

HDFS reliably stores each file as a sequence of blocks across many DataNodes in a cluster (depending on the replication factor). All blocks in a file are the same size except the last block. Replication is meant to provide fault tolerance and recoverability from disaster. The block size and replication factor (dfs.replication) are configurable using a configuration file on the NameNode (hdfs-site.xml). The replication factor can be specified on a per-file basis and can be changed at any time. However, the replication factor cannot exceed the number of DataNodes. Files in HDFS are write-once and strictly have one writer process at any given time. This, as mentioned previously, avoids the tedious tasks of serialization/deserialization, file-hold locking mechanisms, and repeated verification of the continuously growing file.

The optimization of replica placement determines HDFS reliability and performance. This is a feature that distinguishes HDFS from most of the other distributed file systems. The purpose of a rack-aware replica placement policy is to improve HDFS data reliability and availability and provide optimum network bandwidth.

FIGURE 9.5   HDFS architecture

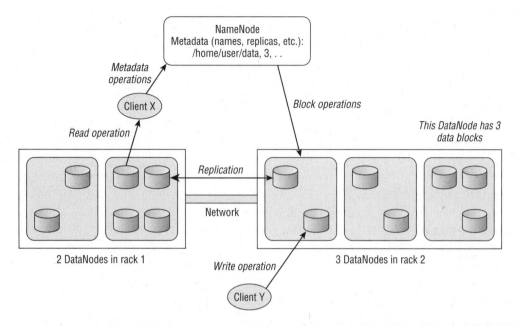

Rack awareness outlines the process by which the NameNode is used to determine the ID of the rack to which each DataNode belongs. One policy is to never place two replicas on the same rack. This prevents data loss in the event of a rack failure and spreads the load all over the racks. However, write cost is high because replicas have to be written across multiple racks. Here, the replication factor comes directly into play and would be directly proportional to the cluster performance. Rack awareness is described further here:

```
http://hadoop.apache.org/docs/r0.18.3/cluster_setup
.html#Hadoop+Rack+Awareness
```

A typical (default) placement policy used by HDFS is to put one replica on one node in a local rack, another on a different node in the local rack, and the third replica on a different node in a different rack. Figure 9.6 shows such a placement policy.

Such a policy limits the inter-rack write traffic, thus decreasing unnecessary network traffic. A rack is composed of many nodes. It is pertinent to note that a failure of the whole rack is far less likely than a node failure. One-third of the replica is on one node, two-thirds on one rack, and the remaining one-third distributed evenly across the remaining racks. The disadvantage of such a policy is that during read operations, the load is compensated by two racks instead of three. However, the write performance is significantly increased because the network connection within a rack is less congested (and thus faster) than the inter-rack network connection.

The HDFS tries to serve a read request from the replica that's closest to the user/reader. A replica on the same rack is preferred, rather than a replica on another rack. If the cluster spans a wide geographical area over multiple data centers, then a replica in the local data center is preferred over a remote replica.

FIGURE 9.6   Data replication and replica management

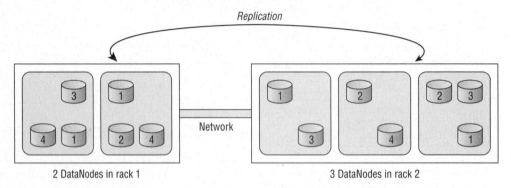

EXERCISE 9.1

Adding, Removing, and Reading Data from HDFS

Before beginning this exercise, please make sure that Java and Hadoop are properly installed and configured on your system (follow the instructions at http://hadoop .apache.org/). A local single-node setup is sufficient for this exercise.

To add files to the HDFS, run the following commands:

```
$ hadoop dfs -mkdir /user/myuser/docs
$ hadoop dfs -put /home/myuser/docs/* /user/myuser/docs/
```

To remove a file:

```
$ hadoop dfs -rm /user/myuser/docs/resume_old.txt
```

To remove the directory:

```
$ hadoop dfs -rmr /user/myuser/docs/
```

The removed files are kept in the .Trash directory for each user. To delete files permanently, without sending them to the .Trash directory, run the following commands:

```
$ hadoop dfs -rm -skipTrash /user/myuser/docs/resume_old.txt
```

```
$ hadoop dfs -rmr -skipTrash /user/myuser/docs/
```

To read a text file, run the following commands (you can avoid spilling text on the terminal by using a pipe):

```
$ hadoop dfs -cat /user/myuser/docs/resume.txt
$ hadoop dfs -cat /user/myuser/docs/resume.txt | less
```

To read compressed (such as Zip) or encoded files (such as TextRecordInputStream):

```
$ hadoop dfs -text /user/myuser/docs/compressed_report.zip
$ hadoop dfs -text /user/myuser/docs/compressed_report.zip | less
```

Killing a Hadoop Job and Avoiding Zombie Processes

To kill a Hadoop job, the user needs the job ID. The job ID is printed when a Hadoop job starts executing. Another, more-formal method is to use the Hadoop Web interface, also known as the job tracker (for a single-node setup, accessible at http://localhost:50030). The job tracker displays information about running jobs, retired or finished jobs, and killed or failed jobs. To kill a job and avoid zombie processes, do the following:

```
$ hadoop job -kill <job-id>
```

Resolving a Common IOException with HDFS

A common Java IOException can occur when the nodes are started or during the execution of a job. This happens due to HDFS's .Trash directory being full. To resolve this issue, clear the HDFS .Trash directory and restart the cluster. Remember that this has to be done through the namenode terminal because the namenode is the master node.

```
$ hadoop dfs -rmr /user/myuser/.Trash/*
$ /bin/hadoop-install-path/bin/stop-all.sh
$ /bin/hadoop-install-path/bin/start-all.sh
```

To check if the nodes (NameNode and DataNodes) have started, do the following on the namenode terminal:

```
$ jps
```

NameNode Conventions

Some of the most important Hadoop NameNode conventions and concepts are introduced in the following list:

Communication Protocols   All HDFS communication uses the TCP/IP protocol suite. A client using the Client Protocol connects to a configurable TCP port on the NameNode. The DataNodes use DataNode Protocol to talk to the NameNode. Both Client Protocol and DataNode Protocol are wrapped by the Java Remote Procedure Call (Java RPC). The NameNode does not initiate any RPC calls. The design is such that it can only respond to RPC requests issued by the clients or DataNodes. This intrinsically makes the DataNodes a lot more secure if a NameNode is compromised.

Safemode   Upon startup, the NameNode enters a special Safemode state. Replication cannot occur when the NameNode is in the Safemode state. The NameNode receives a heartbeat and a block report from the DataNodes. A block is deemed safely replicated when the minimum number of replicas of that data block has checked in with the NameNode. The NameNode exits Safemode once a configurable percentage of safely replicated data blocks have checked in with the NameNode. The NameNode then compiles a list of all those data blocks that have lower than a specified number of replicas. The NameNode then replicates those data blocks to other DataNodes.

Metadata Persistence   NameNode uses a transaction log called *EditLog* to record every change that occurs to the HDFS namespace and file system metadata. EditLog stores an entry to record the creation of a new file, changing the replication factor of a file and other such operations. The entire file system namespace, mappings of blocks to files, and file properties are stored in a file called *FsImage*. Both EditLog and FsImage are stored on the local file system of the NameNode.

The image of the entire file system namespace and a file *Blockmap* is kept in memory. The metadata system is designed to be compact, and 4 GB of main memory is plenty to support a very large number of directories and files.

How this works is that as soon as the NameNode starts up, it reads the FsImage and EditLog from the disk. The NameNode applies all the transactions from EditLog to the FsImage copy kept in memory. It also flushes out this new version, as soon as it is stable, to the disk so that in case of failure of the node, the latest changes have already been written. The EditLog is then truncated, which completes the establishment of a checkpoint.

It is important to note here the role of the DataNode, which is oblivious to the knowledge of HDFS files. Each block of HDFS data is kept in a separate file in its location file system. By design, the DataNode does not create all the files in the same directory but rather uses a heuristic to determine an optimal number of files per directory. The DataNode also creates an appropriate subdirectory structure, which is helpful if there is a large quantity of files. Recall that the performance of I/O operations directly depends on the number of items that need to be read for a given command execution. As the DataNode starts up, it sends a Blockreport to the NameNode. This Blockreport is formed by scanning through its local file system and generating a list of all HDFS data blocks that correspond to local files. The NameNode, already in Safemode, checks the data blocks, exits Safemode, makes a list of data blocks that exhibit a lower replication degree, and stabilizes the file system through data block replication if need be.

Failures   The NameNode exclusively relies on heartbeat messages from DataNodes to maintain a health list of nodes. A network partition can cause some of the DataNodes to lose connectivity with the NameNode. Absence of heartbeats to the NameNode suggests faulty or dead nodes. In such a case, the NameNode stops forwarding any new I/O to presumably dead nodes.

The replication degree of data blocks can drop below the specified value because of reasons such as dead/unavailable DataNodes, corrupt replicas, a disk drive or DataNode failure, and a change of the replication factor of a file. In such cases, the NameNode initiates necessary replication of the affected data blocks.

Cluster Rebalancing   The HDFS maintains balance between DataNodes. If a DataNode is found to fall below a certain threshold of free space, data blocks are migrated from that DataNode to another.

Similarly, in the event of spikes of high demand for a particular file, a scheme might dynamically create additional replicas and rebalance other data blocks in the cluster.

Data Integrity   Data corruption is not new and can be caused by disk drive faults (hard failure), network faults, and buggy application software. It is possible that a data block fetched from a DataNode arrives in a corrupted state. The HDFS client software implements checksum procedures on HDFS files. A checksum of each block of a file is created and stored in the same HDFS namespace. When the client retrieves a file, it verifies that the file checksum matches the checksum stored in the checksum file on the HDFS namespace. If the checksums do not match, the client can opt to retrieve a replica of the block from another DataNode.

Metadata Disk Failure   The FsImage and EditLog are central data structures of HDFS and critical to its correct functional state. The NameNode can be configured to maintain multiple copies of these files (provisioning of a secondary NameNode). Updates to either of these files cause synchronous updates to both. Updating multiple copies may cause degradation of NameNode performance. However, since HDFS applications are typically data intensive and not metadata intensive, the chances of degradation preventing correct behavior is limited. During startup, the NameNode selects the latest consistent copy of FsImage and EditLog.

One of the drawbacks of such a design is that a NameNode can form a single point of failure for an HDFS cluster. However, election algorithms can be implemented that opt to select a secondary NameNode (if provisioned) as the new in-charge NameNode.

Snapshots   Snapshots is a handy feature of HDFS that allows storing a copy of data at a particular instance in time. Some common use cases are data backup, protection against user errors, and disaster recovery.

```
http://hadoop.apache.org/docs/current/hadoop-project-dist/hadoop-hdfs/
HdfsSnapshots.html
```

More technical details about the HDFS design and system can be found on the Apache HDFS design web page:

```
http://hadoop.apache.org/docs/r0.18.3/hdfs_design.html
```

 Real World Scenario

Loading and Processing Archived Data with HDFS and Hive

Sometimes companies archive some of their data to preserve space. Instead of discarding old and rarely used data, companies generally prefer archiving in case they need the data in the future. Data can be archived using compression tools such as GNU Zip (GZIP). Loading compressed (deflated) or decompressed (inflated) data into the HDFS is trivial.

However, Hadoop cannot run multiple jobs for a GZIP file. This is because a GZIP file is considered to be one object. The GZIP replaces repeated text with tokens during the deflation phase. Partitioning this data for processing could create invalid results. Therefore, Hadoop instead prefers to treat it as one file. Imagine the old file being in order of hundreds of GBs. Hadoop or not, processing this file will take ages.

Hadoop recommends a two-step process: (1) loading the compressed data into HDFS, and (2) reloading it from its HDFS source to a sequence file format. The recommended practice is to insert data into a new Hive table, which is stored as a SequenceFile. Hive (http://hive.apache.org/) is a distributed warehouse technology from Apache. It uses HDFS as its base storage system and provides a SQL-like command-line interface (CLI) known as Hive-QL.

A SequenceFile can be split by Hadoop and distributed across multiple nodes (for Map tasks), whereas a GZIP file cannot be distributed. Let us walk through the steps required to accomplish this:

1. First, create a Hadoop directory that our Hive table will use to store compressed file. This is done using the Hadoop command.

    ```
    $ hadoop fs -mkdir /user/myuser/old_data/calllist
    ```

2. Next, using the Hive CLI, create a Hive table to load the compressed file. The
EXTERNAL statement lets the user create the table that does not store data in the
default HDFS location. It also makes sure that whenever the table is dropped, the
data remains intact and is not removed. All other operations such as read and write
work as usual. Moreover, note that the LOCATION statement takes as its parameter the
same path as we created in step 1, but it has to be fully qualified with the HDFS protocol scheme and the cluster name.

```
Hive> CREATE EXTERNAL TABLE calllist (SubscriberID STRING, StartingTime
STRING, EndingTime STRING, InitCell INT, InitSector INT, LastCell INT,
 LastSector INT, CallDirection INT) ROW FORMAT DELIMITED FIELDS
TERMINATED BY '\;' LINES TERMINATED BY '\n' LOCATION 'hdfs://mycluster/user/
myuser/old_data/calllist';
```

3. From the Hive CLI, load the compressed data into the Hive table using the source
compressed file.

```
Hive> LOAD DATA LOCAL INPATH '/mnt/myuser/calllist.gz' INTO TABLE calllist;
```

4. Create an HDFS directory using Hadoop command. The directory will later be
pointed to the new Hive table to store decompressed data in SequenceFile format.

```
$ hadoop fs -mkdir /user/myuser/old_data/calllist_seq
```

5. Create a Hive table that will store files in SequenceFile format. Note that there is a
STORED AS SEQUENCEFILE statement added to the Hive query.

```
Hive> CREATE EXTERNAL TABLE calllist_seq (SubscriberID STRING, StartingTime
STRING, EndingTime STRING, InitCell INT, InitSector INT, LastCell INT,
 LastSector INT, CallDirection INT) STORED AS SEQUENCEFILE LOCATION 'hdfs://
mycluster/user/myuser/old_data/calllist_seq';
```

6. Load the data into the Hive table.

```
Hive> INSERT OVERWRITE TABLE calllist_seq SELECT * FROM calllist;
```

7. Clean up all that is not used anymore. The Hadoop remove command with the
-skipTrash switch will skip the Hadoop trash directory and irreversibly destroy
the data. This command should be executed with caution.

```
Hive> DROP TABLE calllist;
$ hadoop fs -rmr -skipTrash /user/myuser/old_data/calllist
```

EXERCISE 9.4

Using Pig to Group and Join Items Based on Some Criteria

Pig is a distributed high-level Map-Reduce language for expressing data analysis programs to analyze large data sets on HDFS. Before beginning, please make sure that Pig (http://pig.apache.org) is installed along with Hadoop and Java. A single-node Hadoop setup will be sufficient for this exercise.

Let us assume that we have some stock exchange data and we want to analyze it. A sample of data in JavaScript Object Notation (JSON) format is given here. Pig supports a variety of input and output formats, but for this exercise we will use JSON. It is one of the most widely used industry formats.

```
[{"date":"2009-12-31","dividends":"35.39","symbol":"CLI","exchange":"NYSE"},
{"date":"2009-12-30","dividends":"35.22","symbol":"CLI","exchange":"NYSE"},
{"date":"2009-12-29","dividends":"35.69","symbol":"CLS","exchange":"NYSE"},
{"date":"2009-12-28","dividends":"35.67","symbol":"CLS","exchange":"NYSE"},
{"date":"2009-12-24","dividends":"35.38","symbol":"CGW","exchange":"NYSE"},
{"date":"2009-12-23","dividends":"35.13","symbol":"CGW","exchange":"NYSE"},
{"date":"2009-12-22","dividends":"34.76","symbol":"CWW","exchange":"NYSE"},
{"date":"2009-12-21","dividends":"34.65","symbol":"CWW","exchange":"NYSE"}]
```

Once we have copied NYSE_dividends.json to the HDFS, we need to write a Pig script to execute over Hadoop. Let us say we want to group this data by symbol and call this script group.pig. Here symbol represents company stock.

```
--group.pig
divs = load 'hdfs://localhost:9000/user/myuser/NYSE_dividends.json'
using JsonLoader('date:chararray, dividends:chararray, symbol:chararray,
exchange:chararray');
grpd  = group divs by symbol;
store grpd into 'hdfs://localhost:9000/user/myuser/grouped' using JsonStorage();
```

Next we run the script on the cluster. The local switch option tells Pig to run on the single-node cluster deployed on the local machine. In case of the default statement (without the −x switch) Pig would assume it needs to be run in distributed mode and would try to ship the job to the distributed cluster.

```
$ pig -x local group.pig
```

EXERCISE 9.4 *(continued)*

The user can view the data inside the HDFS directory (/user/myuser/grouped) using the Hadoop command. The user can also control the reduce task parallelism by replacing the group statement in the group.pig script as follows. The map task parallelism is dynamically determined by the input file. Usually, there's one map for each HDFS block (default block HDFS size is 128 MB).

```
grpd  = group divs by symbol parallel 12;
```

Now let us assume you have another file called NYSE_daily.json, which represents today's stock trade. What you would like to see is which stocks from NYSE_dividends .json were seen traded today as well. This can be accomplished by doing a join of the two data sets, as shown in the join.pig script. The parallelism option for reduce tasks can be used in Pig with any aggregation or accumulation operation, including group, co-group, and join.

```
--join.pig
daily = load 'hdfs://localhost:9000/user/myuser/NYSE_daily.json'
using JsonLoader('date:chararray, dividends:chararray, symbol:chararray,
exchange:chararray');
divs  = load 'hdfs://localhost:9000/user/myuser/NYSE_dividends.json'
using JsonLoader('date:chararray, dividends:chararray, symbol:chararray,
exchange:chararray');
jnd   = join daily by symbol, divs by symbol;
store jnd into 'hdfs://localhost:9000/user/myuser/joined' using JsonStorage();
```

Choosing from among These Technologies

An obvious problem with the presence of a number of good technologies is the decision-making process. Deciding which technology to use is not always trivial. In fact, such a decision could prove to be critical in terms of an organization's cloud application life cycle.

The decision for a cloud storage technology should take into account three very important factors:

- Nature of the data to be stored (or the type):
  - Is it corporate data, such as customer data, company data, or product data?
  - Is it log data, such as logging or machine-generated data?

- Frequency of data access:
  - How often is a particular set of data accessed? Can it be archived?
  - What is an acceptable delivery time or latency?
- Level of redundancy required:
  - Corporate value of the data. How important is the data to the organization?

Once an organization has determined these three factors, it can make an informed decision for choosing a cloud storage service. Table 9.3 summarizes typical use cases and real-world examples for the aforementioned storage technologies.

TABLE 9.3 Storage technology use cases and examples

Storage Technology	Use Cases	Examples
Amazon EBS	High- and very high-frequency, high-value, corporate data	LinkedIn, Expedia, Dow Jones, Unilever, Adobe, Nokia, Netflix
Amazon S3	High-frequency data, high/medium-value, web-scale query access; large data chunks	Amazon's network of websites, Dropbox, Tumblr, Pinterest, Ubuntu One
OpenStack Swift	Low-frequency data, snapshots, archival, backup	AT&T, CERN, Deutsche Telecom, PayPal, Intel, NASA, Sony, Yahoo!
Apache HDFS	Batch-processing system, low frequency, high value	Facebook, Yahoo!

Cloud Storage Gateway

As enterprises move toward cloud-based storage, new challenges emerge. Cloud storage service providers deliver their services using either Representative State Transfer (REST) or Simple Object Access Protocol (SOAP) application programming interfaces (APIs). Enterprise applications are usually based on block or file data abstraction, which is far different from what the cloud service providers are offering.

A cloud storage gateway is a network server that translates cloud storage APIs such as REST or SOAP calls to block-based storage protocols such as Internet Small Computer System Interface (iSCSI) and Fibre Channel or file-based interfaces such as Network File System (NFS) and Common Internet File System (CIFS). The cloud storage gateways use standard network protocols to integrate existing applications with cloud storage service offerings.

One other use case of cloud storage gateways is to use the gateway as an intermediary to multiple cloud storage service providers. For example, TwinStrata's CloudArray software (`www.twinstrata.com/solutions-overview`) gives enterprises the ability to seamlessly store data across a choice of cloud storage providers. TwinStrata distributes CloudArray as a virtual appliance, meaning that it can reside alongside the existing storage infrastructure.

StorSimple (`www.storsimple.com/solutions-overview/`) and Panzura (`http://panzura .com/solutions/`) work toward appliances that implement technologies to balance storage across on-premises and remote locations. Both the companies offer solutions specific to Microsoft applications, including SharePoint and Exchange. The solution delivers a view of cloud storage as block volumes.

Cloud storage gateways also offer features such as backup and recovery system, caching, compression, data deduplication, encryption, and storage provisioning. Nasuni provides the Nasuni Filter (`www.nasuni.com/how_it_works/storage_controller`), which is a software virtual appliance that resides on the on-premises server. The software encryption and deduplication techniques (such as chunking, data hashing, and primary/secondary storage segregation) are employed before making use of one or many cloud storage providers.

CTERA cloud storage gateway (`www.ctera.com/products/products/cloud-storage-gateways`) is another hybrid appliance solution that transparently combines cloud storage with local storage. The appliance also features NAS capabilities and backup functionality. CTERA uses the on-premises local storage for maximizing performance and local sharing while utilizing the cloud storage for universal access, file sharing, and synchronization and data backup.

Amazon also offers the AWS Storage Gateway solution (`http://aws.amazon.com /storagegateway/`). It connects on-premise applications with cloud storage in a transparent and secure manner. Encrypted data can be stored directly onto Amazon S3 or Amazon Glacier. Moreover, it provides a cost-effective solution that supports standard storage protocols. The AWS Storage Gateway maintains frequently accessed data in on-premise storage infrastructures to provide low-latency performance.

The AWS Storage Gateway supports three configurations:

Gateway-Cached Volumes   Frequently accessed data is stored on premise, and primary data is stored on S3. Advantages include cost savings due to minimization of the need to expand on-premise resources and low-latency access to frequently accessed data.

Gateway-Stored Volumes   All primary data is stored locally, and asynchronous backups of data to S3 is provided. Advantages include durable and inexpensive cloud backup.

Gateway-Virtual Tape Library   Data is stored on limitless collection of tapes. Each tape is backed up by S3 or Glacier. Advantages include inexpensive and virtually unlimited backup facilities.

Cloud Security and Privacy

"TechInsights Report 2013: Cloud Succeeds. Now What?" is a survey-based report commissioned by CA Technologies. It indicates that according to the respondents, "the cloud has moved beyond adolescence and is on the path to maturity in the enterprise" (reported in the *Wall Street Journal*, http://online.wsj.com/article/PR-CO-20130521-906501.html).

The report indicates that the United States leads Europe in terms of experience in cloud technology usage. A total of 55 percent of the respondents in the United States have used the technology for three or more years as compared to 20 percent of European respondents.

The priorities that drive the shift from in-house maintained infrastructures to a cloud platform also differ. For Europeans, the priority was "reduced total costs," whereas the respondents in the United States expressed "increased speed of innovation" and "superior IT performance/scalability/resiliency" as the top objectives for the shift.

However, security remained a concern. Though most (98 percent) of the respondents agreed that the cloud met security expectations across infrastructure, platform, and service architectures, security was cited by almost half of the respondents (46 percent) as a primary reason for not migrating an application or a service into the cloud.

Probably the biggest challenges faced by cloud computing today are related to security, privacy, legal issues, and regulations. Critical voices such as GNU founder Richard Stallman have often warned that the whole cloud system is full of privacy and ownership concerns.

www.theguardian.com/technology/2008/sep/29/cloud.computing
.richard.stallman

Security, Privacy, and Attack Surface Area

Security is a contentious and widely debated issue in the cloud computing domain. The lack of physical control of the public cloud, when compared to complete control over in-house infrastructure (including private cloud), creates multiple issues for companies dealing with sensitive data. Physical control gives operators the ability to inspect data links and check if anything has been compromised. Such issues with control access are incentives for cloud service providers to build and maintain highly secure infrastructure.

Generally, security issues have been categorized as follows:

- Access control policy and secure access to sensitive data
- Multitenancy and clear policy-driven data segregation
- Privacy
- Exploitation through bugs, viruses, and malware
- Malicious insiders

Here are some solutions to these cloud security problems:

- Public key infrastructure (PKI), cryptography, and expiring hashcodes
- Policy-driven data storage architecture and API support for ID-based data object/item access mechanisms
- Anonymization as a tool for enabling and ensuring privacy
- Ensuring the latest security patches and active investigation of any possible threats
- Active surveillance of control staff and use of client-specific PKI-based encryption keys to restrict and control staff access to data.

These issues and their solutions have been mentioned in detailed research works. With greater ease of control for multiple cloud service providers and a plethora of data already in their systems, the risk of data being disclosed either accidentally or deliberately becomes immense. Companies like Amazon deploy country-wide local infrastructures and provide customers with the ability to select Availability Zones. Moreover, articulating clear policy and legislation could help describe how the data of individual cloud users would be accessed and used.

However, there are other architectural and maintenance issues that need to be taken care of. Outsourcing data storage to a cloud storage provider increases the attack surface area.

In a cloud storage platform, data is (automatically) replicated and moved frequently (automatic load balancing) across the entire cloud infrastructure. Though it supports multiple benefits, it does however bring about the risk of unauthorized data recovery (drive reuse, reallocation of storage space, disposal of old hardware, etc.).

Risk of unauthorized access to data can be mitigated by the use of cryptographic techniques and encryption standards such as FIPS 140-2. FIPS Publication 140-2 is a U.S. government computer security standard that provides guidelines for cryptographic modules. It describes four levels of security, from Level 1 to Level 4, without describing what level of security is required by a particular application:

Level 1   The lowest level of security. Basic requirements for a cryptographic module are specified without any physical security mechanisms. An example would be PC encryption board.

Level 2   Improves upon Level 1 and requires features that show evidence of tampering with a cryptographic module. This includes tamper-evident coatings and pick-resident locks and doors that prevent unauthorized access to a facility.

Level 3   In addition to tamper-evident security mechanisms, Level 3 is proactive and puts in places mechanisms to prevent an intruder from gaining access to the cryptographic module. Level 3 is intended to have detection and response to intrusion attempts at physical access and use/modification of cryptographic module. Examples include strong enclosures and tamper detection/response circuitry.

Level 4   This is the highest level of security, with physical security providing a complete envelope of protection around the cryptographic module with the intent to detect and respond to all unauthorized attempts at physical access.

Encryption can be applied to data when it is being uploaded to the cloud. However, encryption has a cost: processing and storage would have to include extra steps to decrypt and encrypt data, respectively. This could cause the service to slow down. This is a sensible compromise for organizations dealing with sensitive user data. Other techniques include zero-filling of disk drives before hardware disposal. Unix- and Linux-based operating systems provide utilities (such as dd) that can write a zero byte to every addressable location of the disk drive. Another similar technique is to overwrite all the disk blocks with random data.

In a cloud storage system, the number of networks increases: LAN, SAN, and WAN are all in play. In a typical cloud storage platform, data from multiple customers will unequivocally pass through the same network channels. Therefore, faulty equipment, software bugs, erroneous actions, and human criminal intent can cause other customers to access data that does not belong to them.

Just as encryption at rest prevents stored data from unauthorized access, encryption based on PKI techniques for data in transit can protect data from unauthorized readable access.

Legal Issues (Jurisdiction and Data)

With cloud computing and its dynamic nature, certain legal issues arise, including trademark infringement and security concerns regarding sharing of proprietary data resources. Moreover, laws vary from country to country and region to region, thus making a user and user data subject to government control and territorial legislation.

During the U.S. government's seizure and shutdown of the MegaUpload cloud storage service, people lost property rights of stored data on the cloud computing platform. The U.S. government's approach to data legislation relies on a combination of legislation, regulation, and self-regulation rather than governmental regulation alone. The data privacy legislation tends to be adopted on ad hoc basis. The United States has no single standardized data protection law comparable to the European Union's Data Protection Directive.

The Data Protection Directive (officially known as Directive 95/46/EC) regulates the processing of personal data and free movement of such data within the European Union. It is an important component of the EU privacy and human rights law. The directive regulates processing of personal data by defining scope and principles. The scope defines personal data as "any information relating to an identified or identifiable natural person (data subject); where an identifiable person is one who can be identified, directly or indirectly."

The principles talk about transparency of processing. Data subjects have the right to be informed when their personal data is being processed. Controllers must provide their name and address, the purpose of processing, the recipients of the data, and all other information required to ensure that the processing is fair.

The principles also talk about legitimate purpose and proportionality. Legitimate purpose regulates that the personal data can be processed only for specified explicit and legitimate purposes. It also specifies that the data may not be processed further in a way that's incompatible with those purposes. Proportionality specifies that the data may be processed only insofar as it is adequate, relevant, and not excessive in relation to the purposes for which it is collected and/or further processed. However, it must be ensured that the data is accurate and, where necessary, kept up-to-date.

One important but generally overlooked problem with data on the cloud is "possession of data." Different cloud storage providers take different positions on this matter. If the provider is the possessor of the data, then the possessor has certain legal rights. This, however, compromises rights of individuals who actually own the data.

Another position for a company is to be a custodian of the data it keeps. In such a case, a different set of rules and rights would apply. Terms of service agreements provided by the cloud computing service providers are either silent or ambiguous on the question of ownership. These agreements should also address what happens when either party (cloud or user) decides to terminate or end the service. The state of the data may become blurred in case of provider insolvencies.

Supplier Lifetime (Vendor Lock-In)

Many cloud platforms and services are proprietary because they are built on specific standards and protocols by particular vendors for particular cloud offerings. Migrating from a proprietary cloud platform can become extremely complicated and even expensive for customers wishing to take the journey. This is typically referred to as vendor lock-in and is not specific to cloud computing.

Three types of vendor lock-in can occur:

Platform Lock-In   Cloud services are built on virtualization platforms such as VMware, Xen, and VirtualBox. Migrating from one to another is not trivial. There is software that might not work, and there are services that might fail and hardware that might not perform the same way.

Tools Lock-In   Different cloud service providers use different tools that are designed specifically to manage their own kind of cloud infrastructure. These tools might not work on a different kind of virtual environment.

Data Lock-In   Data ownership conundrum could cause problems in migrating to another cloud service provider. Acquisition of a service-supplying cloud provider by another company could cause problems because the original service agreement (issued by the acquired company) might not hold any longer.

Heterogeneous cloud computing is a platform that prevents vendor lock-in. Cloud storage gateways provide enterprises with the ability to operate multiple clouds transparently through a unified cloud management system. Companies can choose from among various hypervisors to accomplish their infrastructural goals.

Heterogeneous cloud systems also provide the ability to prevent incompatible APIs to cause vendor lock-in because the data spread is usually consolidated across multiple vendors.

Summary

The process of assigning storage capacity to servers and VMs in a cloud space is called storage provisioning. In this chapter, we introduced some relevant terms related to storage provisioning and explained at length cloud storage provisioning concepts such as cloud storage, SAN storage, and cloud storage provisioning. The chapter also introduced concepts of network configuration and network optimization in the context of the enterprise cloud setup.

We then explained the architectures of various major cloud storage service offerings, such as EBS, Amazon's prime block-level cloud storage offering, and S3, Amazon's web-scale storage system. We described in detail Apache's HDFS, which is a multipurpose highly fault-tolerant and low-cost distributed file system designed to run over low-cost commodity hardware.

The chapter also focused on the importance of cloud storage gateways and security and privacy issues that come along as challenges with cloud storage. In the section "Cloud Security and Privacy," the focus was on preventing security and privacy issues and mitigating the effects of attack surface area. The chapter highlighted the importance of focusing on cloud security issues such as access control policies, multitenancy, and PKI-enabled authorization mechanisms used when designing a cloud infrastructure.

Chapter Essentials

Cloud Storage   Cloud storage provides fault tolerance, better redundancy, and eventual consistency models to guarantee data consistency. Durability of stored data is ensured through versioning and atomicity of operations. Moreover, a cloud storage service provides large cost savings because it eliminates the capital expenditure and maintenance costs.

Storage Provisioning   Storage provisioning is defined as the process of moving data or virtual data centers, applications, services, and VMs to the cloud. Storage provisioning raises security concerns and problems such as isolation, unintended interactions, multitenancy, and attack surface area. These concerns can be addressed using standard guidelines for provisioning storage service. Storage provisioning also offers data management capabilities such as adding more storage, archiving, deduplication, and compression.

Cloud Storage Technologies   Cloud storage technologies form the backbone of an organizational storage infrastructure. There are many storage technologies offered by various companies, and each technology serves a different set of requirements. Organizations should take into account three important factors before deciding on a specific technology. These include the type of data, the frequency of data access, and the required redundancy level. These factors help an organization think about attributes of their data sources to determine the best possible fit.

Cloud Security   Cloud privacy and security is the most debated issue in cloud computing. Cloud security issues have generally been attributed to access controls, malicious software, exploitation through bugs/viruses/malware, and multitenancy. Most of these issues are resolved through access control policies and surveillance, the latest security patches, anonymization for privacy, and ID-based access for stored data objects. Careful planning and policy-driven data storage architecture can help mitigate most of the security and privacy problems.

Data Usage Laws   With the age of big data, a rising concern throughout the computing and information technology domain is compliance with laws and regulations. Different regions and countries have their own distinct laws regarding data capture, procurement, processing, and usage. Organizations should take into account local and international regulations concerning data and information before making any choices for particular cloud service providers. Moreover, it is best for organizations that own or possess private and confidential user data to deploy their own infrastructure or use a cloud service provider that is based in the same region or country where the confidential data is captured or recorded (with consent from the user, such as a telecom operator or a DSL connection provider). This makes it easier for the organization to comply with regional or local legal regulations concerning data and information.

Supplier Lifetime   Another rising concern of cloud storage service is supplier lifetime, also known as vendor lock-in. There are three types of vendor lock-in: platform lock-in, tools or services and applications lock-in, and data lock-in. Organizations should be keen on using heterogeneous platforms to prevent difficult scenarios. For example, where an organization cannot migrate from one platform to another, a service or an application is deemed incompatible for other platforms and data is bound by regional or local regulations where the provider resides.

Chapter

10

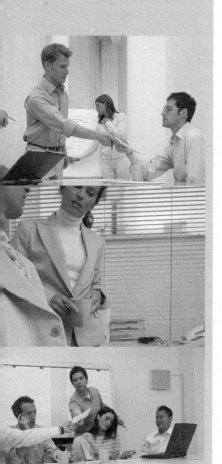

Testing and Deployment: Quality Is King

TOPICS COVERED IN THIS CHAPTER INCLUDE:

- ✓ Overview of deployment models
- ✓ Cloud bursting
- ✓ Cloud management strategies
- ✓ Cloud architecture
- ✓ Cloud deployment options
- ✓ Deployment testing and monitoring
- ✓ Creating and deploying cloud services
- ✓ Organizational best practices

This chapter covers the deployment and testing of cloud computing models. The most popular are private, public, and hybrid models. These models present options for deploying applications in the cloud. Each model presents a different set of options, such as deployed services, security, and accessibility, among others. Moreover, each model also presents different suitability criteria, including location of deployment (on site or off site), sensitivity of data (confidentiality and data security), and costs. This chapter covers cloud computing models and strategies to extend virtualization outside the data center and to the cloud.

Overview of Deployment Models

With emerging cloud implementations, organizations look to expand their businesses and scope, and they need to take advantage of local, offsite, and public cloud offerings. The existing cloud models derive their types from methods of deployment as well as client usage.

National Institute of Standards and Technology (NIST) Special Publication (SP) 800-145 describes four basic models for cloud deployment, as described in the following sections.

Private Cloud

Private clouds reside on a private network that is owned, managed, and operated by the organization itself. Private clouds provide internal users with immediate access to computing resources. Provisioning and scaling a collection of resources is usually performed using a web interface. The cloud computing resources can be situated on or off site and can be managed by an in-house team or a third party.

One of the biggest advantages of having a private cloud is security. In fact, this model addresses the security and privacy issues, due to shared resources and multitenancy, inherent in other cloud models. Because a private cloud is behind the firewall, it is subject to the physical, electronic, and procedural security measures of the organization. Moreover, it offers a higher degree of security for intellectual property (IP) such as code and data.

A private cloud gives network administrators the ability to control performance of the physical machines, thus offering an opportunity to improve efficiency and reduce costs.

However, the biggest downside of this model is heavy setup costs and recurring operational and maintenance costs. In addition, the setup requires special skilled resources such as cloud architect and IT engineers.

Community Cloud

A community cloud is a partnership between related organizations, such as governmental or educational institutions, to share cloud computing resources for a focused purpose (such as research projects). A community cloud is usually set up using local and private resources that can be accessed remotely by partner organizations.

Each partner organization that participates in the setup of a joint community cloud is responsible for the operation and maintenance of their own infrastructure. The biggest advantage of this model is that it provides greater cost savings than a private cloud while compromising some of the stringent security and privacy requirements. This is usually considered fine because there is only a limited group of partners who will have access to the cloud.

This model is well suited for organizations that share similar goals and common security requirements and legal policies. The cloud can be managed by partner organizations or by a third-party provider.

This model, however, comes with a downside. Because each group of members operates and maintains its own part of the cloud, things can become slightly complex. Installation of new hardware/software and troubleshooting and diagnosis can incur issues regarding communication between partners and can cause undesired delays.

Public Cloud

Public clouds reside over host data center resources and are accessible to registered and paying users from anywhere in the world. This is the deployment model that commonly represents cloud computing. In this model, all the physical resources are owned and operated by a third-party cloud provider. Multiple clients—individuals or corporations—utilize these resources through a combination of web interfaces and CLI tools. The infrastructure can be used by clients to dynamically provision services that are billed based on usage.

This model provides two advantages: The first is that it has the highest degree of cost savings because the clients only need to pay for usage (operations) and not for maintenance of infrastructure. The infrastructure cost is shared between clients, thus providing economies of scale. The second advantage is the readiness and availability of the resources.

The biggest challenge (and criticism) of the public cloud model is IP and data control. For organizations that directly deal with people or their personal data, including telecom, finance, and market research, data is the most important asset as well as a liability (if it gets stolen, lost, or corrupted). Data control, security, and privacy are issues that depend on a multitude of factors, including the type of data and how sensitive it is along with industry, local, and federal laws concerning the data. Companies that would like to use a public cloud provider might find themselves limited and restricted by transparent redirection of cloud services to data centers in variable locations. The reason is that the transparent redirection presents regulatory and legislative concerns for local and federal mandates demanding data accountability and governance.

Hybrid Cloud

Hybrid clouds are provisioned by combining one or more cloud models, providing access to multiple infrastructures bridged together by standard or proprietary technologies.

With hybrid clouds, organizations can utilize cost benefits of a public cloud to run services as usual and switch to a private cloud for confidential and sensitive data. For example, an organization may keep sensitive client data in-house on a private cloud setup and interface its private cloud to a public cloud service that processes customer billing.

The biggest advantage of such a model is maintaining segregation between types of applications and data in the public domain and those that stay in private control. The other advantage is to be able to provision or migrate applications or data between platforms as and when required.

The biggest challenge of this approach is to contrive compatibility between two different platforms for applications to run seamlessly and for data to be imported or exported without issues.

Cloud Bursting

Cloud bursting is an application deployment model in a hybrid cloud setup. Local private cloud resources are used for running an application for normal operational load until there is a spike in demand that exceeds local resource limits. When a spike occurs, the application moves, or "bursts," out of the private cloud into the public cloud to manage the overrun.

Cloud bursting is recommended for high performance, non-critical applications that handle nonsensitive information. Another use case for cloud bursting is to move out applications to the public cloud to free up local resources to run business applications.

One of the major limitations of cloud bursting is that the designated public cloud platform should be fully compatible with the private cloud to successfully run the bursting applications. This model works best for applications that do not have a complex delivery mechanism, do not use vendor-specific APIs, and do not require complex integration with other applications and system components.

Another issue with provisioning cloud bursting is the limited availability of management tools that are cross-compatible over multiple platforms. Cloud service providers and hypervisor vendors offer tools to send workloads to the public cloud automatically, but they usually come with multiple strings attached, such as vendor lock-in, limited compatibility, and expensive monitoring tools. Figure 10.1 shows popular cloud computing types.

Cloud Management Strategies

With the growing complexity and variety of private, public, and hybrid cloud-based systems, cloud management strategies help to monitor numerous tasks, including performance, security auditing, disaster recovery, and contingency plans.

FIGURE 10.1 Cloud computing types

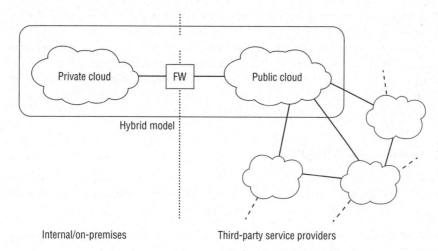

Private Cloud Strategies

Private cloud management requires tools, such as OpenStack, to create virtualized compute resource pools and provide a user self-service portal, security through authentication, dynamic resource allocation, and tracking and troubleshooting.

Forrester Research defines internal clouds as "pools of virtualized machines that can be built upon either virtual server or high-performance computing grid foundations and can be operated to the specific security and process requirements of the business."

```
www.datacenterknowledge.com/archives/2010/04/19/a-guide-to-managing-
private-clouds/
```

Private cloud environments are typically organized in terms of portable workloads. The management tools are usually service driven because the private cloud is highly virtualized.

Community Cloud Strategies

A community cloud is generally not managed in its entirety by one single institution or organization. Instead, parts of the cloud are managed by various responsible parties involved in a joint project or sharing a common concern.

Institutions such as universities and research labs generally have focused groups to deal with issues related to the infrastructure management of the community cloud. These groups collaborate with groups of other partner universities or research labs to achieve set goals, diagnose problems, resolve issues, and prepare contingency plans to adopt in the event of a large-scale failure. However, different partners may not share the same micro-level concerns, such as time limits to fix an issue, prioritizing tasks, and communicating and reporting progress to other institutions.

Having multiple partners collaborating for a community cloud infrastructure can help in terms of the issues and tasks being divided among partner institutions. Also, this helps in spreading the costs. However, the lack of managerial clarity due to a partnership-based approach can reduce productivity, especially when an issue occurs. Moreover, the lack of boundaries defining the managerial domains for the infrastructure on a per-partner basis can affect managerial communication. Last, in the event of an equipment failure, such as the failure of a node or a transceiver, the institute responsible might not be able to fix or replace the affected equipment. This can be attributed to various influencing factors within an institution, including funds, authority, and permission.

Public Cloud Strategies

Public cloud environments are managed by service providers such as Amazon and Microsoft and include servers, storage, networking, and data center maintenance operations. Mainly, there are three basic cloud service management categories for the users to select:

User Self-Provisioning Cloud services are purchased directly from the service provider, and payment is based on a per-transaction model.

Advance Provisioning Customers purchase a set amount of resources and pay a flat fee.

Dynamic Provisioning This is the most popular model. Customers pay on a pay-per-use basis. The provider is responsible for allocating resources when the customer requests them and decommissions them when the user no longer needs them.

Hybrid Cloud Strategies

Hybrid cloud environments, including compute, storage and networking resources, have to be managed across multiple domains. They consist of an internal private cloud and contracted services of one or more public cloud providers. A management strategy should define what needs to be managed, where and how. Over time, the combination of domains might evolve, but the management strategy should remain consistent.

A sound management policy should address a few key issues:

- Installation and configuration policies should specify rules for creating, deploying, upgrading, and destroying virtualized resources.
- Access control policies should specify rights and privileges for private/sensitive data and restricted applications.
- Billing and reporting policies should specify how users receive usage and cost information and stipulate any budgetary controls to prevent unmonitored overrun.

You can find more at the following location:

```
http://searchcloudcomputing.techtarget.com/tip/Hybrid-cloud-management-
tools-and-strategies
```

Management Tools

Cloud management tools become necessary for fairly dynamic environments. There are many cloud management solutions that monitor and provision cloud deployments. Although all the big companies such as IBM, CA, HP, Dell, and VMware provide their own cloud management solutions, they are generally not recommended for a public cloud by cloud vendors themselves. The reasons are costs, compatibility, technology lock-in, and lack of detailed choices.

Most typically a good cloud management tool should support different cloud types, dynamic provisioning and decommissioning of objects (servers, storage, apps), and a management dashboard with system information. A few vendors that offer pervasive approaches in handling provisioning and managing cloud dashboards in private, public, and hybrid environments are listed here:

RightScale   RightScale offers a free edition of its management tool with limited features and capacity, but it's enough to test whether the solution fits an organization's needs. The product is broken into four main components: management environment, cloud-ready server template with a deployment library, adaptable automation engine, and a multi-cloud engine for hybrid environments.

RightScale supports large cloud vendors such as Amazon and Rackspace as well as Eucalyptus and GoGrid.

Kaavo   Kaavo is similar to RightScale and is typically used for single-click deployment of complex multitier applications in the cloud (development, QA, or production). It also provides other useful features, such as handling automatic cloud bursting, management of application infrastructure, data encryption, and work-flow automation to handle runtime production exceptions.

Kaavo supports Amazon, Rackspace, and Eucalyptus.

Zeus Traffic Controller   Zeus was famous for its web server, which despite being rock solid could never compete with Apache Tomcat and Microsoft IIS. Zeus uses its application server expertise and traditional load balancing tools to test availability for spontaneously commissioning or decommissioning instances in the cloud. Zeus currently supports Rackspace and Amazon platforms.

Amazon CloudWatch   CloudWatch works on Amazon's EC2 platform only and therefore does not support hybrid cloud environments. However, it supports dynamic provisioning (auto-scaling), monitoring, and load balancing. It is managed through a central management console, the same one used by Amazon Web Services. The biggest advantage is that an organization using Amazon's cloud infrastructure does not need to install any additional software, nor do they need an additional website to access applications. It provides robust functionality with the only downside being lack of hybrid support.

Cloud Architecture

Cloud architecture is system architecture of software systems that are involved in the delivery of cloud services, such as software applications that use Internet-accessible on-demand services. Cloud architecture typically involves multiple cloud components communicating with each other over a loose coupling mechanism such as a messaging service or queue (one example is Java Messaging Service, or JMS).

Applications built on cloud architecture use the underlying infrastructure to perform a specific job by drawing the necessary resources on demand and then relinquishing the unneeded resources and often disposing them once the job is complete. While in operation, an application might scale up or down depending on the resource needs. Figure 10.2 shows a simple representation of cloud architecture.

FIGURE 10.2   Cloud architecture

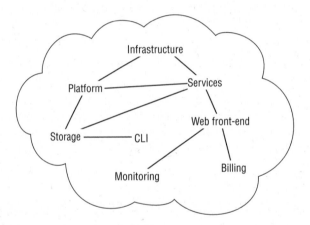

The Need for Cloud Architectures

Traditional data processing techniques suffer from an array of difficulties. It is difficult to commission as many machines as needed by an application as well as provision applications on them. It is tedious to distribute and coordinate tasks on different machines, run processes, and ensure recovery mechanisms. Also, dynamically scaling up or down can create more issues than the issues they are intended to resolve. And finally, decommissioning machines is not as trivial as with traditional architectures. Cloud architectures address all the key difficulties surrounding traditional data processing with large-scale workloads.

The idea is to take advantage of the cloud infrastructure maintained by the service provider, use provider APIs to provision instances, scale up or down, and decommission when done.

Technical Benefits

Cloud architectures offer the possibility of designing applications that could utilize the power of bulk processing systems for various needs. Here are a couple of benefits:

Architecting Real-Time Processing Pipelines   Document processing pipelines can be created to convert documents between formats. This can also empower text indexing for fast search and data mining over millions of records.

Image processing and video encoding/decoding pipelines can be created to process multimedia data.

Architecting Batch Processing Systems   Batch processing systems can be architected to perform efficient and effective log analysis of machine-generated data for performance monitoring and auditing of large-scale compute systems. In addition, log analysis can be used to generate regular reports for administrative and managerial purposes.

Other uses include nightly builds of updated source code repositories, including the newest patches and updates. Another is to automate unit testing and deployment testing for different deployment configurations.

Business Benefits

Cloud architectures offer some clear business-level benefits:

Quick Provisioning Coupled with Zero Upfront Investment   No costs for purchasing machines, storage, networking, power hardware, and operations staff. Organizations can save time because management would not need to approve expenditure before a proposal for new facility can be underway as it would with traditional architectures. The facility currently under use for other operations can be utilized for provisioning new services.

Just-in-Time Infrastructure   Dynamic resource provisioning helps users to control the compute capacity required. Organizations do not need to worry about scaling their infrastructure all the time.

Per-Use Pricing   Utility-based computing comes with utility-style pricing, which allows billing the customers for only the infrastructure and services that have been used.

Efficient Resource Utilization   With the option of dynamic provisioning of resources, users can relinquish cloud resources more efficiently by commissioning those they need and decommissioning the ones not required anymore.

Parallelization   Dynamic provisioning of resources also enables the users to provision instances and use fully distributed and scalable applications for data processing, thus reducing the time it would normally take to accomplish a task on a small number of machines with a nondistributed setup.

Cloud Deployment Options

The cloud servicing industry might be in its nascent stage, but nonetheless there are already some impressive options available from the industry. We will now briefly discuss some of these popular options.

Environment Provisioning

Provisioning a cloud environment and maintaining operability requires answering multiple questions and making informed choices. Apart from selecting the cloud service provider, other aspects have to be taken into astute consideration. Some of the most important aspects include the service provider API, compatibility with applications that need to be migrated, and update scheduling.

In the following sections, we provide an introduction to such issues for the three most popular cloud service providers. Please note that we will not include discussions and comparison based on pricing and some of the vendor specifications because these evolve quickly based on the targeted business and customers.

Windows Azure

Microsoft's Windows Azure provides a Platform as a Service (PaaS) cloud service model. The vendor provides the infrastructure (compute resources, network, and storage) and application development platform, including the OS, database, and web server (IIS). The idea is to have the customer deal with only the application and its issues and remain oblivious to all other platform-specific issues.

Being a Microsoft product, it offers integration with other Microsoft Live tools. Azure works best for enterprise applications designed with service-oriented architecture (SOA) in mind and provides automatic scaling. It also works well for medium-sized mobile apps.

Azure has two approaches to storage: SQL Azure Database (SAD) and Azure Storage. SAD is a relational database, whereas Azure Storage is a nonrelational storage offering. The biggest plus is the compatibility offered during migration from enterprise SQL Server systems to SAD. The cost model is pay per use. The downside is the scalability and database size (hundreds of GBs). Also, the import/export functionality does not guarantee consistency until combined with a live database copy.

Amazon EC2

Amazon's Elastic Compute Cloud (EC2) is based on the Infrastructure as a Service (IaaS) cloud service model. Amazon provides the network, storage, and compute resources and lets the customer take care of everything but the hardware. The customer, thus, is in complete control of the whole environment. EC2 is the most popular cloud service brand in the world because it gives its customers the ability to build their own custom stack from the ground up, operate/maintain it the way they want, upgrade it the way they want, and scale it the way they want. The amount of flexibility is unparalleled.

EC2 offers massive scalability and performance, making it ideal for large enterprise applications that need to support millions of customer queries.

Amazon provides multiple offerings, including Elastic Block Store (EBS), Simple Storage Service (S3), and Relational Database Service (RDS). (We covered EBS and S3 in Chapter 9, "Storage Provisioning and Networking.") RDS offers SQL Server, MySQL, and Oracle storage instances. Apart from providing a list of available relational storage solutions, the two biggest advantages of RDS include availability and database size (200 to 1,000 GBs). When the customer creates a database instance, the Amazon RDS creates a standby replica in another Availability Zone that supports synchronous replication.

This means that the availability of the application that uses the RDS service underneath can continue to operate unless there is a service blackout in two different Availability Zones containing the same replica. However, the only major problem with such a feature is that organizations carrying and processing private customer data and bound by regional laws to not export the data to other countries or regions will have to find another solution or deploy their own.

Other Features

Amazon provides other rich features as well, such as the availability of a more costly database solution that utilizes SSD drives to deliver up to 30,000 I/O operations per second. A maximum of five replicas are supported. Backups are more frequent than they are in Windows Azure and provide snapshots down to the second. Apart from providing standby replicas that support synchronous replication, the RDS comes with the ability to automatically replace dead hosts.

Rackspace

Rackspace is powered by OpenStack, which offers an open and flexible cloud platform. Rackspace provides a responsive API and a good dashboard panel to manage server instances. The OpenStack API used by the next-generation Rackspace cloud service includes new features such as management of server metadata.

Just as with Amazon, the Rackspace customers can choose a region to host their data and services. Regional control also helps in managing availability and connectivity to cloud services. Data replicas are spread across regions to aid with disaster recovery in case of a regional failure.

Rackspace uses OpenStack Swift. Swift is a distributed object storage system for static data objects such as VM snapshots and backup. In design and principle, Swift resembles Amazon's S3 storage technology. Objects are written to multiple drives across the data center. Swift takes care of data replication and integrity across the cluster. In the case of a drive failure, Swift is responsible for replicating data to a healthy drive. This powerful feature is called *self-healing*.

Swift allows objects of 5 GB in size. By design, a proxy handles all the requests and looks up the location of the account, container and object. It then routes the request accordingly. The proxy is also responsible for handling failures.

Container Server

A container server is responsible for tracking lists of objects. Swift containers only know which objects are in a container. An account server is similar to a container but instead keeps track of containers rather than objects.

Swift uses self-healing mechanisms to crawl through the data and replace bad files or objects with healthy replicas. It also makes available statistics of objects through tracking containers.

Deploying a Service to the Cloud

Deploying a service to the cloud involves choosing the deployment target (the need), gathering the requirements, and planning for the steps and processes. We will use an example of deploying a cloud storage service to give an overview of the steps involved in deploying a service to the cloud.

The need for storage cloud arises from at least four major factors:

- First and foremost is the exponential growth of data (customer data, catalogs, activity logs, machine generated logs, etc.).

- Next is limited budgeting. It is not possible to have a separate data center for each different project.

- Legal requirements and regulatory compliance are important factors. For example: anonymized customer data from a telecom operator in the United States cannot be stored in a data center in Europe.

- Heterogeneous storage environments becomes ubiquitous, such as SQL, NoSQL, flat files, and so on.

A cloud storage service can help alleviate all these issues. Cloud storage gives clients the ability to connect, manage, and interact with the underlying storage solutions. The biggest advantage of having a cloud setup is to be able to use multiple storage technologies on a single virtual platform obfuscated to the end user by using a single layer of middleware. End users connect to the middleware, which can then process the user query, connect to the correct underlying storage, retrieve the results, and present the results to the user in human-readable format.

Deployment Steps

There are four major steps to achieving an effective deployment and maintenance scheme. Each step is described in detail:

Step 1: Determine cloud storage use case and deployment model.   The use case depends on what the system will host and how will it be used. For each use case, the capacity, latency, and cost are prioritized. For instance, for a production data cloud, low latency is a much larger concern than cost. Similarly, for a backup data cloud setup, capacity and cost are bigger concerns than latency.

The next step is to choose a deployment model that best suits the organizational needs. Organizations have multiple things to take into consideration before they can arrive at a decision. The biggest concern of them all is data security and confidentiality. Shared infrastructure, multitenancy, and geographical location of the service provider data centers need to be considered.

Organizations that deal with sensitive confidential customer data want to make sure the public cloud provides secure multitenancy at every layer of the IP stack, isolation through private volumes and LUNs, security through firewalls and secure protocols (HTTPS SSL/ TLS), and a final line of defense through data encryption. Figure 10.3 depicts multitenancy in cloud storage.

FIGURE 10.3   Multitenancy in cloud storage

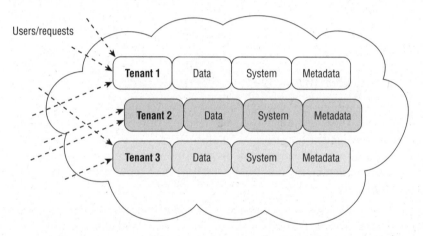

Step 2: Identify bottlenecks and resolve them.   The biggest bottlenecks in most enterprise environments are the network capacity (bandwidth), firewalls, and proxy servers. Apart from that, policies related to data administration can also prove to be big nontechnical hurdles. Sadly, data administration policies are completely subject to the country in which each organization resides.

However, common bottlenecks can be resolved using common solutions. For instance, network capacity can be increased with dedicated connections (FTP/SFTP) to the storage cloud. The caveat is that dedicated connections are generally expensive.

To resolve bottlenecks created by firewalls and proxy servers, a number of solutions can be devised. For instance, the firewall can be programmed to ignore certain IP addresses, thus allowing anonymous bypass for a dedicated connection. The transfer server can be served through a separate firewall. Caching could also be employed by the firewall to make it faster. Figure 10.4 shows how network bottlenecks can be handled.

FIGURE 10.4   Network bottlenecks identified and removed

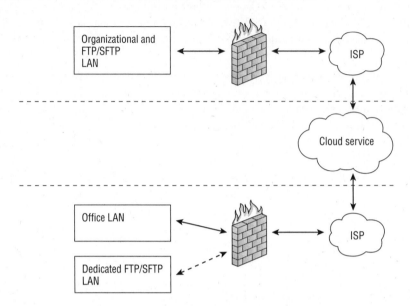

Step 3: Document deployment concerns.   Not all concerns can be resolved during the architecting and design stage. Concerns still outstanding should be put down as part of the deployment documentation. There are usually three types of concerns: security, management, and standards.

Security concerns include legal issues with the retention and location of data, regulatory compliance and data governance (integrity and classification), and data auditing.

Infrastructure management concerns usually include virtual machine management, VLANs, VM migration, application compatibility for cloud-to-cloud migration, and VM multitenancy.

Concerns related to standards include open vs. proprietary cloud service provider APIs and technology, which again points to compatibility and migration. This also suggests risks in terms of vendor lock-in, and organizations have to make a decision whether compromising openness and compatibility is a small giveaway.

Step 4: Design the deployment scheme.   During the design of the deployment scheme, several things need to be considered. The most important issue to be considered is the level of control and access that an organization wishes to maintain over its cloud deployment. The level of administration—i.e., infrastructure level, platform level, or both—is also an important issue.

Deployment Testing and Monitoring

Testing is a critical part of the software development life cycle, perhaps even more so for cloud applications. During the cloud application development process, it is best to do as much testing as possible by using local compute instances and storage. The developers should run unit and ad hoc tests to ensure that the components perform as they are intended. Although the local unit testing environment might not represent the challenges of the cloud environment, it does help to eliminate most of the errors and bugs and introduces the practice of clean production provisioning.

Once done with the unit and ad hoc testing, the development team should deploy the application only to the cloud test environment. The cloud test environment can be a pseudo-cloud setup. The testing is necessary to check the behavior of the final test version of the application. If the application performs as expected and passes the quality control (QC) checks, the administration team can then approve deployment to the production environment.

During the testing phase, the application connects to a test database running in the test environment. This helps the developers and testers to develop and test according to a managed data set that depends on different types of data that can be accepted and their size and repetition. The following sections describe some features for safe and effective cloud application testing.

Test Deployment in a Staging Environment

Organizations can have separate deployments of the test and production environments in the cloud. This helps in maintaining segregation between the two because test environments tend to change quickly. This also helps to manage costs and leverage instances as and when needed. With a separate test environment, the organization can choose to minimize the costs by cutting down on the instances. This can be a fast process because the organization does not need to worry about the consequences on performance of the production cloud.

Functional Testing

Functional testing is a quality assurance (QA) process that tests the specifications of the application.

Black-Box Testing   The idea is to check what the application does, its functionality, without peeking into its internal implementation (white-box testing). The testing can be applied to any level of software testing: unit, integration, system, and acceptance. Usually input is provided to the test subject, which gives an output. The output is then matched against the expected output.

White-Box Testing   This type of testing tests an application for its internal workings and structures as opposed to its functionality (black-box testing). The tests are designed to exercise paths through the code and determine appropriate outputs. White-box testing designs include control flow testing, data flow testing, branch testing, path testing, statement coverage, and decision coverage.

Nonfunctional Testing

Nonfunctional testing is an important part of the overall testing policy as an organization moves into the cloud. The main aim of nonfunctional testing is to test software and applications against a set of nonfunctional requirements such as performance, reliability, and scalability. Most of the risks associated with the cloud emanate from nonfunctional requirements not being met or even not being articulated. The areas of proven vulnerability include performance, security, and disaster recovery.

A plan must be in place to ensure Quality of Service (QoS) for performance and security and to manage possible disasters. For performance testing, traditional tools and techniques can be used, and other factors can also be considered, such as, for example, addressing the surge of sudden loads for an e-commerce website. Similarly, security testing can encompass checking each layer of the architecture—from presentation to data layer—to plug holes and mitigate risks.

Cloud service testing must be carried out at multiple levels to ensure that a service performs the way it is expected when it is stressed:

Performance Testing   Isolates issues when the system is tested by increasing the load from different locations and multiple user operations.

Scalability Testing   Tests an application for its capability to scale up or scale out; that is, what improvement does an application show if resources such as compute power and memory are added to one node (scale up) or when more nodes are added to the whole system (scale out)? Scaling up usually tests an application's ability to utilize hardware, and scaling out tests the ability to parallelize and distribute tasks performed by its processes.

Load Testing   Tests application stability when the user count is increased dramatically.

Stress Testing   Pushes the system to its limits by introducing two or three times the expected stress.

Fail-Over testing   Tests are conducted under anticipated load with component failure to check what happens if an already loaded group of machines experiences failure of one of the nodes.

Latency Testing   Measures the latency or delay between issuing a request (action) and receiving a response.

Browser Testing   Tests client browser software applications to list recommended browsers with minimal issues. This can expose browsers with weak security mechanisms, security vulnerabilities, and platform incompatibilities.

Security Testing   This type of testing is done to check whether it is appropriate to migrate or design an application to run in the cloud. Application dependencies must also be taken into consideration because they can deviate from the actual security policy requirements.

Compatibility Testing   Tests are conducted on the application to evaluate its compatibility with the computing environment. This includes hardware and other applications (e.g., browser compatibility, OS compatibility, database compatibility).

Governance Risk Compliance (GRC) Testing   GRC testing involves listing threats, vulnerabilities, and risks associated with cloud computing (IaaS, Paas, and SaaS) and suggesting controls assimilated from best practices in the industry.

Figure 10.5 shows the application life cycle management in a separate test and production cloud setup.

FIGURE 10.5   Network bottlenecks identified and removed

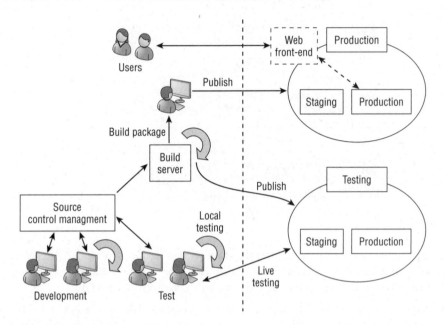

Big Data Testing

Testing of big data technologies is emerging as one of the biggest and most important cloud computing challenges. The problem is multifold as the organizations dealing with big data resources struggle to find what to test and what the corresponding level of tests should be. Thus, testing becomes all the more important to ensure correctness of the procedures and operations involved in processing the data as well as maintaining high credibility internally and externally (with customers who use or exploit the data resources, such as advertising, marketing, etc.).

Functional and nonfunctional testing becomes part of the big data testing routine. This also ensures that the whole process that is being performed on the raw data is within the specified SLA. Figure 10.6 shows level-by-level focus areas of how big data testing should be performed.

FIGURE 10.6 Big data testing—focus areas

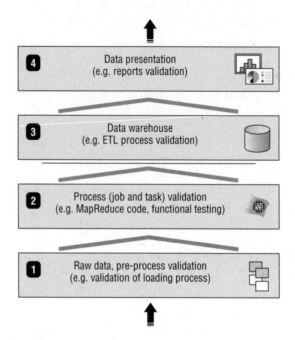

1. The first step is to verify preprocess validation, which involves loading the data into a distributed data store. This involves quality checking (QC) the data for its correctness, necessary format conversions, time-stamp verification, and so on.

2. The second step starts when the data has been loaded to the data store and is ready for processing. This includes functional testing of the data processing chain (code), such as MapReduce programs and job execution.

3. The third step is to test the processed data when extract, transform, and load (ETL) operations are performed on it. This includes functional testing of ETL or data warehousing technologies used, such as Pig and Hive.

4. The fourth and final step is to validate and verify the results and reports produced as a result of the ETL processes. This is done using procedures, such as queries, to verify whether required relevant data is being extracted. Moreover, it is necessary to check if the resultant data set is properly aggregated and grouped.

Creating and Deploying Cloud Services

In the following sections we focus on using hands-on techniques to create and deploy cloud services. We explore two options: using the Windows Azure platform and using Amazon EC2.

Creating and Deploying a Cloud Service Using Windows Azure

In this section we will create and deploy a mock service using Windows Azure Management Portal. We will use the Quick Create method to create a new service and then use the Upload method to deploy the service to Windows Azure.

There are three components necessary to deploy an application or a service in Azure:

Cloud Service Definition File (`.csdef`)   This defines the service model, including roles. You can think of roles as attributes that define how an entity (individual) would behave.

Cloud Service Configuration File (`.cscfg`)   This provides configuration settings for the service and individual roles. It also includes the number of role instances.

Cloud Service Package (`.cspkg`)   This contains the application itself, the source code, and the service definition file.

The first step is to create the cloud service package from the application code and a service configuration file. Each cloud service package contains application files and application configuration files. The Windows Azure software development kit (SDK) provides tools for preparing these files. The SDK can be downloaded from downloads page (www.windowsazure .com/en-us/develop/downloads/) in the preferred programming language.

The three cloud service features require special configuration files before you export a service package:

- To deploy a cloud service that uses secure connections (SSL), the application needs to be configured for SSL.

  http://msdn.microsoft.com/en-us/library/windowsazure/ff795779.aspx

- To enable remote connections to role instances, roles needs to be configured for remote connections.

  http://msdn.microsoft.com/en-us/library/windowsazure/gg433010.aspx

- To configure monitoring for the cloud service, the diagnostics feature needs to be enabled.

  www.windowsazure.com/en-us/develop/net/common-tasks/diagnostics/

The default setting is the minimal monitoring that presents performance counters from the host OS for VMs. Detailed or verbose monitoring gathers additional metrics such as issues or errors that occur during the application life cycle.

Before beginning, please make sure that you have a Windows Azure account set up. A trial or basic account will be sufficient. Figure 10.7 shows a quick glance view of the Windows Azure wizard for creating new cloud, data, app, and network services. In the URL field, enter a subdomain name for accessing your cloud service in production deployments. In Region Or Affinity Group, select a geographical region or affinity group where you wish to deploy the cloud service. Typically, affinity groups help to deploy your cloud service to the same location as other Windows Azure services within a region.

FIGURE 10.7 Windows Azure Quick Create

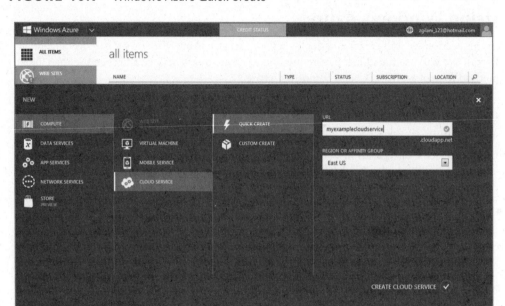

If you select roles (such as administrator) that require a certificate for Secure Sockets Layer (SSL) data encryption, a certificate must be created and uploaded to the cloud service. This should be done before service deployment. Once you upload a certificate, any applications that are running in the role instances can access the certificate. To create an upload a certificate, follow these steps:

1. Select the newly created service and select the Certificates option.

   The next step is to deploy the service.

2. Select the newly created service, and the service dashboard displays. There are two options:

   - Deploy In The Production Environment
   - Deploy In The Staging Environment

3. Generally, it is better to deploy to staging in order to test the service before putting it into production. Choose that option.

4. Install the Windows Azure SDK (www.windowsazure.com/en-us/develop/downloads/) if you have not already.

   The Azure SDK supports client libraries and source code for developing web applications in Java, PHP, Node.js, and other programming languages.

In the staging environment, the service's globally unique identifier (GUID) identifies the cloud service in URLs (e.g., GUID.cloudapp.net). The subdomain name that the user entered while creating the service is reserved to be used with the production environment. Once the service is deployed, users can use the Swap option to redirect client requests to the production deployment. Figure 10.8 shows uploading the service and its associated package (.cspkg) and configuration (.cscfg). We used a C# Hello World example. Both the package and configuration are built and packaged using Microsoft Visual Studio.

FIGURE 10.8   Uploading cloud service package and configuration

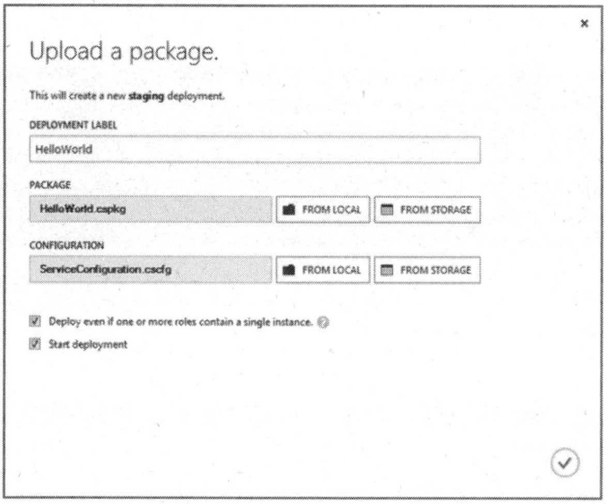

5. If the cloud service will include any roles with only one instance, select the "Deploy even if one or more roles contain a single instance" check box to enable the deployment to proceed.

   Windows Azure can guarantee only 99.95 percent access to the cloud service during maintenance and service updates if every role has at least two instances. The user can add additional role instances on the Scale page after you deploy the cloud service.

The user can monitor the status of the deployment in the notifications area, as shown in Figure 10.9.

To verify that the staging deployment has completed successfully, the user can click the site URL under the cloud service dashboard, as shown in Figure 10.10.

The dashboard gives a number of options to the user, including monitoring, Quick Glance, Operation Logs, Autoscale Status, Usage Overview, Linked Resources, and more.

FIGURE 10.9   Notification area showing the status of the cloud service deployment

FIGURE 10.10   Cloud service dashboard showing Quick Glance and other options

The URL opens the Hello World page generated by the cloud service, as shown in Figure 10.11.

FIGURE 10.11   Hello World cloud service–generated web page

Deploying and Managing a Scalable Web Service with Flume on Amazon EC2

Machine-generated log data is valuable in locating causes of various hardware and software failures. The log information can provide feedback for improving system architecture, reducing system degradation, and improving uptime. For businesses, this translates to cost savings and customer retention. Businesses have recently started using this log data for business insights. In the following sections, we present a how-to guide to deploy and use Flume on a Hadoop cluster (www.ibm.com/developerworks/library/bd-flumews/).

Flume Notes

Flume is a distributed service for efficiently collecting, aggregating, and reliably moving large amounts of streaming event data from many sources to a centralized data store. Flume architecture includes agents (nodes) and events (data flows).

A Flume event can be defined as a unit of data flow having a payload (bytes) and an optional set of string attributes. A Flume agent is a JVM process that hosts the components through which events flow from an external source to the next hop or end destination.

Flume can be used to collect data on a remote location, and a collector can be configured on a Hadoop Distributed File System (HDFS) cluster. This cluster can be used as end storage. Figure 10.12 provides a simple illustration of Flume architecture.

FIGURE 10.12   Flume architecture

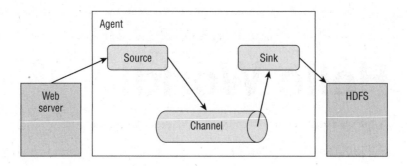

Data Flow Model

There are three main components of a Flume agent: source, channel, and sink:

Source   The source consumes events delivered to it by an external source, such as, for example, a web service. The external source sends events to Flume in a recognizable format. When a Flume source receives events, it stores them into one or more channels.

Channel and Sink   The channel is a passive store that keeps an event until it is consumed by a Flume sink. For example, a file channel uses the local file system, where the sink extracts the event from the channel and puts it in an external repository like the HDFS. Alternatively, the sink can forward the event to the source of the next Flume agent (next hop) in the flow. The source and sink within the given agent run asynchronously with the events staged in the channel.

There can be different formats used by the source for different purposes. For example, an Avro Flume source can be used to receive Avro events from Avro clients. An Avro source forms half of Flume's tiered collection support. Internally, this source uses Avro's NettyTransceiver to listen for and handle events. It can be paired with the built-in AvroSink to create tiered collection topologies. Other popular network streams that Flume uses are Thrift, Syslog, and Netcat.

System Architecture

To set up a scalable web service using Flume, we will need code to read RSS feeds. We also need to configure Flume agents and collectors to receive RSS data and store it in the HDFS.

Flume agent configuration is stored in a local configuration file. This is a text file similar to a Java properties file. Configurations for one or more agents can be specified in the same configuration file. The configuration file includes properties of each source, sink, and channel in an agent and how they are wired together to form data flows.

An Avro source needs a hostname (IP address) and a port number to receive data. A memory channel can have a maximum queue size (capacity), and an HDFS sink needs to know the file system URI and path to create files. An Avro sink can be a forward sink (avro-forward-sink), which can forward to the next Flume agent.

Here we create a miniature Flume distributed feed (log events) collection system using agents as nodes, which get data (RSS feeds in this case) from an RSS feed reader. These agents will pass on these feeds to a collector node that will be responsible for storing the feeds in an HDFS cluster. In this example, we will use two Flume agent nodes, one Flume collector node, and a three-node HDFS cluster. Table 9.1 describes sources and sinks for agent and collector nodes.

TABLE 9.1   Sources and sinks for agent and collector nodes

Nodes	Source	Sink
Agent node	RSS feed	Collector
Collector node	Agents	HDFS

Figure 10.13 shows the architectural overview of our multihop system with two agent nodes, one collector node, and an HDFS cluster. The RSS web feed is an Avro source for both the agents that stores feeds in a memory channel. As the feeds pile up in the memory channel of the two agents, the Avro sinks start sending these events to the collector node's Avro source. The collector also uses a memory channel and an HDFS sink to dump feeds into the HDFS cluster. The code and configurations are provided in Listing 10.1.

The Java code in the listing describes an RSS reader that reads RSS web sources from the BBC news website. RSS is a family of web feed formats used to frequently publish updates (such as blog entries, news headlines, audio, and video) in a standardized format. RSS uses a publish-subscribe model to check the subscribed feeds regularly for updates.

The Java code uses Java's Net and Javax XML APIs to read the contents of a URL source in a W3C document and processes that information, before writing the information to the Flume channel.

Listing 10.1: Java code `RSSReader.java`

```java
import java.net.URL;
import javax.xml.parsers.DocumentBuilder;
import javax.xml.parsers.DocumentBuilderFactory;
import org.w3c.dom.CharacterData;
import org.w3c.dom.Document;
import org.w3c.dom.Element;
import org.w3c.dom.Node;
import org.w3c.dom.NodeList;

public class RSSReader {
  private static RSSReader instance = null;
  private RSSReader() {
  }
```

```
  public static RSSReader getInstance() {
    if(instance == null) {
      instance = new RSSReader();
    }
    return instance;
  }
  public void writeNews() {
    try {
      DocumentBuilder builder = DocumentBuilderFactory
.newInstance().newDocumentBuilder();
      URL u = new URL("http://feeds.bbci.co.uk/news/world/rss.xml?edition=uk#");
      Document doc = builder.parse(u.openStream());
      NodeList nodes = doc.getElementsByTagName("item");
      for(int i=0;i<nodes.getLength();i++) {
        Element element = (Element)nodes.item(i);
        System.out.println("Title: " + getElementValue(element,"title"));
        System.out.println("Link: " + getElementValue(element,"link"));
        System.out.println("Publish Date: "
+ getElementValue(element,"pubDate"));
        System.out.println("author: " + getElementValue(element,"dc:creator"));
        System.out.println("comments: "
+ getElementValue(element,"wfw:comment"));
        System.out.println("description: " + getElementValue(element,"descript
ion"));
        System.out.println();
      }
    } catch(Exception ex) {
      ex.printStackTrace();
    }
  }
  private String getCharacterDataFromElement(Element e) {
    try {
      Node child = e.getFirstChild();
      if(child instanceof CharacterData) {
        CharacterData cd = (CharacterData) child;
        return cd.getData();
      }
    } catch(Exception ex) {
    }
    return "";
  }
```

```
  protected float getFloat(String value) {
    if(value != null && !value.equals("")) {
      return Float.parseFloat(value);
    }
    return 0;
  }
  protected String getElementValue(Element parent,String label) {
    return getCharacterDataFromElement((Element)parent
.getElementsByTagName(label).item(0));
  }
  public static void main(String[] args) {
    RSSReader reader = RSSReader.getInstance();
    reader.writeNews();
  }
}
```

FIGURE 10.13   Overview of multihop system

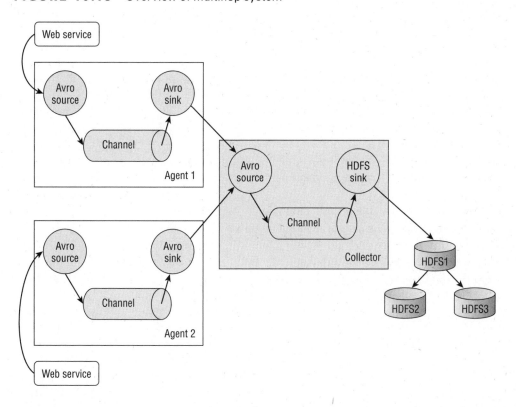

Listing 10.2 and Listing 10.3 show sample configurations for agents (10.0.0.1 and 10.0.0.2). Listing 10.4 shows the configuration for the collector (10.0.0.3). The purpose of the configuration files is to define semantics for source, channel, and sink. For each source type, we also need to define type, command, standard error behavior, and failure options. For each channel, we need to define the channel type. The channel type, capacity (maximum number of events stored in the channel), and transaction capacity (maximum number of events the channel will take from a source or give to a sink per transaction) have to be defined as well. Similarly, for each sink type, we need to define type, hostname (IP of the recipient of the event), and port. In case of an HDFS sink, the path to the HDFS head name node has to be provided.

Listing 10.2: Agent 1 `flume-conf.properties` for 10.0.0.1

```
# The configuration file needs to define the sources,
# the channels and the sinks.
# Sources, channels and sinks are defined per agent,
# in this case called 'agent'
agent.sources = reader
agent.channels = memoryChannel
agent.sinks = avro-forward-sink

# For each one of the sources, the type is defined
agent.sources.reader.type = exec
agent.sources.reader.command = tail -f /var/log/flume-ng/source.txt
# stderr is simply discarded, unless logStdErr=true
# If the process exits for any reason, the source also exits and will produce no
# further data.
agent.sources.reader.logStdErr = true
agent.sources.reader.restart = true

# The channel can be defined as follows.
agent.sources.reader.channels = memoryChannel

# Each sink's type must be defined
agent.sinks.avro-forward-sink.type = avro
agent.sinks.avro-forward-sink.hostname = 10.0.0.3
agent.sinks.avro-forward-sink.port = 60000

#Specify the channel the sink should use
agent.sinks.avro-forward-sink.channel = memoryChannel

# Each channel's type is defined.
```

```
agent.channels.memoryChannel.type = memory

# Other config values specific to each type of channel(sink or source)
# can be defined as well
# In this case, it specifies the capacity of the memory channel
agent.channels.memoryChannel.capacity = 10000
agent.channels.memoryChannel.transactionCapacity = 100
```

Listing 10.3: Agent 2 flume-conf.properties for 10.0.0.2

```
agent.sources = reader
agent.channels = memoryChannel
agent.sinks = avro-forward-sink

# For each one of the sources, the type is defined
agent.sources.reader.type = exec
agent.sources.reader.command = tail -f /var/log/flume-ng/source.txt
# stderr is simply discarded, unless logStdErr=true
# If the process exits for any reason, the source also exits and will produce
# no further data.
agent.sources.reader.logStdErr = true
agent.sources.reader.restart = true

# The channel can be defined as follows.
agent.sources.reader.channels = memoryChannel

# Each sink's type must be defined
agent.sinks.avro-forward-sink.type = avro
agent.sinks.avro-forward-sink.hostname = 10.0.0.3
agent.sinks.avro-forward-sink.port = 60000

#Specify the channel the sink should use
agent.sinks.avro-forward-sink.channel = memoryChannel

# Each channel's type is defined.
agent.channels.memoryChannel.type = memory

# Other config values specific to each type of channel(sink or source)
# can be defined as well
# In this case, it specifies the capacity of the memory channel
agent.channels.memoryChannel.capacity = 10000
agent.channels.memoryChannel.transactionCapacity = 100
```

Listing 10.4: Collector flume-conf.properties for 10.0.0.3

```
Collector configuration (flume-conf.properties on 10.0.0.3):
# The configuration file needs to define the sources,
# the channels and the sinks.
# Sources, channels and sinks are defined per agent,
# in this case called 'agent'

agent.sources = avro-collection-source
agent.channels = memoryChannel
agent.sinks = hdfs-sink

# For each one of the sources, the type is defined
agent.sources.avro-collection-source.type = avro
agent.sources.avro-collection-source.bind = 10.0.0.3
agent.sources.avro-collection-source.port = 60000

# The channel can be defined as follows.
agent.sources.avro-collection-source.channels = memoryChannel

# Each sink's type must be defined
agent.sinks.hdfs-sink.type = hdfs
agent.sinks.hdfs-sink.hdfs.path = hdfs://10.0.10.1:8020/flume

#Specify the channel the sink should use
agent.sinks.hdfs-sink.channel = memoryChannel

# Each channel's type is defined.
agent.channels.memoryChannel.type = memory

# Other config values specific to each type of channel(sink or source)
# can be defined as well
# In this case, it specifies the capacity of the memory channel
agent.channels.memoryChannel.capacity = 10000
```

Execution

Setting up the whole system requires three steps. Note that the configuration files are responsible for how a node behaves (i.e., as an agent or collector).

1. Compiling the Java code and executing two instances, one each on each agent node.

```
$ javac RSSReader.java
$ java -cp /root/RSSReader RSSReader > /var/log/flume-ng/source.txt &
```

2. Starting the agents.

```
Agent node 1 (on 10.0.0.1):
$ $FLUME_HOME/bin/flume-ng agent -n agent1 -c conf -f
$FLUME_HOME/conf/flume-conf.properties
Agent node 2 (on 10.0.0.2):
$ $FLUME_HOME/bin/flume-ng agent -n agent2 -c conf -f
$FLUME_HOME/conf/flume-conf.properties
```

3. Starting the collector.

```
$ $FLUME_HOME/bin/flume-ng agent -n collector -c conf -f
$FLUME_HOME/conf/flume-conf.properties
```

Monitoring

One of the advantages of using a public cloud service provider is that it provides the users with a monitoring interface to track and monitor deployed cloud services. We used Amazon EC2 to deploy the RSS web service. Figure 10.14 and Figure 10.15 show network activity of one of the agent nodes. Figure 10.16 and Figure 10.17 show the collector node, and Figure 10.18 and Figure 10.19 show the master HDFS node.

FIGURE 10.14　Agent 1 incoming data from RSS feed

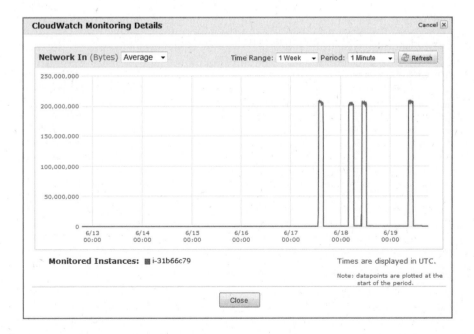

FIGURE 10.15   Agent 1 outgoing data to collector

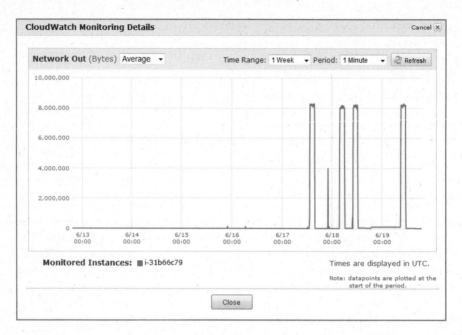

FIGURE 10.16   Collector incoming data from agent nodes

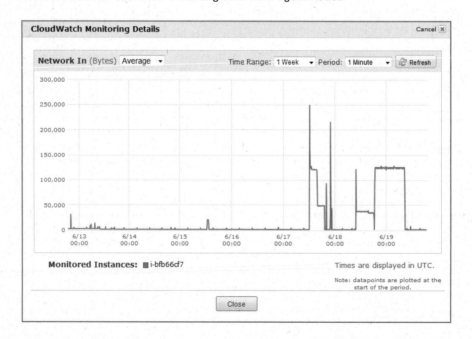

FIGURE 10.17   Collector outgoing data to HDFS

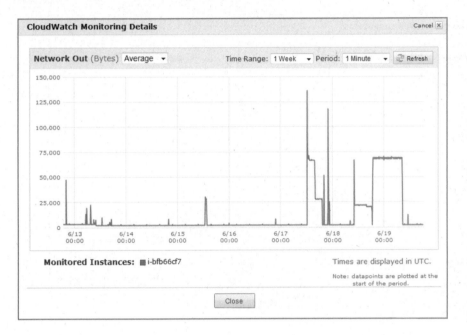

FIGURE 10.18   HDFS node 1 incoming data

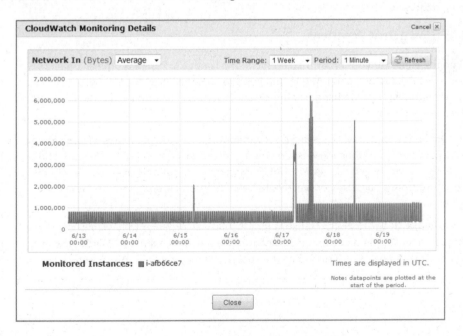

FIGURE 10.19   HDFS node 1 outgoing data

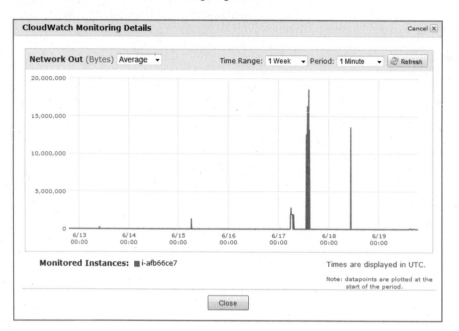

 Real World Scenario

Organizational Best Practices

Adopting the cloud for your enterprise applications is not a trivial task. There are a number of issues, factors, and options that need to be considered for a coherent cloud deployment model. Here we list a few important features to ensure secure deployment and quality assurance (QA).

Service Subscription Policy   Create a policy that prohibits individual users from signing up for business-related cloud services. Instead, individual users should subscribe at the organizational level, which allows account management. It not only protects the cloud infrastructure from a security perspective but also helps in smooth administration of content control.

Service Provider Security Policy   Ensure that the service provider follows industry security standards and implements standard security frameworks (such as OWASP and PCI DSS-type). This mitigates and remedies the security vulnerabilities from the start.

Accounts and Credentials Policy   Making sure your organization implements a strong accounts and credentials policy goes a long way. Typically, long alphanumeric passwords that regularly expire and are consequently changed prove to be a strong remedy against password hacking.

Browser Security Policy   Not all browsers are safe. Most of the cloud services and tools are web accessible. Thus, making sure there is strong security behind browsers is a big plus. Browser vulnerabilities can be mitigated by visiting only trusted websites (with certificates) and regularly updating the browser software.

Data Encryption   Organizations that use cloud storage services for sensitive data must make sure that their servicing chain uses strong data encryption, particularly if public cloud storage is used as the platform or infrastructure.

Service Provider Architecture   Thorough understanding of the cloud service provider architecture not only helps in choosing a provider, it also helps to see how it fits your organizational needs.

Mobile Devices   Mobile devices are fast becoming ubiquitous. The mobile device security policy should adhere to the standard organizational security policy. Mobile applications can be made secure and robust against attacks by ensuring security standards and releasing regular updates and bug fixes.

Cloud Quality Assurance (QA) Policy   The QA involves management of test resources, data storage habits, and network habits of the employees. Management should ensure availability of proper and relevant test resources and techniques.

QA management should be responsible for making sure employees follow a standard way of sharing important files and information (such as through a portal or a version control system). To prevent improper data storage habits, QA managers may need to mandate using a centralized or some sort of a coherent facility.

QA managers may also mandate a proxy server that allows access only to a few relevant resources. This has two main advantages: it prevents network misuse and helps manage network load.

Summary

Deployment and testing are the most important stages for migrating toward the cloud. In this chapter we uncovered models and strategies to exercise deployment from an in-house data center to the cloud. We discussed emerging cloud implementations as organizations look into local, offsite, and public cloud offerings. Private, community, public, and hybrid—all existing cloud models derive their types from methods of deployment. We also discussed cloud management strategies for each of the popular cloud deployment models.

The chapter included cloud architectures and their technical advantages in terms of resource management, resource allocation, task coordination, job scheduling, and scalability. It also included business benefits such as pay per use and capital cost savings.

The chapter then discussed cloud deployment options while keeping in perspective important aspects such as service provider API and compatibility with applications. We further discussed and compared popular commercial offerings, including Windows Azure, Amazon EC2, and Rackspace. We also included discussions of deployment steps and testing and monitoring deployed applications.

The chapter then walked through the steps of creating and deploying applications on Windows Azure and Amazon EC2 cloud services. Last, we discussed organizational best practices for a coherent cloud deployment model to ensure security and quality.

Chapter Essentials

Cloud Models and Management Strategies   Cloud models are derived from their deployment methodologies and their use cases. They help standardize specifications for organizations to adopt and migrate for cloud computing. The cloud management strategies help to monitor tasks related to performance, security, and disaster recovery.

Cloud Architectures   It is the system architecture of software systems that are involved in the delivery of cloud services. Cloud architectures use the underlying infrastructure to perform a specific job by drawing the resources, relinquishing the unneeded resources, and often disposing them once the job is complete. Cloud architectures solve most of the traditional data processing problems such as commissioning machines, provisioning applications, distributing and coordinating tasks, and ensuring recovery mechanisms.

Deployment Testing and Monitoring   Testing the software during the development process of a cloud application using local compute instances and storage helps the development and testing teams avoid most of the issues before the staging process even begins. Running unit and ad hoc tests ensures that the components perform as they are intended.

Chapter

11

Cloud Computing Standards and Security

TOPICS COVERED IN THIS CHAPTER INCLUDE:

✓ Ad hoc cloud computing standards

✓ Security threats and attacks

✓ Access control lists

✓ Virtual private network

✓ Firewalls and DMZs

✓ Encryption techniques

✓ Access control methods

✓ Disabling unneeded ports and services

✓ Secure user credentials

✓ Antivirus software and software security patching

With the advent of the cloud, the IT industry has seen the proposal of many standards. This has led to confusion, despite the standards being largely trivial and mostly insufficient. Furthermore, problems in cloud adoption, security, and interoperability can cause a lack of standardization and coherence in the cloud ecosystem. In this chapter, we describe what cloud computing standards are and explain their importance. We cover important security concepts and tools, encryption techniques, and access control methods. We also explain how to implement guest and host hardening security techniques.

Cloud Computing Standards

The need for cloud computing standards stems from the presence of numerous tech companies in the ever-growing cloud space. There is an obvious advantage to more tech companies: a whole lot of technological innovation due to competition and preferences. However, the downside is that each company will have its own technology based on a set of requirements perceived in a completely different environment and culture than exists in the other companies. It is hard to imagine a coherent cloud ecosystem without a basis for standardization. In the following sections, we'll explain why standards matter, what cloud computing's ad hoc standards are, and what standards are being followed.

Why Do Standards Matter?

Imagine you own a company and have chosen to put an application on a certain provider's cloud platform. Obviously, deploying will require necessary modifications, relevant configurations, and testing. Once all this is done, the application starts working. A few days later you discover another provider that matches your needs in a more comprehensive way and with a lower price tag. Or maybe the provider you chose decides to go out of business, citing major losses. That leaves you, the consumer, in a tricky position. A number of hard questions arise:

- Will you be able to successfully transfer your application and data to a new vendor?
- How hard is it to transfer application and data?
- Is the application using any vendor-specific application programming interfaces (APIs)?
- Is vendor lock-in going to be a concern when you switch to the new cloud provider?
- How will jurisdiction of data pan out?

- Will the physical location of the new provider present any issues relating to the legalities of moving data to the new provider?
- Will the end users get a similar interface to use your company's cloud services?
- How will the end users react to the new change?

There are no straight answers to these questions. And the reason is simple: if there is a lack of standards, the process of moving from one cloud provider to another can be painful, hard, complicated, expensive, and tedious. It could very well be akin to or even harder than building everything from ground up, only because the old and new cloud provider had offerings that were incompatible. In the worst case, which is not so unimaginable, your company could lose most of its customers and be forced out of business.

Cloud standards, like other standards in computing, are meant to resolve incompatibility issues and present solutions. However, interoperability, compatibility, and standardization among different providers are not easy issues to resolve. It is highly unlikely that all of the providers will come to the table agreeing upon a given set of cloud computing standards. One of the major reasons for this is that each provider often uses its own set of principles as opposed to the proposed standards.

Moreover, as with computing standardization drives of the past, the standards that will govern cloud computing in the future are at a nascent stage of development. And as we have experienced in the past with the World Wide Web, the Internet, network technologies, and so on, it will take time—probably years—for the standards to get developed, adopted, and evolved.

Current Ad Hoc Standards

The interesting thing about computing is that technology development is leaps ahead of technology standardization. This holds true for cloud computing as well, which itself is at an early stage of evolution. However, there is no shortage of ad hoc standards for cloud computing proposed by different organizations. Some of these are mentioned here.

NIST Cloud Computing Standards Roadmap   The National Institute of Standards and Technology is a U.S. federal agency that operates under the U.S. Department of Commerce. NIST works toward promoting standards in science and technology. To advocate for the use of specific cloud computing best practices and standards for official/government use, NIST has published the Cloud Computing Standards Roadmap.

www.nist.gov/manuscript-publication-search.cfm?pub_id=909024

IEEE Standards Association Working Groups   The Institute of Electrical and Electronics Engineers (IEEE) Standards Association develops and advances worldwide technologies. IEEE has set up two specialized working groups for cloud computing standards and interoperability. The P2301 workgroup (http://standards.ieee.org/develop/project/2301 .html) is involved in standardizing cloud management and portability with the use of various interfaces and file formats. The P2302 workgroup (http://standards.ieee.org /develop/project/2302.html) is focused on interoperability and federation.

The Green Grid   The Green Grid (www.thegreengrid.org/about-the-green-grid.aspx) is a collaborative organization committed to bringing together technology/service providers, utility companies, facility architects, cloud policy makers, and end users to present a set of standards. These standards aim to improve the resource utilization efficiency of data centers and cloud computing ecosystems.

Cloud Security Alliance (CSA)   CSA (https://cloudsecurityalliance.org/about/) presents best practices for cloud computing security with a special focus on cloud applications and data security. CSA also provides education on the uses of cloud computing. CSA is led by a broad coalition of industry practitioners, corporations, associations, and other key stakeholders.

DMTF Open Virtualization Format   The Open Virtualization Format (www.dmtf.org /standards/ovf) suggested by the Distributed Management Task Force (DMTF) provides a method for migrating virtual machine images from one platform to another. The aim of the Open Virtualization Format is to provide a simplified and error-free VM migration and deployment across platforms.

SNIA Cloud Data Management Interface (CDMI)   The Storage Networking Industry Association (SNIA) provides the CDMI specification (www.snia.org/cdmi), which defines the functional interface that applications can use to create, retrieve, update, and delete data elements from the cloud. CDMI provides protocols that describe how an organization can use this interface to manage containers and the data and metadata that is placed in them. The protocol also describes how data should be moved between public and private cloud environments. The International Organization for Standardization (IOS) has already approved the CDMI.

For both academia and industry, IEEE P2301 and P2302 should serve as the preferred guidelines to follow. For additional guidance, the NIST Cloud Computing Standards Roadmap can be consulted to acquire government-recommended practices and principles.

Security Concepts and Tools

In the following sections, we start by looking at common security threats and attacks such as the ping of death, denial of service, and distributed denial of service. We then look at enforcement of security through obfuscation, access control lists, and virtual private networks. Last, we look at the options for making networks secure, such as using firewalls and provisioning demilitarized zones.

Security Threats and Attacks

Some of the common security threats and attacks are valid for cloud computing systems as well, though the means of attack might be different. We cover three of the most common security attacks here: ping of death, ping flood (or denial of service), and distributed denial of service.

Ping of Death

A *ping of death* is a type of a security attack that is carried out on a target machine by sending a malicious ping to a computer (http://en.wikipedia.org/wiki/Ping_of_death). A ping is an Internet Control Management Protocol (ICMP) echo request. A correctly formed ping message is 56 bytes in size (84 bytes when the IP header is included). Earlier systems could not properly handle a ping packet larger than 65,535 bytes (64 KB). Therefore, a ping packet larger than this limit could cause a system to crash.

According to RFC 791 (www.ietf.org/rfc/rfc791.txt), sending a packet larger than 65,535 bytes violates the IP regulations. However, such a packet can be sent if it is fragmented. This would require the target machine to reassemble the packet, which can cause a buffer overflow (a kind of memory overflow), which in turn can cause a system crash.

Here is how it works:

1. When fragmentation is performed, each IP fragment carries information about the part number of the original packet it contains.

   This information is kept in the fragment offset field in the IP header.

2. A single IP fragment is given an offset in 8 byte units.

   A single IP fragment should not have more than 7 bytes of data.

3. A malicious user sends an IP fragment with the maximum offset and with much more data than 7 bytes, as large as the physical layer allows it to be.

   This causes buffer overflow problems that can result in a system crash.

In order to correct this problem, checks are added to the reassembly process. The check for each incoming IP fragment makes sure that the sum of fragment offset and total length in the IP header of each fragment is smaller than 65,535 bytes. Any fragment having a sum larger than this size is invalid and is therefore ignored. This check can be performed by firewalls to protect internal network and machines. Another nonstandard fix is to break the limit of the specification and use a memory buffer larger than 65,535 bytes.

Ping Flood

A *ping flood*, or *denial of service (DoS)* attack, tries to overwhelm the victim with a large number of repeated ping packets (http://en.wikipedia.org/wiki/Ping_flood). The most effective way is to use the ping flood option that sends ICMP packets as fast as possible without waiting for response messages. The ping flood attack is most successful if the attacker has more bandwidth than the victim.

The attack is even more effective if the victim responds with ICMP echo reply packets that would consume both outgoing bandwidth as well as incoming bandwidth on the victim's network. Moreover, if the victim's system has a slower processor, chances are the ping flood would consume enough CPU cycles to cause the target system to slow down considerably.

Alternatively, network administrators can use a ping flood to diagnose network packet loss and throughput problems.

To prevent a ping flood, a firewall can be set in place to examine the IP address of the attacker. The IP address can be blacklisted if any malicious activity is detected by the firewall. (See the section "Firewalls" later in this chapter.)

Another technique to prevent such attacks is to minimize the attack surface area by closing down unneeded ports. Moreover, ICMP echo messages can simply be ignored by dropping ICMP requests.

Distributed Denial of Service

A *distributed denial of service (DDoS)* is a sophisticated security threat that floods the bandwidth or processing resources of a target system using multiple compromised systems (also known as zombie systems).

`http://en.wikipedia.org/wiki/DDoS#Distributed_attack`

A collection of compromised systems is usually referred to as *botnet*, which is a number of computer systems controlled by a malicious program. The main purpose of a DDoS attack is to overload a server system with so many false connections that it can no longer accept legitimate connections.

This attack is sophisticated in nature because the attacker is able to launch an attack using multiple machines rather than just one. It is hard to distinguish between good and malicious requests. Additionally, it is even harder to track or detect the behavior of such machines. By making the behavior of each attack machine stealthier and more adaptive, the attacker has a huge advantage over the target server's defense mechanisms. For example, purchasing more incoming bandwidth to increase the servable volume could be completely futile because the attacker can add more machines by spreading the malicious program to other hosts on the Internet. Figure 11.1 depicts a DDoS attack with attacker, handler hosts, the botnet, and the victim.

FIGURE 11.1   A simple representation of a DDoS attack

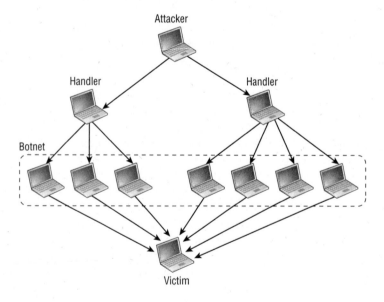

A DDoS can be carried out through TCP SYN floods from different machines with different IP addresses. A TCP SYN message is a message in which the TCP header has the SYN bit set on. This lets the receiver know that the sender wants to establish a TCP-based connection. The server replies with a SYN/ACK message to acknowledge it has received the initial SYN message.

Such flood attacks do not require completion of a TCP three-way handshake process; they attempt to exhaust the destination SYN queue or bandwidth of the targeted server by not completing the three-way handshake process. It is important to know that the source IP address can be spoofed, and an attack coming from a number of hosts could actually originate from a few zombie hosts or even just one host (in which case it will be referred to as a DoS attack). One of the common ways to mitigate a TCP SYN flood is to enhance SYN cookies.

Defensive responses to DDoS attacks involve planning and designing advanced combinations of attack detection, traffic and behavior classification, and response mechanisms. The purpose of these defensive measures is to block traffic identified as illegitimate while still allowing legitimate traffic to flow freely. For this purpose, firewalls, ACL-enabled routers and switches, application front-end hardware, and intrusion prevention systems (IPSs) are employed. These are described in the following sections.

Obfuscation

Obfuscation refers to methods used to semantically preserve transformation of a data payload into such a form that hides extraction of information from the data. Obfuscation can impede understanding of algorithms and data structures and therefore is widely used in cryptography and information hiding.

Moreover, obfuscation can reduce the size of your assembly by reusing pointers for different words. It can prevent or limit tools from reading the obfuscated data.

Some examples of obfuscated code and algorithms can be found on the IOCCC website (www.ioccc.org/years.html).

Access Control List

An *access control list (ACL)* is a list of permissions attached to an object. The ACL of an item specifies the following items:

- Which users are granted access to the object
- Which system processes are granted access to the object
- What operations are allowed on given objects

Note that there are three major access types; *read*, *write*, and *execute*. Each entry in a typical ACL specifies a subject and an operation. An example would be an ACL that contains {Alice, read/write} over the file example.dat.

There are two major implementations of ACLs for different use cases:

Filesystem ACLs These were developed to administer file permissions in file systems. Each kind of operating system implements its own ACLs, using a standard design. The use of a standard ensures that the ACLs provide compatibility across different operating systems and architectures.

Networking ACLs Networking hardware such as routers and switches implement ACLs. These ACLs are used to list rules that are applied to port numbers and IP addresses available on a host or other layers. The ACLs can be used to control the list of hosts and networks that are permitted to use different services. In this way, ACLs might act somewhat like routing tables. Moreover, ACLs can be used to control both inbound and outbound traffic. In this context they can be thought of as similar to software-based firewalls, although they are more trivial.

Virtual Private Network

A *virtual private network (VPN)* is a secure private network that operates over the Internet. (See *Cloud Essentials: CompTIA Authorized Courseware for Exam CLO-001* [Sybex, 2013] by Kalani Kirk Hausman et al.) A VPN uses two main techniques to secure communications over a public network:

- A limited-access IP tunnel is created from source to destination.

  Limited access means that only those users who have been granted access with proper permissions and privileges can use the network. Users have to authenticate themselves to use the network and access resources.

- The IP tunnel is secured via encryption.

  Requests across the VPN are encrypted at the source and decrypted at the destination. System administrators have the option of selecting the encryption algorithm as well as the level of strength.

The biggest advantage of VPN networks is that the users can select or use cloud resources securely and remotely from any location using proper authentication credentials (Figure 11.2). However, it is essential for the users to have a VPN client available and configured on their machines. Moreover, organizations need to have VPNs set up so that their virtual network gateways can properly identify and recognize user machines.

Firewalls

A *firewall* is a machine (hardware based) or an application (software based) that allows or blocks incoming traffic based on a configurable rule set. (See *Cloud Essentials: CompTIA Authorized Courseware for Exam CLO-001* [Sybex, 2013] by Kalani Kirk Hausman et al.) The main job of a firewall is to inspect and regulate incoming traffic on specific ports and to/from specific hosts. It does so by examining against this rule set a number of attributes of the incoming packet, such as the origin/source of the packet, destination of the packet, header attributes (size, encoding, etc.), and payload.

FIGURE 11.2   Illustration of a secure IP tunnel in a virtual private network

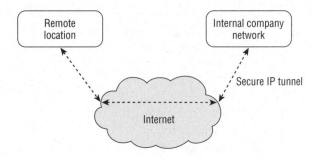

Firewalls for cloud computing need to keep up with its demanding nature. Compared to traditional firewalls, cloud firewalls need to have the ability to scale, should have redundant network connections, and should be connected to alternate standby power sources and be more robust.

Firewalls can be broken down into two main categories:

Stateful Packet Filtering   This type of firewall analyzes both inbound and outbound traffic based on the given rule set. *Stateful* means that the firewall keeps track of the session state. This in turn makes sure that the only packets that enter the internal (protected) network are those that were requested from a machine residing inside the network.

Stateless Packet Filtering   Just like the stateful firewall, the stateless packet filtering firewall analyzes incoming traffic and decides whether to allow or deny access to the internal network based on the given rule set. *Stateless* means that the session state is not maintained, thus enabling the firewall to block particular types of incoming connections completely. This is especially important if a rule set is to be implemented for a system that should not be accessible via certain protocols and does not offer connections for certain services. These include blocking HTTP (port 80 or 8080) to disable web access, blocking FTP/SFTP (port 21) to disable file transfer service, and blocking SSH connections (port 23) to disable Secure Shell access.

So far we have discussed only hardware-based firewalls. As noted earlier, firewalls can also be software based. A common software-based firewall is called a virtual firewall, and it is designed to protect virtual hosts. There are two modes in which a virtual firewall can operate: bridged and hypervisor.

Bridged   The bridged firewall is deployed just as a traditional firewall would be, that is, within the network infrastructure.

Hypervisor   In hypervisor mode, the virtual firewall resides only within the hypervisor environment and thus only monitors the traffic to and from the virtual machine. Figure 11.3 shows a virtual firewall setup.

Apart from different kinds of firewalls, there are systems used for hardening security in the internal network.

FIGURE 11.3   A virtual firewall setup

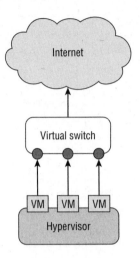

An intrusion detection system (IDS) is a machine or software application that passively or actively monitors incoming traffic or system activities for malicious software and unusual activity such as security violations and policy disagreements. The primary job of an IDS is to detect unusual activity and send alerts to system administrators. There are two main categories of IDSs: network-based IDS (NIDS) and host-based IDS (HIDS).

Network-based IDSs are placed at strategic points within the network to monitor traffic, such as on the subnet where firewalls are located to check for potential threats to the firewalls.

```
http://en.wikipedia.org/wiki/Intrusion_detection_system
```

Alternatively, a host-based IDS runs on individual machines and only monitors the traffic to and from the host. It takes a snapshot of the existing system and matches it to the previous snapshot to check for differences. If critical system files were modified or deleted, an alert is generated for the system administrators to investigate.

IDSs can also be passive or active. In a passive system, unusual activity such as security breaches are detected, logged, and signaled to the system administrator. In an active or reactive system, also called an intrusion prevention system (IPS), the system itself launches an auto-response to the detected malicious activity by reprogramming the firewall or resetting the connection. The idea is to protect the firewall and the internal network by blocking network traffic from the suspicious source.

```
http://en.wikipedia.org/wiki/Intrusion_prevention_system
```

Commonly, the term *IDPS* is used to refer to a system that can both detect and prevent suspicious activity.

Demilitarized Zone

A *demilitarized zone (DMZ)*, or a *perimeter network*, can be a physical or logical sub-network that contains and exposes an organization's external services to a larger and untrusted network, usually the Internet.

The idea of a DMZ is to have an additional layer of security by segregating a LAN from the infrastructure in the perimeter network. By doing this, an organization can restrict an external attacker to only the perimeter network rather than the whole network infrastructure.

Generally, any service that is being provided to the users on the external network can be placed in the perimeter network. The most common candidates are as follows:

* Web servers
* Email servers
* FTP servers
* VoIP servers

Some enterprises install a proxy server with the perimeter network. This serves two purposes: security and monitoring. And it has additional benefits:

* Internal users are obliged to use the proxy server for Internet access.
* Proxy servers maintain a local cache of web content, and therefore Internet access bandwidth requirements can be reduced to some extent.
* Monitoring and recording of user activities is simplified.
* Web content filtering is centralized.

There are two basic methods to design a network with a perimeter network: a single-firewall layout and a dual-firewall layout (see Figure 11.4). The two layouts are described in the following sections.

Single-Firewall Layout

In this layout, three network interfaces are used to create a layout containing a perimeter network. The firewall stands as an interface for the ISP, the internal network, and the perimeter network. The advantage is that this setup is simple to deploy and manage and requires minimum changes to the existing network. However, the disadvantage is that the firewall becomes a single point of failure for the entire network because it must be able to handle all the incoming and outgoing traffic. Another disadvantage is that one firewall is a single line of defense. If attackers can get through the firewall, they can get to the internal network.

Dual-Firewall Layout

To mitigate security concerns in a single-firewall setup, a dual-firewall approach is used. The first firewall is the front end (or perimeter) firewall that provides an interface for the ISP, the perimeter network, and a second firewall.

FIGURE 11.4   Single-firewall layout vs. dual-firewall layout

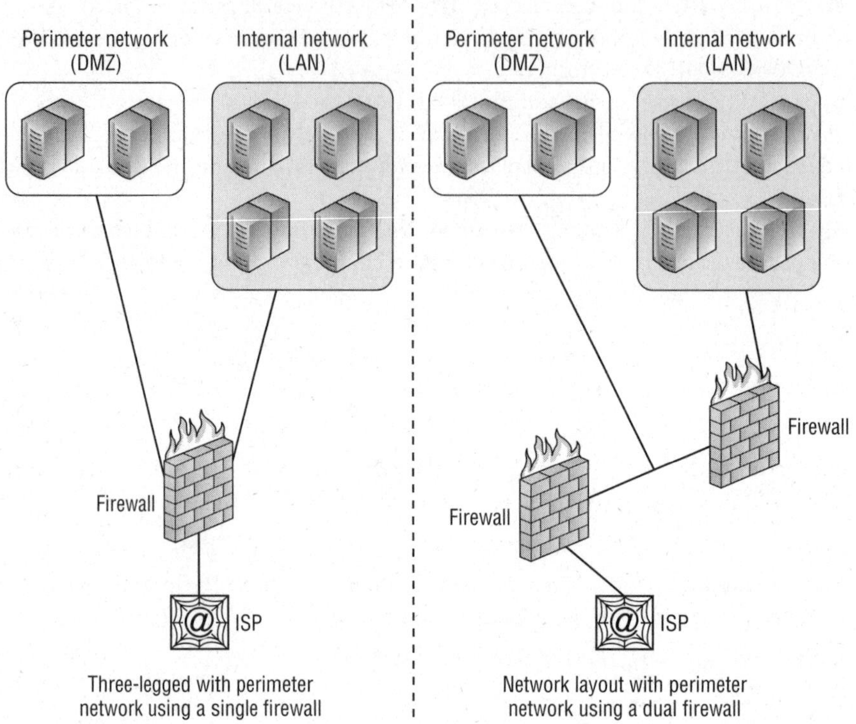

The second firewall provides an interface for the internal network, the first firewall (for outgoing connections), and the perimeter network. This layout is more secure because it mitigates the chances of the entire network being compromised in the event of an attack. Security can be further improved if two firewalls are provided by two different vendors because it makes it less likely that both machines suffer from same security vulnerabilities. This is commonly referred to as a defense-in-depth security strategy.

Encryption Techniques

To prevent data from unauthenticated use, encryption techniques are widely used for IT services and products. In the following sections, we cover public key infrastructure, IPSec, Transport Layer Security (TLS), and a few widely used cipher algorithms.

Public Key Infrastructure

A *public key infrastructure (PKI)* is a cryptographic technique that enables users to securely communicate on an insecure public network. It is an arrangement that binds public keys with user identities by means of a certificate authority (CA).

http://en.wikipedia.org/wiki/Public_key_infrastructure

The IEEE defines PKI as a set of hardware, software, people, policies, and procedures needed to create, manage, distribute, use, store, and revoke digital certificates.

PKI requires that the user identity is unique within each CA domain. Keys are bound with identities through a registration authority (RA). This registration and issuance process is carried out depending on the assurance level of the binding. The RA ensures *non-repudiation* by binding the key with the user identity to which it has been assigned. This means that the users can authenticate and the system can recognize the authentication process as being genuine. A PKI consists of the following collaborating entities, as shown in Figure 11.5:

- The certificate authority (CA) issues and verifies digital certificates.

- The registration authority (RA) verifies user identities by requesting information from the CA.

- The central directory is a secure location to store and index keys.

- The certificate management system is a central or distributed database that stores certificates.

- The certificate access control policy specifies access control for certificates, that is, how a certificate can be accessed, such as, for example, via user credentials (username and password).

FIGURE 11.5 Illustration of a public key infrastructure

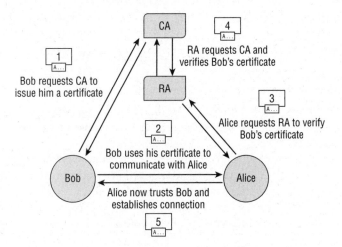

Internet Protocol Security

Internet Protocol Security (IPSec) is an Internet layer protocol suite that uses authentication and encryption techniques for secure IP communications (http://en.wikipedia.org/wiki/IPsec). IPSec protects data flows between two hosts across a network (host to host), between gateways (network to network), or between a security gateway and a host (network to host).

IPSec supports the following features:

- Network-level peer authentication
- Data origin authentication
- Data integrity
- Data confidentiality
- Replay protection

Software applications can be secured by using IPSec at the IP layer. However, without IPSec, TLS/SSL protocols must be used for each application for security.

Secure Sockets Layer/Transport Layer Security

Secure Sockets Layer (SSL) and its current version *Transport Layer Security (TLS)* are cryptographic protocols designed to provide communication security over the Internet.

http://en.wikipedia.org/wiki/Transport_Layer_Security

TLS works at the Application layer. It uses X.509 certificates and asymmetric cryptography to authenticate the host with which a user is communicating.

Asymmetric, or public-key, cryptography uses two separate keys per user to identify and authenticate each user securely.

http://en.wikipedia.org/wiki/Public-key_cryptography

Asymmetric refers to the opposite nature of functions, one the inverse of the other, that are used to create the keys:

- One of the keys is public, which is uploaded to the host to which a user wants to communicate.
- The other is a private key, which is kept secret by the user.

The two keys are different but mathematically linked. A public key is used to encrypt communication or to verify a digital signature. A private key is used to decrypt ciphertext or create a digital signature.

Public-key cryptography uses a PKI to verify a certificate and its owner via a CA. A PKI is also used to generate, sign, and administer the validity of certificates. When a PKI is used, forward secrecy is maintained, which means that short-term session keys cannot be derived from private keys. TLS is widely applied for web browsing, email, faxing over the Internet, instant messaging (IM), and Voice over IP (VoIP).

Ciphers

A *cipher* is a cryptographic algorithm used to perform encryption or decryption through a series of mathematical steps. When data is converted from plain text to ciphertext or code, the procedure is known as *enciphering* or *encoding*. Similarly, when cipher or code is converted to plain text, the procedure is called deciphering or decoding.

Ciphers can be categorized in a couple of ways:

Block or Stream Ciphers   Ciphers that work on blocks of data or on a continuous stream of data.

Symmetric or Asymmetric Key Algorithms   Ciphers that use a key for enciphering and deciphering. Cipher algorithms that use the same key for both encryption and decryption are called symmetric key algorithms. Similarly, algorithms that use different keys for both procedures are known as asymmetric key algorithms.

Symmetric key algorithms require that both sender and recipient share the key. This could be a security hazard because the key has to be shared. Asymmetric key algorithms prevent loss of confidentiality due to the public/private key property of such ciphers.

Table 11.1 shows some ciphers with their respective properties and aspects.

TABLE 11.1   Ciphers and their properties and aspects

Cipher	Category	Key size (bits)	Block size (bits)
Advanced Encryption Standard (AES), 2001	Block cipher, symmetric key algorithm	128, 192, 256	128
Data Encryption Standard (DES), 1970s	Block cipher, symmetric key algorithm	56 (+8 parity)	64
Triple Data Encryption Algorithm (3DES/TDEA), 1998	Block cipher, symmetric key algorithm	168, 112	64
Ron Rivest, Adi Shamir, and Leonard Adleman (RSA), 1977	Asymmetric key algorithm	1,024 to 4,096	
RC4	Stream cipher	40 to 2,048	
RC5	Block cipher, symmetric key algorithm	0 to 2,040	32, 64, 128

Access Control Methods

Generally, *access control* is the selective restriction of access to a place or resource. The act of accessing may be entering, consuming, or using. Permission to access a resource requires prior authorization. Specifically, access control is identifying a person doing a specific job. This involves authentication by proof of identification and granting access to accessible resources only. The proof of identification would be username, password, and key files. Access privileges would refer to the right level of permissions per resource granted to the user to perform the job.

The following access control models are used to grant the allowed privileges to individuals:

- Role-based access control (RBAC)
- Mandatory access control (MAC)
- Discretionary access control (DAC)
- Rule-based multifactor access control (RB-RBAC)

These models are explained in detail in the following sections, and we will also look at multifactor authentication, single sign-on, and federation.

Role-Based Access Control

The *role-based access control* model provides access based on the position of an individual in an organization. Template profiles are created and used to assign permissions automatically. For example, if a person holds the position of a manager in an organization, the role profile of the manager would be enough to assign permissions to that person. This makes life easier for the system administrator and DevOps team. However, an issue arises if the manager requires access to some other resources that the role does not allow by default. In this case, a manual workaround is needed to allow supra-role permissions.

Mandatory Access Control

With the *mandatory access control* (MAC) model, the end user has no control over any settings that configure privileges for anyone. There are two security models associated with MAC: Biba and Bell-LaPadula. The Biba model is focused on the integrity of the information, while the Bell-LaPadula model focuses on the confidentiality of the information.

Biba is used when a user with low-level clearance can read higher-level information (commonly referred to as *read up*) and a user with high-level clearance can write for lower levels of clearance (called *write down*). Biba is commonly used in organizations where employees can read managerial or executive stuff and managers or executives can write to inform employees.

The Bell-LaPadula model is set up so that a user can write only to a level they belong to but no lower (called *write-up*). However, the user can read at lower levels (called *read down*). This model is used in government and military organizations.

Discretionary Access Control

The *discretionary access control (DAC)* model allows individuals complete control over any resources or objects they own along with programs associated with those objects. The DAC is the least restrictive model and therefore is weak in a couple of areas:

- First, users are allowed complete control over security levels for other users. This could result in some users having higher permissions than they are supposed to have.

- Second, since the permissions over objects are inherited into other programs, the user can execute malicious software intentionally or unintentionally. Moreover, malware can take advantage of potentially high-level privileges to launch and kill user processes.

Rule-Based Access Controls

Rule-based access controls (RB-RBAC) dynamically assign roles to users based on criteria defined by the system administrator. This model is ideal if a user has to be allowed access to certain files during certain hours of the day. However, the catch is that the rules need to be custom specified into the network by the system administrator. An example use case would be a freelancer working for an organization during certain hours of the day.

Multifactor Authentication

Multifactor authentication, also known as two-factor authentication, is an attempt to maximize security and minimize unauthorized access. This is achieved by increasing the number of required items or factors for successful authentication and access. The approach requires the availability and presentation of at least two of the three authentication factors described here:

- Something only the user knows, such as password, PIN, pattern (token generators, one-time pads, etc.)
- Something only the user has, such as smart access card, mobile phone
- Something only the user is, such as a biometric characteristic like a fingerprint scan, or iris scan

Upon presentation, each factor is validated by the system for authentication to complete.

Single Sign-On

Single sign-on is an access control method or property that allows a user access to all linked systems without being prompted to log in or sign in at each one of them. Such a scheme is typically accomplished by using shared access and privileges directory services such as the open-source and vendor-independent *Lightweight Directory Access Protocol (LDAP)* or the proprietary Windows-based Active Directory. These SSO application protocols share centralized authentication servers that all linked software applications and systems use for authentication purposes. Conversely, a single sign-off property logs out or terminates access to multiple linked systems.

For example, cookies can be stored to achieve a simplistic version of single sign-on on the same domain. The requirement of the single sign-on model is that the system handling it must internally translate and store credentials for different mechanisms to enable consistency of service to users.

There are three major benefits of using single sign-on:

- It reduces password fatigue caused by different username and password combinations for different systems.

- It reduces time spent reentering passwords for the same identity.

- It reduces IT costs due to lower number of IT help desk calls about lost or forgotten passwords.

Federation

Federation, or *federated identity*, is the means by which a person's electronic identity and attributes are linked across multiple distinct identity management systems. Single sign-on (SSO) is an example of federation.

Federated identity management (FIDM) is used to maintain a common set of policies, practices, and protocols for managing identity in IT systems and devices across organizations. There is also a need to manage trust between users and the organization, which can be achieved by promoting best practices and policies and educating employees about the advantages and disadvantages of technical interoperability between users and IT systems.

Implementing Guest and Host Hardening Techniques

Guest and host hardening involve security techniques and algorithms that should be applied to secure host and server systems. In the following sections, we cover disabling unnecessary ports and services that could potentially become an opportunity for security attacks. We explain why secure user credentials are important and how they can be enforced. Antivirus software and security patching are also important aspects of implementing host hardening techniques.

Disabling Unneeded Ports and Services

Disabling unnecessary ports and services reduces the risk of malicious attacks. Unix- and Linux-based systems come with multiple utilities that can be conveniently used to see which ports and services are open and running, respectively. Here we will list a few commonly used utilities for such purposes.

netstat   netstat is a utility used to print network connections, routing tables, interface statistics, masquerade connections, and multicast memberships. The following command can be used to view local addresses and ports, foreign addresses and ports, the state of the connection, and timer information. We have also included example output.

```
$ netstat -an
Proto Recv-Q Send-Q Local Address          Foreign Address         State
tcp      0      0 127.0.0.1:953          0.0.0.0:*               LISTEN
tcp      0      0 0.0.0.0:25             0.0.0.0:*               LISTEN
tcp      0      1 10.0.0.254:46692       10.0.4.22:5666          SYN_SENT
tcp      0      0 10.0.0.254:38127       10.0.3.104:8807         TIME_
WAIT
```

nmap   nmap is another network exploration tool and port scanner. A user can run the following command on the local machine to see which ports are open and listening.

```
$ nmap localhost
PORT       STATE SERVICE
22/tcp     open  ssh
25/tcp     open  smtp
53/tcp     open  domain
80/tcp     open  http
443/tcp    open  https
3306/tcp   open  mysql
5666/tcp   open  nrpe
8083/tcp   open  unknown
8443/tcp   open  https-alt
8649/tcp   open  unknown
8651/tcp   open  unknown
8652/tcp   open  unknown
```

inetd   inetd listens for connections that are on Internet sockets that are defined by the port numbers. The ports are listed in a configuration file located on the host system at /etc/inetd.conf. A user can activate or deactivate ports and services by commenting out lines from the configuration file. Upon creation of a connection, inetd invokes a server process with the service socket as its standard input (STDIN), output (STDOUT), and error (STDERR) descriptors. To see which ports are open, a user can execute the following command.

```
$ grep -v "^s*#" /etc/inetd.conf

printer stream tcp nowait lp /usr/local/libexec/cups/daemon/cups-lpd
cups-lpd -o document-format=application/octet/stream
```

rc.d　rc.d is a utility that is used to automate the boot process. A user can activate or deactivate a port and its associated server process by commenting out lines from the configuration files. Furthermore, /etc/rc*.d directories can be found on host systems (where * is any number from 0 to 6, each denoting a run level). These directories contain symbolic links (symlinks) to server startup scripts. Deleting a symlink will prevent the rc.d utility from starting that server process. The following shows the output of listing rc*.d directories.

```
$ ls -lh /etc/rc*.d
/etc/rc0.d:
total 4.0K
lrwxrwxrwx 1 root root  17 Mar  7  2013 K08tomcat7 -> ../init.d/tomcat7
lrwxrwxrwx 1 root root  17 Nov 28  2012 K09apache2 -> ../init.d/apache2
..


/etc/rc1.d:
total 4.0K
lrwxrwxrwx 1 root root  17 Mar  7  2013 K08tomcat7 -> ../init.d/tomcat7
lrwxrwxrwx 1 root root  17 Nov 28  2012 K09apache2 -> ../init.d/apache2
lrwxrwxrwx 1 root root  17 Jan 15  2013 K20jenkins -> ../init.d/jenkins
..


/etc/rc2.d:
total 4.0K
-rw-r--r-- 1 root root 677 Jul 26  2012 README
lrwxrwxrwx 1 root root  15 Nov 28  2012 S15bind9 -> ../init.d/bind9
lrwxrwxrwx 1 root root  20 Nov 28  2012 S20apt-cacher -> ../init.d/apt-cacher
..


/etc/rc3.d:
total 4.0K
-rw-r--r-- 1 root root 677 Jul 26  2012 README
lrwxrwxrwx 1 root root  15 Nov 28  2012 S15bind9 -> ../init.d/bind9
lrwxrwxrwx 1 root root  20 Nov 28  2012 S20apt-cacher -> ../init.d/apt-cacher
..


/etc/rc4.d:
total 4.0K
-rw-r--r-- 1 root root 677 Jul 26  2012 README
lrwxrwxrwx 1 root root  15 Nov 28  2012 S15bind9 -> ../init.d/bind9
lrwxrwxrwx 1 root root  20 Nov 28  2012 S20apt-cacher -> ../init.d/apt-cacher
lrwxrwxrwx 1 root root  17 Nov 26  2013 S20foreman -> ../init.d/foreman
..
```

```
/etc/rc5.d:
total 4.0K
-rw-r--r-- 1 root root 677 Jul 26  2012 README
lrwxrwxrwx 1 root root  15 Nov 28  2012 S15bind9 -> ../init.d/bind9
lrwxrwxrwx 1 root root  20 Nov 28  2012 S20apt-cacher -> ../init.d/apt-cacher
lrwxrwxrwx 1 root root  17 Nov 26  2013 S20foreman -> ../init.d/foreman
..

/etc/rc6.d:
total 4.0K
lrwxrwxrwx 1 root root  17 Mar  7  2013 K08tomcat7 -> ../init.d/tomcat7
lrwxrwxrwx 1 root root  17 Nov 28  2012 K09apache2 -> ../init.d/apache2
..
```

Secure User Credentials

User credentials are a combination of two or more pieces of information, some or all of which are stored in encrypted state. User credentials usually involve username, password, and/or security questions. Credentials are used to access target systems such as hosts, application servers, databases, and logs to view or run tasks and management activities.

To apply and maintain secure user credentials, companies and organizations implement a strong password policy. A password policy can be defined as a set of rules dictating password requirements and how passwords must be set. These rules are designed to encourage users to employ strong passwords and use them properly (http://en.wikipedia.org/wiki/Password_policy). A password policy is usually a part of official regulations or even part of the employee contract.

There are two main types of password policies:

Advisory Policy   An advisory policy is not implemented by technical means and is only meant to be a guideline.

Mandated Policy   A mandated policy is technically implemented and can have different requirements before a password can be set and accepted. Some of these requirements are using upper- and lowercase letters, numerical digits, and special characters and discouraging the use of dictionary words.

The number of requirements for a password policy defines its complexity. The level of complexity of a password policy determines its level of popularity and success. A downside to a complex password policy is that it can be much harder to enforce and maintain. An organization must find the right balance between security and complexity to enable adaptation.

Antivirus Software

Antivirus and anti-malware are types of computer software designed to prevent, scan, detect, and remove viruses, worms, Trojans, adware, and other types of malware.

> www.webroot.com/us/en/home/resources/tips/pc-security/security-what-is-anti-virus-software

Given that new malware is created daily, antivirus software is an essential tool to have.

Computer security companies such as Norton, McAfee, Kaspersky, Panda, and others build and offer a variety of tools with functions such these:

- Scan for viruses and malware
- Schedule scans to run automatically
- Detect and remove malicious software
- Meter the health of the host machine

However, antivirus tools can have some drawbacks:

- Computer performance is affected.
- Antivirus programs are not usually up-to-date all the time and are not a 100 percent guarantee against all new viruses and malware.
- Antivirus programs run with special permissions to gain access to all processes and files, which may become a potential threat on its own.
- Some sophisticated viruses particularly attack antivirus programs.

Despite these drawbacks, antivirus programs are a good option to have on hosts for security and protection. Security companies nowadays focus on creating lightweight tools that can be readily and regularly updated without requiring reboots. This enables maximum protection against evolving threats.

Software Security Patching

A *patch* is a piece of software that is designed to update, fix, or improve a computer program or its supporting data (http://en.wikipedia.org/wiki/Patch_%28computing%29). Patches can also be used to deliberately break functionality in a program by removing certain components for which the provider is no longer licensed or paid. It can also be used to dynamically disable a device.

Patching is widely used for fixing emerging and newly found security issues. Generally, a security patch is applied to a software application to fix weaknesses caused by a vulnerability. Large software engineering enterprises such as Microsoft, IBM, Apple, Red Hat, and Oracle have security teams that are dedicated to releasing security patches to fix vulnerabilities.

One of the important techniques used in dynamic server environments is *hot patching*, also known as *hot fixing* or *live patching*. The idea is to apply patches to software applications without system reboot. This technique addresses the unavailability and downtime issues of a software application or a service.

Summary

The need for cloud computing standards arises from the presence of numerous entities in the cloud space. Because each company can have its own technology, it is hard to imagine a coherent cloud ecosystem without a basis for standardization. Therefore, standardization attains utmost importance.

Similarly, security threats and attacks pose major threats to cloud computing becoming a ubiquitous infrastructure. In this chapter, we covered topics related to important security concepts and tools, including obfuscation, access control lists, virtual private networks, firewalls, and DMZs. We also discussed encryption techniques, public key infrastructure, IPSec, Transport Layer Security, and widely used cipher algorithms.

Security techniques and algorithms need to be applied to hosts and server systems to make them secure. Special consideration and importance must also be given to secure user credentials, antivirus software tools, and security patching. Access control and privileges must be strictly enforced to ensure maximum security.

Chapter Essentials

Ad Hoc Standards   Ad hoc standards for cloud computing are proposed by different organizations. These include the NIST Cloud Computing Standards Roadmap, IEEE Standards Association Working Groups, Cloud Security Alliance (CSA), DMTF Open Virtualization Format, and SNIA Cloud Data Management Interface (CDMI).

Security Concepts and Tools   Some of the most common security threats and attacks include ping of death, denial of service, and distributed denial of service. Techniques for ensuring secure communications include obfuscation, access control lists, and virtual private networks. Other options for making the whole network infrastructure secure include firewalls and provisioning demilitarized zones.

Encryption Techniques   Encryption techniques are widely used to prevent data from unauthenticated use. These include public key infrastructure, IPSec, Transport Layer Security, and a few widely used ciphers algorithms such as AES, DES, RSA, RC4, and RC5.

Unnecessary Ports and Services, Secure Credentials, and Security Patching   Security techniques and algorithms need to be applied to secure host and server systems. Disabling unnecessary ports and services is an important aspect of securing network-wide systems, which could otherwise pose security vulnerabilities. Secure user credentials and strong password policy should be enforced because authentication is only as strong as the credentials themselves. In addition, antivirus software tools and security patching are essential aspects of implementing host hardening techniques.

Chapter 12

The Cloud Makes It Rain Money: The Business in Cloud Computing

---

TOPICS COVERED IN THIS CHAPTER INCLUDE:

✓ The nature of cloud business

✓ Cloud service business models

✓ The enterprise cloud

✓ Disaster recovery and replication

✓ Business continuity and cloud computing

Cloud computing is a business model that brings new technologies together to solve complex, modern-day business problems. The aim to achieve ubiquity pushes the cloud to offer on-demand services as required by the user. This business model and these services help organizations expand their outreach into new markets and try out new brands in established markets. In this chapter, we will start with the nature of cloud business and cloud business models. We will then take a look at how the enterprise cloud provides new opportunities to organizations willing to utilize cloud computing for competitive advantage. Finally, we'll discuss the essential topics of disaster recovery through replication and redundancy and business continuity in the cloud.

The Nature of Cloud Business

The cloud is not only about technology. Understanding cloud business is a key to understanding the nature of cloud computing and its associations. In the following sections, you will learn about the service nature of cloud computing and about doing business with open-source software (OSS) and explore white label branding.

The Service Nature of the Cloud

A common question today is about the nature of cloud business and cloud computing services—is it about technology or is it more of a business model? The truth of the matter is that it is not as much about competing technologies as it is about a new business orientation. However, without the technology aspect, the business model will not exist.

The business model is basically about computing services being provided on demand, when they are needed, swiftly and efficiently and in a cost-effective way. This can be thought of as a business-scale policy that ensures that a business has the IT support it needs for services, terms, and costs. Previously, the discussion revolved around the number of servers needed, the IT specialists required, the number of licenses to be bought, and the time needed to make things happen. Now, though, it is much more about provisioning cloud resources, acquiring cloud expertise, and making the solutions accessible as cloud services.

The technology plays a key part in making cloud computing possible. At its core, cloud computing is all about IT capabilities providing the same resources, applications, infrastructure, and platform but in an ultra-ubiquitous and scalable way using the Web as the access medium. This helps organizations migrate the worry (i.e., developing an understanding about IT capabilities) to the cloud and concentrate on the business itself.

Cloud computing faces challenges in terms of both software and hardware, but it also serves as a driving force for technological progress to respond to demands in a flexible manner covering diverse services and an infrastructure with a continuously increasing number of devices. Moreover, this challenge makes the IT services industry more aware and requires professionals to become more business savvy along with being technically sound.

Making Money with Open-Source Software

Open-source software (OSS) is used widely by many software vendors, value-added resellers, and hardware vendors (OEMs or ODMs) for their proprietary, for-profit products and services. Customers are willing to pay for the licenses, commercial-grade quality assurance (QA), and professional support, training, and consulting.

There are several different business models for making a profit using OSS:

Selling Support Contracts   In this model, a company makes the application freely downloadable but may charge for expert consulting. Consulting might cover setup, maintenance, and enhancements.

Service contracts can be customized to varying levels of support. Companies can charge more for immediate phone support and offer lower rates for email-based support. Examples include Red Hat and IBM, both of which make some of their applications freely available and instead sell services such as export consulting.

Value-Added Enhancements and Services   The application might be free, but the add-ons and add-on services that provide additional productive value can be made available for sale. This model allows both the creators and third parties to make a profit from enhancements.

Examples include Skype selling add-ons and credit for cheap VoIP phone calls.

Selling Subscriptions to Software as a Service (SaaS)   Another related method is to sell subscriptions to online accounts, services, and server access instead of selling the software. Using the SaaS model, neither the source nor the binaries are released, which could be inherently constrictive for software or service users.

Microsoft sells its cloud-based office product suite, called Office 365 (`http://office.microsoft.com/en-us/`), using this model.

Selling Binaries   Typically, for large, complex projects the source code needs to be compiled into a binary. The source code might have multiple dependencies related to external libraries, modules, and other resources. Resolving these dependencies can easily become a tedious task, especially if the environment is distributed and components need to be deployed to multiple different machines across a cluster or data center.

Companies that release OSS for free can make money by selling binaries and associated licenses. Examples of such companies include Microsoft, Apple, IBM, Oracle, and many others.

Selling Documentation   Documentation is an essential part of software and the software development life cycle. Making the source code available for free does not obligate a company to give away the documentation for free as well. Purchasing the documentation can make it much easier for users to learn an application.

Another way of making money is to share expertise about an application by authoring a book and selling it either through e-publishing channels or traditional book publishers. The author does not have to be the developer of the software, just an avid user.

Consultancy   A developer with experience installing, using, or customizing any open-source application—all marketable skills—can sell their expertise by being a consultant. Organizations are mostly on the lookout for project-based help from experts. Online resources such as Elance and Guru provide freelance portals that put employers and expert resources in touch with each other.

Dual Licensing   Software can be released under both an open-source license and a separate proprietary license for, say, an enterprise edition. For customers, the open-source, free edition can be a part of an upsell to a commercial enterprise edition. An example of this is the MySQL database, which is dual-licensed by Oracle under a commercial proprietary license and GNU Public License version 2 (GPLv2).

Ad-Supported Software   Companies can advertise supported software against a compensation sum in return. For example, Google funds the AdBlock Plus add-on for web browsers, which prevents white-listed acceptable ads from being removed by the browser. Another example is SourceForge, an open-source project service provider that advertises banner sales on its website.

Voluntary Donations   With the donation model, funds are collected for large-scale projects requiring additional money. The campaigns are also used for projects that do not have other major funding sources. For example, *Wikipedia* launches a donation campaign every year to pay off its annual salaries and expenses. In 2004, the Mozilla Foundation had a fundraising campaign to support the launch of the Firefox 1.0 web browser.

Selling Merchandise   Some open-source organizations also sell branded merchandise articles such as T-shirts and coffee mugs to collect additional funds and expand the user community. Wikimedia Foundation, Mozilla Foundation, and Ubuntu Foundation are all organizations that sell merchandise.

White Label Branding

White label branding is the rebranding and sale of a product or a service that is not manufactured by the seller. The product/service is purchased by a marketer (a company) from a producer (another company) along with selling rights to the product/service.

Marketing and manufacturing companies follow a business-to-business (B2B) model. Some marketing companies may offer products without any investment in the technology or infrastructure. This can increase the sales for a manufacturing company by having a marketer sell a white label version of its product or service. The biggest gain for a marketer is the addition of another product or service, thus enlarging the portfolio.

A major example is Dell, for whom multiple manufacturers produce and assemble computer displays. Dell issues a model number for each display despite the fact that it may not have actually manufactured it.

A white label cloud service provider sells its customers resources that they can, in turn, offer to their own customers under their own brand name. The third-party company has control over appearance, administration and security policy, support, and access to infrastructure.

Cloud Service Business Models

Cloud services bring immense benefits and cost savings to businesses. Cloud service models help consumers organize their needs and goals in a coherent manner. Businesses can relieve themselves of worrying about costs and return on investment (ROI) and just focus on the actual task of doing business. They can test their ideas by designing and prototyping solutions, possibly maturing them if they see a potential for growth or discarding them altogether in the case of unmet targets.

In the following sections, we present well-known and emerging cloud service models from a business perspective.

Infrastructure as a Service (IaaS)

In this model, the consumer does not deal with the infrastructure; instead, the responsibility of all the hardware is outsourced to the service provider. The consumer is charged on a pay-per-use basis. IaaS is often utilized as a horizontally integrated service including server, storage, and connectivity domains. While the consumer may deploy and run their own operating system and applications, the IaaS provider is responsible for replication, backup and archiving, compute resources, network, load balancing, and firewalls. Some of the popular vendors and their solutions are shown in Table 12.1.

TABLE 12.1   IaaS vendors and their solutions

Vendor	Solution/Product
Amazon	AWS, EC2
AT&T	Synaptic Compute, Synaptic Storage
GoGrid	Range of cloud products: servers, storage, load balancers, and network
HP	BladeSystem Matrix

TABLE 12.1   IaaS vendors and their solutions *(continued)*

Vendor	Solution/Product
Joyent	SmartDataCenter, Compute Service, Manta Storage, Private Cloud
Rackspace	Range of cloud products: servers, storage, load balancers, backup/archival, monitoring, and network OpenStack
Eucalyptus Systems	Eucalyptus Cloud
Verizon	Range of cloud products: compute and storage
Terremark	Enterprise cloud products including compute, storage, and network
Akamai	Range of cloud products: servers, storage, load balancers, monitoring, and network

Platform as a Service (PaaS)

PaaS provides the capability for consumers to have applications deployed without the burden and cost of buying and managing the hardware and software. These are web-accessible applications or services created using standard languages and tools supported by the PaaS provider. The PaaS service consumer has control over the deployed application or service and even the hosting environment in particular circumstances. Services can be provisioned as integrated solutions over the Web, offering a quick time to market. PaaS facilitates immediate business requirements such as application design, development, and testing at a fraction of the normal cost. Most popular PaaS vendors and their solutions are shown in Table 12.2.

TABLE 12.2   PaaS vendors and their solutions

Vendor	Solution/Product
Amazon	Elastic Beanstalk
Appistry	CloudIQ
CA Technologies	AppLogic
Flexiant	FlexiScale (mostly video streaming, social networking, IPTV, VoIP)

Vendor	Solution/Product
SalesForce	Force
Google	Google App Engine, Google Apps
GigaSpaces	Cloudify
Microsoft	Windows Azure
VMware and EMC corporation	Cloud Foundry (part of Pivotal)
OrangeScape	OrangeScape Studio, Visual PaaS
ServiceNow	Cloud computing IT service management

Software as a Service (SaaS)

SaaS offers on-demand applications or services accessible through a thin client such as a web browser. The consumer has no management or control of the infrastructure as well as no control over the application's management and capabilities. SaaS providers were previously known as application service providers (ASPs). SaaS is an efficient delivery model for key business applications. These include customer relationship management (CRM), enterprise resource planning (ERP), human resources (HR), and payroll applications. Table 12.3 shows most popular SaaS vendors and the products they offer.

TABLE 12.3 SaaS vendors and their solutions

Vendor	Solution/Product
Abiquo	anyCloud
Akamai	Akamai SaaS
AppDynamics	Range of application performance management products
Cloud9	Cloud9 Analytics
NetSuite	Range of SaaS products: finance, accounting, CRM, inventory, and e-commerce software applications

TABLE 12.3 SaaS vendors and their solutions *(continued)*

Vendor	Solution/Product
Oracle	Oracle On Demand (delivers CRM, managed applications, and other SaaS offerings)
SAP	Business ByDesign (delivers on-demand ERP and CRM cloud systems)
Workday	Human capital management, payroll, and financial management

Data as a Service (DaaS)

DaaS is based on the concept that data can be provided on demand to the user regardless of geographic or organizational separation of provider and consumer. It is much akin to SaaS. Service-oriented architecture (SOA) has made the platform carrying the data almost irrelevant. DaaS was primarily used in web mashups, but it is now being utilized both commercially and within organizations such as United Nations (UN).

```
http://unstats.un.org/unsd/statcom/statcom_2010/Seminars/Communication/
Data%20as%20a%20Service.ppt
```

Organizations have typically used data stored in a self-contained onsite repository for which software was specifically developed to access and present the data. The result of this paradigm is bundling both the data and the software needed to interpret it into a single package. As a number of packages were made to suite different needs, enterprise application integration (EAI) provided a way for much required interaction among the packages. However, the EAI tools often encouraged vendor lock-in. The result of combined software and data consumer packages along with required EAI middleware has increased the amount of software organizations must manage and maintain. Cascading updates of all required tools to conform to the latest data formats and data schemas makes it a more difficult and a time-consuming affair. DaaS addresses the need to allow for the separation of data cost and usage from specific software or a specific platform. Table 12.4 lists a couple of DaaS vendors and their solutions.

TABLE 12.4 DaaS vendors and their solutions

Vendor	Solution/Product
dinCloud	SaaS and storage services
Apps4Rent	Project collaboration, document sharing

Communication as a Service (CaaS)

CaaS enables the consumers to utilize enterprise-level VoIP, VPNs, private branch exchange (PBX) systems, and unified communications without the need to purchase and manage the infrastructure. This avoids both capital and operating expenses. Table 12.5 lists a couple of CaaS vendors and their solutions.

TABLE 12.5 CaaS vendors and their solutions

Vendor	Solution/Product
Interactive Intelligence	Telecom software
NICE Systems	Communication services

Monitoring as a Service (MaaS)

MaaS provides the ability to use a web-based dashboard hosted by a service provider to monitor the status of key consumer applications. This can be done using a thin client such as a web browser. The advantages, apart from avoiding capital and operating costs, is the easy setup and purchasing process. Table 12.6 lists a couple of MaaS vendors and their solutions.

TABLE 12.6 MaaS vendors and their solutions

Vendor	Solution/Product
ScienceLogic	Monitoring software solutions
Zyrion (acquired by Kaseya)	Cloud monitoring, systems monitoring, network monitoring, managed service monitoring

Business Process as a Service (BPaaS)

Business process outsourcing (BPO) that utilizes any of foundational cloud computing service models (IaaS, PaaS, and SaaS) is known as Business Process as a Service (BPaaS). Traditionally, BPO was aimed at reducing labor costs. However, BPaaS reduces the amount of labor through increased automation, thus cutting the cost of the whole process. Services that can be outsourced and fall under the BPaaS umbrella include HR functions, finance (including payroll and benefits administration), procurement, advertising, marketing, and industry operation processes.

BPaaS delivers business processes based on the cloud service models. These cloud services include SaaS, PaaS, and IaaS. BPaaS sits on top of these three foundational cloud services. Table 12.7 lists several BPaaS vendors and their solutions.

TABLE 12.7 BPaaS vendors and their solutions

Vendor	Solution/Product
Oracle	Business Process Services: full stack of cloud services and application, database, and middleware technologies
Accenture	Industry-specific business process utilities
Cognizant	BPaaS
CSC	Business process services

Anything as a Service (XaaS)

The delivery of IT as a service by utilizing cloud computing is known as XaaS. It is basically intended to be a reference to one or more of the combinations described in the preceding sections. The term is quickly gaining popularity as services that were previously separated on different cloud models are becoming transparent and more integrated. Table 12.8 lists two XaaS vendors and their solutions.

TABLE 12.8 XaaS vendors and their solutions

Vendor	Solution/Product
Citrix	CloudPortal Business Manager
CloudFX	CloudConsult, CloudSelect, CloudData&Analytics

Service Model Accountability and Responsibility

Cloud computing introduces a paradigm shift in providing and supporting services, including shifts in responsibility and accountability of services and service outages.

In the traditional model, applications and services were offered by vertically integrated enterprises and service providers. The supplier bundling hardware and software together was accountable and responsible if a service went down or crashed.

The cloud environment has changed that altogether. Figure 12.1 shows a comparison between traditional and cloud deployment models. The integrated approach is replaced by decoupled model where the software is dissociated from the hardware resources. The resources can be pooled together to enable greater efficiency, convenience, economy of scale and can be offered to multiple cloud consumers. If there is an outage of a cloud service, who should be held accountable—the infrastructure provider, the cloud consumer who purchases the infrastructure service, the software provider, or the network service provider?

FIGURE 12.1   Traditional model vs. cloud model

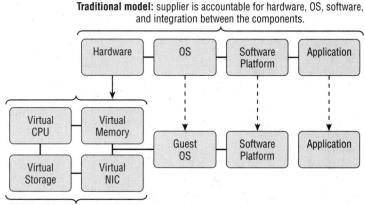

Some existing distribution of service accountability can be adapted to the new environment. All bodies operating in the cloud need to be aware and aligned on the basic principles involved. SLAs can then be established to clarify accountability and ownership of responsibility for different layers.

Cloud computing is interaction between many layers formed by applications, platforms, infrastructure, and network. The layers can be offered by different providers, which may expand beyond their usual business activities. Figure 12.2 shows different service models and cloud roles.

- Suppliers develop equipment, create software, provide integration.

- Network service provider owns and operates network and equipment for delivering the service to the consumer.

- Cloud service provider owns and operates the compute, storage, and internal network resources used to deliver the service to the consumer.

- Cloud consumers offer applications to the end users. End users pay for consuming the services.

- End users use services and applications hosted in the cloud.

FIGURE 12.2   Service models and cloud roles

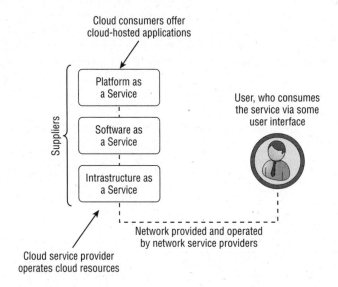

Service Impairments and Responsibilities

Service impairments are caused by vulnerabilities in the software, hardware, power supply, environment, application payload, networking, operational policies, application data, and user data and by natural disasters and human error. There are three outage categories generally identified for accountability:

- Outages associated with hardware or software, known as product-attributable service outages. This includes scheduled outages necessitated by system design.

- Service-provider-attributable outages. This includes procedural errors, environment problems, and security problems.

- External outages such as natural disasters, malicious attacks, and so on.

Consideration of Accountability and Responsibility

The often vague split between cloud consumer and service provider makes accountability difficult. This is even made more complex because many more service providers can be involved in the service delivery. The following list offers factors that can be used to consider accountability on a layer-by-layer model:

Cloud Consumer   The consumer is responsible for properly provisioning, configuring, and operating their applications. They are also responsible for their operational policies and the correctness of their data.

Virtual Appliance Supplier   Software vendors are responsible for ensuring that their applications are stable and reliable.

Infrastructure Supplier   The resource provider for compute, storage, network, load balancer, monitoring, and platform software resources are responsible for ensuring that their systems are robust and reliable.

Cloud Service Provider   The cloud service provider is responsible for robust and reliable operation of the cloud infrastructure and facilities. This includes their data centers, any or all virtualized hardware platforms, and the consumers' data.

Network Service Provider   The network service provider is responsible for making sure the network is available, reliable, and running robustly.

End user   The end user is responsible for their equipment.

The Enterprise Cloud

The enterprise cloud utilizes cloud computing for competitive advantage and breakout opportunities. It allows business innovation with unprecedented speed and agility. It empowers improved collaboration among business partners and customers. It allows reducing costs considerably, especially capital and maintenance expenses. And it offers a larger revenue stream while dramatically cutting risks and startup expenses.

Moreover, it offers massive scalability and elasticity, which gives companies a sandbox to try out new innovative ideas without capital expenses. Companies are empowered and can scale up instantly if their idea succeeds or shut down quickly if it fails.

In the following sections, we will share the most crucial components of the enterprise cloud: enterprise applications, collaboration, and telepresence.

Enterprise Applications

The term *enterprise applications* is used to describe applications or software suites that an organization uses to solve enterprise problems. The term refers to a large software platform that is complex and used by individuals or small businesses.

Enterprise applications are designed to integrate with other enterprise applications used within the organization. They can be deployed to different networks, including the Internet, intranets, and corporate networks. Enterprise applications have to meet strict security requirements and administration management guidelines because they usually deal with sensitive corporate data in either an in-house or public cloud setup.

Use of enterprise application service providers (ASPs) is quickly becoming prevalent. The enterprise application is designed by a third-party ASP and leased to an organization as an in-house or a hosted SaaS service. Organizations can also move the enterprise application to the cloud so that services are delivered to the in-house computers and devices through the Internet as an on-demand service. Another option is to choose the hybrid solution, where cloud applications are integrated with in-house systems.

The following types of enterprise applications are among the most common:

- Customer relationship management (CRM)
- Enterprise resource planning (ERP)
- Business intelligence (BI)
- Business continuity planning (BCP)
- Enterprise application integration (EAI)
- Automated billing systems
- Email marketing systems
- Messaging and collaboration systems
- Content management systems
- Payment processing systems
- Call center and customer support systems
- HR management
- Enterprise search

Cloud Collaboration

An emerging method for sharing and coauthoring documents and files, cloud collaboration uses cloud storage with customized permissions. Cloud collaboration technologies allow users to upload, comment on, and edit documents, thus collaborating within the cloud storage.

The biggest advantage for enterprises is to have members of a team work simultaneously on a particular task, thus increasing productivity. However, collaboration has become technologically complex with the need for team members to work in real time on a variety of documents and using different devices.

Even though the cloud collaboration sector has been growing rapidly, it has reached a point where is it less about the current technology and more about the choices and reluctance of team members to collaborate in this way. In a report for Giga Information Group, Erica Rugullies points out five reasons for reluctance to collaborate ("Overcome People Related Challenges For Success With Team Collaboration Software" by Erica Rugullies, Giga Information Group, 2003):

- Resistance to sharing knowledge
- Preference for using email as the primary electronic collaboration tool

- No incentive to change collaboration behavior
- Lack of strong leadership to drive collaboration
- Lack of interest by senior management in team collaboration initiatives

Cloud collaboration tool providers have created solutions to address these issues. These include integration of email alerts into collaboration tools and the ability to see viewers of a document. Tools are also put into one piece of software to reduce complexity and support task management.

Organizations now prefer to use single software solutions for solving all their collaboration needs rather than relying on multiple different solutions. Cloud collaboration providers are now replacing a complicated mix of email clients, FTP clients, and instant messengers. The best cloud collaboration tools include the following features:

- Real-time commenting and messaging features for timely project delivery
- Presence indicators to identify members active on shared documents
- Allowing users to set permissions and manage activity profiles
- Allowing users to set personal activity feeds and email alert profiles to keep track of the latest activities per resource (document) or user
- Allowing public space to share and collaborate with users outside the company firewall
- Adherence to the company security and compliance framework
- Auditing of documents shared within and outside the organization
- Reduced number of workarounds for sharing and collaboration on large files

Gartner in 2011 outlined a five-stage model on the maturity of firms with regard to cloud collaboration tools (*Maturity Model for Enterprise Collaboration and Social Software*, Gartner, 2011):

- A *reactive* firm is one with only email as a collaboration platform and a culture that resists information sharing.
- A *basic* firm is one where technology support teams are established and activities are stabilized.
- An *emerging* firm is one where new and emerging technologies are evaluated as possible choices on a qualitative basis.
- An *expanding* firm is one where new and emerging technologies are evaluated as possible choices on a quantitative basis.
- A *pervasive* firm has universal access to a rich collaboration toolset and a strong collaboration culture.

Collaborating with Telepresence

Telepresence is a set of technologies that allow people across geographical distances to communicate and collaborate with each other in real time using various multimedia types such as voice and video.

The six defining benefits of telepresence are as follows:

- Reduced travel expenditure
- Reduced carbon footprint and environmental impact
- Improved employee work and life balance
- Accelerated problem resolution
- Improved customer service
- Improved productivity

Rather than traveling to have face-to-face meetings, telepresence is now common in the industry for collaborating and managing projects. It uses a multiple-codec audio/video system in which each member or party *dials in* to join a call. This brings huge time and cost benefits and greatly enhances the interaction during conferencing. For instance, a speaker has tools available to present slides or show videos or animated presentations to the audience and engage them in real time. This is superior to phone conferencing, where audio is the only means to share information.

Teleconferencing and videoconferencing are the most popular forms of telepresence technology. They deploy a degree of technical sophistication and require improved fidelity of both audio and video. Technical advancements have extended telepresence capabilities to handheld mobile devices such as tablets. Although these mobile devices are still less reliable and lack the professional practicality of a true videoconferencing boardroom, they do offer a location-independent alternative.

With the cloud becoming ubiquitous and companies having resources (both manpower and infrastructure) spread over vast geographical areas, teleconferencing has become an everyday tool for meetings, collaboration, and management. The most popular teleconferencing tools used by the industry are listed here:

Microsoft Lync   Figure 12.3 shows Lync, formerly called Office Communicator, which is a teleconferencing client used with Microsoft Lync Server or Lync Online. It is part of the Microsoft Office suite and include features such as instant messaging, VoIP, videoconferencing with multiple users, contact book, onscreen document viewing, desktop sharing, document sharing, whiteboards, and collaboration through PowerPoint sharing. The downside is that there is a limit to how many people can join a call (typically 250).

Adobe Acrobat Connect   Acrobat Connect (Figure 12.4), from Adobe, is similar to Microsoft Lync. It is a powerful videoconferencing tool that includes a number of useful features comparable to Lync's. The upside is that a user can host a videoconference with a virtually unlimited number of people. However, compatibility issues with documents other than PDFs become a nuisance.

Skype   Skype (Figure 12.5) is a free service for one-to-one videoconferencing. It offers standard features such as instant messaging, VoIP, videoconferencing, file sharing, and screen viewing, but only for one-to-one calls. To participate in multiparty videoconferencing, users need to pay for the service. However, there are no supported options for desktop sharing and whiteboards. Moreover, Skype's messaging system is not very reliable and often has problems with the correct sequence of messages between people who are present in different time zones.

FIGURE 12.3   Microsoft Lync sign-in window

FIGURE 12.4   Adobe Acrobat Connect window

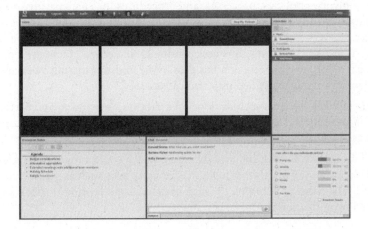

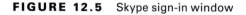

FIGURE 12.5   Skype sign-in window

Disaster Recovery

Disaster recovery involves policies, processes, and procedures that prepare organizations for the continuation of the vital technology infrastructure after a disaster or a set of major failures. Disaster recovery is a subset of business continuity, which focuses on the IT systems that support business functions. Business continuity, in general, focuses on planning to keep functional all or most aspects of a business in the midst of disruptive events.

Generally, disasters can be classified into two categories.

- The first are natural disasters such as floods, hurricanes, tornadoes, and earthquakes. Planning for natural disasters is focused upon mitigation measures to avoid or minimize damage.

- The second category is human-induced disasters, which could range from hardware- to software-level failures. This also includes malicious attacks such as viruses, malware, and hacking. The focus of planning for such disasters is prevention through strict policies followed by mitigation through surveillance.

Control measures are taken in the form of a disaster recovery plan (DRP) to eliminate or reduce such threats for an organization. IT disaster recovery control measures are usually classified into three types:

Preventive Measures Aim to prevent a disruptive event from occurring

Detective Measures Aim to discover unwanted events

Corrective Measures Aimed at correcting or restoring the system after a disruptive event

Organizations should document and exercise these three types of measures regularly to have a sound DRP in place when disasters strike. In the following sections, we will focus on topics such as redundancy and replication as a means of preparing for failure, backup and recovery, and geographical diversity.

Preparing for Failure: Disaster Recovery Plan

Cloud computing is an enabler for cloud-based disaster recovery resources. This is especially true for companies that are low on IT resources due to operating costs and sizeable user base. Although cloud-based disaster recovery eliminates the need for data center space, it does come with a few challenges involving data security, user authentication, regulatory requirements, and network requirements. Availability of the cloud provider and its ability to serve your users when a disaster strikes are also key considerations.

Every organization is unique in the applications it runs and the relevance of those applications to its business. Therefore, a DRP blueprint has to be specific to the business and needs of each organization. The process of DRP depends on determining the acceptable downtime for each application and data resource to the lowest acceptable threshold beyond which significant business impact can occur. DRP process involves identification and prioritization of application tools, services, and data resources. It should be noted that it is very important to keep the DRP as focused as possible to minimize costs and enable regular testing. This means not including applications and data resources that are not vital or are irrelevant. Application priority and required recovery time objectives (RTOs) can then help shape the DRP.

The RTO (http://en.wikipedia.org/wiki/Recovery_time_objective) can be defined as the duration of time and a service level to which a business process must be restored following a disruption. The purpose of RTO is to avoid undesired and unacceptable consequences due to service disruption. The RTO could depend on repair times of a number of failed components or devices, called mean time to repair (MTTR). The MTTR (http://en.wikipedia .org/wiki/Mean_time_to_repair) measures the average time required to repair a failed device or component. It can also be thought of as a factor of total corrective maintenance time and total number of corrective maintenance actions in a given time period.

Backing up to and restoring from the cloud is yet another cloud service feature that can be utilized by organizations to back up or archive applications and data into the cloud. With this approach, applications and data remain on premises for normal work, while the backup is in the cloud when a disaster strikes. The backup in the cloud thus becomes a substitute for off-site or tape-based backups.

However, the challenging aspect of using cloud-based backups is the recovery procedure. With bandwidth limitations and a lot of data to recover, getting data restored on site within defined RTOs can be tough. To minimize the recovery time, an option is to use local backups that are copied to the cloud as well. In this way, the backup in the cloud becomes a secondary offsite backup.

Service features such as compression and data deduplication make data restores from the cloud to the on-premises infrastructure a viable option. Another practical option is to back up and restore applications and data using VMs or virtual disk images (VDIs). Prestaging disaster recovery VMs and keeping them relatively up-to-date through scheduled restores can help in cases where a string of failures strike. This can help in a situation where aggressive RTOs need to be met.

Replication is the key for applications that require quick recovery time and recovery point objectives (RPOs) while supporting application awareness. An RPO (http://en.wikipedia .org/wiki/Recovery_point_objective) can be defined as maximum tolerable time period for which data might not be available from an IT service because of a major disruptive event. This means that the system design should take into account a limit to work toward. The system design should also include off-site mirrored backups, which must be continuously maintained.

There are two types of replication procedures (http://en.wikipedia.org/wiki/ Replication_(computing)):

Synchronous (or Eager) Replication   Synchronous or eager replication focuses on preventing conflicts. For example, if a record is simultaneously changed on two or more nodes, an eager replication system would be able to detect the conflict. The system will then abort one of the transactions before committing the other.

Asynchronous (or Lazy) Replication   Asynchronous or lazy solutions perform conflict resolution. For example, if a record is simultaneously changed on two or more nodes, a lazy replication system would first allow both transactions to perform commit. The system will then execute a conflict resolution resynchronization phase from periodically. The conflict resolution resynchronization phase could be based on a number of factors, such as transaction timestamp or node hierarchy.

Backup Sites and Geographical Diversity

Recovery can take place only if there is a location from which it can take place. This location is known as a backup site. In the event of a disaster, a backup site is both where an organization's data center will be re-created and the location from which that organization will resume to operate for the entire length of the disaster.

There are three different types of backup sites, cold, warm, and hot, referring to the effort required to begin operations at the backup site:

Cold Backup   A cold backup site is something akin to a properly configured space in an office building. Everything required to restore service to users must be procured and delivered to the site before the recovery process can begin. The delay to reach full operations can be substantial. However, this is the least-expensive backup site solution.

Warm Backup   A warm backup site is already stocked with hardware. However, to restore the service, the latest backups from the offsite storage facility must be delivered and bare metal restoration must be completed before the recovery process can begin.

Hot Backup   Hot backup sites are really a virtual mirror image of the current data center, with all systems configured and waiting only for the latest backups of data from an offsite storage facility. A hot site can often be brought up to full operation in significantly less time, typically a few hours. However, this type is the most expensive of them all.

Backup sites can come from three different sources:

- Companies specializing in providing disaster recovery services
- Other locations owned and operated by an organization
- A mutual agreement with another organization to share data center facilities in the event of major disasters or failures

Each approach has its pros and cons:

Using Disaster Recovery Specialists   Contracting with a disaster recovery specialist often comes with access to professional skills, which can help in guiding organizations through the process of creating, testing, and implementing a DRP.

Using Another Facility of Your Organization   Using space in another facility owned and operated by your organization is cost effective in terms of capital expenses, but stocking the backup site and maintaining its readiness is still an expensive proposition. Nevertheless, if the site is being used for other operations and projects, then the cost of operation can be covered by funds from those operations and projects. In fact, this empowers an organization with geographical diversity, such that it has sites in two or more distant geographical regions that maintain backups for one another. It provides a number of technical advantages as well:

- Additional redundancy
- Network proximity
- Performance enhancement
- Legal diversity, getting around regional legal issues

Sites in distant geographical regions are more likely to survive a disaster, especially a natural one, if only because of their different locations.

Sharing Data Centers with Another Organization   Last, crafting an agreement to share data centers with another organization can be inexpensive, but it may create a lot of administrative and managerial friction. Long-term operation might not be possible because the operation of the host's facility might different than the other organization's operations.

The selection of the backup site is therefore a compromise between cost and the needs of the organization.

Real World Scenario

The Importance of Cloud Backup and Task Documentation

In a development team, it can often be the case that a common user account is shared in the cloud between multiple developers who work on the same project. Apart from the obvious advantages of being able to execute and monitor jobs in the cloud, there could be some consequences, despite the presence of expert users and caution.

Deleting important processed data accidentally is one such consequence of a shared account. However, it is not always possible to copy processed data for backup somewhere else, given the sheer size of some data as well as the network time required to complete the process. It's possible to face such a situation when transforming/processing data and loading it into a Hive table. Hive is a distributed data warehouse technology from Apache. It is based on the MapReduce framework and uses Hadoop Distributed File System (HDFS) as its underlying file system.

The decision that generally has to be made is whether to keep the unprocessed/raw data or to discard it. Not all data can be stored for too long. Therefore, the decision is governed by three factors: the future relevance/importance of the raw data, the size of the raw data, and the time required to archive it. We usually go for compression and archival, even if there is a semblance of doubt that the data will be required in future.

Suppose that during an ongoing task you had to create a few intermediate external Hive tables that would then be used for joins (per criteria) to create another external Hive table loaded with processed data. An external table is one that stores just the schema and location of the table. If the table is destroyed or dropped, the data stays intact and is not removed. However, some other team member used the same account to accidentally delete the entire directory path underneath the HDFS that those tables were reading as input source. The team member had no knowledge of the Hive tables and thus even cleared the HDFS trash directory, while mistakenly assuming that the data can be discarded.

Luckily, the raw data was archived and stored in another HDFS directory path. In addition, the documentation was already in place when the tedious task (which required mathematical operations and time zone conversions in long complex queries) was performed. What followed was just the exercise of automating the task of raw data reprocessing and putting it back into the missing HDFS directory path.

Change-Over Mechanism: Failover and Failback

To protect a business, critical application and data servers can be fully replicated to secure cloud environments using cold, warm, or hot backup options. Servers and data can be kept current using continuous and scheduled replication procedures. Change-over mechanisms can also be put in place to automatically handle small or medium failures and prevent large-scale or elongated service disruptions.

There are two types of change-over mechanisms: failover and failback.

Failover Service   In the case of a service failure, downtime, or a complete site loss, a failover service can be set up to automatically redirect data and users to replica servers. These servers can be configured to operate in failover mode for the duration of the downtime event. Users will be able to securely access the replica servers from any location and continue to work seamlessly, as they normally would. However, users may experience some nonrepeating delay in accessing the service the first time it goes down.

Failback Service   Failback refers to getting a service back from the recovery environment after a planned or an unplanned outage. Failback is fast and transparent to the end users, who can continue to work without any interruption. The biggest plus of the failback process is that it synchronizes the changed data in real time and on-the-fly while users continue to access their applications and data. It then seamlessly redirects the user traffic back to the production environment once it is restored.

Change-over mechanisms such as failover and failback can improve the mean time between failures (MTBF) and mean time to failures (MTTF) of the overall system. MTBF is usually calculated as an arithmetic mean time between inherent failures of a system during operation, assuming that the failed components are repaired immediately as a part of renewal process. The MTTF, on the other hand, measures average time to failures with the assumption that the failed system has an infinite repair time.

Business Continuity and Cloud Computing

Implementing failure-resilient systems is not easy. Quickly moving operations from one infrastructure to the next during peak load or in the advent of a failure is a huge design challenge. The problem is twofold:

- Allowing new resources (compute, storage, and network) to operate as a part of the service
- Maintaining up-to-date copies of the data that the users and customers depend on

This is the key to business continuity in the cloud.

Business Continuity in the Cloud

Generally, business continuity is a set of planning and preparatory activities intended to ensure uninterrupted operation of organization's critical business functions despite disruptive events or disasters. Business continuity includes three key elements:

Resilience   Critical business functions and infrastructure are designed and engineered to transparently handle disruptions such as, for example, replicated systems and redundant capacity.

Recovery   Arrangements are made for restoring critical business functions.

Contingency   Readiness capability is established to cope with disruptions, disasters, and other major incidents. This is generally a last-resort response if resilience and recovery arrangements prove to be inadequate.

Business continuity is a crossover of a few interconnected and related fields such as management, governance, information security, and compliance. Risk and business impact analysis are core considerations and usually drive the priorities, planning, preparations, and management activities.

A general approach that works for business continuity is to combine redundancy in design with automation in cloud management. The architecture needs to withstand failures of individual components, including individual nodes. Each component then needs to be considered independently and designed with the realities of data center infrastructure, bandwidth, cost, and performance in mind.

The next step is to decide which parts of the system can respond automatically to failures and which parts cannot. The challenge is to seamlessly fail over to another component and keep operations running if a disk drive, server, network switch, SAN, or an entire geographical region goes down. Operational excellence is determined by automation.

To achieve the maximum level of automation, the design requires that the components and configuration is easily replaceable. Servers, for instance, need to be redeployable in a predictable way across heterogeneous cloud infrastructures.

Companies can practice outage scenarios and how to respond to them by doing artificial drills from time to time. Open-source tools are also available to help simulate component failures and mass system outages.

Procedures, standards, supporting policies and guidelines, and program development are all foundations of business continuity practice. In order to be equipped to tackle wide-scale or elongated disruptions and disasters, all system design, engineering, implementation, support, and maintenance should be based on these foundations. This coherent practice of business continuity and disaster recovery across all levels of an organization will help in minimizing damage and loss and achieving maximum operational ability amidst chaos.

Workshifting in the Cloud

Workshifting is a strategy to get work done in the right place by the right people at the right time. Cloud computing decouples all the constraints that prevent this flexibility from being achieved. The cloud offers architectures, models, and tools that enable an easy flow to resources for the users. Operations, applications, and data can be moved from location to location and at will. The concerns of operability, manageability, security, and location are removed, which enables the users to focus on the job at hand. The following are a few reasons for adopting workshifting.

Drive Business Growth   A virtual computing infrastructure allows organizations to bring new locations online in a short amount of time and provision applications and services in a matter of hours. This enables capturing a large market base without capital expenditures and related worries.

Enable Virtual Borderless Collaboration   Teams spread over multiple geographical regions play vital roles in many organizations. Timely and real-time collaboration between geographically distributed teams is necessary for business productivity, affectivity, and growth. Apart from saving travel costs and enabling virtual availability, cloud resources offer a common platform for sharing documents and information. Moreover, this enables a consistent set of up-to-date data and helps in engaging in coherent communication and making informed decisions.

Move Processes to Optimal Locations   Business processes can be moved to the most suitable locations. Virtual systems can be designed that fulfill the need for tools and services required for a particular job or project. Those systems can then be replicated and deployed to any number of users and locations.

Improve Customer Service Quality and Speed   Workshifting empowers enterprises to deploy resources according to customer requirements rather than requiring customers to adapt to their constraints. Task-aware and relevant experienced consultants can be placed on site with important customers for providing solutions to customer problems. Moreover, replication and redundancy of resources (compute, storage, and network) can help minimize service downtime, which grows customer business and improves customer satisfaction.

Bring Your Own Device

Bring your own device (BYOD) is the policy of permitting employees to bring personally owned mobile devices such laptops, tablets, and smartphones to their workplace and use them to access privileged company information and applications.

BYOD is significantly changing how people work. In high-growth and emerging markets, 75 percent of employees use their own device at work compared to 44 percent in developed markets.

http://cxounplugged.com/2012/11/ovum_byod_research-findings-released/

A recent study by Cisco partners (`http://bit.ly/1fCSQXF`) found that 9 out of 10 Americans use their personal mobile device for work. They also found that the highest percentage of people using BYOD for work (95.25 percent) is in education and academia.

A study by IBM

`www.ibm.com/mobilefirst/us/en/bring-your-own-device/byod.html`

says that 82 percent of employees feel that smartphones play a critical role in business. It also shows that BYOD increases productivity, employee satisfaction, and cost savings for the company. The increased productivity comes from a user being more comfortable with a personally owned device. It allows them to carry one device as opposed to several. The company can cut costs because they do not have to provide devices and maintain them.

However, BYOD comes with a lot of issues, most of them security related. Because the devices are owned by users, the users themselves are solely responsible for security patches, preventing leaks, and data breaches. Moreover, the company can neither enforce their own security policies nor handle the possibility of providing assistance and maintenance to each device because the hardware and software platforms vary considerably. A related issue is enterprise application compatibility across multiple platforms because employees will have different environments running on their personal devices.

Organizations that allow BYOD usually require employees to sign a BYOD policy document, which presents legal binding for employees to prevent them from sharing sensitive and classified data with other users or to other devices. For organizations, the challenge is to define exactly what constitutes sensitive company information and which employees should have access to that information.

Summary

Cloud computing helps bring new technologies together to solve complex business problems. Cloud business models offer need-based on-demand infrastructures, platforms, and services to help organizations carry out or grow their businesses. In this chapter we looked at cloud service business models and how they can help businesses perform while outsourcing all the worries of managerial and administrative work, costs, and ROI.

You then saw how cloud computing is really a combination of all these layers of infrastructure, platforms, applications, and network technologies. This can create problems during disruptive events where multiple providers could be responsible for various layers. We explained how the roles have to be properly defined for all service providers, consumers, and end users.

Next, we explored what the enterprise cloud is and how it helps shape business processes for organizations. Last, we focused on one of the most important aspects of cloud computing infrastructure and resource planning: business continuity and disaster recovery. You learned that business continuity policies and procedures must be defined to assist an organization during disasters. In addition, disaster recovery policies and procedures must focus on operability and availability of critical IT systems. These are essential for continual operation of important business functions during disasters and must be ensured via various levels of control measures.

Chapter Essentials

Cloud Service Business Models   Cloud service business models help organizations arrange their requirements in a manner that reflects their needs. Businesses can focus on the actual task of doing business rather than worrying about costs and ROI. Ideas can be quickly prototyped without worrying about the need for all the long and tedious managerial and administrative steps. Cloud business models include IaaS, PaaS, SaaS, and XaaS.

Service Model and Accountability   Cloud computing is interaction between many layers formed by applications, platforms, infrastructure, and network. Each layer can be offered by different providers, which may go beyond their usual business scope. This makes things complicated if there is an outage; for example, who is responsible and to what extent? Therefore, roles need to be decided for suppliers, network service providers, cloud service providers, cloud consumers, and end users.

The Enterprise Cloud   Utilizing cloud computing for breakout opportunities and competitive advantage is the defining aspect of the enterprise cloud. It empowers fast business innovation and improved collaboration while reducing costs. This is made possible through massive scalability and flexibility, which are inherent properties of the cloud concept.

Business Continuity and Disaster Recovery   Business continuity focuses on keeping functional all or most aspects of a business in the midst of large-scale disruptive events. It depends on three key elements: resilience, recovery, and contingency. Disaster recovery is a subset of business continuity and focuses on keeping operational the most critical IT systems that support business functions. This is achieved through preventive, detective, and corrective control measures.

Chapter 13

Planning for Cloud Integration: Pitfalls and Advantages

TOPICS COVERED IN THIS CHAPTER INCLUDE:

- ✓ Work optimization and reducing costs
- ✓ Choosing a suitable cloud service model
- ✓ Choosing the right cloud model
- ✓ Adapting organizational culture for the cloud
- ✓ Potholes on the cloud road

Cloud integration is a process that needs to take place at multiple levels in an organization. It affects the overall culture, business, and technical aspects of an organization. It carries with it advantages and pitfalls. Company culture is the embodiment of company values, traditions, and goals. It defines a company uniquely, but it can also be sensitive to change. Understanding a company's culture can assist in integrating the new culture that cloud computing brings. It can also help in establishing and affirming changes. In this chapter, we'll cover optimizing to improve work effectiveness while reducing costs. We will also cover suitable cloud service models and present criteria for making informed choices. Last, we discuss issues that can be raised with cloud integration and adaption.

Work Optimization

Migrating to the cloud can be challenging on multiple levels. These have been covered extensively in Chapter 10, "Testing and Deployment: Quality Is King." The whole migration process is made easy and simple by the manner in which the cloud operates. Public cloud business space is essentially an IT services industry. On a higher level of abstraction, moving to the public cloud space can be as easy as a two-step process: migrating business applications and paying the monthly bill.

However, optimization is another chapter of this story. Is an organization spending more than it should to accomplish its business objectives? Will the system be able to effectively and dynamically respond to urgent requests? Will the system upscale and downscale correctly and satisfactorily for each customer application? Is the billing flexible enough to handle dynamic changes in the environment?

In the following sections, we address the issues related to optimizing cloud usage, the flexibility of dynamic environments, cloud capacity, and reducing operational and maintenance costs. We also address the most suitable cloud service models by outlining a variety of dependencies and needs.

Optimizing Usage, Capacity, and Cost

Optimizing usage, capacity, and expenditure is achievable through a measured approach. Here we present a few key optimizations that can be applied to business applications when moving to the cloud, particularly the public cloud.

Choosing Cloud Instances

Administrators can make a choice from among various levels of compute, memory, storage, and networking instances. Some public cloud vendors, especially the ones offering PaaS and IaaS models, offer certain types of instances at lower prices. For instance, Amazon EC2 offers Spot Instances, which are spare instances that provide excess capacity at a lower price than normal ones. You can find out more at the following locations:

`https://aws.amazon.com/ec2/purchasing-options/spot-instances/`

`http://docs.aws.amazon.com/AWSEC2/latest/UserGuide/using-spot-instances.html`

Amazon says that the customer simply bids on spare Amazon EC2 instances and runs them whenever the bid exceeds the current Spot Price. The price for such instances fluctuates periodically depending on supply and demand for Spot Instance capacity. For this to be useful, however, business applications should have flexibility for when applications will run. This is because the instance runs only when the customer's maximum price is greater than the current Spot Price. If so, the instances will run and terminate only if one of the two conditions is met: the customer terminates them or the Spot Price increases above the customer's maximum price.

At the time of this writing, the potential savings for using Amazon Spot Instances against Amazon Reserved Instances was between 200 and 800 percent per hour (`http://aws.amazon.com/ec2/pricing/`). This statistic is for general-purpose instance types (medium, large, and extra large) depending on utilization requirement (light, medium, and heavy). Moreover, Spot Instances do not accompany any upfront costs.

Similarly, Rackspace offers a monthly rate for faster cloud block storage on a per-GB basis, versus its cloud backup service. The potential savings for using the backup service instead of block storage is around 120 percent. More information is available at the following location:

`www.rackspace.com/cloud/public-pricing/#cloud-block-storage`

It is important to survey and spend time experimenting with the application in order to determine the optimal level of compute, memory, and storage that is required. And it is equally important to know which applications can be deployed on spare instances and which cannot. For instance, Spot Instances make perfect candidates for daily batch processing systems or as short-term storage for machine logs that need not be kept for long time periods. An interesting use case will be to utilize spare instances for processing machine-generated log data for regular maintenance tasks.

Balancing Required Service Levels

Each application has its own service-level profile: its general purpose and functions. For example, a publically accessible e-commerce website will have a different level of service requirements than an internal employee portal. Evaluating the costs of public cloud instances against the service levels needed for various applications can help in optimizing the public cloud costs.

Preparing for Outages

Although it's more of a disaster planning and recovery concern, preparing for outages is relevant and of utmost importance in the context of cost and capacity optimization. Public cloud outages can cause huge losses in revenue for a company. They can even alienate an organization's main customers. Companies should generally follow three key principles: prepare for failure, design for failure, and have an alternative.

Engineers should have a good understanding of the weak points of the system. They should also be prepared for real disaster, and one way to do that is to carry out service outage drills. Cloud environments are composed of multiple machines, and machines fail. The system must be designed to handle failure, and although it may be expensive, it might pay off in the end.

Furthermore, a few of the mission-critical services can be deployed and served out of the alternative data centers if necessary. This helps in minimizing the risk of "total blackout" during an outage of a particular public cloud data center housing an organization's applications. One option could be to deploy applications in multiple regions and in isolated locations within those regions, such as by using Amazon's Regions and Availability Zones. The idea is to spread the chances of failure over a number of locations, which automatically reduces the probability of total blackout. This is because failures are usually isolated to specific locations and do not spread outward to other regions. See the following location for information on Amazon's Regions and Availability Zones:

```
http://docs.aws.amazon.com/AWSEC2/latest/UserGuide/using-regions-
availability-zones.html
```

Fine-Tuning Auto-Scaling Rules

Applications that are able to automatically scale the number of server instances offer flexibility and great opportunity for optimization. For example, you could have an auto-scaling rule that spawns a new instance once CPU utilization reaches 80 percent on all current instances and another that spawns once average CPU utilization reaches 50 percent.

However, how do businesses know whether 80 percent and 50 percent are the right percentages? There are two methods to determine the right percentage. The first is based on the trial-and-error method. An organization stress tests its application and determines loads under which the response time of an application starts lagging behind the usual response time or causes a noticeable delay. The second approach is to calculate the maximum number of tasks, users, or processes an application can simultaneously handle and convert that to a percentage in terms of compute capacity. Factors other than compute capacity can also be included, such as memory footprint, network utilization, and disk utilization.

Nevertheless, you may still need to experiment with different combinations to get it absolutely spot-on and then be able to perform considerable optimization.

Refactor Code to Address Necessary Changes in the Execution Environment

Public cloud vendors charge for compute, storage, and network resources and also for read and write disk operations. Applications can require disk accessibility for storing data, disk caching, and swapping data in and out of memory. Therefore, it can be fruitful to gather reads and writes and bunch them into single operations whenever possible.

In fact, this serves two more purposes apart from saving costs. First, application developers can think in terms of atomicity of operations and bunch together those operations that reflect the atomic nature of events. *Atomicity* means that in a series of outstanding uncommitted operations, either *all* occur or *nothing* occurs. Second, an I/O operation such as reading from disk or writing to disk is the most expensive operation in terms of time consumed and latency incurred. Bundling such operations can cause a considerable drop in I/O time and in the process make the application more responsive.

Moreover, other optimization techniques can be used that utilize the concepts of multi-threaded programming, concurrency, and in-memory processing to cut down not only on response times and latency but also on the usage of compute and storage resources.

Which Service Model Is Best for You?

The cloud covers a wide spectrum of services and delivery models. Therefore, it is highly relevant to understand the variety of cloud services and choose the service model best suited to your organization's needs. Here, we outline the three foundational cloud service models and their best use cases.

Infrastructure as a Service (IaaS)

IaaS provides basic computing resources and allows the customer to transfer an existing workload to the cloud with minimal changes. Here are two use cases for IaaS:

Extra Capacity for Short-Term Peak Workloads   In an e-commerce or retail business, workloads can be expected to peak at certain times of the year, such as Christmas, Thanksgiving, Easter, Black Friday, and so on. These shopping peaks could also coincide with aggressive advertising campaigns. Quickly provisioning capacity during these times is important to keep up with the buying pace. IaaS cloud service models can use the elastic ability of the cloud to add virtual resources to boost the capacity. The linchpin here is traffic monitoring because of the variance in user traffic that occurs.

Storage System for Storing Media   Some domains consume huge amounts of storage capacity, including for audio and video files. Typical use cases involve a film production house, a music production house, or even a video-enabled security surveillance system or a security company offering such a service. In addition to the files being stored, the service could allow storing metadata about the videos and make them accessible on demand.

Platform as a Service (PaaS)

PaaS provides an environment to the customer to build and deploy custom cloud applications and services. A customer can focus on the business idea and applications and worry less about setting up the environment. Here are a couple of suitable use cases for PaaS:

Testing New Business Ideas and Services   Enterprises usually go through a proof-of-concept evaluation of new business ideas before committing to put them in production. The biggest hurdle to testing implementation of a new business idea used to be setting up the whole physical environment or upgrading the facility. Most enterprises lacking financial resources resorted to either limiting the scope of the test implementation or completely bypassing it altogether. Without proper evaluation, good business ideas may not even leave the drawing board. The PaaS model makes this easier by providing the necessary resources to implement the business idea and an infrastructure to perform testing, and allows saving images for future usage.

Website Hosting   Web-site hosting is still the most common business use case for the PaaS cloud service model. While companies can host their web presence on their own data centers, the scale and ability to grow and reach new markets is an immense advantage gained through the use of a cloud solution. Moreover, if a website or web service is built for the cloud, it will be inherently prepared to scale and grow based on demand.

Software as a Service (SaaS)

SaaS provides an application or service that can be accessed over the Web using a variety of thin clients (web browsers) on either computers or smartdevices (phones and tablets). The major benefits include the immediate availability of a working solution and no upfront investments. Major disadvantages include loss of governance, data privacy issues for customer data. Some of the most suitable use cases for SaaS model are mentioned in the following list:

Web Services Such as Email, Social Media, and Blogging   These are classic use cases for the SaaS model. Email services, social media services, and blogging websites are the most suitable because SaaS provides the scalability, availability, and accessibility required by these services.

File Storage, Synchronization, and Sharing   Online file storage and synchronization services are becoming increasingly common because users can access them from anywhere with a device and an Internet connection. Small to medium-sized companies prefer to using such services so they can keep their data and files with one service vendor.

Finance, E-commerce, Accounting, Inventory, CRM, and ERP Software Applications
Some companies want to increase their sales by enabling shopping carts. Others want to keep an eye on their accounts and inventory. And still others want CRM and ERP systems in place. Options are straightforward: either develop and deploy in-house or purchase cloud services with all their benefits, such as scalability, availability, and accessibility.

Enterprise Collaboration Tools   Enterprise can host their projects on SaaS solutions. This allows an enterprises to not only establish a common platform on which all of its employees can collaborate but also to also monitor progress and develop using common development tools. However, a big disadvantage is vendor lock-in for IT projects that use vendor-specific APIs.

Cloud Monitoring Applications   Organizations are usually interested in monitoring their applications for performance and failures. They can employ the use of SaaS-based cloud monitoring services to set up self-configuration and self-healing solutions. Custom alerts for problems that cannot be automatically fixed may also be set up, as can scheduled automatic system maintenance for planned outages.

The Right Cloud Model

Organizations need to understand how to best deliver IT services by means of various cloud deployment models. It is a huge challenge to determine which cloud model fits their business needs. In the following sections, we evaluate the three cloud deployment models—private, public, and hybrid—and present useful information to assist in the decision-making process.

Let us first look at a few factors that could help in leading up to the decision. First, companies need to evaluate their existing infrastructure. The infrastructure depends on all application requirements, the environments needed for testing applications, the duration of testing, and the migration to production setups. This is important because testing applications, staging them, and migrating to the production environment could be a long and challenging endeavor.

Once that has been ascertained, budget becomes the next factor. It is important to determine whether an organization could and would move from a *capital expenditure (CAPEX)* model to an *operating expenditure (OPEX)* model. This includes the willingness for allocating budget for investments in the cloud and flexibility in terms of contingencies.

The next factor is the need to look into scenarios that would provide an ideal fit for applications for each cloud deployment model. The scenarios for the three primary cloud deployment models are covered in the next sections.

Private Cloud

The private cloud model is subdivided into two models, the enterprise private cloud and the virtual private cloud. We will cover both.

Enterprise Private Cloud

The enterprise private cloud is a cloud resource pool that is physically deployed within an organization's network and firewall. For all purposes, it can be thought of as a company-created, owned, and operated data center. Companies may also create private cloud resources from existing hardware.

Advantages:

- Optimal utilization of existing hardware assets
- A high level of data security and custom compliance with regulations and standards set by the company
- On-demand provisioning of resources

Disadvantages:

- Extra resource management load
- The need for special skills and expertise in cloud solutions
- Additional capital expenditure required to set up the infrastructure (hardware, software, and other tools and services)

Best for:

- Large organizations with underutilized hardware resources
- Medium-sized organizations requiring platforms

Usual applicability scenarios:

- Organizations willing to invest in resources such as hypervisor platforms, cloud resource management tools, storage, and server machines
- Organizations willing to spend funds on acquiring long-term cloud expertise and willing to manage future demands of infrastructural expansion

Virtual Private Cloud

These are third-party public clouds that have additional features for security and compliance.

Advantages:

- Minimum vendor lock-in concerns.
- Zero management requirements because the cloud provider takes care of it.
- On-demand provisioning of resources with zero capital expenditure.
- Strong compliance with data security, privacy, standards, and regulations. Though these are public cloud instances, they are not shared with other organizations that may also be subscribers of the same cloud provider.

Disadvantages:

- Additional compliances might be required, such as the SAS 70 validation from the cloud service provider. The Statement on Auditing Standards (SAS) No. 70 is a widely recognized auditing standard developed by the American Institute of Certified Public Accountants (AICPA). See http://sas70.com/sas70_overview.html.

- Though having a virtually private setup, it still exists in public space. Businesses that are customers of organizations using such a platform might be deeply concerned with their data security and choose to change their service providers.

Best for:

- Organizations of any size that do not deal with or operate highly sensitive and confidential customer data

Usual applicability scenarios:

- Organizations unable or unwilling to make capital expenditure for a privately owned infrastructure
- Organizations that do not own any hardware assets
- Organizations that have the responsibility to comply with standards, regulations, data privacy, and security

Public Cloud

The public cloud is a cloud deployment model where the cloud infrastructure and resource pool is in the public space. The public cloud is built by a vendor for the purposes of operating it as a commercial service.

Advantages:

- No special hardware resources requirements for managing the public cloud because the cloud service provider is solely responsible for it
- On-demand provisioning with no capital expenditure

Disadvantages:

- Vendor lock-in concerns
- Data privacy, security, and compliance concerns
- Standards and regulation concerns

Best for:

- Companies that want to have a fast and dynamic environment on a per-project basis
- Companies that want to quickly prototype or test new ideas and solutions
- Companies that want to move quickly from staging to production (and thus require quick provisioning of resources)

Usual applicability scenarios:

- Small and medium-sized companies that do not own any infrastructure, are unable to allocate capital funds, or are unwilling to spend capital on infrastructure
- Companies short on specialized hardware resources

Hybrid Cloud

The hybrid cloud model is a combination of multiple cloud deployment models that capitalizes on advantages of all the employed models while considerably reducing the disadvantages of any one model.

Advantages:

- On-demand provisioning on a per-need basis, thus improving efficiency (improved private cloud utilization) and minimizing costs due to underutilization (of public cloud instances).
- Long-term infrastructure can be managed within the private setup, while short-term infrastructure can be managed in the public cloud without additional capital costs.
- Sensitive, private, and confidential customer data can be retained in private cloud space, while additional data can be kept in public cloud space.
- Data security, privacy, standards, and regulations can be used to choose private or public cloud spaces.
- New solutions can be prototyped and tested easily without worrying too much about capital costs.
- Companies can quickly move from staging to production by dynamically provisioning resources.

Disadvantages:

- Public and private cloud integration is not easy because it requires software that can establish interaction between the two entities.
- Troubleshooting problems in applications that use resources from both platforms can be problematic.

Best for:

- Organizations that have traditional data centers or their own private cloud setup for mature projects and want to set up a public cloud environment for new long-term or short-term projects.
- Organizations that expect large sporadic increases or spikes in traffic to their services and applications. This is most suitable for organizations engaged in electronic commerce business.

Usual applicability scenarios:

- Large or medium-sized organizations capable of investing in their own private infrastructure as well as public cloud space. Typically organizations that are technology savvy.
- Organizations that comply strongly with data privacy, security, standards, and regulations.
- Organizations that want to outsource infrastructural management for nascent or new projects.

Adapting Organizational Culture for the Cloud

Organizational culture is the collective values, principles, visions, norms, working language, systems, symbols, beliefs, and habits that have evolved with the organization. David Needle, in *Business in Context: An Introduction to Business and Its Environment* (Learning Business Press, 2004), opines that this is a product of factors such as history, product, market, technology, strategy, types of employees, management style, regional/national cultures, and so on.

Although a large firm usually has its own unique culture, there might be diverse and conflicting subcultures that coexist within the firm. This is due to different projects and the characteristics of different departments and teams. Organizational culture also constitutes the behavior of employees who are part of an organization as well as their thought and work habits. This affects the way employees interact within departments or teams, with clients, and with other stakeholders. The negative and positive aspects of an organization's culture can also greatly affect employee perceptions and how they identify with the organization.

According to Daniel P. Modaff, Jennifer A. Butler, and Sue DeWine in *Organizational Communication: Foundations, Challenges, and Misunderstandings, Third Edition* (Pearson, 2011), the organization sees its culture as a root metaphor created through communication and symbols or competing metaphors. Just like personal experience, culture also produces a variety of perspectives.

The organizational communication perspective on culture includes three different views:

Traditionalism   Culture is viewed through objective things, such as stories, symbols, and work rituals.

Interpretivism   Culture is viewed through a network of shared meaning; that is, members of an organization share subjective meanings.

Critical interpretivism   Culture is viewed through a network of shared meanings as well as power struggles created by a competing network of shared meanings.

In the following sections, we will discuss how to determine your current organizational culture and map out plan for adapting to the changes in culture due to the integration of cloud technology. We will also discuss how to ensure propagation of the cloud-influenced culture and maintain the new cloud-influenced culture.

Finding Out the Current Culture

Understanding different types of cultures and their attributes is essential to finding organizational culture. Several management studies have classified organizational cultures. Fons Trompenaars and Charles Hampden-Turner, in *Managing People across Cultures* (Capstone, 2004), propose four cultural archetypes. These archetypes can help an organization to benchmark its culture and execute an effective strategy to use the culture for growth.

Trompenaars and Hampden-Turner's model proposes two dimensions. The first dimension discusses hierarchical against egalitarian organizational structure. The second discusses innovation against efficiency, which balances individual talent and process (i.e., person versus task). They used these dimensions to define four types of cultures:

Incubator   These are the companies that spawn new ideas. Ideas are discussed openly, workplaces are usually casual, and discipline is driven more by trust and less by rules. Examples include Silicon Valley startups, including the ones with large funding and impressive market valuations.

Guided   These are companies that have egalitarian structure and whose mission and vision defines processes and guides high-level decisions. Ideas are appreciated but at a lower level. Missions and projects are central and crucial to organizational goals. NASA is an example of a guided culture.

Eiffel Tower   These are the companies that have a classical hierarchical culture that practices explicit delegation of responsibilities and tasks. Communication is generally top-down rather than bottom-up. People moving into this culture from other cultures require time to adjust. Examples include many successful commercial firms.

Family   This is a hierarchical archetype that displays family or family-like close relationships controlling major decisions and strategy. Criticism is handled privately. Examples include very successful Japanese and Chinese firms.

Figure 13.1 shows different organizational cultures. Note that hierarchical and egalitarian cultures can implement the same practices; they just do so differently. Also note that in an incubator culture, a wiki can be used to share knowledge and discuss or debate ideas. The role of the management is to let the wiki grow. However, in a family culture, wiki content has to be filtered through a workflow process.

FIGURE 13.1   Different organizational cultures

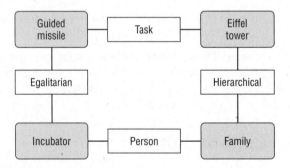

Mapping Out an Adaption Plan

The cloud is disruptive, and it is important to acknowledge that moving to a cloud-based service model is a major shift in organizational culture and thinking. Adapting to the cloud is both a quantitative (costs, etc.) and qualitative (processes, etc.) change. It renders some of the established metrics and concepts obsolete while introducing new ones. As an example, consider cloud testing and monitoring as opposed to the same activities in a non-cloud layout.

Most organizations are very capable of adapting incremental changes. This is because most are usually in a *self-learning* phase amidst new projects. Therefore, changes are a part of the routine. However, this model rarely works for cloud transformations due to the steepness of the learning curve as well as the requirement of learning new attitude and approaches.

Another factor is the inherent resistance to change in individuals, and as individuals form organizations, aversion to change is a common reaction. This is the fear of new demands and new knowledge. In order to get through this resistance and promote cultural evolution, effective communication and planning needs to be done differently and carefully.

To encourage and empower organizational learning, some key principles can be followed. Employees tend to be goal oriented, and it helps to paint early a compelling vision for the future of the organization. The vision should be supported by concrete, applicable information. This can help employees see how the evolution will help their daily activities.

Moreover, employees may also bring substantial prior knowledge and experience. They will try to relate new knowledge to their past experience. Introducing cloud models in comparison to traditional models can help in displaying the worth of adapting. Also, it is important to leverage positive group dynamics. People naturally listen to and model leaders in their teams, departments, and organizations. Therefore, including visible, charismatic, influential managers can assist a great deal.

Communication is the linchpin of the whole adaption process. The following few actionable recommendations can help in optimizing communication to facilitate culture change:

- Enlist visible and influential people as responsible team members for cloud adaption.

- Encourage regular communication for eliminating gaps in understanding of the core team members.

- Use different methods of communication to develop deep understanding (visual aids, text, etc.).

- Resistance is natural. Give people time to cope with the learning process. Answer concerns and questions. This is a great opportunity to turn skeptics into vocal supporters.

Culture Adaption, Propagation, and Maintenance

There are three important aspects to consider for successfully incorporating cloud computing within an organization's culture:

- The leadership and management involved needs to act strategically in order to encourage people to collaborate toward a shared goal. Employees are stakeholders, and they need to be aware of what is going to evolve, why, and how.

- Employees need to be encouraged to actively adjust and organize their work toward adaption. This involves training sessions, work drills, and exercises. Documentation is the key here and forms a basis for meaningful productive communication.

▪ The organization might need to rethink how to organize its tools, use its techniques, and procure and access its data sources. This is where the actual work lies, because it essentially requires reinventing or adapting old narratives to new ones.

Embodying this new culture involves establishing, affirming, and keeping the new changes. For large organizations, replacing old tools and techniques with new cloud-based ones can be a huge challenge. This is not only because of the culture that evolved along with using these tools and techniques but also because of the revenue stream that the company depends upon.

Figure 13.2 shows models for adapting changes to organizational tools, techniques, and resources. The first model is the standard model, which builds on the shared assumptions and present knowledge of an organization. Change is viewed as an external or alien entity until the organization goes through learning, teaching, and training exercises to incorporate the change. This model may have a disadvantage in moving slowly toward the goal of change adaption, but it promises the greatest stability in uncertain situations.

FIGURE 13.2   Adaption models

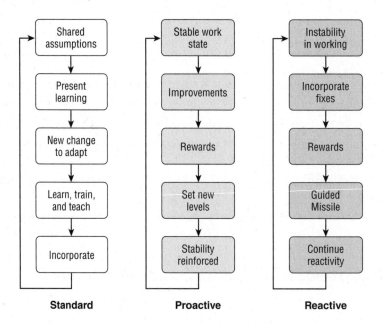

The proactive adaption model applies to organizations that have already perfected and matured their procedures. It starts with a stable working state with occasional or scheduled improvements. Once the improvements have been executed and affirmed, new levels of standards are set. These new standards now serve as the benchmarks and entry points for new changes. This, in return, maintains and reinforces stability.

The reactive model applies to organizations that have instability in their work processes and need to incorporate fixes rather than changes. Once the fixes are executed, reactivity continues to find new issues to fix.

The process of change and propagation is shown in Figure 13.3. First and foremost, an understanding of the problem has to be established (which in this case is adapting or changing a technique). This is followed by development and implementation of the changes. Then the changes have to be evaluated and validated. Corrective measures need to be taken into account and applied. Feedback ensures smooth sailing and communication is used as a tool for early detection of issues and problems.

FIGURE 13.3   The change regime

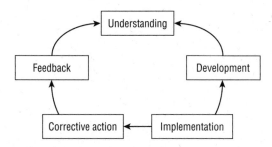

With time, an organization will absorb even large changes given detailed planning and relevant resources to implement those changes. Once that happens, most organizations will then have to put in place recommended practices for their departments, teams, and employees to follow. This serves two purposes and carries major advantages:

- The whole organization can move toward standard work practices, thus making it easy for different departments to communicate and collaborate in a coherent manner.

    We often see that it is the case with large organizations that projects and goals involving multiple departments suffer from long and tedious procedures and are therefore victims of slow progress. Adaption of new changes might resolve such issues as projects begin.

- Procedures and interdepartmental communication can outline various areas to further improve. This can also help an organization find new opportunities for initiating projects.

Potholes on the Cloud Road

A business might not need a certain piece of functionality today, but how does it know if it might need it tomorrow? Planning is finding a convergence point among business goals, vision, and daily work routine. In the following sections, we discuss issues that hinder business cloud integration and adaption.

Roadblocks to Planning

A variety of roadblocks can obstruct companies wanting to achieve successful changes. These obstacles can be as diverse as the efforts by companies to introduce change. Since cloud adaption and integration have to take place at multiple levels in an organization, it can cause problems at any of those levels. Here we'll cover some of the common roadblocks:

Resistance to Change   Businesses have constant pressures like product deadlines, bottom-line results, increasing market competition, market presence, and regulatory issues. They can either emerge more efficient and effective or become paralyzed and succumb to the pressure to deliver.

There will be resistance whenever a new change is proposed. This is natural because people tend to be afraid of change. "It won't work here because our organization is different" say the naysayers. The problem here is that it is hard to separate resistance from truth, and vice versa. Some people will always find excuses to dismiss an effort that will require them to detach themselves from their comfort zones of work and behavior. However, resistance must be detached from those who speak in terms of realistic possibilities.

The key here is to validate proposed changes by explaining the intentions in terms of achievements. The approach depends on the organization and must be tailored accordingly.

Function versus Process   Businesses can be organized across functional lines as well as processes. In a functionally organized businesses, people become focused solely on their functional area. This discourages interaction with groups that are upstream or downstream in the overall process. Moreover, even if there is cross-department communication, it is mostly on the basis of the requirements of one department for the other.

This type of workflow prevents individual groups from contributing to the end-to-end process that might directly serve the customer base. Instead of focusing efforts toward improving products and services for customers, traditional hierarchical setups can promote a culture of interdepartmental competition. This can cause disruptions for undertaking projects and resistance to overall change. The key here is to promote collaboration through interaction and communication.

Group Reporting   This is slightly related to the preceding points. It is difficult to be responsible for improvements or change initiatives for a group that does not report directly to a manager handling changes. The real issue is the failure in getting the message across various groups of how new changes might affect the way they work.

The key point here is to disseminate relevant information through departmental meetings that present detailed explanations regarding "why" and "how." It is also pertinent to clarify doubts and answer questions of groups who will be directly involved throughout the transition.

Support the Change   Tangible change in a constructive manner is achieved through the support of senior management. Leadership will always be felt if senior management is actively involved. Good leadership will promote good governance, which eventually translates to support. Moreover, middle management should also assume responsibility for ownership of their functions.

Training and Documentation   It is absolutely necessary for organizations to offer training to their employees for new changes. Investment in employees, who are resources of an organization, can help them save time and money for an organization. In fact, this approach will eventually lead to improved output and better utilization of provisions of the new changes.

Possible and Most Common Problems   Budget cuts, changing requirements and needs, and alternative approaches to traditional methods keep things uncertain. These are the most common problems faced during planning, and how do you plan for such fluctuation in an uncertain, continuously changing and shifting environment?

One way is to prepare prefeasibility and feasibility studies that focus on evaluating and analyzing the potential of a proposed change. The study is based on investigating and researching to support the process of decision making.

Another is to involve stakeholders, such as top management, middle management, and senior and new employees to get their perspective. This serves two purposes: it provides a sense of belonging and responsibility in employees, and it helps in getting the message across.

It is also important to embrace what cannot be controlled. Explicit micromanagement and control is hardly ever fruitful. The key is to plan and then go with the flow. This means having a plan and all the requirements (budget, alternatives, legal/statutory) in place but also having enough flexibility to change during the course of change proceedings.

Convincing the Board

The board or the top management of an organization is at the core of effective strategic planning and governance. They need to think and plan smartly to lead an organization forward. It is imperative for the board to focus on critical issues and policy challenges. However, the board should also concern itself (but to a lesser extent and only from time to time) with lower-level administrative details and process implementation.

Any plans that disturb the equilibrium of processes in place for achieving the agreed-upon goals can meet resistance. The board needs convincing and persuading in a manner that supports new changes within the framework of an overall fulfillment of their goals. Some of the following points might be helpful in planning a convincing campaign:

Creating Change for Good   Well-planned proposed changes usually begin with articulation of the problems faced by the organization and how the new changes can effectively help in resolving those problems.

Arranging for the Best Use of Staff   If the new changes bring about a good work process and a sound strategic planning process, it will most certainly get employees engaged. This will help them invest time in the organization and be more productive because they will understand their unique contributions to the goals of the organization.

Getting the Board Moving   New changes can reinvigorate enthusiasm among the board of directors. The board can provide a plethora of resources through their expertise and networks and by sharing ideas. They could also provide a broader vision and guide employees about the purpose of their work. A good plan will get the board excited, actively involved, and committed to their role in making things happen.

Figure 13.4 shows four phases of persuasion. Phases 1 and 2 bank on convincing that change is necessary and probably even critical to an organization's growth. Convincing is followed by preparing a preliminary plan, gathering feedback, and revising the plan into a final plan.

FIGURE 13.4   Four phases of persuasion

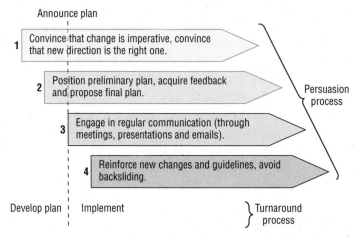

Four phases of persuasion campaign (*Harvard Business Review*), http://hbr.org/hbrg-main/resources/images/article_assets/hbr/0502/R0502F_B.gif

Phases 3 and 4 concentrate on communication to keep the plan rolling forward. In this phase, guidelines and new changes are used as a tool for reinforcements and avoiding lapse.

In order for the change to be convincing, it should satisfy all the requirements of an organization's mission, vision, goals, strategies, and objectives.

 **Real World Scenario**

Avoiding the Potholes: The Dos and Don'ts

Companies that wish to stay relevant in the cloud-based world will need to redefine their approach, business models, policies, and even culture. Focused aspiration is great, but unplanned ambitions can be disastrous. Here are *dos* and *don'ts* to provide guidance on avoiding hurdles.

Do start with a strategy, and evaluate and reevaluate organizational maturity for migration.   Start with a sound and board-approved plan and strategy. The key is honest assessment of IT tools, policies, procedures, and business models. The assessment also drives organizational planning for cloud adaption.

Do automate infrastructure; buy instead of reinventing the wheel. When a company embarks toward a journey of cloud-based operations, it should focus on automating its infrastructure. Automation saves time, effort, and costs. Another very important thing is to set aside any ideas of reinventing the wheel. If standard solutions or products are available off the shelf (whether paid or open source), then it is much more advisable to use those instead of spending time and money on making something customized.

Do solve business problems. Addressing business demands and solving related problems trumps the traditional motto of achieving greater efficiency, higher utilization, agility, and flexibility. During the earlier stages of transitioning toward a cloud-based model, the focus should be entirely on business demands.

Improving efficiency, utilization, and so on, should be secondary concerns and must be addressed only when a transition to the cloud has been fortified to some extent. However, it is not recommended at all to ignore these things. Instead, the key is to focus on transition and only when it looks promising, start including other important issues as well.

Do retool, retrain, restaff. Because the transition is a change, organizations will need to arm themselves with new resources, including new tools and products for their business. They will need to retrain their staff for future cloud operations and probably even restaff to acquiring new human resources for task relevance.

Do be inclusive. Include all the appropriate stakeholders early in policy making and culture evolution. Also, include stakeholders often for major or critical decision-making routines.

Do be realistic. Even though all the bases might be covered, there might be delays and lower-than-expected outcomes. A good management team evaluates and reevaluates its expected outcomes against a realistic frame of reference. This avoids not only unnecessary expenditures and unfocused and uncompounded efforts but also a hierarchical chain of disappointment. Moreover, it maximizes the chances of success as a sequence of small steps rather than large leaps in a short time.

Don't jump in before certain level of readiness. Readiness is important before taking the next step. This requires a certain level of refinement in an organization's procedures and tools and how it goes about its daily processes.

Don't forget people, policies, and processes. It is not certain that a cloud migration will definitely succeed for an organization if it has a sound technical platform. What the organization offers might not be ready for the cloud. This is where people (employees), organizational policies, and business processes become relevant. They should be considered before the organization leaps onto any major endeavors.

Don't be impatient. Once an organization nears the completion of the transition, it should allow time for people and processes to have an effect and become mature. It is easy to mistake process immaturity for failure.

> **Don't underestimate the challenges.**   It is often the case that management or middle management underestimates the challenges in working with legal departments and information security departments. On top of that, collaboration, coordination, communication, and progress reporting within two departments can be a major challenge. Moreover, don't underestimate the power of resistance to change by the employees. It is natural to be afraid of change initially because actors such as leaving the comfort zone, extra effort, fear of job loss, and even fear of failure.
>
> **Don't overpromise.**   To overpromise is to expect too much of a team within a given time frame. It is a good practice for both upper and middle management to recognize realistic goals. This minimizes tangible (expenses) as well as intangible (effort, time, confidence) losses.

Summary

Cloud integration can be a tricky business. Therefore, planning plays an essential part in the overall integration process. It involves optimizing organizational resources to reduce costs and improve efficiency. Administrators need to weigh the amount of resources used against company or project requirements. Choosing from among a number of candidate cloud models and services depends on multiple factors, such as projects, services, users, and processes. All factors must be considered to better address the needs of an organization.

Competitive advantage, consistency, and team cohesiveness can be directly associated with an organization and its culture. However, the culture can be an advantage as well as an occlusion. To integrate cloud-based IT infrastructure, the current culture needs to be assessed, understood, and transformed in a frictionless manner. Change can be a daunting undertaking because the current culture can be an embedded part of an organization and there might be a certain level of inertia. Leadership, communication, and employee motivation must be the points of concentration because they play very important roles in carrying out such a challenging change.

Chapter Essentials

Optimization to Improve Efficiency and Reduce Costs   If an organization is spending more than required on resources to accomplish its objectives, it should consider optimizing usage and capacity and reducing costs. Administrators can choose from among various levels of resources (compute, memory, storage, and networking) to better suit their needs. To avoid full-scale blackouts, businesses can deploy mission-critical services at alternative data centers. This avoids total dependency on a single cloud provider.

Calculating Requirements and Choosing a Cloud Service Model   One method of calculating requirements and fine-tuning is to stress-test applications to determine load parameters and response times. Another method is to calculate the maximum number of users and processes an application can handle simultaneously. You can choose from a variety of cloud service models, and your choice will depend on multiple factors. All factors must be kept in focus to better address an organization's needs.

Choosing a Cloud Model   Companies need to evaluate their existing infrastructure to ascertain the kind of cloud model (private, public, or hybrid) that best suits their requirements. The enterprise private cloud is best for large organizations with underutilized hardware resources. The virtual private cloud best suits the needs of an organization that does not deal with very sensitive data. The public cloud is best for companies that want to have a fast and dynamic environment for their projects. The hybrid cloud should be chosen by organizations that have traditional data centers or a private cloud setup for mature projects but want a platform for executing new projects.

Organizational Culture and Business Issues   Organizational culture is composed of values, principles, visions, norms, working language, systems, symbols, beliefs, and habits that have evolved with the organization. To chart-out a plan for adapting to changes in culture, the current organizational culture should be recognized. Adapting to the cloud is both a quantitative and qualitative change. To successfully incorporate the cloud within an organization's culture, three important things need to be adopted. Leadership needs to communicate and act strategically. Employees need to be encouraged to adapt and adjust. Businesses need to rethink their tools and techniques. Planning for future functionality is another critical aspect. Finding a convergence among business goals and daily work is critical for effective planning.

Appendix

The CompTIA Cloud+ Certification Exam

TOPICS COVERED IN THIS APPENDIX INCLUDE:

✓ Preparing for the CompTIA Cloud+ exam

✓ Registering for the exam

✓ Taking the exam

✓ Reviewing exam objectives

As mentioned in the introduction to this book, cloud computing is increasing in relevance and becoming ubiquitous at the same time. It is becoming key to the corporate and business world, not to mention the IT world. The cloud provides infrastructure, platform, and services that are critical to business needs. And like any other IT domain, it requires skilled and trained professionals who can deploy, integrate, support, and manage cloud environments. One way to demonstrate your ability in this area is to attain the CompTIA Cloud+ certification.

To achieve this certification, you need to pass the CompTIA Cloud+ exam (CV0-001).

The CompTIA Cloud+ certification is an internationally recognized validation of the knowledge required of IT practitioners working in cloud computing environments. This exam will certify that the successful candidate has the knowledge and skills required to understand standard cloud terminology and methodologies; to implement, maintain, and deliver cloud technologies and infrastructures (e.g., server, network, storage, and virtualization technologies); and to understand aspects of IT security and use of industry best practices related to cloud implementations and the application of virtualization. Cloud+ certified professionals ensure that proper security measures are maintained for cloud systems, storage, and platforms to mitigate risks and threats while ensuring usability. The exam is geared toward IT professionals with 24 to 36 months of experience in IT networking, network storage, or data center administration. It is recommended that CompTIA Cloud+ candidates have CompTIA Network+ and/or CompTIA Storage+ Powered by SNIA certification. It is further recommended that Cloud+ exam candidates have familiarity with any major hypervisor technologies for server virtualization, though vendor-specific certifications in virtualization are not required.

This book covers all the exam objectives, plus more, to enable you to pass the exam and be successful in your career as a cloud systems administrator, cloud IT specialist, cloud manager, and cloud architect.

Preparing for the Exam

Preparation is key to being successful. Now that you've read this book and are ready to pass the exam, it's a good idea to consider how the exam will look and feel so that nothing takes you by surprise.

We highly recommend that you visit the CompTIA website before taking the exam because details about the exam can change. The CompTIA website for this exam is here:

`http://certification.comptia.org/getcertified/certifications/cloudplus.aspx`

The first thing to be aware of is that the exam is kept as vendor neutral as possible. There are no vendor-specific questions with respect to particular proprietary technology from various companies. They're universal and conceptual. That is a good thing because the information you've learned in this book is transferrable across most, if not all, vendors.

The exam is 2 hours and 30 minutes long and consists of 70 multiple choice questions. There are no hands-on exercises or lab simulations. To pass, you need a score of 70 percent or more.

The exam is broken into the domains of expertise shown in Table A.1.

TABLE A.1   Exam objective categories

Expertise Domain	% of Exam
1.0 Cloud Concepts and Models	12%
2.0 Virtualization	19%
3.0 Infrastructure	21%
4.0 Resource Management	13%
5.0 Security	16%
6.0 Systems Management	11%
7.0 Business Continuity in the Cloud	8%

Looking at the objectives table, if you feel you're weak in any particular area, do some more homework so that you can go into the exam as confident as possible.

Taking the Exam

As we go to press, the CompTIA Cloud+ exam can be taken only at Pearson VUE testing centers. Pearson VUE is a leading global training company with more than 5,000 testing centers around the globe.

To book your exam, you simply go to www.pearsonvue.com/comptia and follow the online procedure. The website enables you to locate your nearest testing center, book the test, and pay for it. To complete the procedure, you'll need a Pearson VUE account (which can be set up on the website) and an electronic payment method. The exam costs around $200 (or the local equivalent in whatever country you are in).

After your exam is booked, you need to sort out a few other important things:

- Plan your route to the testing center—you do not want to arrive late!
- Be sure to bring the required identification. You cannot take the exam without providing identification documentation that has a photograph of you and your current valid signature.

Once you know where the testing center is and you have the required identification, you're ready for your exam.

On the day of your exam, do yourself a favor and arrive at the testing center early. The last thing you need is the stress of running late. Be prepared to surrender all personal electronic devices; they will be stored in a secure locker while you take the exam.

After signing in at the testing center, you'll be taken to a secure room, where you'll be logged in to a computer and asked to complete a short computer-based survey. The time required to take this survey does not count toward the time you have to take the exam, so you don't need to rush through the survey. The answers you give in the survey do not influence your exam marks.

After you've completed the survey, it's time to take the exam. As mentioned earlier, the exam consists of multiple-choice questions. If you're unsure of the answer to a question, you can mark it for review, and after you've answered all other questions, the system will allow you to go back to questions that you've marked. Do your best to answer all questions! There is no advantage in leaving a question unanswered. An unanswered question is automatically considered incorrect. If you guess at the answer, you stand a chance of guessing right. So answer all questions!

After you've answered all questions and clicked the Complete button, you'll be shown your score and find out whether you've passed the exam. Hopefully you've passed and the system will automatically print out your score card. You'll then receive an email outlining your results and giving you the option of having a certificate mailed to you. In the event that you do not pass the exam, you are able to retake it at any time that's convenient to you and your chosen testing center—there is no requirement for a waiting period between your first and second attempt at the exam. However, if you do not pass on your second attempt, you will need to wait a minimum of 14 days before any further retakes.

Reviewing the Exam Objectives

Table A.2 lists the CV0-001 exam objectives along with the chapters in which they are covered. You can test yourself on the exam objectives by using the flashcards and practice exam on the book's companion website, www.sybextestbanks.wiley.com.

TABLE A.2 Exam CV0-001CompTIA Cloud+ objectives map

Objective	Corresponding Book Chapter
1.0 Cloud Concepts and Models 1.1 Compare and contrast cloud services.	Chapter 12

- SaaS (according to NIST)
- IaaS (according to NIST)
- PaaS (according to NIST)
- CaaS
- XaaS
- DaaS
- BPaaS
- Accountability and responsibility based on service models

1.2 Compare and contrast cloud delivery models and services.	Chapter 10

- Private
- Public
- Hybrid
- Community
- On-premise vs. Off-premises hosting
- Accountability and responsibility based on delivery models
- Security differences between models
  - Multitenancy issues
  - Data segregation
  - Network isolation
  - Check laws and regulations
- Functionality and performance validation based on chosen delivery model
- Orchestration platforms

TABLE A.2   Exam CV0-001CompTIA Cloud+ objectives map *(continued)*

Objective	Corresponding Book Chapter
1.3 Summarize cloud characteristics and terms.	Chapters 1, 10

- Elasticity
- On-demand self serve/just in time service
- Pay-as-you-grow
- Chargeback
- Ubiquitous access
- Metering resource pooling
- Multitenancy
- Cloud bursting
- Rapid deployment
- Automation

Objective	Corresponding Book Chapter
1.4 Explain object storage concepts.	Chapter 1

- Object ID
- Metadata
- Data/blob
- Extended metadata
- Policies
- Replicas
- Access control

2.0 Virtualization

Objective	Corresponding Book Chapter
2.1 Explain the differences between hypervisor types.	Chapter 2

- Type I and Type II
    - Bare metal vs. OS dependent
    - Performance and overhead considerations
    - Hypervisor specific system requirements
- Proprietary vs. open source
- Consumer vs. enterprise use
    - Workstation vs. infrastructure

Objective	Corresponding Book Chapter
2.2 Install, configure, and manage virtual machines and devices.	Chapter 7

- Creating, importing, and exporting template and virtual machines
- Install guest tools
  - Drives
  - Management tools
- Snapshots and cloning
- Image backups vs. file backups
- Virtual NIC
  - Virtual network
  - IP address
  - Default gateway
  - Netmask
  - Bridging
- Virtual disks
  - Limits
  - SCSI/ATA ID
- Virtual switches
  - VLAN
  - Interface configuration
- VLAN
  - Assign IDs
  - Bind interfaces
- VSAN
  - Assign IDs

TABLE A.2 Exam CV0-001CompTIA Cloud+ objectives map *(continued)*

Objective	Corresponding Book Chapter
2.3 Given a scenario, perform virtual resource migration.	Chapter 7

- Establish requirements
- Maintenance scheduling
- Reasons
    - Performance issues
    - Testing
    - Upgrading
    - Utilization
- Storage migration
    - Virtual vs. physical
- Online vs. offline migrations
- Physical to Virtual (P2V)
- Virtual to Virtual (V2V)
- Virtual to Physical (V2P)

2.4 Explain the benefits of virtualization in a cloud environment.	Chapter 7

- Shared resources
- Elasticity
    - Time to service/mean time to implement
    - Resource pooling
    - Scalable
    - Available
    - Portable
- Network and application isolation
- Infrastructure consolidation
- Virtual datacenter creation

Objective	Corresponding Book Chapter
2.5 Compare and contrast virtual components used to construct a cloud environment.	Chapter 7

- Virtual network components
  - Virtual NIC
  - Virtual HBA
  - Virtual router
- Shared memory
- Virtual CPU
- Storage virtualization
  - Shared storage
  - Clustered storage
  - NPIV

3.0 Infrastructure

3.1 Compare and contrast various storage technologies.	Chapters 8, 9

- Network Attached Storage (NAS)
  - File level access
  - Shared storage
- Direct Attached Storage (DAS)
  - Block level access
  - Dedicated storage
- Storage Area Network (SAN)
  - Block level access
  - Shared storage
  - HBAs
  - LUN masking
  - Zoning
  - WWN
  - Fiber channel protocols
- Different access protocols
  - FCoE
  - FC
  - Ethernet
  - iSCSI
- Protocols and applications
  - IP
  - FCP
  - iSCSI
- Management differences

TABLE A.2   Exam CV0-001CompTIA Cloud+ objectives map *(continued)*

Objective	Corresponding Book Chapter
3.2 Explain storage configuration concepts.	Chapter 8

- Disk types
  - SSD vs. spinning
  - Interfaces types
  - Access speed
- Tiering
  - Performance levels of each tier
  - Policies
- RAID levels
  - RAID 1
  - RAID 0
  - RAID 1+0
  - RAID 0+1
  - RAID 5
  - RAID 6
- File system types
  - UFS
  - EXT
  - NTFS
  - FAT
  - VMFS
  - ZFS

3.3 Execute storage provisioning.	Chapter 9

- Creating LUNs
- Creating network shares
- Zoning and LUN masking
- Multipathing
- Implications of adding capacity to a NAS and SAN
  - Impact to operations
  - Downtime
  - Best practices

Objective	Corresponding Book Chapter

3.4 Given a scenario, implement appropriate network configurations.   Chapter 9

- NAT
- PAT
- Subnetting/Supernetting
- VLAN and VLAN tagging
- Network port configurations
- Switching and routing in physical and virtual environments
  - Routing tables

3.5 Explain the importance of network optimization.   Chapter 9

- WAN
- LAN
- MAN
- QoS
- Bandwidth
- Latency
- Compression
- Caching
- Load balancing
- Devices on the same subnet

3.6 Given a scenario, troubleshoot basic network connectivity issues.   Chapter 5

- Tools
- Review documentation and device configuration settings
- Review system logs

TABLE A.2 Exam CV0-001CompTIA Cloud+ objectives map *(continued)*

Objective	Corresponding Book Chapter

- Work optimization and reducing costs
- Choosing a suitable cloud service model
- Adapting organizational culture for the cloud
- Potholes on the cloud road
- Trunk ports
- Port binding/aggregation
- Common ports
  - 80
  - 21
  - 22
  - 25
  - 53
  - 443
  - 68
- Common protocols
  - HTTP
  - FTP
  - HTTPS
  - FTPS
  - SFTP
  - SSH
  - DNS
  - DHCP
  - SMTP
- Types of networks
  - Intranet
  - Extranet
  - Internet

Objective	Corresponding Book Chapter

3.8 Explain common hardware resources and features used to enable virtual environments.   Chapter 7

- BIOS/firmware configurations
- Minimum memory capacity and configuration
- Number of CPUs
- Number of cores
- NICs quantity, speeds, and configurations
- Internal hardware compatibility
- HBAs
- Storage media
    - Tape
    - SSD
    - USB
    - Disk

4.0 Resource Management

4.1 Given a scenario, implement and use proper resource monitoring techniques.   Chapter 4

- Protocols
    - SNMP
    - WMI
    - IPMI
    - Syslog service
- Alert methods
    - SMTP
    - SMS
    - SNMP
    - Web services
    - Syslog
- Establish baselines and thresholds
- Automated responses to specific events
- Examine processes usage / resource usage

TABLE A.2   Exam CV0-001CompTIA Cloud+ objectives map *(continued)*

Objective	Corresponding Book Chapter
4.2 Given a scenario, appropriately allocate physical (host) resources using best practices.	Chapter 8

- Memory
- CPU
- Storage and network allocation
- Entitlement/quotas (shares)
  - Hard limit
  - Soft limit
- Reservations
- Licensing
- Resource pooling

Objective	Corresponding Book Chapter
4.3 Given a scenario, appropriately allocate virtual (guest) resources using best practices.	Chapter 7

- Virtual CPU
- Memory
- Storage and network allocation
- Entitlement/quotas (shares)
- Hard limit, soft limit
- Reservations, licensing
- Dynamic resource allocation
- Resource pooling
- CPU affinity
- Physical resource redirection and mapping to virtual resources
  - Serial
  - USB
  - Parallel port mapping

Objective	Corresponding Book Chapter
4.4 Given a scenario, use appropriate tools for remote access.	Chapter 10

- Remote hypervisor access
- RDP
- SSH
- Console port
- HTTP

Objective	Corresponding Book Chapter

5.0 Security

5.1 Explain network security concepts, tools, and best practices.   Chapter 11

- ACLs
- VPNs
- IDS/IPS hardware/software-based firewalls
- DMZ
- Review / audit logs
- Attacks
    - DDoS
    - Ping of death
    - Ping flood

5.2 Explain storage security concepts, methods, and best practices.   Chapter 11

- Obfuscation
- Access Control Lists
- Zoning
- LUN masking
- User and host authentication
- Review/audit logs

5.3 Compare and contrast different encryption technologies and methods.   Chapter 11

- PKI
- IPSEC
- SSL/TLS
- Ciphers
    - AES
    - 3DES
    - RSA
    - DSA
    - RC4
    - RC5
- Encryption for data in transit and encryption for data at rest

TABLE A.2 Exam CV0-001CompTIA Cloud+ objectives map *(continued)*

Objective	Corresponding Book Chapter
5.4 Identify access control methods.	Chapter 11

- Role-based administration
- Mandatory access controls
- Discretionary access controls
- Multifactor authentication
- Single sign-on
- Federation

Objective	Corresponding Book Chapter
5.5 Implement guest and host hardening techniques.	Chapter 11

- Disabling unneeded ports and services
- User credentials
  - Changing default passwords
- Host-based/software firewalls
- Antivirus software
- Patching
- Deactivating default accounts

6.0 Systems Management

Objective	Corresponding Book Chapter
6.1 Explain policies and procedures as they relate to a cloud environment.	Chapter 4

- Network and IP planning/documentation
- Configuration standardization and documentation
- Change management best practices
  - Documentation
  - Configuration control
  - Asset accountability
  - Approval process
  - Back-out plan
- Configuration management
  - CMDB
  - Approval process
  - Configuration control
- Capacity management
  - Monitoring for changes
  - Trending
- Systems life cycle management
- Maintenance windows
  - Server upgrades and patches

Objective	Corresponding Book Chapter
6.2 Given a scenario, diagnose, remediate and optimize physical host performance.	Chapter 8

- Disk performance
- Disk tuning
- Disk latency
- Swap disk space
- I/O tuning
- Performance management and monitoring tools
- Establish baseline and create documentation with appropriate tools
- Hypervisor configuration best practices
  - Memory ballooning
  - I/O throttling
  - CPU wait time
- Impact of configuration changes to the virtual environment
- Common issues
  - Disk failure
  - HBA failure
  - Memory failure
  - NIC failure
  - CPU failure

6.3 Explain common performance concepts as they relate to the host and the guest.	Chapter 8

- IOPS
- Read vs. write files
- File system performance
- Metadata performance
- Caching
- Bandwidth
- Throughput (bonding/teaming)
- Jumbo frames
- Network latency
- Hop counts
- QoS
- Multipathing
- Load balancing
- Scaling
  - Vertical vs. horizontal vs. diagonal

TABLE A.2   Exam CV0-001CompTIA Cloud+ objectives map *(continued)*

Objective	Corresponding Book Chapter
6.4 Implement appropriate testing techniques when deploying cloud services.	Chapter 10

- Test replication
- Test latency
- Test bandwidth
- Test load balancing
- Test application servers
- Test storage
- Test application delivery
- Service performance testing and application performance testing
- Penetration testing
- Vulnerability assessment
- Separation of duties during testing

7.0 Business Continuity in the Cloud

7.1 Compare and contrast disaster recovery methods and concepts.	Chapter 12

- Redundancy
- Failover
- Geographical diversity
- Failback
- Replication
- Site mirroring
- Hot site
- Cold site
- Warm site
- Backup and recovery
- Archiving and offsite storage
- Replication types
  - Synchronous
  - Asynchronous
- RTO
- RPO
- MTBF
- MTTR
- Mission critical requirements

Objective	Corresponding Book Chapter
7.2 Deploy solutions to meet availability requirements.	Chapter 9 and 10

- Fault tolerance
  - High availability
  - Local clustering /geoclustering
  - Non-high availability resources
- Multipathing
- Load balancing

Exam objectives are subject to change at any time without prior notice. Make sure you visit the following site:

`http://certification.comptia.org/getcertified/certifications/cloudplus.aspx`

If the URL for the exam has moved, Google probably knows where it is!

Good luck with the exam!

Index

Note to the reader: Throughout this index **boldfaced** page numbers indicate primary discussions of a topic. *Italicized* page numbers indicate illustrations.

Free Online Learning Environment

Register on Sybex.com to gain access to the free online interactive learning environment and test bank to help you study for your CompTIA Cloud+ certification.

The online test bank includes:

- **Practice Exam** to test your knowledge of the materials

- **Electronic Flashcards** to reinforce your learning and provide last-minute test prep before the exam

- **Searchable Glossary** gives you instant access to the key terms you'll need to know for the exam

Go to `http://sybextestbanks.wiley.com` **to register and gain access to this comprehensive study tool package.**

SYBEX®
A Wiley Brand